Practical Apartment Management

Third Edition

Joseph T. Lannon
Publishing and Curriculum Development Manager

Caroline Scoulas
Senior Editor

Stephanie J. Mathurin
Project Editor

Practical Apartment Management

Third Edition

Edward N. Kelley, CPM®

Institute of Real Estate Management
of the NATIONAL ASSOCIATION OF REALTORS®
430 NORTH MICHIGAN AVENUE · CHICAGO, ILLINOIS 60611

This publication is designed to provide accurate and authoritative information in regard to the subject matter covered; however, due to the changing and varying nature of federal, state, and local laws, independent legal and other professional advice should be sought in the application of the information covered in this book. Forms or other documents included in this book are intended as samples only; neither IREM nor the author endorses their use. This publication is sold with the understanding that neither the author nor the publisher is engaged in rendering legal, accounting or any other service. If legal advice or other expert assistance is required, the services of a competent professional should be sought.

The opinions expressed in this text are those of the author, Edward N. Kelley, CPM®, and do not necessarily reflect the policies and positions of the Institute on Real Estate Management.

Library of Congress Cataloging-in-Publication Data

Kelley, Edward N. 7/90 B&T 34.95
    Practical apartment management.

    1. Apartment houses–Management.   I. Title.
TX957.K44   1990   647'.92'068   89-83353
ISBN 0-944298-40-0

Printed in the United States of America

      1 2 3 4 5 6 7 8 9 10 Printing / Year 99 98 97 96 95 94 93 92 91 90

Contents

Foreword

The Institute of Real Estate Management of the NATIONAL ASSOCIATION OF REALTORS® is dedicated to assisting and advancing the careers of professional property managers through the development of extensive educational courses and materials. This new edition of *Practical Apartment Management* has been prepared as part of that professional program.

ABOUT THE AUTHOR

Edward N. Kelley's thirty years in property management serve as an inspiration for those who are beginning careers in real estate. In need of income and housing while he attended college, Kelley accepted a position as the resident manager of a small lakefront property on Chicago's north side. Kelley made the most of the irregular hours of a student and succeeded in leasing this building to capacity—even though it was in a highly competitive market. Soon, he was promoted to larger and more difficult properties, eventually becoming supervisor of one hundred properties while working for one of Chicago's oldest and most prestigious full-service real estate companies. From a part-time job, Edward Kelley became one of the top officers of the firm.

After thirteen years in the business, Kelley changed positions and took charge of a nationwide management organization with more than 44,000 apartment units and a significant portfolio of office buildings and shopping centers. The properties were located in 137 cities and thirty-seven states; annual rent collections exceeded $100 million.

In 1973, Kelley founded the firm E.N. Kelley & Associates and began building his own investment portfolio. Recognized nationally for marketing successes, Kelley and his firm are frequently called on to assist institutions and individual owners alike. In 1984, Kelley joined with David Lehr to form Kelley/Lehr & Associates. Their company has three offices in the Chicago area and provides advisory and asset management services to a growing list of the country's largest lending institutions, universities, corporations, and private investors.

Mr. Kelley's reputation for developing innovative approaches to property management is widely known. He has written comprehensive investment analysis computer software; his articles identifying market trends appear regularly in many industry publications; and he has written four well-read books. A dynamic speaker, Edward Kelley is asked to present his ideas and concepts to real estate professionals at an ever-growing number of conventions and educational gatherings.

Mr. Kelley, a CERTIFIED PROPERTY MANAGER®, is an active member of the Institute of Real Estate Management of the NATIONAL ASSOCIATION OF REALTORS® and has served on many of its committees, including the Executive Committee and the Governing Council. He has served three terms as an IREM Regional Vice President and is a former president of the Chicago chapter of IREM. A frequent contributor to the *Journal of Property Management* published by the Institute, Mr. Kelley has twice received the *Journal's* coveted Author of the Year award. In 1982, Mr. Kelley was honored as the first recipient of the IREM Foundation's Louis L. and Y. T. Lum Award for his dedication to advancing professionalism in the industry and his many contributions in real estate management education. Mr. Kelley is a Senior Instructor on the National Faculty at IREM and received the Lloyd D. Hanford Sr. Distinguished Faculty Award in 1989. These IREM awards are among many that Mr. Kelley has received for his leadership in the industry.

When one asks Ed Kelley what might occur next in his career, he expresses a hope to continue to study the business and to organize and quantify past lessons for the benefit of apartment residents, managers, and owners. In this new edition of his book, Kelley shares many new ideas for the professional management of residential properties. The Institute of Real Estate Management is pleased to be the publisher of yet a third edition of *Practical Apartment Management.*

ACKNOWLEDGMENTS

The publisher wishes to acknowledge the contributions of the following individuals. Property management professionals who reviewed the entire manuscript: Douglas F. Collins, CPM®, Principal, Tooman Collins Associates, Inc.,

Tulsa, Oklahoma; David C. Nilges, CPM®, President, David Nilges Interests Inc., Denver, Colorado; Beverly A. Roachell, CPM®, Senior Vice President, Rector Phillips Morse, Inc., Little Rock, Arkansas; Vyetta Sunderland, CPM®, Vice President, United Management (Canada), Ltd., Calgary, Alberta, Canada; and Lyn E. Weiland, CPM®, of St. Augustine, Florida, one of the authors of *The Successful On-Site Manager,* published by IREM. Those who did special topical reviews: R. Bruce Campbell, CPM®, President, Wallace H. Campbell & Co., Inc., Baltimore, Maryland; Anthony R. Diana, CPM®, President, Diana Management Inc., Bel Air, Maryland; Lowell E. Pinney, CPM®, of Indianapolis, Indiana; and Randy Rosen, CPM®, President, Rosen Realty & Management Co., Chicago, Illinois. Jonathan T. Howe and Henry M. Schaffer of IREM's counsel, Howe & Hutton, Chicago, Illinois, for their legal review of selected text material. Attorneys Lawrence M. Mages, David Saltiel, and Gregory Shroedter of Bell, Boyd & Lloyd, Chicago, Illinois, for their help and advice throughout the project. Russell Schneck Design of Glenview, Illinois, for the graphic design.

DISCLAIMER

We would like to remind the reader of the temporal nature of some of the information presented in this book. Today, the apartment manager witnesses a constantly changing legal picture. To begin with, laws often vary from one locality to another. Over time, these laws and their interpretations are often modified or reinterpreted. It is imperative that all apartment managers maintain an awareness of laws unique to their state or city and any changes in these laws. Professional counsel should be obtained when questions or problems arise.

Throughout the text the author addresses you, the reader, as the property manager. He may at times instruct *you* to perform certain tasks, when in fact your employees will be executing the duties described. The author's recommendations are presented to *you* because you ultimately assume responsibility for the property as the property manager.

Introduction to Apartment Management

As you opened this book, two questions might have come to mind: "Why was *Practical Apartment Management* written?" and "What was the reason for creating a new Third Edition?"

First, I'll answer question number one. More than twenty years ago, I was responsible for a very large portfolio of rental property; it included tens of thousands of apartment units handled by hundreds of property managers spread across the country. Managing apartments was a tough business, one that wasn't known for generous salaries. Employee turnover for certain positions and situations would commonly approach 100 percent per year and this meant a never-ending training process. Some problems were clearly industry-wide, and I thought that the apartment management business could benefit from a uniform set of policies and procedures—but such a source did not seem to exist. People entering the field were expected to learn by experience and make decisions on their feet. Many of those quick decisions proved to be incorrect and some were even damaging to the long-term viability of the properties managed. People new to the industry needed a central source of information regarding the common problems and workable solutions associated with the management of rental apartments—so I wrote *Practical Apartment Management*.

I wanted to present an organized discussion of the situations that commonly occur during the management of an apartment property. One of the complaints frequently expressed at gatherings of property managers was the absence of a book that could be given to people about to enter the business, a book new employees could read before reporting to work. Over the years, people in the industry have tried different solutions to common problems and learned valuable lessons that are easier to read about than they are to experience. Why should people struggle with old problems? *Practical Apartment Management* was written to help the apartment manager understand common problems and their solutions.

If these problems are so common, then why is a Third Edition necessary? When I first wrote the book, I thought that it would continue to answer frequently asked questions for many years to come. When it became necessary to revise *Practical Apartment Management* for the Second Edition, I tried to "lead" the future by making some predictions; this was done in part to keep the book contemporary for a longer period of time. Some of my forecasts were on the mark and others were less accurate.

In both cases, I didn't anticipate the tremendous number of changes that have taken place. I reasoned that rental housing had been around for more than a millennium—so how many changes could there be? In fact, there are countless situations in which the action called for is completely different from the response that would have been appropriate a few years ago. The Third Edition will help keep the practitioner current and point to areas of the business that are changing.

THE BUSINESS OF PROPERTY MANAGEMENT

Real estate and wealth are terms that are frequently used as synonyms. Investment real estate is considered the ultimate in personal and financial attainment. Unfortunately, real estate ownership is not a typical career path; it is most often the result of success in another field. This sets up a rather interesting relationship—one person provides the necessary funds and assumes the primary risk, while a second person provides the imagination, skill, and energy to maximize profits. The latter is you, the property manager.

While I didn't realize it at the time, I received some sage advice from one of my first employers when I was still in high school. The man's name was Vic and he operated an auto parts store. He advised me to choose a business that offered a product that was in high demand and wore out rather quickly—just as his auto parts store offered such items as tires, spark plugs, lubricating oil, etc. Vic often cited positive examples from other industries; for example, he would point to razor blades and explain to me why a razor blade company would sacrifice profits on the sale of blade handles to encourage future purchases of special-fitting blades. How does this story relate to the apartment business? Rental apartments are certainly needed by a large segment of the population, but they don't wear out like razor blades—or do they?

It has taken me a long time to focus on this point, but I am now learning that apartments <u>do</u> wear out and lose their usefulness and appeal. In the past, an apartment was an apartment. Granted, some units were nicer, larger, or better located; but basically an apartment was a simple "box" that was designed to accommodate the basic needs of residents. If well-maintained, a rental apartment could be recycled time and again with virtually no loss in appeal while the rent escalated regularly and almost kept pace with the units in newer buildings. Today, building age has a profound impact on apartment rents and rental property values. Apartments built in the 1960s or 1970s cannot compete effectively with buildings built in the 1980s and 1990s. Most rental units look much like they did when they first came into the marketplace because owners have been woefully slow in discovering that their apartments are wearing out and barely meet today's needs. At first, lowering the rent of older units adjusts for any deficiencies; but the owner remains saddled with increasing maintenance costs at the same time that the rent is decreasing.

In the past, buyers of rental apartment complexes made few allowances for the age of the property and often believed that properties of different ages had the same operating expenses. Consequently, a number of rental dwellings have worn out and now need to be replaced. Values for these older buildings are going down, contrary to the belief of some investors. We shouldn't be surprised by this, because we have seen the same pattern of decay in the hotel and motel business. A lot of money is going to be lost in the rental housing business while people reach the realization that the commodity being offered <u>does</u> wear out and must be regularly updated or replaced.

My former employer, Vic, offered advice that definitely applies to the rental property business. First of all, there is a huge market for rental units (over thirty-two million households and that number is rising faster than the number of homeowners). Secondly, apartments do wear out and many are doing so with alarming speed. This sets the stage for the future. Managing and repositioning rental housing units will become a significant career opportunity in the future. People who understand what is happening will surface and succeed. Profit will not be available to those who choose to wait in the hope that their aging properties will somehow become rejuvenated. The policies that we have employed in the past won't work either; we need a completely new approach.

So what can we expect in the field of apartment management? The owners will change. The policies and procedures will change. The product will change as well. This doesn't mean that more than thirty million rental units will be demolished. Decisions should be based on the location and basic structure of each building—many buildings will be completely reworked to fit changing lifestyles. Facades will undergo dramatic and innovative changes, interior layouts will be modified to fit household requirements, many bathrooms will be doubled in size, kitchens will be made more efficient, and the importance of privacy and identity will be emphasized. All of these changes should be made using up-to-date materials and colors.

People in the apartment management business who work with renters every day are learning what is acceptable and what is not. This knowledge is extremely valuable to developers and potential buyers. The advice of skilled property managers will be sought prior to the purchase or repositioning of investment real estate. Such advice wasn't as crucial during the days of syndications and large tax shelters—decisions were driven by a different set of motivators then. We, as property managers, will participate in the process of salvaging billions and billions of dollars worth of poor decisions that were a result of times of plenty. The apartment manager will also profit from the thousands of new and repositioned units that will be created and offered to fill the needs of today's renters. The necessary marketing process will be much more sophisticated than efforts in the past.

One of the most important reasons for selecting apartment management as a career is that *a single individual can make a difference.* There are very few industries or job opportunities that offer that advantage. A dedicated and skilled property manager can take on the responsibilities of an apartment community that is in physical or fiscal trouble and, often within months, restore the community's viability, direction, and reputation. Real estate investments are often in the millions of dollars, so there is a great deal of money at stake. Developers and owners will pay handsome rewards to individuals who produce better-than-average results.

When property managers achieve some success, they are in a position to capitalize even more on their acquired skills. Unlike the successful business professional I spoke of earlier, property managers can invest their surplus funds in their own field. Isn't that the ideal goal, to learn a craft that essentially creates more and more investment value? You should market your skills to others who are desperately searching for help managing their investments, and charge accordingly. Then, take some of your fees and invest the money in properties that require your help—only this time your skills will be used for your own benefit.

Property management offers a career opportunity with an unusual amount of stability plus enormous growth potential. As a property manager, you have control over your destiny, and your proficiency can mean the difference between mediocre and dramatic results. Finally, the fact that you can apply property management skills to your own investments certainly adds to the positive aspects of being a part of the industry. If I had the chance to do it all over again, I would select the same career path. I would only change two things: I would choose to work a little harder and be a bit more daring. Now, with that introduction, let's begin our study of the subject of practical apartment management.

PROPERTY LOCATION

Virtually every discussion dealing with the subject of real estate quickly outlines the importance of a property's location; this book is no exception. Basically, location will dictate most of the success or failure of a given property, not the skills or programs introduced by the owner or manager. You can apply the basics that I will outline in this book to a routine property in an excellent neighborhood and be very successful. On the other hand, you can heap imagination and energy onto a property in a declining or marginal location and realize only limited success.

For those unseasoned real estate investors and developers who disregard this warning, a natural trap awaits. The lure involves the fact that properties and land in poor locations are comparatively inexpensive and, thus, appear to be bargains. Realizing that it may be difficult to find buyers for their poorly situated real estate, sellers are inclined to take back financing or offer other purchase incentives. To many novices, a lower price and special purchase arrangements present an irresistible offer. Nevertheless, poorly located property is seldom a bargain and usually produces mediocre profits at best.

As a property manager, you will frequently be offered opportunities to increase the value of investment real estate by applying your creative skills. You must understand that even the most highly skilled property manager will find it nearly impossible to overcome a poor location. Every property can be improved, but the real turnaround success stories always start with ailing properties in choice locations.

THE PROPERTY

The nature of the management style required for different properties is clearly influenced by several factors. The type of structure that is typified by the development (e.g., low-rise or high-rise structure, townhomes or suburban garden apartments) is one such influence. The stage is set further by the property's character: Design, unit mix, unit layout, and equipment package shape the character of a property. Regardless of how poorly a property is located, designed, or equipped, there is nevertheless an optimum level at which it can be operated. That is the point at which income is at a maximum and expenditures are at a minimum. The property manager must take the necessary action to reach this point and produce the greatest possible net operating income.

Property Type

Height is a good starting point to distinguish different types of apartment buildings. Where land is relatively cheap and the developer is under little or no pressure to increase the number of housing units per acre, shorter buildings can be constructed and spread out over a large area. As land costs increase, the developer starts to think of getting more units onto a piece of land, so taller buildings are constructed. In this book, buildings of various heights are identified as follows:

- *Low-rise*. Buildings with one to five stories. If the building has an elevator, it is an elevator building. If it has no elevator, it is a walk-up.
- *Mid-rise*. Buildings with six to nine stories. Elevator service is assumed unless otherwise stated.
- *High-rise*. Buildings with ten or more stories.

Unit Size, Area, and Layout

A prospect setting out to rent an apartment is interested in a number of apartment measurements: unit size (number of rooms), unit area (square footage), and the apartment layout (functionality of the space).

Apartment size is expressed by the number of bedrooms and bathrooms that a unit contains or by its total number of rooms.

A small apartment without a bedroom is referred to as an *efficiency* or *studio* apartment. (In some parts of the country, a studio unit means a small apartment with two levels.) Most often an efficiency apartment contains a small walk-in or Pullman kitchen (a kitchen built along a wall), a combined dining and living room area (that also serves as a sleeping area), and a bathroom. A larger efficiency apartment—the convertible—has also become very popular. The identifying feature of a convertible is an unusually large living room in an "L" shape or with an alcove that serves as a sleeping area.

There is a prescribed way to make a *room count*. The kitchen, no matter how small, is considered one room. A bathroom that contains a toilet, wash basin, and tub or shower stall is a full bath but is not included in the room count. A bathroom with just a toilet and basin is classified as a half-bath and is not included in the count either. A living room is counted as a room, as is a separate, formal dining room. A living and dining room combination is counted as one and one-half rooms, unless the combined space exceeds 300 square feet, in which case it is counted as two rooms. Dining or dinette space smaller than 100 square feet is regarded only as a half-room. Each bedroom with its own separate entry off a hall is counted as a room. A den or family room is counted as one room, too. Outside patios or balconies are not included in the count, nor are closets, no matter how large.

The following example illustrates this room count method:

An apartment containing a combined living-dining area, a kitchen, a bedroom, and a bath is referred to as a one-bedroom apartment. The presence of one complete bathroom is assumed and not mentioned, unless one is not included, or unless more than one is provided. The room count then is as follows:

Living Room and Dining Area	1½ rooms
Kitchen	1 room
Bedroom	1 room
Unit size	3½ rooms

Many apartment managers have adopted a short-cut method to determine an apartment's room count. This approach assumes that all apartments contain two and one-half rooms plus bedrooms. An efficiency apartment, for example, would equal just two and one-half rooms since it has no bedroom, while a one-bedroom apartment would be equal to three and one-half rooms: two and one-half rooms for the apartment plus one for the bedroom. This system is much easier and surprisingly accurate.

The area of an apartment is stated in terms of its *rentable square feet*. This measurement is determined by multiplying a unit's length by its width. No deduction is made for partitions, plumbing chases, or other small niches. Neither should an apartment's square-foot area include balconies, patios, or unheated sun porches.

To a seasoned renter, an apartment's layout is really more important than its area in square footage. When comparing two apartments of identical area, one is often more functional than the other. Some layouts simply accommodate furnishings and belongings better than others and are more desirable because of their distribution of space. An example of this is the *two-bedroom split layout*; this type of apartment has enjoyed great popularity in the 1980s and is expected to remain in favor throughout the 1990s. Unlike the standard two-bedroom apartment that contains one larger and one smaller bedroom, the two-bedroom split layout features two equal bedrooms, two equal baths, and closet facilities that are separated by the living and dining area and kitchen. In addition to providing equal sleeping quarters, this layout affords a greater degree of privacy for residents than the standard two-bedroom unit with bedrooms that are next to each other. This makes it ideal for roommate situations, parents and a growing child, or visiting relatives, or space for a den or stereo room.

Unit Mix

Almost every apartment building or complex contains a number of different-sized units. This distribution, whatever it is, is referred to as the *unit mix*. The unit mix can greatly affect the character, ultimate use, direction, and success of a particular property type. Any one of the property types described would take on a different character if it contained only one size of dwelling unit. For example, a building with only efficiency units would have a distinctly different resident profile than one with, say, only two-bedroom units.

A building's location and intended market should influence the builder's decision when establishing the optimum unit mix. Differing economic conditions also affect the desirability of and demand for particular unit sizes. An example of this can be seen during periods of a depressed economy, when efficiency apartments and convertibles enjoy their greatest demand. Many people decide to scale down their living accommodations to small apartments in desirable buildings rather than moving to one-bedroom apartments in older, less-expensive buildings or losing privacy by taking in roommates to help share costs.

During periods of especially high inflation, even the mainstay one-bedroom apartment suffers vacancies as people opt for efficiency units, two-bedroom units with rent-sharing roommates, or a return to their parents' homes in an effort to save money. Families requiring two bedrooms will settle for apartments with one bath and the two-bedroom split unit will outrent the standard two-bedroom apartment. Likewise, two- and three-bedroom townhouses will be in short supply as occupants wait for the economy to improve before purchasing a home.

At any point in time, economic conditions will affect the demand for the various types of units, and, therefore, the definition of the optimum unit mix will always be changing. Obviously, no one unit mix will remain at the same level of demand continuously. The goal is to provide a wide range of unit types, in varying percentages, to sustain a healthy occupancy and demand over a rental building's long life.

The long-range plan for the property also has an impact on the unit mix. If, for example, the developer had the idea of eventually converting the property to condominium ownership, a specialized unit mix would be advisable.

Managers seldom have the chance to establish the unit mix of a development. Still, they should be aware of the differences of each and the respective advantages and disadvantages of one opposed to the other.

Nonyield Space

Every apartment building contains some nonyield space. This space costs money to build and is essential to the operation of the building, but it does not produce direct revenue. Obviously, the less nonyield space, the better.

The ratio between a property's gross building area (length times the width of the structure(s) times the number of floors with living space) and the rentable area (the sum of the areas of all the apartments) is termed the building's *efficiency factor*. For example, a building with a gross building area of 100,000 square feet and a rentable area of 85,000 square feet has an 85 percent efficiency factor.

$$\text{Efficiency Factor} = \frac{\text{Rentable Area}}{\text{Gross Building Area}}$$

$$= \frac{85{,}000 \text{ square feet}}{100{,}000 \text{ square feet}}$$

$$= 85 \text{ percent}$$

Efficiency factors of apartment buildings vary for a number of reasons. Some architects are more skilled than others at minimizing nonyield space. On the other hand, a designer may intentionally provide more non-yield space than is necessary in a luxury building in an effort to establish a feeling of opulence through conspicuous waste (e.g., large lobbies or extra-wide corridors).

Generally, the most efficient housing type is the townhouse built on a slab. Its efficiency factor is usually in the mid-90 percent range, with losses due only to the exterior wall thickness and any outbuildings such as storage, laundry, or recreation facilities. High-rise and mid-rise build-ings have comparatively lower efficiency factors than walk-up apartments. This is due to their greater proportion of interior common spaces plus their large, more sophisticated, and space-consuming mechanical equip-ment areas.

Climate also has an impact on efficiency. Properties in northern re-gions usually have much lower efficiency factors than those in southern regions because of vestibules and interior corridors that are added as pro-tection from the elements. These properties also frequently require addi-tional nonyield space to house larger heating and mechanical apparatus. In northern regions, efficiency factors between 70 and 85 percent are common. Buildings in warm or moderate climates typically enjoy an effi-ciency factor in the 85 to 90 percent range.

TYPES OF RESIDENTS

The life of a residential property is marked by the fact that it is occupied by people. Because residents add a dimension to the character of a prop-erty, it is necessary to understand the resident's role, differentiate be-tween the various types of residents, and apply management skills to create a property's character through sensible resident selection.

Before discussing different types of residents, let's address the issue of word choice: How do you identify the people who live in the properties you manage? There has been a movement to replace the word "tenant" with another designation such as occupant, resident, or lessee. This tendency is, in part, a response to the opinion that a tenant is a second-class citizen—a view held by many Americans in the early days of rental property. It is also an effort to de-emphasize the financial relationship between owner and tenant (notice that I also choose to use the word "owner" rather than "landlord" because the latter seems dictatorial).

Such a negative view of tenants is obviously inaccurate; consider the fact that some of the world's largest corporations are tenants in the premises they occupy. Nevertheless, it is important for the property manager to be aware of the sensitive nature of the word and use it with discretion— especially in conversation. This is why I have chosen to use the words "resident," "occupant," and "renter" with a fair degree of frequency.

The fact remains that the word "tenant" is really the only word in the English language that specifically refers to a person who gains the privilege of occupying land or a building by paying rent. After all, every tenant is a resident, but not vice versa. There are hundreds of years of landlord-tenant laws, but no owner and occupant laws. As a result, it is absolutely necessary to employ the word "tenant" in legal contexts.

There are many types of residents: singles and families, students and the elderly, never-nesters and empty-nesters, quiet and loud, more desirable and less desirable, and so forth. Since experience has demonstrated that each of the groups can be expected to behave in a certain predictable way and make certain demands, managers of residential rental properties must be able to recognize the resident types and know which ones are preferred occupants for given properties. The type of resident for which a building is designed will affect many aspects of management, including marketing, maintenance, and resident relations.

Some people may object to categorizing residents, claiming that every one is an individual human being and must be treated as such. True, residents are individuals. Still, insurance companies categorize people by height, weight, gender, medical history, occupation, etc. on the principle that groups demonstrate certain tendencies; scientists make similar generalizations when studying behavior. Property managers are justified in doing the same.

Residents can be grouped in two broad categories; namely, *renters by choice* and *renters by circumstance.* Renters by choice are likely to stay longer, cause fewer problems, and make better residents. They choose a place to be their home and back this up with commitments of money and energy.

In the other category are apartment dwellers who are not necessarily happy with renting. They accept the arrangement only as a temporary compromise until they can achieve other long-range ambitions. Frequently, the real wish of these people is to achieve the American dream—to own a home.

No doubt, the special attraction that owning real estate holds for most people reflects the common attitude of buying before all the land is "used up." It also reflects the viewpoint that property owners are the ones who have succeeded in life. This belief has had a very compelling influence on the renter who perceives his or her present housing arrangement as a rude indication of a lack of achievement.

Many housing analysts and demographers are predicting that there will be more renters in the future. As the cost of purchasing and financing a new or existing home increases dramatically, it may well slow the transition from renter to homeowner. Renters will not lose their desire to purchase their own homes; they simply will be unable to afford them. Whether this prediction is accurate or not, there will always be a need for rental housing and managers to operate it.

Renters by Choice

Career people, settled people without children, couples whose children have grown and left home, and retired people are typically renters by choice. For some, the situation is one in which the extra space available in purchased housing is not needed. Others want the freedom provided by renting. Still others choose to rent because it is the most economical means of living in the area of their choice.

Their choice, however, is not necessarily absolute. If high-quality housing and its accompanying services are not available, renters by choice can and have been swayed to buy—particularly cooperative and condominium units where exterior maintenance is provided. Owners, and especially managers, must be alert to the fact that this resident group demands quality accommodations and will be constantly wooed by real estate brokers with housing to sell.

Still, the resident types described below have one thing in common: They prefer to rent. Their priorities, lifestyles, and conditions of age and health are such that the desire to become homeowners is negligible, perhaps entirely absent. Maybe they do not want to cut the grass. Maybe they are convinced that, in the long run, there is greater economy in renting. In any case, these renters are either satisfied with their situation or have more or less permanently resigned themselves to renting.

Empty-Nesters.   Given complete freedom to select residents, an experienced property manager would try to fill all his or her units with empty-nesters. Typically, these are married couples who have raised their children—perhaps in single-family homes—and have chosen the carefree ways of apartment living. They invest in furnishings to provide comfort and convenience. They pay the rent promptly, live in peace and harmony with neighbors, and pose few management problems. As the most selective of all renters in choosing their living quarters, they insist on quality in housing, services, and management. Before renting they shop around, since they are looking for accommodations that will remain satisfactory for the long run.

Empty-nesters make up a steadily increasing segment of the prospective resident market. Unfortunately for the property manager, many empty-nesters are buying townhouses, coach houses, manor houses, and condominiums rather than renting. They have learned to enjoy the value appreciation and the tax benefits of owning, and they regard ownership as the preferred alternative. Nevertheless, empty-nesters represent an important segment of the market—not all empty-nesters are buyers, and those who do choose to rent are the best possible renters.

Career People.   Next in terms of resident desirability are established career people whose numbers are also increasing. These people can be single men and women or childless couples. A relatively homogeneous group, their lifestyle is career-oriented. They have chosen to be renters rather than homeowners. The character of their homes is important to them and to their small circle of close friends. They tend to choose smaller apartments in established neighborhoods that are convenient to work and entertainment activities. Because of their career orientation, these residents may move from time to time, so their occupancy does not offer the same stability that empty-nesters provide to management.

Senior Citizens.   Senior citizens—married and unmarried—who have regular retirement benefits are also a favorite resident type. This group tends to make little noise, pay bills promptly, and keep their homes clean. Such people are also inclined to choose small apartments, especially when they are constrained by fixed, inflation-eroded incomes. Budgetary limitations may keep senior citizens from living in preferred neighborhoods; still, they will be discriminating about finding a place where basic daily needs can be met. It is true that the medical problems associated with advancing age may present some management problems. Beyond that, senior citizens form a most desirable segment of the market.

Renters by Circumstance

Offsetting renters by choice are those residents who rent because of their current circumstances. A student attending college away from home, for example, needs temporary housing. Many young families want a place to live until they can save enough money to make a down payment on a home, and singles who anticipate being married someday often do not want to be tied down to a house. In each of these cases, rental housing is occupied on an interim basis. Decisions about ultimate living arrangements are still to be made. Because of the temporary aspect of the choice to rent, there is a reluctance to commit time, money, and energy to create a home-like environment. When rental units are occupied without an ongoing commitment, management problems increase dramatically.

From management's point of view, the desirability of different groups of residents by circumstance is measured by the duration of occupancy and the absence of the costly problems such tenants often present. After all, with good service, renters by circumstance may be transformed into more permanent renters by choice. Every time the need to rerent is avoided, net operating income increases.

Families with Children.   Families with children make up a substantial part of the rental market. This becomes increasingly true when the cost of buying and maintaining a single-family home is rising faster than most families' ability to meet these expenses. Renting often becomes the interim solution while a family postpones their goal of homeownership.

Families with children are less mobile than other residents, meaning that the need to deal with move-outs will be minimized. Also, the rate of skip-outs (residents who leave without paying rent) tends to be lower with families. With a creative management program that channels the energies of youngsters in nondestructive directions, a property manager can take advantage of the relative stability of this segment of the market.

Families with children may be renters by circumstance, but there are a lot of them, and they are good residents in many cases. You should be reminded that The Fair Housing Amendments Act of 1988 included an amendment that prohibits discrimination based on familial status (the only exceptions are made for housing that satisfies specific requirements for older persons). Thus, it is not merely prudent to consider including families with children in your development, it is required by law.

One- and Two-Person Households.   The people in these two categories represent the vast majority of all renters. In fact, single people living alone account for 25 percent of all households—it's the fastest growing segment of our population. Couples, either married or living together, are the largest single household grouping. Both of these groups are maturing, with an average age well into the thirties. As these groups age, their lifestyles will mellow, their possessions will grow in number, and their abilities to discern quality accommodations will sharpen. Most rental developments focus their advertising and marketing efforts directly toward this audience. New appointments, features, services, and amenities are offered to attract people who have more money to spend on rent, are concerned about health and fitness, and have limited extra time.

A substantial number of these people will not become homeowners; renting will be their way of life. While these people may start out moving from one complex to another, they eventually find themselves looking for a place to call home for a number of years.

Students.   The most temporary of all resident types is the student. Students come in large numbers to college towns, bringing with them few possessions and even less money. Their stay is short. This, and their lack of commitment to the place they are renting, present management problems that only those who specialize in the student market will care to face. Occupancy terms are for ten months or less. Rent collections are often challenging. Wear and tear creates enormous maintenance problems. There is also the competition to cope with, because the colleges themselves may offer lower-rent housing (e.g., dormitories, student and staff apartments, etc.). In periods of declining school enrollments, investment properties that rely on student renters are left with more and more vacancies.

Income Group

The discussion of resident types so far has made no reference to income. It is a sensitive subject, and one I will address in more detail in chapter 9 when I discuss setting and raising rents. One fact is clear: Managing housing for low-income residents is different from and can be more demanding than managing apartments occupied by those more able to afford housing. It is beyond the scope of this book to deal with the socio-economic reasons for this observation, but for completeness, the matter must be mentioned.

It should also be stated that the management of a property that has been financed with government subsidies or has residents whose rents are subsidized requires a thorough knowledge of the regulations established by the United States Department of Housing and Urban Development (HUD) or other governmental housing agencies. This book does not attempt to address the myriad issues that are unique to the management of subsidized housing.

Categorizing the people who comprise the rental market, especially using a small number of classifications, is arbitrary and obviously very general. The exceptions to these descriptions are many and varied. In the final analysis, the quality and desirability of each resident can be gauged only by individual performance.

GOALS OF OWNERSHIP

When you undertake the management of a real estate investment for either yourself or others, the first order of business is to understand exactly what you expect to accomplish. If you are being hired by the owner of an apartment complex, what does he or she want? "To make as much money as possible" is not a very precise answer and it's one that will not help you very much in preparing a management plan. Some owners need regular monthly income while others would rather reinvest surplus money into the property in hopes of dramatically increasing the ultimate resale value some time in the future. Let's explore some of the more important goals of ownership and discuss their differences.

Periodic Income

This means a steady return in the form of cash. An owner risks equity by investing in real estate. In return, he or she expects to receive monthly, quarterly, or annual cash dividends that represent the profits or surplus revenue derived from the property's operation. In addition to real estate, there are many competing types of investments such as bonds, stocks, investment trusts, and even bank accounts that yield regular income. Many of these are insured, guaranteed, or backed by years and years of payment patterns. Real estate, on the other hand, is very unpredictable and most sensitive to market "winds" and the impact of management skills. Those seeking regular and predictable returns often opt for buildings with long-term commercial or industrial leases rather than risking the more frequent turnover experienced with rental apartments or small offices. The *rate of return* is generally dictated by the probability of predictable and sustained periodic returns. In other words, an investor will usually seek a much higher return if there is a degree of uncertainty about either the rate of earnings or the return of the original equity invested. Real estate investments, including rental apartments, have those risks; such investments must be structured to deliver a higher rate of return.

As we enter the 1990s, investors are searching for cash generators. They are looking for apartments and other forms of rental real estate that will produce a steady flow of cash as a return or reward for invested capital. The problem is that there are few properties that qualify as continuous moneymakers and many investors are in search of them. Whenever there are too many bidders, the price goes up and an increased price lessens the property's ability to deliver the desired return. The alternative is to look for properties that have been poorly managed, or ones that have been so loaded down with debt in the past that they have a dismal record of returning periodic cash. A great many properties fall into this category, and most experienced real estate buyers spend their days searching for the properties offering the opportunity of periodic cash returns.

Appreciation in Value

When investors search for real estate investments that will, with reasonable probability, grow in value at a faster rate than inflation, the process is commonly called "playing long ball." As a group, these investors are typically successful in their primary career and they look to real estate investment as a way of building equity and staying ahead of or at least even with inflation. Most people who invest in land are looking for appreciation in value because that is the only promise land speculation offers. Others wait for an economic upturn after purchasing buildings in up-and-coming locations or properties that need an infusion of new money and imagination. Some investors pay too much to capture a trophy building in a prime neighborhood and are forced to wait for rents and eventual values to catch up. The goal of appreciation is present in each of these examples.

Think about the difference between the management techniques employed to satisfy the goals of an owner who is more interested in the ultimate property appreciation and those employed to satisfy the owner who is only concerned with the monthly generation of cash return. Usually, the management techniques employed for an owner looking solely for periodic return are far more conservative than they are for the investor speculating and building for the future.

Control of Investment

An investment in real estate probably offers the investor more control than any other form of investment short of a passbook savings account. When you purchase stocks or bonds, you are clearly at the mercy of a great many influences over which you have absolutely no control. When a particular stock plummets or panic selling begins in the market, investors may not see the warning until it is much too late to avoid losses. Bonds, gold, and collectibles often follow patterns that are difficult to predict and impossible to control. With real estate, however, the investor can exercise some degree of control. If there is a surplus of unfurnished apartments in the market, the answer may be to offer some units as furnished or corporate units. If two-bedroom apartments with one bathroom are slow to rent, perhaps the second bedroom can be modified into a den or an extension of the living room. The owner or agent can attract more customers by adding some punch to the entranceway landscaping. An apartment operator can always exercise control over occupancy levels—and sometimes influence profits—by adjusting rent rates.

Some aspects of real estate are beyond the investor's control. Real estate markets, mortgage rates, and availability are a few examples. Tax laws, environmental issues, and neighborhood influences all change; they too are usually beyond the immediate control of the real estate investor. Nevertheless, real estate offers a far greater degree of control than most other forms of investment and you, as a manager, will be called upon to participate in that control.

Pride of Ownership

For many people, being able to demonstrate success and a high level of achievement is a common desire. Over the centuries, real estate has been used by many successful people to display wealth and power within a community. While considering this concept, several names probably come to mind—people who have named towers, developments, or even entire communities after themselves. On a less grand scale, there are many real estate owners who are more motivated by the pride they have in their properties than by the dollars they can earn. As a manager, you will probably come in contact with the type of owner who regularly sacrifices maximum profits while making a property more and more of a showcase. To such an owner, decisions regarding an effect on the property's appearance always seem to outweigh the immediate effect on the bottom line. All the same, it can be said that pride of ownership is another form of appreciation in value; meticulously maintained properties almost always command premium prices at resale.

For Use by Owner

This ownership goal is not nearly as prevalent in rental apartments as it is with office, commercial, or industrial real estate; but it does occur. There are owners who prefer living in a multifamily building and do not want to trust their lifestyle to the typical landlord. These owners may have friends who also choose apartments that can be modified or customized to their liking. Usually, properties that are owned and used in part by their owners enjoy better locations. Also, a much more strict set of criteria is used to screen prospects who wish to rent in these properties. One of the most difficult assignments a property manager can undertake is handling the affairs of a rental apartment property in which the owner or owners reside. This arrangement usually involves two sets of rules—one set for the owners and a distinctly different one for the rent-paying residents.

Financing Leverage

One of the attributes of real estate ownership is that an investor can leverage a considerably larger investment through borrowing. In its heyday, mortgage financing of 90 and even 100 percent was not uncommon. An investor who made a relatively small cash down payment could control real estate worth much more. Any cash return was substantial when compared to the actual cash at risk. Many books and even television shows have been created to show the world how to become rich through the use of other people's money. Leverage or mortgage borrowing is fine when the cost of the money (the interest rate) is close to the earning rate of the property. The problems begin to escalate quickly, however, when a property can only earn, say, 7 percent and borrowing the money costs 10 percent or more. Another sure indicator of trouble is when the mortgage payments are so high that they begin to "steal" money away from needed operating revenues. During inflationary times, many owners choose to burden their properties with additional debt in order to gain the advantage of acquiring cash today; this allows them to pay back the debt with cheaper, inflation-diluted dollars. Managing investment real estate that has been the subject of such financing schemes and extremes is a most difficult undertaking. After the debt service has been paid, there is often little left to properly operate the investment.

Income Tax Shelter

For a period of some forty years, investment real estate enjoyed a unique advantage over almost all other ventures. Owners were allowed to *recover the cost of their investment*—often at an accelerated rate—and offset any resulting losses against their other income including salaries and the like. Tax laws allowed investors to be creative and aggressive in their interpretation of these regulations. Property values regularly exceeded the properties' ability to earn a return because investors sought the advantages granted by the favorable tax climate. The tax-saving aspects of real estate ownership negated a consideration of the basics of location and the particular property's ability to generate any return. Many managers were pushed past the point of reason when investors insisted that tax-driven investments continue operating in an effort to avoid the negative consequences of recapture should the property fail and fall into receivership. After the shock of a new set of tax laws, it took some time to convince investment property owners that the tax-shelter advantage had been neutralized and real estate must again stand on its own merits.

Hedge on Inflation

Whenever there is a hint of inflation and its erosion of the strength of the dollar, investors begin a shift to collectibles; and one of the most popular and most tangible is investment real estate. Rents historically parallel inflation, thereby protecting the earning power of real estate. Single-family homes often lead price increases in an inflationary period and reach a point at which they become unaffordable. When people can't afford their own homes, the alternative generally is renting; this strengthens the income potential of rental apartments.

OWNERSHIP DISADVANTAGES

There are disadvantages, too, to purchasing real estate as an investment. A wrong decision in the original purchase or in the method of operation may be enough to wipe out the investment. Market conditions—fluctuating as they do—as well as local laws and ordinances can adversely affect the situation. Rent control, specialized health and safety requirements, and significant changes in property tax rates, for example, can be damaging blows to real estate investment. More than that, real estate ownership means the loss of the liquidity of investment capital. For example, while stocks, bonds, and savings accounts can be cashed quickly when funds are needed elsewhere, real estate may require sixty days or more to liquidate—and then perhaps at a loss because of the quick sale.

Ownership of income-producing real estate involves business management problems that do not appear in most other forms of investment. In addition to the professional management needed to operate the property, there must be supervision of the management itself. More than that, investors in real estate face the fact that bricks and mortar do not last forever. Ultimately, all that will be left is the land itself. Clearly, few investors expect to live long enough to face this eventuality.

Despite these formidable shortcomings and the fact that many owners are not making money on real estate investments, private investments in multifamily housing properties still offer opportunities for profit. In fact, it can be said that investment in all forms of real estate provides an attraction shared by no other form of investment. This is because land, with or without improvements, is something tangible and inexhaustible that historically has appreciated in value.

FORMS OF OWNERSHIP

The form or structure of the entity that holds title to the property is independent of the type of property, its location, or the resident who selects it for occupancy. Here are some of the more common forms of apartment ownership together with a short description of their unique features or approaches to ownership.

Individual Investors

Most people who invest in income-producing apartment buildings come under the classification of sole owners. These individuals frequently use the income from other business pursuits or employment income as the investment ante that allows them to enter the real estate world. Their investment choice is influenced by the allure of real estate and all the advantages outlined earlier.

Partnerships

When two or more entities invest in a property, it is said to be held by a partnership. All partners in an ordinary partnership are *general partners*. By having more people involved, the risks to each individual are reduced, and larger purchases can be made that may be more profitable because of the economies that come with size. In the case of partnerships, there is always the problem of how to control and deal with disenchanted partners. Written partnership agreements help but are never adequate when disagreements arise.

Some partnerships are formed involuntarily through inheritance. These arrangements can be most difficult for the property manager because the goals and objectives of the various partners and their attitudes toward risk often are at odds. Hence, the manager is thrust into the position of mediator. This generally is not a problem with a voluntary partnership whose participants have similar goals and objectives, although even here disagreements do occur.

Limited partnership is another popular form of ownership. Unlike the general partnership, with partners whose liability is not limited, the limited partnership involves two classes of ownership: one or more general partners and the limited partner(s). Essentially, the general partner is the quarterback who organizes and calls the plays (i.e., controls the property and makes up any operating losses that may occur). Meanwhile, *limited partners* invest capital in an agreed-upon amount, and this amount becomes the limit of their liability. The limit, however, applies only so long as the general partner is solvent and performs as expected. If the general partner fails to do this, the limited partners, who otherwise are passive investors, may have to assume responsibility to protect their investment; however, they are under no legal obligation to do so. Property managers who deal with properties owned by limited partnerships take their direction from the general partners, not the limited partners.

Joint Venture

In the joint venture, the skills and assets of two or more individuals or entities are brought together for one specific project. Typically, one furnishes the investment capital while the other furnishes services or know-how. Builders and developers frequently supply their construction knowledge and capabilities, while their joint-venture colleagues come up with the cash. Many large lending institutions and other major corporations have funded such operations as investments. No rules dictate how profits are split, as each case is negotiated separately. The success or failure of a joint venture rests solely with the attitude and skills of the partners involved.

Corporate Ownership

There are several different types of corporations; a corporation can be nonpublic or publicly traded, for-profit or not-for-profit, it can have C corporation or S corporation status. All corporations are legal entities that are chartered by their states.

Many corporations over the years have plunged into the business of owning multifamily rental housing. These attempts at diversification have not always been successful—despite the general tendency for real estate to appreciate in value with the passage of time. Real estate entrepreneurs and developers succeed more often than not because of a certain degree of daring. They move quickly in ways that are dynamic, even flamboyant. These are not operational characteristics of corporations—especially large ones—whose structure prevents making intuitive decisions. When major corporations suffer substantial losses, it takes time for them to forget their disillusionment.

A few large corporations have entered the multifamily housing business, not as an investment, but as a way to provide convenient, safe, and clean residential accommodations for their employees. In some cases, special holding companies may be formed to conceal the real ownership and thereby avoid the adverse publicity of creating a "company town."

Insurance Companies and Lending Institutions.   Some of the largest companies in America are to be found in the residential housing business as owners. These include insurance companies, banks, thrift institutions, and the government—the prime lenders of the capital needed to finance apartment housing. Often this ownership is involuntary—the consequence of having to foreclose on delinquent accounts. Ownership that develops in this manner is usually the interim or caretaker type: The goal is to wait out the bad times and resell the investment at a price that minimizes the loss. The difficulties associated with financial failure and differences in goals and objectives add a complicating dimension to the business of handling foreclosed properties.

Increasingly, insurance companies and lending institutions are acquiring real estate as investments. In an inflationary economy, these institutions are less inclined to accept the fixed, long-term yield associated with providing mortgage financing. Instead, they are choosing to take equity positions. They are adding real estate investments to their portfolios because such investments produce income and appreciate in value.

Real Estate Investment Trusts

Real estate investment trusts, referred to as REITs (pronounced REETS), are another form of ownership. Through a pooling of funds to create substantial investment capacity, REITs give small investors the profit opportunities and the advantages that come from participation in real estate ownership. However, the REIT investor has almost no voice in the management.

In their operation, REITs get approval from the Securities and Exchange Commission to make a public offering of shares of beneficial interest. The funds so generated then are put into the purchase of investment real estate (i.e., equity REITs) or used as short-term mortgage money for real estate properties (i.e., mortgage REITs). Because the value of an investment in a REIT is subject to fluctuations similar to the stock market and not tied exclusively to the values of the properties themselves, an important advantage of real estate ownership may be missing.

In the early 1970s, REITs quickly plunged millions of dollars into real estate without proper research and knowledge. In the declining real estate market of 1974 to 1975, major losses were felt both by REITs and their investors. Since that time, REITs steadily have been rebuilding their image in the investment community, and today their portfolios reflect a healthier and more conservative investment attitude.

Condominium and Cooperative Ownership

Condominiums and cooperatives are forms of mutual ownership that center on personal benefits, not profit. Although many condominium buyers hope their investments will appreciate, the owners are primarily users, not investors.

Condominium and cooperative ownership presents a most difficult challenge to professional management. This is because the two essential ingredients for successful management are lacking.

The first ingredient is knowledge of the property. To be successful, the property manager must know more about the property than anyone else—especially the residents. This is very difficult to do when the condominium owners live in the building and the manager does not. The manager is forced to assume a defensive posture when the unit owners constantly search out problems and flaws in management and make complaints.

The second ingredient is authority. The management of a business enterprise is most successful when it is run, to a degree, as a benevolent dictatorship; in other words, when there is one boss. However, most cooperatives and condominiums are operated by an elected board of directors and a collection of committees—in spite of the fact that they have hired professional management. Instead of restricting themselves to major fiscal matters and long-range policy, the board and its committees feel compelled to get involved in the day-to-day operating problems. This is less true in very expensive condominiums, whose units typically are owned by successful businesspeople more accustomed to delegating authority. The problem also lessens with time as the condominium association stabilizes and the succeeding boards come to realize that professional managers possess the skills to operate their property. Unfortunately, it usually takes several changes in management before this occurs.

Foreign Ownership

Balance-of-payment deficits have sent hundreds of billions of United States' dollars overseas. Many foreign investors have chosen to return these dollars to the United States by investing in American real estate, which they regard as an extremely attractive investment. Typically, they search for stabilized commercial and industrial properties and invest relatively few dollars in rental apartment developments. Apartments are shunned because of the intensive management required to operate them and the fear of rent control that might be imposed. Still, some management opportunities in rental housing do exist with foreign investors.

TYPES OF MANAGERS

A manager is primarily an *agent*—an extension of the owner he or she represents. The owner's interest always should be uppermost in the professional manager's mind. When faced with decision making, the property manager ought to ask: "What would I do if I owned this property?" The manager who has acquired experience and specialized skills is in a much better position than the owner to produce a qualified answer. As a professional substitute for the owner, the property manager is like any other professional whose specialized skills are applied in the owner's best interests.

The basic goal of the property manager is to produce the highest possible net operating income (NOI). This is defined as collections less operating expenses. Some owners would like the property manager's role expanded to include the production of the highest possible *cash flow,* which is net operating income less debt service (mortgage payment). The amount and payment of debt service has little to do with successful management. The property manager who has produced maximum rent collections and has kept operating expenses to an effective minimum has done the job, regardless of the debt service the owner must pay.

So with the goals and responsibilities of management in mind, let us look at what is involved in property management. First, a professional property manager must be equipped with a storehouse of information about the property and its location, the market area, operating expenses, maintenance techniques, reporting procedures, and a host of other items. The principal ingredients that make a capable property manager are common sense, resourcefulness, and a willingness to work hard. The sole purpose of this book is to offer managers time-tested knowledge that has been gained by others through years of experience.

The most exciting part of the management business is the handling of investment properties for profit. While caretaker assignments and not-for-profit housing offer their own opportunities and challenges, in the main, this book is directed at managing income-producing multifamily housing.

Investment housing is intended to generate profits. In fact, the value of investment real estate is in direct proportion to the property's ability to generate net operating income. The manager's role is to produce the highest possible net operating income over the economic life of the property.

The skills in managing profit-producing housing are more demanding and more fulfilling than those needed for caretaker or not-for-profit management. In fact, managing the caretaker or not-for-profit properties can be very frustrating because of the absence of a material goal. Without the motivation of producing a profit, the manager is often deprived of the purpose and spirit required to succeed.

The differences between the types of managers really reflect varying degrees of knowledge possessed at the different levels. Granted, the amount of authority also changes, but this is just a further reflection of a particular manager's skill and experience.

Managers are employed in one of two ways: as direct employees of owners, who can be individuals, partnerships, corporations, or even the government; or as employees of real estate companies that are in the business of property management. The first type covers the greatest number of property managers.

The managers described below may belong to either group. They are the people who are engaged in the practice of property management and enjoy career opportunities rarely found today. The success or failure of privately financed investment real estate falls on their shoulders. Those who learn their lessons well will be rewarded both financially and in the satisfaction of performing a vitally needed service.

Executive Property Manager

An executive property manager is a supervisor who oversees and directs other property managers who are in the field handling the operational affairs of various properties. The executive's primary concern is with running a business that manages properties rather than with the direct management of those properties. Knowledge for this position is usually acquired from long and broad experience in the actual management of investment real estate. This knowledge is used to establish long-range policies and fiscal plans and to guide the company's property managers in resolving difficult situations.

The executive property manager is frequently an officer of the company and, in fact, might be its owner. Typically, compensation is by a regular salary; additional incentive bonuses are common.

Asset Manager

This is a comparatively new job description in the business of property management. Asset managers answer the need for finely-tuned skills in the planning, analysis, and financial tracking of investment real estate. These managers are often charged with the long-range planning and preparation of business plans for rather substantial investment portfolios. It's common to combine the use of an asset manager with a full complement of management personnel. For example, a 200-unit apartment community might have a site manager who works for a supervising property manager who, in turn, reports to an executive property manager. At the top of this "ladder" might be an asset manager who is coordinating that 200-unit property with the other properties in his or her portfolio. Matters such as capital improvements, cash management, market analysis, rent structuring, budget tracking, plus short- and long-range goal attainment are a few of the responsibilities of the asset manager.

Sometimes an individual or company will hire an asset manager to directly supervise or at least monitor the activities of the people or firm doing the actual management of a property. One of the problems with this arrangement is that some asset managers distance themselves from the daily problems and pressures of residential management and make decisions based on business textbook guidelines. Rental housing is a consumer product that is emotional as well as volatile. Careful tracking of rents and expenses along with comparative studies of neighboring properties will frequently help an analyst to develop a financial plan, but there is no substitute for a thorough understanding of the property and its marketplace. This knowledge comes with years of hands-on experience. Hence, the asset manager whose analytical skills are combined with day-to-day property involvement can deliver significantly better bottom-line results.

Property Manager

The individual who is directly responsible for managing a particular property is called a property manager. In effect, the person holding this title is the chief operating officer or administrator of a particular property or group of properties. A property manager is responsible for fiscal planning, setting rents, establishing marketing and maintenance procedures, supervising site managers, and reporting to and maintaining liaison with owners and superiors.

Site Manager

At the next level of management is the site manager. Responsibilities of a person in this position include day-to-day dealings with residents, renting units, making collections, and follow-through supervision of maintenance. The site manager is truly the person on the firing line.

Some people refer to the site manager as the on-site or resident manager, which implies that the person lives on the site. This is not always true. The place of residence has nothing to do with the responsibilities of this position. In this book, the term "site manager" will be used to refer to this level of management.

"Ma and Pa" Management

So called "ma and pa" management, originally popular in small hotel-motel buildings, is well on its way to extinction in apartment operations. Typically, one spouse performs renting and bookkeeping duties, while the other handles maintenance and perhaps problem collections or disturbances. While less expensive in the short run than professional management, this arrangement is frequently inadequate and ineffective in today's demanding times—especially for major investments.

THE MANAGEMENT AGREEMENT

When any of the types of manager are employed directly by the owner, the duties and responsibilities are commonly spelled out in a job description. When the manager is an employee of the management company that is acting as the managing agent for the owner, the duties and responsibilities are defined in what is referred to as a management agreement. At its most basic level, this document accomplishes several functions:

- It serves as an employment contract between the owner and the managing agent.
- It establishes an agency relationship, giving the managing agent the right to act in the owner's behalf and to assume obligations in the name of the owner.
- It spells out the rights, responsibilities, and limitations of the managing agent.
- It stipulates the managing agent's compensation.
- Finally, it provides for the agreement's termination.

To undertake the management of real estate without a management agreement is hazardous. The main reason for having an agreement is that it sets out everything in writing, thereby reducing the chance of misunderstandings. The agreement is more for the managing agent's protection than for the owner's.

Powers

A managing agent is far more than the owner's representative. The agent, in effect, acts for the owner and has the same powers as the owner would have.

As the owner's agent, the manager has the authority to set rents; to execute, extend, and cancel leases; and to make settlements with residents. The authority to collect money and spend it on behalf of the property is also granted. The manager has a fiduciary responsibility to the owner to act honestly and in good faith, which requires a precise accounting of collections and expenditures.

The management agreement also gives the agent the authority to execute contracts for building services, keep the property in good condition, and make repairs. What is spent on maintenance and repairs may be limited by a dollar amount, beyond which the owner's further approval is needed. The exception would be emergencies when life or property is threatened.

The manager also has the authority to hire, fire, and supervise personnel. Staff employees are generally employees of the property owner, not direct employees of the managing agent. However, even when this is the case, you may be considered an alternate employer because of your authority to hire, fire, and supervise. For instance, you may be held responsible for observing all requirements of the federal and state Wage and Hour Laws. This obligation cannot be avoided, even though the personnel are employees of the owner. Along with the manager's authority to hire, fire, and supervise, there is a corresponding responsibility to see that all employment conditions required by the law are fulfilled. The owner in turn holds the manager responsible for fulfilling all the obligations that are specified in the agreement.

The extent and limitations of the agent's authority to act on the owner's behalf should be set forth clearly in the management agreement. This authority is needed for three specific reasons:

1. *To establish the manager's authority to execute a lease.* A tenant may challenge your authority to do so. By referring to the management agreement you can support this authority.
2. *To meet Internal Revenue Service requirements for filing employee tax payments.*
3. *To distribute net proceeds to the owners.* This can be complicated. You must get specific direction from all of the owners for any percentage distribution of net proceeds. It's not uncommon for a managing agent to receive a contract from two owners, only to discover later that there are other owners who demand their share of the proceeds. The only protection you have is to identify all of the owners and make sure that they all sign any distribution instructions.

Independent Contractor.   When soliciting new management accounts from a lending institution that has a portfolio of foreclosed properties or from a major investment institution that owns apartment properties, you may be asked to sign an agreement that is not the typical form management agreement but a contract that identifies you as an *independent contractor.* The reason for this is that these institutions often do not want you to be acting in an agency capacity but rather as a hired vendor. There is a world of difference between the status and liability of an independent contractor and that of an agent. Be sure to carefully review such a document with your attorney to determine whether or not this change in capacity is acceptable to your firm. Many independent contractor contracts are thinly veiled agency agreements that will be interpreted as such by the courts. Be sure to seek a professional legal opinion before proceeding.

Obligations

The manager's overall obligation is to act in a professional manner with the owner's interest as the first objective. Most management agreements place obligations on the agent to:

*   Ensure that the property achieves maximum occupancy with the most economical outlay of operating expenses.
*   Collect rents.
*   Pay bills incurred for the property.
*   Submit a report to the owner of collections and disbursements.
*   Make sure that the necessary property and liability insurance is maintained.
*   Pay real estate taxes from building funds.

- File employee payroll tax returns.
- Maintain the property with building funds.
- Notify the owner of the property's shortcomings and defects as well as citations.
- Maintain records such as leases, tax payments, mortgage payments, original paid invoices, and insurance policies, all of which are the owner's property. Correspondence files and books of account that the managing agent generates in the course of managing the property remain the property of the agent, not the owner.

Associated Risks

A managing agent is exposed to certain risks. The hold-harmless provisions of the management agreement are designed to minimize these risks by placing many responsibilities on the owner and providing for the payment of legal defense in certain matters, unless the agent has been negligent. These matters generally include:

- Actions stemming from the owner's refusal to advance needed funds.
- Building code violations.
- Civil rights suits.
- Wage and Hour claims.
- Occupational Safety and Health Act (OSHA) claims.
- Lawsuits in general.
- Harmful or improper acts of employees.

Compensation

The most common method of compensation for property managers is a flat percentage of total collections from a property's operation (less security deposits). It's also routine to have an established "floor," so that the manager has a guaranteed minimum fee. This method is traditional and it gives the managing agent an incentive to collect the maximum rents.

In addition to covering the managing agent's fee, *the agreement should also spell out who pays for on-site administrative help.* Usually, this is the responsibility of the owner, not the managing agent.

Finally, *the agreement should contain any specifics on commissions for renting apartments and bonuses for renewals.*

Termination or Cancellation

The management agreement can be terminated in one of four ways:

- When the term of the agreement expires.
- By notice from either the owner or the managing agent according to contract provisions.

- By mutual agreement. If cancellation is negotiated, one party may ask for payment from the other in return for early termination.
- When the purpose is ended. A common reason for terminating agreements is the sale of the building. Owners retain agents to manage their property, but if a property is sold, the purpose is gone and the contract normally is ended. The managing agent may seek protection against early termination by having the agreement state that a sale of property does not affect the contract, or if the building is sold, that the agent will receive a specified sum as liquidated damages.

The management agreement is an important document, one that should be kept in a safe place. However, it doesn't guarantee continuous employment. Only effective performance will do that.

2

Establish Policies for Smooth Operations

Every business, large or small, is confronted constantly with situations and problems that demand decisions. One way of handling this decision-making responsibility is with *policies,* which are prepared answers to anticipated problems. Some of these policies will eliminate many problems in the first place. Others will permit recurring problems to be dealt with swiftly and competently.

The development of proper policies is critical to the smooth functioning and successful marketing of multifamily housing. Every property management organization needs to have policies. Even a one-person management operation needs them, because it will face the same problems that the large management company faces. For the large company with hundreds or thousands of units to manage, problems are much the same in kind; they simply are more numerous. Without policies, management would have to make decisions on a case-by-case basis. Not having policies would not only lead to chaos and be time consuming but also produce inconsistent results.

Policies help to eliminate all this. They clear the air. Policies let all persons involved know where they stand, what's expected of them, and what will be done when something goes wrong.

The right policies permit the scheduling of management activities on a routine basis and thus enable the manager to concentrate on the really demanding aspects of the business. Certainly policies have to be developed in accordance with the owner's goals and objectives, but the best policies are shaped by the expertise of a professional property manager.

With policies, it is not necessary to spend time constantly reinventing the wheel, so work becomes more efficient. Once a pattern has been set, it can be followed until something occurs to indicate the policy is no longer useful.

Yes, policies should be reviewed and changed when necessary. Policies are guidelines, not straitjackets. It is not possible to anticipate every contingency. From time to time, you will encounter problems that cannot be dealt with unless policies are bent a little or changed entirely. But for the most part, policies will save you the trouble of making time-consuming decisions on an individual basis.

Policies are also important because they compel you to study your business and understand it thoroughly. Good policies cannot be made until you know everything about your business. When taking over a property for the first time, you must do a lot of creative thinking—just like a chess player does—to plan moves and consider alternatives.

Policies are important not only for you, the manager, but also for rental agents and the maintenance staff, prospects and residents in the building, as well as the owner. Each has a right to know what to expect. The time to examine those expectations is before a crisis erupts when there is time to reach a cool, unimpassioned decision rather than being forced to act in haste.

To be useful, policies should be in writing and made available to everyone concerned. When policies are changed, these changes should be communicated to all appropriate parties. Confusion can be prevented by dating your printed policies and including revision dates on all changed pages.

Policies should be reasonable and enforceable. The manager's position will be weakened if policies are established that cannot be enforced, and he or she will appear dictatorial if the policies are unreasonable.

You do not have to rely entirely on your own ability to anticipate problems. In the beginning, property management had to innovate, because there was no history of professional expertise. You are more fortunate since you can learn from the experiences of others.

The following discussion will focus on some policies that ensure high levels of efficiency. In a very real sense, much of this book is a delineation of policies that address the various aspects of apartment management. Special areas that call for policies will be pointed out, and alternative policies will be suggested. In some cases, specific policies will be recommended. But in the end, it is often up to the manager to determine the policies best suited to a particular situation.

To ensure an efficient management operation, general policies are needed in several major areas. Specifically, policies should cover the rental and management office, recreational facilities, amenities of the property, and parking. When these policies are formulated, they will be a useful framework from which specialized personnel, rental, and resident-related policies can be approached.

THE OFFICE

Let's begin with policies that relate to the rental and management office. Apartment complexes may have one or two such offices depending on the size of the development. One thing is certain: Policies are as important to the management of an apartment building with a single office as they are to a building with two offices.

Office Location

There probably will be several possible locations for the rental and management office. Since the purpose of the office is to serve both prospects and residents, it should be located where it will be easy to find, especially for prospects. From this standpoint, the closer the office is to the road or visitor parking lot, the better.

One of the best places to locate the office is close to or in the property's recreational facility. There are several advantages to this arrangement.

- It ensures that prospects will see the recreational facilities. In the later stages of a rental program, agents showing the property may skip that part of the tour. The prospect who must come to the recreational area to get to the office sees the facility, which should be a real plus in the marketing program. Unfortunately, in some properties, the recreational facility is closed or even locked during daylight hours.
- You can supervise the recreational facility without adding the extra staff you would need if the office and facility were separate.
- Finally, when the office is located in the recreational facility, you can easily check on its maintenance and make sure the facility is kept clean at all times.

Complexes without recreational facilities obviously exist; and in these cases the office should be in an easy-to-find location—probably close to the main entrance. Ideally, the office will have a separate outside entrance so prospects do not have to enter the building lobby.

Some managers like the idea of making the rental office part of the model apartment or setting up the office in a regular apartment next to the model. When alternatives are available, these are poor choices. They breach security by bringing outside visitor traffic into the building and by having a commercial purpose intrude into a residential area.

Combining the office with the model apartment usually destroys the merchandising appeal of the model. If only one unit is available, it would be better to have only an office and no model. Taking over a next-door apartment for the office eliminates the rental revenue from that unit. Circumstances may force you into this situation, but avoid it if possible.

One Office or Two?

The function of the rental office, or, as it should be known, the *rental information center,* is to serve prospects; the function of the management office is to serve residents. For this reason, you may consider having two separate offices. However, it is generally better to combine the two functions in a single office, since such an arrangement uses personnel more effectively. If, at slack periods, there is only one person in an office, there would be no staff present if that individual had to leave for a few minutes. When the two functions are combined, rental and management people can fill in for each other when necessary. This arrangement also allows the staff to gain a better understanding of the property's total operation. Possible exceptions are extremely large complexes.

Some managers prefer to separate the two functions in all cases to avoid the risk of having a complaining resident come into the office and discourage a prospect who overhears the complaint. Most managers do not encounter this problem frequently, especially when their properties are operated properly. If a resident complains, it's generally at the time of rent payment (usually early in the morning or late in the day) or just before a major holiday (like Thanksgiving or Christmas) when it's important to get things looking right for visiting friends and relatives. These are light rental periods when prospects are not apt to be present.

If the thought of having residents and prospects running into each other is still a concern, a private area in the same office can be set aside for residents. The fact remains that a combined office is more efficient than two separate ones.

Office Appearance

Despite the old saying, "you can't judge a book by its cover," people can and do judge by appearance. A disorderly management office with service requests stacked in the file tray, half-empty coffee cups lying around, wastebaskets overflowing, and old plumbing parts on the floor may make a rental prospect wonder just how well the rest of the building is maintained.

Maintaining an attractive appearance is essential. Desks should be clean and uncluttered. Ashtrays should be emptied several times a day and wiped clean each time. Coffee pots and cups should be kept out of sight, except when coffee is being served. If there are magazines for prospects to read while they are waiting, the copies should be current and appear fresh. Windows should be sparkling and the floor cleaned or vacuumed daily. Good housekeeping in the rental office will pay off in increased prospect confidence.

Office Hours

Again, because the office exists to serve prospects and residents, the hours of operation should conform to the habits of the people being served.

Consider prospects first. My experience shows that Sunday is the day when you can expect the greatest activity. Some managers dispute this. They say they never see any prospects on Sunday. (Why? Probably because their offices are not open!) Don't doubt the importance of Sunday; it is almost always the busiest day.

Holidays are as important as Sundays. The only exceptions are Thanksgiving Day, Christmas, and New Year's Day, when most people stay home. But Easter, Memorial Day, Fourth of July, and Labor Day bring out apartment hunters.

Monday evening is another prime time for prospects. Saturday, contrary to what some may believe, is a relatively poor day, because people reserve it for grocery shopping and other chores.

Knowing this, it's a good idea to keep the rental office open on Sundays and holidays in addition to weekdays. That means seven days a week. A study of prospect traffic in our office revealed that few people show up before 11:00 A.M. So generally, with rental hours from 11:00 A.M. to 6:00 P.M., you'll catch most of the prospect traffic. When establishing your hours, avoid changes from one day to the next. Consider the fact that it's unwise to show apartments after dark. You may want to extend your hours in the summer when daylight saving time is in effect. Also, you should post your rental hours so prospects know when the office is open.

Quite possibly, rental hours may differ from actual office hours. For example, even with rental hours of 11 A.M. to 6 P.M., the workday might begin as early as 7:30 A.M. This allows the office staff to plan the day and start work before problems begin to take precedence.

Banks and landlords were probably two of the last holdouts against adjusting business hours to meet customer needs. Banking institutions today are certainly open and ready to serve their clients at all sorts of odd hours. Apartment managers should follow suit. We need to be open when the customer is most likely to have free time. That will include early mornings, some evenings, and all weekends. Be aware that service is the property manager's goal. If you need to change hours to better serve prospects and residents, do so!

RECREATIONAL FACILITIES

From the single room with a ping-pong table to a lavish clubhouse, all the property's recreational facilities need policies to govern hours of use, guests, and fees. Otherwise, these facilities will be uncontrolled, a situation that will irritate residents and reflect poorly on management.

In setting hours, consider residents' preferences as well as the effect on those who live near the facility. For example, it would not be wise to permit the clubhouse to be open until midnight if it is immediately adjacent to dwelling units.

Guests can be a problem. There is a thin line between being so restrictive that residents will be discouraged from having guests (and may move out for that reason) and being so relaxed that the entire neighborhood can use the facility. A policy that many managers have found workable is to limit guests to two at a time in the company of a resident.

As for guest fees, avoid them if possible. Residents dislike them, and they make your place seem unfriendly. Guest fees, a negligible revenue source, also create extra bookkeeping work.

Do not staff the facility with any more personnel than absolutely necessary. Once you do, you've established a precedent that you may have to maintain. Unless you are legally required to have a swimming pool lifeguard, don't hire one unless it's a service you wish to extend indefinitely.

If your development has a nice facility, make sure that the established policies allow the residents to use it. Sometimes management is reluctant to let the residents use the recreational facility for fear it will become less "showable" to prospective renters. If this feature cannot be used by residents on a regular basis, it really will have little value in the rental process.

The character of recreational facilities has really evolved over the years. They are used less for seasonal parties, or as space to be rented for private gatherings. Many have been converted to private clubs for the residents and their guests. Evening offerings such as snacks, beverages, and entertainment (piano music, for example) are often used to attract residents. Renting the facility to one resident prohibits its use by all others. The private club concept benefits all residents and encourages a general camaraderie among them; this, in turn, prompts residents to renew their leases.

Neighboring rental developments may get together to develop jogging trails or, more commonly, exercise courses in which participants run or walk between guideposts and complete exercises on various apparatus. Few developments have the acreage to make an interesting and challenging course. Together, several competing apartment complexes can easily provide the land needed for something that will be beneficial to all.

Some types of equipment such as basketball standards and pool tables can attract groups that behave like gangs; this certainly should be avoided in apartment complexes. If the manager sees unruly teenagers beginning to congregate around apartment facilities, a change in the rules or removal of the equipment should be considered. It's always better to take the initiative than to be forced to respond to complaints.

Finally, establish a policy governing use of the recreational facilities by special-interest groups, such as political organizations or commercial enterprises. Generally, such use should be discouraged.

SUPPORTING AMENITIES

Most properties have supporting amenities designed to meet basic resident needs and make life more comfortable. Carefully consider what policies are needed for these facilities.

Laundry Room

This is a basic facility that is important in satisfying residents and will be of interest to prospects. Expect it to get heavy use.

Equipment is of primary importance. Availability of off-site facilities will influence your need for laundry room appliances, but a good method of defining equipment requirements estimates the ratio of washers and dryers to residents by taking resident type into account:

Young families	One washer and dryer per ten to twelve apartments
Career people	One washer and dryer per twelve to sixteen apartments
Upper rent level	One washer and dryer per twenty to twenty-four apartments
Senior Citizens	One washer and dryer per thirty to forty apartments

Dryers should be the single-load, stack-on variety rather than the large double-load models. The latter type is hard on clothes and does not offer the flexibility or revenue potential of the smaller dryers. Provide a sorting table, clothes hanging rods, and laundry tub in adequate numbers for the size of the facility. The laundry room should be properly ventilated, brightly decorated, well lit, and cleaned daily. To encourage neatness, add a wide-mouth trash receptacle. For resident convenience, a bulletin board is a good idea; but do keep an eye on the items posted and remove the undesirable ones. The laundry room should remain open the maximum number of hours each day, depending on its location. For security reasons and to minimize the disturbance to nearby residents, 11 P.M. is a typical closing time. If conditions permit, consider keeping it open twenty-four hours a day; residents who work odd hours will appreciate this. It may be necessary to keep the laundry room locked at all times. If so, residents should be issued laundry room keys; residents' apartment keys can also be designed to operate the laundry room lock.

Soap dispensers are usually cheaply made and are subject to failure and pilferage. Residents who come to depend on them will be irritated when the machines are empty or not working. It's best not to install them. In the absence of dispensers, residents will bring their own soap. Also, avoid having the management office make change; you might find yourself constantly interrupted by people asking for change. In my experience, most residents prefer using only one type of coin to operate the machines, even if it means paying slightly more.

Should the property own the laundry machines? From a financial standpoint, it is better to do so. But the burden and expense of maintenance, plus the risk of coin theft, are major drawbacks. If a manager deals with a concessionaire, he or she should reserve the right to approve prices charged to operate the machines. Otherwise, residents may become irritated and blame the manager if the concessionaire raises prices unreasonably.

Vending Machines

Cigarette, candy, soft drink, and ice dispensers are appreciated by many residents. These machines are best housed in a separate facility, preferably in or near the recreation room or clubhouse, in their own separate room, or in the laundry room.

The disadvantage of these vending machines is that they are subject to vandalism and theft. In time they create a maintenance problem and become unsightly, especially if exposed to the weather.

Pay Telephone

This can be a big convenience to residents on moving day, employees on the site, delivery people, and subcontractors. But it should be located outside the building in an out-of-the-way spot. If it is inside, the telephone may become a gathering place and will probably collect litter.

If you feel strongly about locating a pay telephone indoors, the laundry room is a good location. The lack of privacy in the laundry room would discourage people from spending too much time using the phone. Remember, a pay telephone in a locked laundry room is of no use to outsiders. Admitting other individuals to your laundry room to use the phone creates a breach of security.

Pay telephones are subject to vandalism and seldom generate enough revenue to pay for themselves. Cost is a consideration. Telephone companies offer different kinds of pay telephone service. "Public" phones do not necessarily involve a monthly fee; but there are requirements to meet (e.g., proximity to a business, a minimum number of daily calls). If these requirements can't be met, the alternate service is likely to involve installation fees as well as a monthly charge. Obviously, phone companies are your source of information regarding service and fee structures.

Storage

A well-kept, organized, brightly lit, and secure resident storage facility is a building asset. Some complexes have a storage room that's nothing more than a large room where residents can store items at random, without benefit of lockers or other separation. This arrangement has a major drawback: Even though the lease may have a disclaimer denying landlord responsibility for items stored in the facility, there still may be liability for theft or damage.

It is better to have separate resident lockers. They should be identified by apartment number to avoid confusion and to help the manager locate a particular residents's locker. To prevent residents from using unauthorized lockers or more than one locker, all vacant lockers should be kept securely locked until assigned.

PARKING

Parking is one of the perennial problems of management. Unsupervised parking of automobiles, motorcycles, boat trailers, and bicycles is a major detraction from the neat appearance of a property and adversely affects marketing. We'll pursue the subject of parking again in reference to readying your property for residents. For now, we'll make one key policy-making recommendation: Don't establish reserved parking. This rule always applies, except where parking spaces are enclosed or specially delineated, as in high-rise garages, covered carports, or individual garages.

The reason for this recommendation is simple: Reserved parking is extremely difficult to enforce. Residents who have reserved parking spaces naturally expect them always to be available. If they find another car in their space, they become upset and create a scene; this usually occurs late at night. Reserved parking that cannot be enforced is bound to irritate residents. You should avoid such policies because they erode good resident relations. Throughout this book, you will see examples of the importance of building your relationship with residents.

3

Human Resources

It is your staff who must make things work. Personnel policies in themselves will not make employees work harder or more skillfully; they will help minimize disputes and confusion while ensuring uniform treatment of employees and establishing a professional level of employment practices. The following discussion focuses on the key areas these policies should address.

HIRING

Before making any hiring decisions, it is wise to check the qualifications of all applicants. Be aware that federal law prohibits discrimination in employment. Complaints by applicants or employees claiming discrimination can be filed through a state commission, an office of the Equal Employment Opportunity Commission (EEOC) or federal court (state laws on filing vary). It's important to treat all potential employees the same, so none of your actions can be interpreted as discriminatory. The "EOE" (Equal Opportunity Employer) abbreviation is something you may want to include in advertising and application materials. Know the laws as they apply to your situation.

Screening Applicants

Obviously, it pays to find the right employees and there are means to locate the best people. Consider the following items.

- *Application form.* Be aware of what you can and cannot ask; check federal, state, and local laws governing hiring. In most cases, the standard application form you can purchase from local stationery or office supply stores will meet current requirements.
- *References.* Talk to the applicant's previous employer, if possible, or a reference who is not a relative. If the applicant has worked in property management before, ask the previous employer to list the applicant's strong and weak points. Pay particular attention to the answers you get.
- *Credit bureau.* A credit bureau check can provide information regarding judgments, bankruptcy, and general credit history. The information should not be used for making the decision of hiring unless it is relevant to the job (e.g., when the employee will have access to money or merchandise). If used for hiring there are specific disclosure requirements that must be followed as outlined in the Fair Credit Reporting Act. It is illegal in most states to refuse employment because of an employee's past; therefore, a credit check is of limited value and only serves to forewarn you that there may be trouble ahead.
- *Criminal check.* This can be done when required by business necessity (e.g., bonding requirements). Prior convictions should not be an absolute bar to employment. Consideration must be given to the nature of the position, how serious the prior offense was, and how recently the offense was committed.
- *Bonding.* Any employee who deals with money or is responsible for major expenses should be bonded.
- *Tests.* Some companies require applicants to take a battery of psychological and personality tests. These have their limitations but may be useful in giving you more insight regarding the applicant.
- *Polygraph tests.* Federal law prohibits the use of employee lie detector tests in most business situations. This practice, when used previously, almost always had a negative effect on the employees, so the loss of this technique should not be missed. In situations in which the employer has suffered an economic loss, polygraph tests are permissible after providing notice and meeting a number of other restrictions.

A much surer way of avoiding dishonest personnel would be to simply take a little extra time, carefully performing reference and background checks prior to making hiring decisions.

Matching the Individual to the Job

Employees must fit the development. The reverse is also true. Before you make a decision regarding employees, you should sit down and write a description of the types of people who currently reside in the complex.

Your choice for manager should be shaped by that resident profile. The manager should be comfortable with the rent levels being charged. For example, if the rents are in the $900 range, your manager should be comfortable with that figure; someone who would only pay a rent of $450 may not be. The subject of value will constantly surface; it is essential that the manager is not intimidated by a high rent or, on the other hand, does not belittle the residents because the rent level seems low.

Follow the same advice when choosing leasing agents. This position is one of the most important posts that you will fill. The rental agent is the only staff member whose job is to bring in new residents. The wrong choice can mean poor rental results, the wrong clientele, or both.

I conducted a series of rental agent evaluations for one of my major clients—a developer of comparatively high-rent apartments for successful professionals—and the results were startling. The agents had all been through rather extensive training and knew the neighborhood and product well. However, they were uncomfortable with the rent level and would only announce the rents timidly when asked directly. Our survey revealed that because these people were being paid by the hour, and most of them worked part-time, they were troubled by the concept of monthly rent exceeding their total monthly earnings. If a leasing agent is at all troubled by the rent level, it will be virtually impossible for that agent to help a prospect over that hurdle, or for that matter to understand the motivations of people in higher income brackets.

The leasing agent's demeanor should match your tenant profile. People need help and counsel in making major decisions about housing, but they will rarely take advice from someone who is not at least their age or who has not attained their achievement level. Don't expect an inexperienced rental agent to be able to provide the right touch or invoke the necessary urgency with an established, very sophisticated renter. Don't confuse a very helpful, energetic, and highly personable clerk with a professional rental agent who can make the difference between a signature and prospects who leave "to think about it." When times are tough, the match-up of the rental agent to the desired customer is critical. This is especially true at the high end of the market.

Job Descriptions

A job description is rarely a complete list of job responsibilities. Although most personnel manuals recommend that you have job descriptions, it's important to be aware of the problems that job descriptions may create; difficulties arise from the restrictive nature of any finite job description. Management personnel are called upon to perform a variety of duties, some of which can't be anticipated or formalized into a job description. An employee may balk at a request to perform a certain activity because "it wasn't in the job description." When you choose to put a job description in writing, be sure to make it as broad as possible.

PERSONNEL POLICIES

Policies are necessary tools for managing any staff. Like other policies in apartment management, employee policies are usually developed by the owner or in cooperation with the owner. It's a good idea to provide employees with a handbook setting guidelines for behavior and explaining the benefits provided.

Scheduling

When scheduling staff, remember that the apartment management business must be able to effectively serve both the prospect and the existing residents.

It is amazing that some residential management professionals will complain of poor rental results and search for ways to increase prospect traffic, but they won't work on the most important day of the week, Sunday. Granted, there are situations in which Sunday is not a business day, but these are rare occurrences indeed. More often than not, a manager will say that Sunday is not a business day in his or her area when in fact business could be brisk on Sunday if the office were open. Also, you must be aware that your Sunday staff must be top notch. A property simply cannot afford to have the rental office staffed with part-time rental agents during the times when most prospects do their serious looking. Some managers choose not to work on Sunday, even though the office is open. Sunday may not be producing any better results than other days, but it might be because the second-string staff is on duty then.

Besides renting, there are many other duties that can be better accomplished on Sunday. For example, most managers complain that there is a lack of uninterrupted time in which they can accomplish much needed planning or paperwork. Between 7:30 and 9:30 A.M. on Sunday morning, the manager is almost guaranteed some "quiet time." Sunday is also an excellent time to get out and meet the residents and handle renewals, solve problems, etc. This does not mean a six-day week. The work week of a great many managers runs from Sunday through Thursday.

Just as the presence of the manager is needed on Sunday, the property should have the benefit of its maintenance chief all day on Saturday. Many residents are reluctant to have people in their apartments when they themselves are not present. Perhaps they are experiencing a problem that is complicated and is best explained in person. Saturday is often perfect for that. Saturday service in an apartment complex is a must if you plan to retain the maximum number of existing residents. The convenience of your maintenance chief should not be a factor in deciding the level of service you're offering to your customer. The Saturday schedule should not be a partial day even though the rental office may not be open the full day. Typical hours for maintenance staff might be 7:30 A.M. to 4:00 P.M. Tuesday through Saturday.

Determining On-Site Staff

Living on-site was almost standard for apartment managers in the early years of the rental apartment business. The managers, often a "Ma and Pa" team, handled all rental and maintenance duties. This was basically a seven-day-a-week commitment. As apartment developments grew larger, the staff grew as well. Living on-site remained commonplace, but there were many exceptions. In this section, we'll examine the pros and cons of living on-site.

With a manager living on-site, you will always have someone available to handle the inevitable after-hours problems. The manager can witness the ways different facilities are used or abused during peak activity times. Monitoring parking patterns and night lighting is often ignored when the manager returns home at the end of the workday.

There are distinct disadvantages to having someone live on-site, burnout being perhaps the greatest. Working and living in the same place, especially in a business that involves a constant flow of problems, takes a heavy toll. Some managers become hermits and practically hide from tenants in an attempt to preserve some semblance of a private life. Some become hostile in an effort to keep intrusions to a minimum, while others strike up acquaintances with the existing residents. All of these reactions will have a negative impact on the complex. Many managers want to own their own homes. Others may have families too large for the apartments available. Rules requiring the on-site residence of a manager or a maintenance chief should be flexible. In most developments of any size, on-site personnel are important. Nevertheless, latitude should be exercised when assigning on-site duties.

It is a problem when staff members think themselves better than the residents and prefer not to live with them; this is almost instantly detected by the residents. Ultimately, there will be associated costs when residents sense that the staff has a low opinion of them. Turnover is almost certain to increase—it's difficult for people to feel good about their homes when the management displays even a hint of a belittling attitude.

When staff members live on-site, the location of their housing unit is the next decision to be made. Most managers live very close to the rental office or in a building that has a special view or some extra feature or appointment. This happens for two basic reasons. First of all, the manager's apartment was most likely part of the initial construction package. These early buildings often received very special treatment as they were being used to demonstrate the quality standards that were to follow.

After a period of time, the building begins to show wear. The process is much slower in the buildings immediately adjacent to the on-site employee's unit. The reason for this is simple. These areas and the various building components are in daily view of the manager and the necessary corrections are ordered. Many owners or supervisors who visit the property look only at the buildings surrounding the clubhouse and rental center. Owners authorize repairs or replacements in these areas to avoid losing prospects as a result of a bad first impression of the complex.

Another sure indicator of trouble occurs when the staff members choose to live in the very best units. To understand this, assume that a complex has fifty one-bedroom and forty two-bedroom apartments plus ten townhouses. The townhouses are in the least supply and probably in the greatest demand, plus they rent at top dollar. These units should be reserved for the tenants and not for the staff. The staff units should be the most difficult to lease rather than the exceptional apartments.

Socializing with Residents.   All employees should be discouraged from socializing with residents. This policy is particularly hard on employees who live on the site, but it's necessary. Socializing with residents, becoming personally involved with residents, or having an occasional drink are all seemingly innocent practices bound to affect an employees' judgment.

Posting Notices, Keeping Records

At this juncture, it is important to take note of the existence of some employee-related legal requirements. Managers must be aware of local, state, and federal regulations regarding the posting of certain notices and licenses. Here are some examples of commonly required postings.

1. Local business license
2. Real estate salesperson and broker's license
3. Unemployment insurance notice
4. Worker's compensation notice
5. Occupational Safety and Health Act notice (OSHA)
6. Equal Employment Opportunity (EEO) notice
7. Fair Housing notice
8. Employee Polygraph Protection Act poster
9. Fair Labor Standards Act (FLSA) poster
10. Age Discrimination in Employment Act (ADEA) poster

These notices primarily address issues concerning prospective employees and existing employees. Such posters must be placed in an area accessible to your staff. Those notices that pertain to residents and prospects must be similarly accessible to the "audience." Stay current: Laws change and there may be state regulations to keep in mind (e.g., your state Department of Labor probably has information-posting requirements).

There are also numerous laws that prescribe requirements regarding employee records, and these laws frequently change and expand. Some of these requirements are an outgrowth of The Occupational Safety and Health Act (OSHA) of 1970. OSHA includes definite record-keeping requirements for employers—including managing agents—and fines are imposed for violations. Since laws are changing constantly, the local U.S. Department of Labor office should be contacted for details. It is sound business practice to always maintain adequate employee records. Here are examples of items that should appear in the file of every employee, including part-time workers.

1. Employee application form
2. Job description
3. Current W-4 form for withholding tax
4. Benefit application
5. Time records
6. Pay records, including regular pay, overtime, bonuses, commissions, and raises
7. Vacation and sick-day records
8. Social security payments
9. Union benefits
10. Accident reports
11. Review and evaluation reports
12. Promotions, transfers, layoffs, and discharges
13. Commendations and complaints
14. Records of disciplinary action
15. INS Form I-9 (proof of citizenship)

Employment records should be maintained for at least five years after the employee leaves. Many management firms keep employee records indefinitely. In situations where the people working at a complex under your management are technically the employees of the property and not of your company, prepare a duplicate set of records for your own files. By doing this, your files will be complete if you should lose the management account and be required to turn over the original employment records.

Licensing

Many states have real estate license law provisions that say, in effect, that persons who "lease or offer to lease" real estate must be licensed. In most states, this requirement does not extend to direct employees of the property owner, but it almost always includes employees of a managing agent. In the future, licensing requirements definitely will become increasingly stringent. Currently, there is a movement under way to require the licensing of property managers. Licensing requirements vary from state to state, and it is important to know whether the licensing specifications in your state include continuing education requirements. Be aware of the laws in your area and be alert for upcoming changes in those laws.

Compensation

It is not unusual for property management employees to receive several forms of compensation, including salary or wages, free rent, free utilities, and other noncash items. Some owners hold the opinion that salary or wages can be lower if other noncash benefits are offered. Thus, as some owners put it, you can hire a site manager for $1200 a month, provide a $500 per month apartment, toss in $80 worth of free telephone service and utilities a month, and claim to be paying the employee $1,800 a month. Let's see if this is true.

Free rent.   The idea of giving an apartment rent-free to an employee came about in the days when empty apartments were more plentiful than money. When the practice started, it was common for employees not to report the value of their apartments as income. But laws have changed. The IRS now includes an apartment's value as taxable income, unless the employee is required by the owner to live on the site. If the apartment is provided for the owner's convenience, it cannot be counted as part or full compensation for services rendered.

In most cases, providing a free apartment is simply a matter of giving the employee something extra to make up for an otherwise low salary or wage. Under those circumstances, the employee will have to pay taxes on the value of the apartment. So "free" rent is not exactly free.

Now let's examine it from the employee's standpoint. An employee earning $1200 a month normally would spend no more than $360 a month for an apartment (using the rule of thumb of paying 30 percent of gross income for housing). So, if you provide a $500 per month unit, the employee can only credit you with the $360 he or she would normally spend on rent; the other $140 of value is nice, but the employee probably would prefer cash to pay other normal living expenses. The disadvantage to giving an employee a free apartment is that the value may not be appreciated.

Employee Discounts.   One way to avoid the problems created by offering free rent is to rent the apartment to the employee at its regular value less an *employee discount*. This is a method used by retailers for their employees, and it results in making the employee aware of value. Also, in most cases, a modest employee discount is not taxable compensation.

The IRS allows some flexibility when it comes to taxing the benefits of an employee discount. Clear this with a tax law authority before establishing your policy regarding such discounts. The general rule followed in the apartment industry is that an acceptable discount amount would be roughly equal to the money spent on a per unit basis for promotion plus an allowance for profit. For example, an apartment that leases to the general public for $600 per month might be discounted by $40 to $50 when rented to an employee without incurring income tax liability on the benefit.

In all events, discounts should be offered to all employees equally. Discounts can not be used as a method of rewarding one set of employees and not others.

Free utilities.   Free utilities are offered to employees in cases where they are not normally included in the apartment rent. In my experience, employees who receive this benefit seldom appreciate it as part of their income. Ask them what they earn and they'll quote their salaries or wages, not what the free utilities (and free apartment) are worth. Because they may not be aware of the value and don't appreciate it, employees may not see the benefit.

Other Noncash Benefits.   The same holds true of other noncash benefits such as free gasoline for employee cars. It will not be appreciated and is apt to be wasted. Use a mileage allowance instead.

Salary.   A manager is better off paying an employee a straight salary or wage and forgetting about free apartments and free utilities. As for the amount of the salary or wage, set it at a level that will attract the people you want. This level will vary from one area to another. When property management businesses underpay employees, they pay for it dearly in inefficient operations. An informed owner wants a manager who is competent and businesslike. There are no bargains in low wages.

Salary or Commission?   This question will come up when setting out to hire a leasing agent. My advice is simple: Choose salary.

Commission would appear to have much in its favor. The complex only pays for results, and commission jobs have a way of weeding out those with little confidence. A person who works hard will rent more units and make more money. So where is the problem? There are several. First of all, very good real estate sales people are selling houses, rather than renting apartments, because the financial rewards are significantly greater. There are certainly some exceptions; there are situations in which a person with some of the inborn skills decides to try renting apartments. Getting started in apartment rentals takes a lot less time than it does to begin as a home seller. Unfortunately, most people who apply for a commission-only leasing agent position see it as something to fall back on, an interesting sideline. To attract a top-quality rental agent, the commission per lease must be respectable; this way, any kind of success will cover the startup period and the inevitable slow weeks. If the agent does obtain lots of rentals—either because of superior ability, market trends, or both, the income achieved frequently exceeds the manager's. Obviously, this is the beginning of another problem.

Commission-only leasing agents get paid exclusively for prospects who become residents. It doesn't take long to learn which prospects the manager will accept on the basis of income and past history. As a result, agents may steer application answers to fit the manager's expectations. Also, a commission-only rental agent may refuse to handle resident calls, act as a receptionist, or even take a rent check from an existing resident during busy times in the office. Offering fixed salaries to your leasing agents not only provides employment security to the agents, but also allows you the freedom to assign additional duties.

When rentals are plentiful, there's no problem; but if prospect traffic falls off, agents may search for greener pastures. When times are tough and you need the most help, the commissioned agent's pay will be at its lowest; and you will probably be searching for someone new. There are many individuals who will develop into top rental agents who need and want employment security and a regular salary. You can sweeten an agent's paycheck with a small bonus after an exceptional week, but let the fixed salary represent most of the compensation package.

Wage and Hour Law

It is absolutely essential to be familiar with the Fair Labor Standards Act. This is frequently referred to as the Federal Wage and Hour Law. The requirements of this law are significant. Likewise, the penalties for failure to comply are severe. Contact the Wage and Hour Division of the Employment Standards Administration of the U.S. Department of Labor to secure information on the law and its requirements.

The comments in this section amount to a broad interpretation of the Wage and Hour provisions. Specific wage and salary amounts have been avoided, as they are subject to change. Interpretation of specific situations by regional Wage and Hour offices will differ, making a complete discussion of the subject even more difficult.

The Federal Wage and Hour Law generally prevents paying a property management employee a fixed salary so that the employee can work unlimited amounts without additional compensation. Almost all apartment buildings are covered by this law, which states that *employees must be paid the minimum hourly wage* and that *you must compensate employees at the rate of time-and-a-half,* for all hours in excess of forty worked each week (with certain exceptions). Even if you pay employees monthly, the federal agency simply will take the monthly salary, multiply it by twleve months and then divide by 2,080 hours (forty hours a week multiplied by fifty-two weeks a year) to arrive at an hourly rate.

Consider some implications of the Wage and Hour Law. Your objective is to avoid paying for overtime, if possible. You can do this by giving compensating time off within the workweek. This means that an employee who reaches forty hours before the end of the week can be given time off for the rest of the week. You can't give compensating time off during the following week; the law says each week must stand on its own.

In most industries, the workweek begins on Monday and ends on Sunday. If you follow this system and you need employees to work on weekends—the time when most emergencies occur—you'll probably wind up paying overtime. You are better advised to *declare your workweek to begin on Friday and end on Thursday*. This means if employees must work on the weekend, you have the less-hectic remainder of the week to grant time off for compensation. Such a policy can save you many overtime hours. If you do this, it is more efficient to pay employees weekly or every two weeks, because then your records will conform more easily to a workweek.

Take the time to study how the government calculates minimum wages and overtime. The Wage and Hour people may consider both the salary and the value of an apartment when calculating the hourly rate and testing for the minimum wage. The apartment value only counts if the apartment is provided for the *employee's—not the employer's—convenience*. If this is the case, then the IRS will expect taxes withheld on its value. You can't have it both ways.

Test to see that you are meeting the minimum wage requirement. Assume you provide an apartment for an employee and that this apartment normally rents for $600 per month. Assume further that a reasonable profit and promotion allocation attributable to the unit is $50 per month. You then subtract this amount from the monthly rent ($600 − $50 = $550) to arrive at the apartment's value, which is added to the monthly wage for the purpose of satisfying minimum wage requirements. Continuing the example, a person receiving a monthly salary of $450 and an apartment with an adjusted value of $550 is effectively being compensated $1000 per month or $12,000 per year. By dividing $12,000 per year by 2,080 hours, you arrive at an hourly rate of $5.77. If this is less than the current federal minimum wage, you must increase this person's wage at least enough to equal the minimum wage. If your property is in a state that has a different minimum wage than the federal rate, the higher of the two rates prevails. It should be noted that the employee will be required to pay income tax on the $550 per month apartment value.

Using the same example, but assuming the apartment is provided for the owner's convenience, only the $450 monthly salary may be considered as the employee's compensation. This amounts to $5,400 a year and, when divided by 2,080 hours, produces an hourly rate of just $2.60, which is considerably less than the current minimum wage and violates the law. The salary must be adjusted upwards to comply with the law. Federal taxes on the apartment value need not be withheld in this situation as it is furnished for the owner's convenience.

When computing overtime compensation, the government requires you to use the total hourly rate that includes the adjusted apartment value. This figure will be multiplied by 1.5 to arrive at the hourly wage to be paid for all hours worked in excess of forty during one workweek. (The preceding example is an extremely simplified examination of one particular situation; it is imperative that you seek legal advice to learn how the law applies to your unique circumstances.)

You must be very careful in keeping track of both wage levels and hours worked. If the government suspects you are violating the law, it will study all of your employees' pay records for the past two years (in some cases, for the past three years) and hold you liable for any underpayment of the minimum wage plus any premium or overtime pay that was not paid during those years. If it can be proved that you acted willfully in underpaying your employees, the government can go back three years and force you to pay double the wages due.

The best practice is to have each employee fill out a weekly timecard detailing the hours worked each day. Employees should sign their cards at week's end. Retain these cards as a permanent record, and pay overtime when necessary.

The Wage and Hour Law does provide that certain employees meeting specific criteria can be exempt from the overtime provision. In property management, these exemptions come under one of two classifications: executive or administrative. The government has published a special booklet dealing with these exemptions (Regulations, Part 541). Copies are available from the Wage and Hour Division of the U.S. Department of Labor.

In a very broad interpretation of exemption requirements, a person must at least meet the following tests to qualify for exemption from the overtime provision.

1. The primary duties of the employee must be management-related.
2. The employee must supervise two or more employees.
3. The employee must not spend more than 20 percent of the workweek performing manual or nonmanagement-related activities.
4. The employee must receive a guaranteed weekly wage of at least a specified amount. This figure has two levels and is subject to change. The wage must be guaranteed at this level and must not be subject to deductions for sick pay or short hours. The test of this wage level may not include any apartment value.

A thorough reading of the government's pamphlet on this subject is recommended before determining which, if any, of your employees can be classified as exempt.

Don't take the Wage and Hour Law lightly. The law is written to protect the employee, whose word often will be upheld against the employer's. Be sure you know and understand the law thoroughly and be careful to document your actions.

Salary and Wage Adjustments

Ideally, you will make it a policy to review salaries and wages for each employee at least once a year. At that time, you can determine whether an employee should get a merit or cost-of-living increase. Job performance and local job market conditions will help you decide the amount.

In keeping with what was said earlier about paying a competitive wage or salary, your policy should be to reward good performance and to pay your people well and in accordance with their responsibilities.

Incentives and Bonuses

Regular incentives and bonuses are self-defeating. Employees learn to count on them and expect them. They become regarded as part of employees' regular income and lose all value as incentives for extra effort. For this reason, any kind of regular bonus, including a Christmas bonus, is discouraged.

Instead, consider random bonuses geared to short-range goals, such as leasing a certain number of apartments, obtaining renewals, or collecting rent in a short, specific period. Such incentives build excitement and vary the pace of activities. Employees usually will welcome the challenge and respond with extra performance. Bonuses needn't be paid in dollars; they can be just as effective in the form of merchandise, commendations, or travel.

Gifts, Kickbacks, and Commissions

You need an absolute policy for gifts, commissions, and kickbacks in order to head off trouble and ensure that whatever you purchase from vendors is based on price and quality, not favoritism.

Vendors historically have offered management employees bonuses for orders, knowing that the employees' traditionally low pay scale may tempt them to accept. Many companies that sell cleaning supplies and chemicals, for example, continue to follow such practices. Some furniture leasing companies pay a bonus to the manager or rental agent for every resident who rents furniture; the companies then may pressure the manager to let the furniture remain after a resident moves, hoping that the apartment will be re-leased and the company's furnishings with it. This practice saves the furniture company money because they don't have to pick up the furniture. Nevertheless, waiting for someone who will accept the furnishings may cost the property owner money in lost rent. And you must consider the fact that residents who have their own furnishings are often more stable than those who do not.

Commissions, gifts, and bonuses—indeed, any form of kickback from vendors—are unacceptable for several reasons. First, they may encourage employees to order more than is needed in order to qualify for a gift. Second, employees may disregard quality, costing the property more money in the long run. Third, if there are any reductions in price, these rightfully should be credited to the building account in the form of a discount rather than going into employees' pockets.

To make sure that all relations with vendors are on a strictly businesslike basis, employees should be forbidden to accept any kind of money payments from them. They should also be instructed to refuse any free tickets to entertainment or sporting events and to turn down any free dinners or other invitations to socialize. You may wish to permit the acceptance of "token" gifts at Christmas time.

Gifts or tips from residents should be refused; they could lead to special treatment and unequal service, a source of many resident complaints. If holiday tipping and gift-giving to employees is already practiced, establish a kitty so that all employees benefit and individual residents are not identified.

Holidays

Let your rental employees know right away that they will be expected to work Sundays and on summer holidays. Thanksgiving, Christmas, and New Year's Day generally are poor rental days, when you might just as well remain closed.

The maintenance staff usually can be minimal on all holidays.

Vacations

It's a good idea to establish a vacation year in which any earned vacation time must be taken. An employee usually earns one day of vacation for each full month of employment, up to a total of ten days (employees with greater tenure should be allowed to accumulate some additional vacation time). Employees should be required to take these vacation days within a certain period. For example, many management companies allow vacation time to be accumulated through April 30; employees then have to take their vacations before March 31 of the following year. This policy prevents employees from combining two weeks of vacation at the end of one year with two weeks at the beginning of the next to make a four-week vacation. Here are some other vacation policies to consider:

- Employees must schedule their vacations around those of other employees, so that you are not left shorthanded at any time. If a conflict develops, seniority rules.
- Any vacation time not taken is lost forever. It is not carried over into the next year or compensated by money.
- If an employee resigns without sufficient notice or after less than one year of employment, all accrued vacation time is lost.
- An employee who is terminated receives any accrued vacation pay as severance.
- If an employee dies, the heirs receive any accrued vacation pay.

Death of a Relative

If an employee's immediate relative dies, consider granting up to three days off with pay. "Immediate relative" includes spouse, mother, father, mother-in-law, father-in-law, son, daughter, sister, or brother. If the employee needs more time, allow an authorized leave of absence. Absence due to the death of any other relative or friend should be without pay.

Sick Days

It is virtually impossible to set a foolproof sick-day policy. Some companies allow employees five sick days during a calendar year. For each day they take, they are paid. For each sick day not taken, they receive one day's additional vacation, up to five days. Any sick days taken beyond five days are without pay.

Whatever sick-day policy you establish, be sure to record sick days carefully to avoid disputes.

Employee Insurance

Employee insurance, such as a health and hospitalization plan, is rare for many management and maintenance-associated employees because of the typically small size of the work force. Most group plans require ten or more people. This may put you at a hiring disadvantage, since many employees expect this kind of coverage. However, even if you do provide insurance, employees won't give you full credit for what it costs. Again, they generally think only of their wages or salaries, not the full cost of any benefit you offer.

Some community health groups have been set up to provide medical coverage. If your community has one, it might be a good idea to have your employees enroll on a fifty-fifty basis. That is, you offer to pay 50 percent of the premium while the employee pays the other 50 percent. In this way, the employee gains a better appreciation of the value of the coverage. An employee also should pay any premium for coverage of dependents.

In some cases, employers are obligated to provide a Health Maintenance Organization (HMO) option. This requirement only applies to those employers who already provide health insurance benefits. Under the Health Maintenance Organization Act, an employer may be required to offer an HMO plan if the employees involved exceed a specified number and a written request has been received from a qualified HMO. An employer who fails to comply can be subject to substantial fines. The changing law in this area serves as a reminder that the entire insurance picture is in a state of flux; it's very important to stay up-to-date and seek professional advice.

Education and Tuition

Employers usually benefit by encouraging their employees to pursue education to improve their on-the-job skills. This education can include formal day or evening classes, seminars, dinner programs, and short-term training programs. Administrative, rental, and maintenance people should be included in the education policy.

The policy must be thought out carefully and enforced, or you may find yourself paying for education that has no relation to the job. Some owners find this acceptable; they believe that *any* course an employee takes will pay off in better job performance.

The typical education policy requires an employee to get approval from a supervisor before enrolling in the course. The employee then pays for tuition, books, and other expenses in advance. When the employee presents evidence of having successfully completed the course, the employer calculates the reimbursement due using a predetermined percentage of the tuition cost (e.g., 50 percent). Books and expenses are typically not reimbursed. This policy encourages the employee to make a personal financial commitment, rather than get a free ride at the employer's expense. It also encourages the employee to take the course more seriously.

Professional Memberships

You may decide to encourage your employees to join a professional association, perhaps one with which you yourself are affiliated. In this case you can establish a policy to pay for part or all of the employees' membership fees and subsequent dues. Professional organizations provide a forum for exchanging ideas and an opportunity for members of your staff to learn about the industry through the experience of other property managers. Providing this benefit may be quite costly, but it frequently pays off in the form of a skilled and enthusiastic staff.

Permanent, Part-time, or Seasonal Employees

Unless your operation is very small and is not subject to federal and state Wage and Hour regulations, employees cannot work more than forty hours a week without being paid time-and-a-half for overtime. In many cases, it doesn't take much overtime to make you realize that you'd be better off with another full-time person.

Overtime in general should be discouraged. If it becomes routine, employees will come to expect overtime pay as part of their regular income and will be disappointed when they don't get it. Try to streamline your operation with efficient planning and scheduling so all routine work is performed during the regular workweek. There may be certain periods due to weather, untimely breakdowns, or seasonal traffic when short-term needs justify overtime. If overtime becomes a regular requirement, add another full-time or part-time person to your staff.

Reporting to Work and Breaks

You have a right to expect employees to be at work on time. Your policy should state that if an employee is sick or delayed, the supervisor must be notified no later than thirty minutes after the appointed starting time. Similarly, if an employee must leave work before the designated break, lunch period, or quitting time, the supervisor must be notified. Your policies should clearly state the number of violations of these rules that is cause for dismissal.

A common response from an employee found not working is "I am on my break." If you wish to eliminate this excuse, establish uniform time periods in the morning and afternoon for breaks. Typically, these would be from 9:45 to 10:00 a.m., and 2:30 to 2:45 p.m. You also may establish a set lunch period. At all other times of the workday, you should expect to find employees working.

Uniforms

Policies on uniforms vary widely. Some firms require rental personnel to be dressed in blazers. Whether you make this your standard or not, you should require a professional appearance in dress and grooming and spell this out in as much detail as necessary.

It's generally a good idea to require maintenance and service people to wear uniforms while on duty, because that makes them easy to identify and also contributes to the well-managed appearance of the property. It also saves on wear and tear of their own clothing.

If you decide on uniforms, select a *readily available style and color* and provide each employee with two or three sets. Employees should be responsible for washing and cleaning; you should be responsible for replacing worn out uniforms. Giving the employee a standard *name badge* is also a good idea.

You must provide appropriate safety equipment (shoes, goggles, helmets, etc.) if the nature of an employee's work requires such items. Here again, you must be aware of the Occupational Safety and Health Act of 1970.

Radios

One of the quickest ways to spot an unprofessional work environment is by the playing of radios. Workers will often bring radios and play their favorite music while they work. Whatever rules you establish regarding radios should apply to both employees and vendors. These people are being paid to work, not to entertain themselves. The sound of a radio is often loud and annoying to residents and visitors. You won't see employees or other outside workers in top hotels playing radios or even wearing earphones, so why should you allow it?

Tools

Maintenance personnel should be *required to provide their own tools.* If they are first-rate workers, they will have their own hand tools and take care of them. Ask to see the tools before you hire the person. If the tools are in good condition, you can feel reasonably confident that the person is competent. If you must provide tools, don't expect workers to care for them as they would their own. The exceptions are specialized or expensive heavy-duty tools that should be provided as equipment of the property.

Guns

It is recommended that you *prohibit employees from carrying guns* or having them anywhere on the premises at any time (i.e., an employee can't store a gun in his or her desk or locker during the day). The sight of an employee toting a gun creates the wrong image for your property: Would you rent an apartment if you saw the manager wearing a gun? Guns can be misused, leading to tragedy and possibly a lawsuit against you and the property. It is even questionable whether bona fide security employees should be allowed to carry guns.

Controlling Employee Purchases

Property managers often establish accounts with local vendors such as hardware, electrical, and plumbing supply stores. This can create problems since employees may take advantage of these accounts to buy items for themselves. Some property managers attempt to deal with this situation by setting a dollar limit on each order, but it's a simple matter for an employee to get around such a restriction by coming in at different times with smaller orders.

The recommended way to control purchases is to require vendors to refuse any orders that are not itemized and signed by the manager. This makes it difficult for any unauthorized person to buy something for personal use. The same rule applies to purchases of capital equipment.

Pilfering and Petty Theft

Because of the supplies, equipment, petty cash, and coin meter collections kept on the premises, a property management business is vulnerable to pilfering and petty theft. Employees should know that you realize this temptation exists and that you will use every means available to reduce losses. Furthermore, let them know that if they are caught pilfering, you will terminate them. If the theft involves a substantial amount, you should prosecute.

These are some steps you can take to reduce the possibilities of petty theft:

- *Keep supplies to a minimum.* Don't order a gross of brooms and expect them to remain; order one or two at a time, as they are needed. You can give your vendor a blanket purchase order to arrange drop shipments of small quantities.
- *Keep supplies locked in cabinets.* Give the keys to only one or two people.
- *Buy bulk quantities.* It's easy to steal a gallon of paint or a quart of household cleaner. But if you buy in larger containers, such as thirty-gallon drums, theft becomes more difficult. It's often cheaper to buy in large quantities anyway.
- *Bank money daily.* Don't hold checks, or cash, other than petty cash, for more than eight hours. Keep petty cash in a locked desk.
- *Log coin collections.* Normally, there is little variation in monthly collections from year to year. If there is a sharp drop in this income, you can suspect theft.
- *Never authorize site personnel to sign checks.* They should only make deposits. Any exception to this recommendation virtually guarantees accounting problems and money irregularities.

MANAGING YOUR STAFF

The subject of staff management is an expansive one. Your level of management ability will depend on your aptitude in a wide variety of skills. For starters, a manager must be able to organize, communicate, solve problems, and relate to others. There is a proliferation of courses and books addressing this topic—many of them can be helpful. For that reason, I will explore a few management issues without devoting much time to management techniques.

Labor Unions

In certain areas, particularly in major cities, labor unions have made and are continuing to make efforts to organize apartment property personnel, especially maintenance workers. Unions seek out the larger complexes because the numbers of employees make it worth the effort.

The best approach is to avoid union organizing in the first place. One way to do this is through fair and reasonable personnel policies uniformly applied, regular salary and wage reviews, good supervision, and communication with your employees. Give them more advantages than they would have as members of a union, and you'll eliminate any need for them to organize.

If a union does approach you with notice of its intention to organize, *contact a labor attorney immediately* before you do anything else. This is not the time to get tough or make threats. The federal government has strict rules governing union organizing, and these are best interpreted by a labor attorney. You should contact a labor attorney immediately before you take any action, including discussing the situation in any manner with personnel.

Employee Termination

Most of us are employees ourselves and we understand the family crisis that can result from losing a job. We also know that our complaints about the people we supervise rarely express the total picture. In other words, most people do some things better than others. Perhaps an individual possesses a high level of skill working with customers and is hopelessly inaccurate when dealing with money or arithmetic. You may want to restrict that employee's activity to the areas of strength, or you may provide additional training and supervision. However, in a small operation you may not have the time to provide the necessary extra attention.

Sometimes an employee claims to be indispensable. Perhaps this individual knows something about your building equipment that no other staff person appears to understand. However, there are few things in an apartment building that cannot be quickly figured out by professionals.

Certainly, nothing is so mysterious that you should put up with a difficult employee. In fact, terminating the so-called "indispensable" person almost always results in the discovery of a grand omission on the part of the departing employee. Correcting these problems obviously benefits the property.

Countless situations exist in which a valuable employee threatens to quit. A good many of these threats are ongoing and often said in a joking fashion. Nevertheless, the message is clear. When this happens, the time has come to stop the comments or terminate the employee. You absolutely do not need an employee who walks around telling others it's time to quit if changes aren't made. Allowing this to continue means you will lose control and respect. We have all witnessed children who do this to their parents and we may wish we could influence those parents with our advice. When it comes to an employee threatening to quit, our advice would be to grant one written warning (and no more than one) before termination. Remember to check all your termination policies with a lawyer.

Before you terminate an employee, it is crucial to document the incidents that led to the discharge—that way you'll have the proper records should a disgruntled former employee accuse you of discrimination. When you must terminate someone, handle the situation with dispatch. If circumstances dictate severance pay, then issue a check and dismiss the employee. The final check should not be turned over, however, until the employee gives back all keys, vehicles, tools, and any property of the complex. If you're providing the employee with living quarters, naturally you must take possession of the space before handing over the final check. Know your state laws because there may be notice requirements when living quarters are involved. In general, don't give a two-week notice. If a person is being terminated, your best, safest, and most humane course of action is to make the termination effective immediately. The terminated employee will only do harm to your relationship with other employees, vendors, or residents during those two weeks. Also, it's absolutely foolish to have a person who is leaving involuntarily train a replacement.

As a final note, you do not need to crush a person's self-esteem with a recitation of every weakness and fault, nor do you need to quantify the damages that have been caused to the property. It is sufficient to say that things haven't worked out. This person now has the problem of having no job and an interrupted income; don't inflict more pain or embarrassment with a sermon.

Employee Turnover

Turnover is an expensive affair. With each change, the training process starts over again, and usually a little something is lost with each new training session.

Your residents notice such turnover. Finding a new set of players with each trip to the office can be frustrating. Residents are forced to bring the new staff up to date regarding the chronology of their occupancy and to adjust to the personality and temperament of the new workers.

The advice for achieving greater longevity is the same advice we'll offer for selecting new residents: Slow down. Don't jump at the first hiring opportunity. Complete thorough background and reference checks. If a person has held a number of positions in the past year or so, you should be alert. Hiring and working with people involves personal chemistry. So, while it is possible that you will succeed where others have failed, the odds aren't good. You will solve an immediate problem if you can quickly replace someone who leaves your operation. Nevertheless, it's crucial to be aware that you waste time and money when you train someone who ultimately won't stay.

Assure yourself through investigation that the individual is capable of doing the job. Start out with a trial period during which both parties know that they must prove themselves. A large company can offer advancement and a multifaceted benefit package. A single apartment complex cannot compete with those terms, but it can certainly respond with a good compensation program, greater individual recognition, and freedom from the politics of working for a large organization.

Turnover is often driven by a need for a particular strength. The four basic disciplines in the management of investment residential real estate are marketing, staffing, organization, and renovation. Each of these areas demands unique strengths. Therefore, as the need for help within a given discipline changes, so does the need for a person with different skills and interests. Finding someone with a flair for all or most of the four disciplines usually doesn't work because such individuals typically have their own operations.

The need for a particular skill often comes and goes in a period of about eighteen months. For example, consider an apartment complex that has been allowed to deteriorate. First, there is a need for a manager who possesses considerable experience in identifying the work to be done and the skill to direct people to accomplish established goals. Such an individual would be ideal initially, but as the work is completed, the personnel needs change. Next, the complex could benefit from a person with carefully honed marketing skills. As occupancy levels climb, the challenge to your marketing specialist wanes. You might switch to building a staff capable of providing top service to the customer, or you might need to develop an organization to correct deficiencies in bookkeeping, scheduling, or record keeping. If you pause to reflect upon your own experiences, you will probably recall individuals who exhibited competence in one of the four skill areas while demonstrating weaknesses in aspects of the other three.

Shifts occur as the need for different skills arises. Of course, large companies have the advantage in this area because they can rotate their employees according to specialization and need. In general, however, some turnover at the managerial level is inevitable in the business of apartment management.

The Importance of Building Morale

Morale is a hidden force that can push your efforts forward or stop any chance of success. Instilling positive morale requires the kind of leadership and motivational skills that are the envy of managers in all aspects of the business community. It's also the subject of countless training courses and books. We need to address the damaging effects of low morale and the ways the motivation level of your staff can be eroded. In a service-driven business, low morale is surely the beginning of the end.

Nonpayment or slow payment of bills does more damage to the staff's morale than anything else. When a maintenance person is turned away at the hardware store because previous bills remain unpaid, the psychological damage is substantial. People need to feel good about their jobs and they need to feel secure. If a small hardware bill isn't paid, the newspaper has refused any more insertions, or units have been left unpainted because of a lack of money, there's no way the staff can feel secure or enthusiastic. Sometimes the owner of a group of properties will put on sales training or motivational sessions in an expensive hotel in an effort to brighten the spirits of the staff. People may want to go, but they can't sidestep the fact that it would be more helpful to use the money to pay bills rather than funding the sales training. If there are problems with money, they must be dealt with at the highest level. Once financial problems become known to the staff, any positive spirit in the office is lost.

Morale is also damaged by hiring or promoting staff members who are unqualified for their positions. Relatives are sometimes given jobs ahead of staff members with much more experience. Nepotism is a dangerous practice. You should also discourage the possibility of staff members having intimate relationships; office romances often cause breakdowns in morale and operations.

Displaying a lack of sensitivity is another way to harm employees' spirit. Firms that have policies that cheat residents of their security deposits are in fact hurting their staff as well as their residents. People do not like unfair policies or methods. Employees may appear to support unfair policies (because they want to keep their jobs), when in fact they may disagree vehemently. This sets up a lack of respect that will weave its way through virtually every employee action.

Employee Burnout

Managers and maintenance people are often subject to employee burnout. Ours is a business of basics that must be repeated every day. We clean up the mess of residents who have moved so that we can quickly attract new ones. The more the property is used, the greater the need for cleaning. Good residents seem to leave and difficult residents seem to stay. Properties continually decay, and a property's ability to attract maximum rents drops just when the operational costs begin to increase. Deteriorating conditions bring less responsible residents, who often cause more damage and are more mobile. Thus the cycle continues at an extremely rapid pace.

When this pattern sets itself in the minds of the employees, the burnout syndrome has begun. At that point, employees (owners are certainly not immune) no longer put a lot of thought behind their actions. Suddenly, the excitement of maintaining and improving the property is gone. The challenge of learning what prospects want in their housing has been lost. The rewards of resident comments and praise stop. The winning attitude has vanished.

The way to defeat burnout is to constantly experiment with new improvements. When a vacancy occurs, don't paint the unit white, try something special. You might change the carpet, or add some new woodwork or built-ins. If you always plant geraniums in the front yard, try creating new flower beds with a totally different arrangement. Redecorate the rental center or recreational facility, or start over completely and create the most provocative models you and your staff can.

You can learn from the continual progression of department store displays. Even better, watch the most popular fast food restaurants and note the constant evolution of the hamburger, a much more mundane product. Making changes in your product or your marketing approach adds the needed spark to prevent burnout.

The job of initiating change falls to those in supervisory positions, but don't get caught waiting for someone else. Share your ideas for innovation; create an opportunity to heighten your own sense of job satisfaction as well as that of others. Soon we'll discuss the value of making changes in the context of retaining residents. Obviously, making progressive changes in your complex will pay dividends beyond the prevention of employee burnout.

Product Preparation

The chapters in this book contain suggestions and methods to achieve the best results in the operation of rental apartments. The advice in this chapter is the most critical to a successful operation. A mistake in adopting a certain office policy, the wrong marketing strategy, or even the wrong rent level will not damage the property's performance to the same degree as poor preparation. Learning the job of preparing a complex for marketing is the most important single lesson.

UNDERSTANDING WHY PEOPLE RENT

For a number of years, I have conducted surveys tracking apartment renters who have just made the decision to rent at a particular development. Such studies are very important because they help to pinpoint the "hot button" or primary reason for leasing one apartment as opposed to another. Without fail, each survey has revealed almost the same set of priorities in terms of influences on the final decision.

Location

Location has always scored as the single most important motivation. People choose the area they want to live in for a number of reasons. Quality of lifestyle is the most common one. Other popular responses to questions regarding location include proximity to the workplace, quality schools, friends, relatives, highways, or airport.

Appearance

Appearance of the community has always followed as the next most important deciding factor. The physical condition of a complex has more to do with the quality of the resident that it attracts than any other factor. After conducting thousands of interviews, I can tell you it's commonplace to hear that prospective renters were attracted to an area by the advertisement for a complex and then lost interest after viewing the property. The prospects might have been pleased with the neighborhood but were dissatisfied with the property itself. They found alternative accommodations with a more pleasing appearance. It's quite possible that the owner or property manager who ran an ad last week to attract prospects and then lost them, is struggling today with an ad for next week in hopes of generating more traffic.

Reputation

Reputation is also mentioned as a reason that people choose to rent at a particular development. This might include the reputation of the property, the owner, the manager, or a combination of the three. Further questioning of new renters often modifies our interpretation of this response. Properties that appear nice and are well cared for are frequently given credit for a good reputation. The response is based on the assumption that a nice appearance must be the result of quality residents as well as responsive and sensitive management. Actually, that is almost always a valid assumption. When questioning prospects about the reputation of a management firm, negative responses are practically nonexistent; prospects would not have visited the complex in the first place if they had been aware of problems with reputation. When word gets around that a particular operator is unfair or unreasonable, prospects never make it to the rental office.

Apartment Layout and Features

Apartment layout and features are next in order of stated importance. In a discussion of this response, it's important to be aware of the means by which people judge an apartment's features. Actually, the most critical criterion is the condition of the apartment shown. Remember, this discussion concerns the factors that contributed to people liking a complex and choosing to lease an apartment in it. Let's talk about the reverse of this: Consider an exit interview to question prospective renters who have decided against leasing in a complex. In this case, you would be alarmed by the number of prospects who were disappointed by the shoddy condition of the apartment rather than the neighborhood, appearance, or rent. *The*

Primary Attraction in Decision To Rent

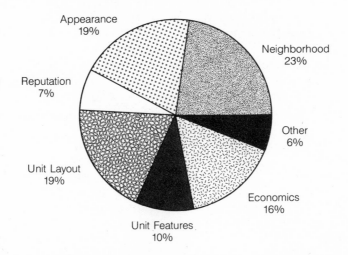

Appearance 19%

Neighborhood 23%

Reputation 7%

Other 6%

Unit Layout 19%

Economics 16%

Unit Features 10%

condition of the apartment shown contributes to losing prospective renters more than any other factor. In fact, in regularly conducted surveys, more than 70 percent of the rental apartments shown are not in market-ready condition. The importance of an apartment's layout or features does not make an impact until the matter of condition satisfies the prospect. The prospect who finds fault with the condition of a potential rental apartment often cites the layout or the lack of a particular feature as the reason for not renting. When conditions are a turnoff, prospects usually want to make a quick exit, and they prefer to refer to missing features as an excuse for not renting. This is a more effective way for prospects to get away from the site because complaints about the apartment's condition will invariably prompt a promise by management to correct the problems.

Rent Level

Rent level is a rarely stated reason for renting a particular unit. This is not to say that rent is not very important in the overall decision process. Rent is relative. Better neighborhoods command higher rent than less-desirable neighborhoods. Well cared for apartment complexes bring higher rent than do poorly maintained ones. Vacant units that are fixed up rent for more than units requiring a great deal of imagination. So, as potential renters are clearing the various hurdles involved in choosing apartments, they are also going through a qualifying process for themselves in terms of the final rent level.

Surveys have also tracked prospect behavior to determine whether patterns exist in the decision-making process. It appears that they do.

In one situation, a developer purchased a tract of land and commissioned a builder to construct three five-story, semi-luxury, elevator buildings. The developer's architect was also told to create an elaborate entryway for the development. When completed, this entryway included a gatehouse, expensive planting, and a large rock formation complete with a spectacular waterfall that fed meandering creeks that ran throughout the property. The cost of the waterfall was estimated to be more than $500,000. The builder dutifully constructed the buildings and the waterfall, but openly ridiculed the developer for wasting so much money on the pretty but useless waterfall.

Later, the builder, who had a parcel of land across from this property, decided to construct a similar three-building development for himself. However, the builder chose to save money by omitting the waterfall and, instead, installed a better line of appliances and an expensive grade of carpeting. The units were offered at a lower rent, even though the project was nearly two years newer than the project across the street.

Less than three years later, the rent differential between the two developments was more than $75 per month for comparable apartments. The development with the waterfall displayed some significant advantages: its developer was collecting at least $200,000 more per year than the competitor across the street, had the first choice of residents, and enjoyed a very long waiting list. Conclusion: People who want nice housing are willing to pay a premium for it. Many times people will really be paying for a well-presented idea or a bit of glitz (as in the waterfall example). This reflects the value of status, a subject I will address further in chapter 9.

Maintaining a property in quality condition has other benefits. Consider a well-located but somewhat run-down suburban apartment complex with relatively expensive rents for that particular area. A sizable portion of the prospect traffic was woefully unqualified for the rent levels. In fact, on more than one occasion, quality prospects were lost because the rental center and models were filled with lookers who obviously were not qualified financially.

As a result, the property manager decided to embark on a major upgrading program that included large expenditures for landscaping and the creation of a new entryway. The development acquired a new look, the occupancy level rose quickly, and turnover rates dropped. The most interesting benefit, however, was that the unqualified prospect traffic dropped to nearly zero. People judge whether a place is within their means by its appearance. The same is true of restaurants, hotels, jewelry stores, and other business establishments. When a development looks exceptional, people of limited means don't stop to look. You don't face the problem of having to turn these prospects down and they won't serve as a turnoff to qualified prospects.

Analyze successful rental properties carefully, and you will discover they all have something in common: They look superior, inside and out.

Professionals refer to this as *curb appeal* or *frosting*. This means the property offers more than better architecture; it also has superior housekeeping, which is evident from the moment you drive through the front entryway. Now take a look at properties that have vacancies, and you will almost always find they suffer from poor housekeeping. They may have lower rents, more amenities, and better apartments, but their down-at-the-heels appearance drives prospects away.

If your development is going to attract prospects, you have to prepare your product. In other words, make it as attractive as possible. This is essential if you are to capture drive-by traffic, which accounts for most prospects.

If you doubt the importance of drive-by traffic, run a check of prospects visiting a successful development (or any development for that matter). You will usually find that more than 54 percent were just driving by and were attracted by the overall appearance; the remaining prospects are attracted by all other means combined, including newspaper advertising.

Imagine two almost identical apartment developments across the street from each other. The apartments and rents are virtually the same. Manager A invests a lot of money in advertising to draw prospects but ignores product preparation. Manager B does no advertising but takes the same amount of money Manager A spends on advertising and spends it on product preparation instead. What happens? The prospects come out to see Manager A's property, but, on the way, they notice Manager B's property across the street. They may go in to see Manager A's apartments, but most of them will rent from Manager B. In short, Manager A hands prospects over to Manager B, who captures them with a better-looking product.

Besides having more renters, Manager B is better off in three other ways.

1. The better-looking complex will attract a better-qualified resident, who will cause less wear and tear, stay longer, and present fewer problems.
2. Improvements made to a property have a long life and multiple advantages. The benefits derived from advertising expenditures are very short-lived and rarely exceed a few days.
3. The better-looking property can command substantially higher rents.

In short, Manager B's complex will rent up faster and attract more qualified residents; and Manager B will be able to charge higher rents, have fewer resident problems, be required to do less policing, and have fewer maintenance and record-keeping problems. All of these factors add up to more net operating income (NOI) for the owner.

Product preparation is important from another standpoint: It helps to convey a status image for the property. Remember, prospects are looking for more than a place to live. They're seeking a home that reflects their lifestyles and roles in life—real or imagined. People don't want to make excuses for their apartments to themselves or to their friends. Status can be another important factor in anyone's decision to rent, and readying your property and apartments helps to establish confidence in the status your property offers.

These remarks pertain to both existing and new apartment properties. A new property, if it is to command the premium rent necessary to pay its way, must be presented as a finished product. Prospects who visit new properties should not encounter obstacles—construction litter, partially completed buildings, lack of landscaping, half-finished parking lots, mounds of earth and mud, and every other conceivable item that can discourage them. Most new complexes are opened prematurely, a fact that causes permanent damage to their economic potential. It is better to wait until the property is ready; the more complete and perfect a new development is when it is opened, the more successful it will be.

There is no excuse for an apartment complex that doesn't look its best. If it does look bad, then the manager automatically risks the loss of a good portion of the potential drive-by traffic.

Details can make a significant difference in prospects' perceptions of your property. Call it nit-picking, but your prospects often have sharper eyes than you do for things that don't look right or are out of place. Likewise, they are probably more aware of the added touches that make a building and grounds look appealing.

To prove this, consider the example of two identical used cars for sale. The dealer gives one a routine wash and polish job to make it shine. The second car gets the same wash and polish treatment, plus a little extra attention. The crew does some detail work, going over all the hidden nooks and crannies to remove dirt and apply polish. They clean the edges underneath the hood, under the trunk lid, and on the inside edges of the doors. They carefully remove any traces of dried polish that may have accumulated between the chrome trim and the paint. They remove all rust spots on the bumpers. They steam clean the engine and shampoo the upholstery. As a result, the second car looks better and probably will sell faster and for several hundred dollars more than the first car, even though the two are basically the same. Product preparation and appearance absolutely make all the difference.

The same principle applies to an apartment property. Make it look better, and it will rent faster. Remember that your job is to lease apartments at the best possible rent. Empty apartments result in money being lost forever. When an airplane takes off with empty seats, the revenue from those seats can never be recovered. When a month begins with empty apartments, you cannot go back in time and rent those apartments for the previous month. So, everything you can do to see that apartments are rented when the month begins is money in the bank.

The following sections call attention to aspects of your property that may need consideration and will also suggest things you should do to keep it in first-class condition.

EXTERIOR PREPARATION

Let's start with the outside of your property, since that is what prospective residents see first.

Landscaping

I said earlier that 54 percent of prospect traffic is attracted primarily by the appearance of the property as people drive by. While architecture certainly plays a role, landscaping is the major ingredient in forming a favorable or unfavorable first impression. The good news is that a manager, even operating with a tight budget, can have a considerable effect on landscaping.

The best advice is to find the money to commission a landscape architect to prepare an overall scheme. The architect should have experience with rental apartments as opposed to single-family homes. Make it clear that the plan will be implemented over a period of years as money becomes available. A good architect will typically specify plants that are too small when purchased but in time will grow to the right size. While this is correct, an apartment manager is looking for quick, lush results. You're probably better served with fewer plants, large-sized and grouped in a rather tight ring. There is rarely enough money in the construction budget to do the proper landscaping job all at once. As a result, landscaping is an expense category that should receive a regular and significant amount in the annual capital budget for the first ten or fifteen years of a property's life.

Here are a number of points to keep in mind:
- *Don't rely on grass to cover acreage.* Grass needs mowing and constant maintenance and can look drab in many climates. Break up the monotony with beds of plants and clumps of trees. Establishing tiny forests where there is space to accommodate them often allows you to use wild plants rather than nursery grown ones. This way you get plenty of impact for fewer dollars. These forest areas also serve as visual breaks, something that is highly coveted by today's renters.
- *Flower beds or perimeter plantings should be regularly tilled and edged to give the richest appearance.* Ground cover looks good for a

few weeks, but it tends to look neglected as the summer progresses. However, this treatment may be essential in areas that withstand extreme heat during the summer because the ground cover often holds the precious moisture needed to keep plants alive.

• *Strive for a pleasing color effect all year.* Use evergreens in addition to trees with gray, yellow, brown, and red bark.

• *Use concentrated flower beds for accents.* Perennials, including flowering bulbs, provide a welcome note of color at the end of a dreary winter, when color is most needed. One note of caution about tulip bulbs: They bloom later and have a more limited life span than other flowering bulbs, leaving you with flowerless plants for an important period in the spring when you would prefer to have annuals in bloom. Many parks or large shopping centers that present flower shows each year get around the problem by digging the tulips up each year. There is another reason for digging up tulips every year: Tulips tend to come up crooked in subsequent years, so it's best if they are replanted every fall. The optimal plan would be to keep the flowering bulbs you plan to dig up in a separate flower bed. This way you avoid disturbing the other plants.

• *Choose strong colors and plant masses of the same color.* This maximizes the visual impact. Mixing flowers and colors is a nice treatment in the backyard of a home, but in a rental complex the best results are obtained with large groups of the same flower in solid color arrangements.

• *Avoid using boulders unnaturally.* Too many owners and managers use boulders as a form of traffic control. Some even paint them bright white so they can be seen at night. If you need curbs to control cars, then add curbs, not boulders. For a different reason, avoid using stones and gravel as a ground cover. Gravel is dangerous underfoot, especially when it spreads to your paved surfaces. Also, children will often find stones tempting ammunition to use against light fixtures and windows.

• *Allow your residents to use direct routes.* Universities learned long ago that it is foolish to try to dictate how a person will approach a building or facility. They watch the wear patterns that soon become evident and they construct walks to accommodate the traffic. Planting bushes and adding barricades rarely blocks shortcuts, and such things end up frustrating the manager. Walks should always be for the convenience of the person using the building or facility.

• *Landscaping and playgrounds don't mix.* Try sand or shredded bark for the playground area. You might even explore interlocking rubber mats that are made for this purpose.

• *Plan landscaping for easy maintenance.* Lay out lawns, tree clumps, shrubbery, and flower beds so that machines can be used rather than costly hand labor. Avoid narrow strips of grass along buildings and walls, as these usually require hand trimming.

• *Use water to your advantage.* Running or moving water is not only an effective way to deaden obtrusive noise but it is also one of the most relaxing sounds. Fountains, decorative pools, streams, and even water from lawn sprinklers help create a quiet and peaceful environment. Setting up sprinklers in highly visible areas on weekends and other high-traffic periods will pay multiple dividends. Lawns will look greener and fresher, sidewalks and paved surfaces are more attractive when whey are wet, and the property will appear cooler. In addition, sprinkling clearly demonstrates that the property is being maintained for the enjoyment of its residents. This, of course, presumes there are no restrictions on water use.

These suggestions can be helpful if you have the opportunity and budget to improve the property's landscaping. If your budget is too low for immediate improvement, then try to enhance the landscaping gradually. Remember, some sort of regular budget is needed to pay for seeds, fertilizers, and replacements for dead or damaged plants. Even with a minimum budget, try to maximize the appearance of your landscaping with careful maintenance.

Remember, with landscaping it's important to do things one at a time. There are few owners who can afford to invest large amounts of capital in the improvement of a rental community. The secret is to have a plan and to spend any available funds slowly and steadily to carry out that plan. Choose an area to begin with and work that area until it is complete. Then, expand by shifting your attention to a section immediately adjacent to the finished area. Don't skip around and don't dilute your money or effort by trying to treat too large an area. There will be tomorrow, next month, and next year. Success is determined by steady progress and an ever-increasing level of quality.

Paved Area

A prospect who is attracted by the lushly landscaped appearance of your property will proceed to the paved area, which probably covers the second largest amount of ground. What prospects see and feel provides them with another clue to the kind of property you're offering.

Driveways and parking areas should be as smooth as possible. Potholes and puddles caused by poor drainage are discouraging and may make the prospect turn around and leave.

The condition of paved surfaces is often determined when the project is built. The paving may have been inadequate in the first place. The base of gravel may be too thin, or perhaps it wasn't allowed to settle before the asphalt *lift* or *topping* was applied. Overloaded trucks may have broken down the surface in spots.

Whatever the situation, your job as manager is to do the best possible job of restoring the surface and keeping it in good condition. The site maintenance personnel should be instructed to handle minor patching as the need arises. Inserting hot asphalt materials into a pothole is far superior to using cold materials. Most patches do not last very long and are unsightly because a vertical edge was not cut prior to filling the patch. Using a circular saw with a special blade, have the maintenance staff cut a square or vertical edge in a rectangular pattern around the hole, remove all materials to a depth of at least three inches and then pack-in the new materials. Ideally, your maintenance people would also roll or tamp the patch until it is even with the adjoining surfaces.

As the surface develops cracks, the cracks should be routed and then filled with a hot sealing compound. This work is expensive, but when done correctly and in a timely fashion, it will add many years to the life of an asphalt surface. Again, look for help in matters such as these from your fellow managers or from managers of large institutions who deal with this particular problem regularly.

If the surface is worn, but still usable, perhaps it should be *resealed* with a film of liquid driveway coating. When you do this, be sure to alert residents and arrange for cars to be moved so that the coating truck has proper access. Be aware that people will pick up the coating on their shoes and track it onto sidewalks and into buildings; it can be a messy procedure. For paved surfaces that are beyond surface treatment, *a new layer of asphalt* can be applied. This is an expensive process, but it should produce a paved surface that will serve for at least five years.

What does the prospect see first upon driving into the parking lot? Bright *parking stripes* can make a world of difference; these stripes and any fire lane indications should always look bright and fresh. *Concrete wheel stops* are another asset and are needed to keep cars in orderly rows and prevent them from running onto lawns. Avoid half-size concrete stops that are intended to halt only one wheel. A car can miss the stop and run onto the lawn. If snow covers the half-stop, a small plow may miss it and destroy the lawn. Stay away from asphalt wheel stops. While these are less expensive than concrete, they deteriorate fast and can be gouged by snowplows. Also, they often have rounded edges that permit car wheels to ride over them. Concrete curbing around the parking lot is no substitute for wheel stops. Without stops, a car's front or rear end can hang over the sidewalk next to the curb. This is annoying to visitors and residents.

Provide parking for the handicapped, and identify the space or spaces with both the approved sign and the wheelchair glyph on the pavement. If two such spaces are side by side, there is a considerable savings in their combined width. Many managers place these spaces at the main entrance of the building to assist the person using the space. This often opens up and better identifies the entrance since these spaces are frequently empty.

If your development has surplus parking, or if residents crowd the parking nearest the building entries, consider striping the remote sections of the parking lot to provide eleven-foot-wide spaces. Residents with nice cars will often trade proximity for the protection that a wider parking space offers.

Some roadways and drives have *speed bumps.* These ridges of asphalt give a jolt to cars traveling at high speeds and are very effective in warmer climates. In northern climates, however, these ridges can upset a snow plow or be removed by a plow's blade. Concrete depressions across the road can provide another impediment to speeding cars.

A prospect may be discouraged if there are a lot of motorcycles, campers, and boats parked in the lot. You can counter this by establishing *separate parking areas* for these vehicles. For motorcycles, construct a rack of 2½-inch galvanized pipe and embed the ends of the pipe in concrete; motorcyclists will be receptive to this because they can chain their cycles to the rack. Set aside a distant area of the parking lot for boats and trailers. A row of boats lined up not only solves a parking problem, but also gives your property a neat and organized appearance. Do the same for campers and recreational vehicles.

Junk autos should not be tolerated in your parking lot, nor should auto repairs. Check local laws on junk autos before you do anything; but, in general, if there is a car in your lot that is not currently licensed and drivable, ask the owner to remove it. Autos being repaired in the parking lot will attract prospects who like to be auto mechanics, but this will also turn off other prospects. Your rules and regulations should prohibit auto repairs; the only exception to this rule is car washing.

Historically, it was difficult to collect sufficient parking fees to warrant the construction cost of either carports or full garages. That is not the case today. The more-expensive rental developments can usually keep garages and carports full at rather attractive monthly rents. Perhaps that is something for your development to consider.

Outdoor Lighting

Lighting provides safety and is also used to accent and beautify. Lighting standards and fixtures rarely receive any maintenance other than the changing of bulbs or gas mantles. Typical eyesores are parking lot standards that are dented, knocked askew, or broken off altogether. Light poles along sidewalks, set in loose earth or with light concrete ballasts, may be leaning over. Fixtures on buildings may be twisted. The glass in many lighting fixtures may be dirty, broken, missing, or filled with insects. If any of these conditions apply to your property, the response is obvious—correct them. If lights near parking lots are forever being knocked down by cars, install guard posts or move the lights.

Lighting can be attractive as well as functional if it is located properly and maintained well. Landscape lighting, for example, with bollard fixtures (indirect lighting in which a mirror reflects a hidden high-intensity bulb) and spotlights around plants and pools can create a pleasant aura. This lighting must be maintained; to reduce breakage problems, consider using plastic panels and globes instead of glass. The plastic costs more initially, but it lasts longer and requires less maintenance.

Parking lots require minimum levels of moon-bright illumination. Residents may want the light to be brighter for safety reasons, but you needn't increase it to a shopping center level. The higher level will only make your lot look commercial and safety isn't likely to improve.

Many exterior lighting fixtures are controlled automatically by timers or photoelectric cells. Photo cells generally are more practical because they respond to darkness regardless of the time of day or season of the year, as long as they are shielded from the lights they operate.

There are some disadvantages to photo cells, however. Occasionally it will get very dark during the day, just before a thunderstorm for example; and the lights will come on when the natural light level is still adequate. This doesn't happen very often, so wasted power is minimal. Also, some developments only burn every other light or every third light after a certain hour, say 2:00 A.M. To override the photo cell switch in this setup, these lights must be equipped with a timer.

Motion and sonic detectors have found their way into the lighting scheme in rental property and are often attached to light poles. If there is no activity in the middle of the night, this device would shut off unneeded lights. With electricity costs heading the list of expense increases, alert managers are continually searching for ways to cut consumption.

Timers will probably remain the primary method of controlling exterior lighting. This means that clocks must be checked on a regular schedule. It's a basic industry standard to check and adjust timer clocks every other Monday in a pattern that includes the Mondays following the changes to and from daylight saving time. Obviously, your staff must be alert to periodic power outages that will require resetting your timers.

Rubbish

Even if the prospect has been favorably impressed by your landscaping and paved areas, that impression may be offset by the presence of rubbish. You cannot eliminate refuse, but you can make it as orderly as possible.

In a large building with central trash-collection facilities, trash is not much of a problem, at least outside. Residents deposit refuse in a chute that leads to a collection bin where it's stored, perhaps compacted, for the crew to remove.

In most garden apartments, however, residents carry their garbage outside to randomly located dumpsters. Usually these receptacles are unsightly and hard to keep clean. They are often dirty, streaked with garbage drippings, and dented by the trucks that service them. Some managers put the dumpsters behind fenced enclosures that are subsequently damaged by the garbage trucks. To try to prevent residents from simply tossing garbage into dumpsters, a manager may install a wire fence that extends above the enclosure. This rarely stops the problem; and if the garbage hits the wire fence and scatters, the situation is even worse.

There are other problems associated with dumpsters and enclosures. A manager could install a gate to keep refuse from blowing out. But residents who come to the enclosure laden with two bags of garbage will not appreciate the gate. Neither will the collection crew, who may refuse to pick up the dumpster unless the manager or one of the on-site personnel opens the gate for them. A tight enclosure that's closed all the way to the ground will keep refuse inside; however, if a resident confronts an animal that has been trapped in the enclosure, the consequences could be serious. It's better to have an opening at the bottom of the enclosure so animals can escape.

Finally, the manager may opt for a large dumpster because it is more efficient and holds more refuse without overflowing. WARNING: A large dumpster can be a deadly trap for a child. Furthermore, a large dumpster requires a large truck to pick it up, and the truck is apt to damage the asphalt surface.

Whatever size dumpster you choose, it should be *pressure-washed and painted inside and out* whenever necessary. If possible, the dumpster should be placed on a *concrete pad* so it won't indent the asphalt and set within a three-sided enclosure. Dumpsters should be located *away from heavy-traffic areas* and particularly away from the main entrance to each building, the rental office, model apartments, and the recreational area.

Don't bother to add plantings around the dumpster enclosure. Planters almost certainly will be broken and will catch windblown papers. It's much more important to have on-site personnel police dumpsters three or four times a day. Dumpsters are never attractive, but people will tolerate them if they are neat.

INTERIOR PREPARATION

Stop and think about the reasons some properties are allowed to run down, even when their owners and managers believe they are doing a good job of maintenance. Perhaps it's because they don't realize that a building, like other consumable products, has a limited life. A candy bar may be consumed in three minutes; an automobile may wear out in seven years. Compared to these, the life of a building is very long, perhaps more than forty or fifty years. Many managers are lulled into thinking a building never wears out because the deterioration or consumption occurs so slowly. But like all consumable items, a building begins to deteriorate even before the day it is completed. That is why maintenance to counteract the effects of age and decay is so important.

Another point that many owners and managers may overlook is that the "consumption" of real estate occurs most quickly in the places of greatest use. These are public areas—entryway, stairs, halls, corridors, and elevators. The areas of greatest use are also the places of greatest abuse and, therefore, the areas where deterioration is likely to be most visible to your prospects.

The Entrance Door

The main entrance door to your building is used more often than any other door in the entire structure. If the building has fifty units, the entrance door will get fifty times the use and require fifty times the repairs of any other door. Therefore, the door itself should be selected on the basis of the heavy-duty service it will be required to give. The hardware should also be substantial enough to withstand constant locking and unlocking. If the door and hardware are not heavy-duty, even greater maintenance will be required.

Be sure the door is hung so it opens into the wind. Otherwise, a sudden gust can yank the door from a person's hand, possibly injuring the person and damaging the door. If the door is not hung properly, have it rehung on the reverse side, or else build something to shield it. Make sure the door closer is in working order. These devices require frequent adjustments and must be well-maintained. The alternative is a spring-loaded hinge device like those commonly installed on hotel and motel doors. While these cost less and are fairly easy to install, one often has to increase the tension to close the door against brisk winds. This results in loud, annoying slamming.

Vestibule

In some apartment buildings, the entrance door opens into a vestibule, and people open a second locked door before stepping into the apartment hall or corridor. A vestibule has certain advantages; it provides better security and permits the installation of mats to collect moisture and dirt that might be tracked into the building. Without a vestibule, the hall carpeting quickly becomes soiled, and any heat or air-conditioning levels are quickly disturbed.

Also, the lock on the vestibule door is subject to abuse because residents often open it by pulling on their keys rather than on the knob. In a short time, the lock mechanism wears out. If you have a vestibule, consider installing the lock cylinder in the jamb rather than in the door itself.

Doorway Glass and Fittings

Glass panes in the entrance and vestibule doors are subject to constant handling, fingerprints, smudges, water streaks, dirt, and breakage. Prospects will notice whatever is wrong with the glass, so it must be clean at all times. Don't ignore transom glass either; just because it's overhead doesn't mean it's out of sight. You may overlook it, but the prospect won't.

To reduce breakage, some managers have switched to sheet plastic. This is expensive and genuinely attractive when new. Unfortunately, plastic is easily scratched and, in time, becomes so badly marred that is never looks clean. I recommend you avoid it.

Most entrance doors are made of anodized aluminum or painted steel and retain a bright appearance with minimum care. Some doors have brass or bronze fittings, hardware, and kickplates that become tarnished. These should be polished first and then coated with lacquer to keep them looking bright for as long as possible. Weathered metal detracts from the sharp appearance of your property.

Mailboxes

Mailboxes should be *uniformly labeled* by management. Boxes indiscriminately identified with business cards, plastic tape, hand printing, and stickers only detract from the building's appearance. The exteriors of the boxes should be kept neat and clean.

One problem you'll discover with mailboxes is that *handbills* cannot be placed in them. In fact, only items officially sent through the mail can legally be inserted in mailboxes. This means that handbills will be dumped on the floor beneath the boxes. Handbills are an unfortunate fact of life in apartments. You can't get rid of them, but you can provide a special box, rack, or shelf where handbills can be placed.

It's a good idea, too, to have a small *waste receptacle* near the mailboxes and a *shelf* below the boxes. Residents will find the shelf handy when sorting their mail, and the waste receptacle will be convenient for disposing of junk mail that otherwise might end up in the entrance or on the hall floor. Daily pickup of this material should be part of the maintenance schedule.

In the newer single-entry apartment buildings, the Post Office requires a small mail room that is separate from the vestibule. The mail delivery person must have an area to access the open side of all mail boxes (which is not accessible to residents). Only postal personnel, residents, and those admitted by staff have access to separate mail rooms, and this would preclude the accumulation of handbills and avert solicitations.

Directory

If your building has a directory, be sure it is up-to-date and has the residents' names arranged alphabetically for the convenience of visitors. For security, I recommend using a code rather than apartment numbers. Incorporating a two-way speaker system permits identification and acceptance of visitors. Residents can give directions to their apartments at that time.

Elevator Cabs

Because of the concentrated use they get, there is more wear and tear in elevators than in any other area of the building. The numbers on the call buttons may be worn away. Inspection certificates may be stolen, gum wrappers are often stuck into openings in the walls and ceiling, and graffiti mysteriously appears on the walls. The carpet gets intensive wear.

The elevator shaft acts as a flue, and a layer of dust will build up on the edges of the elevator doors and the outer frames on each floor. If there is no separate freight elevator in the building, passenger elevators have to be used for moving. Many managers protect elevator cabs by *hanging protective pads* when people move furniture in and out. Be sure to take down these pads when the moving is over. Leaving them in place creates two risks: (1) The pads will impair the residential look of the property, and (2) they may be stolen.

Furnishings, Plants and Artwork

Not too many suburban garden complexes have lobbies spacious enough to accommodate furnishings, but you'll often find such lobbies in larger buildings. *Furnishings should be built-in or permanently fastened* to walls or floor to prevent theft. To discourage lounging, chairs should be backless; furniture should be scattered, not grouped for conversation. Choose fabrics for their durability and ease of maintenance; flame-retardant fabrics should also be sought. Of course, everything should be spotless.

Whether you opt to furnish your lobby or not, there should always be wall-mounted or weighted *cigarette receptacles* in the main entrance hall and near elevator doors.

Plants can add decorative interest, but use them only if they can be fastened securely. The same applies to paintings and sculpture.

Floor Mats

Well-managed buildings will have *runners* or *mats* that are put out during inclement weather, especially in regions that experience periods of ice and snow. A small rectangular mat is better than nothing, but it will do little to protect corridor carpeting. To be effective, the mat or runner has to be about twelve feet long because it takes at least three full strides for shoes or boots to begin drying. These mats also serve a safety function on hard surfaces such as quarry tile, marble, or granite that can be slippery when wet. Well-managed buildings use mats during inclement weather; they do not use them when the weather is fine. This means that mats must be picked up and stored when the weather is dry.

Doorway mats may be acceptable outside of apartment doors in buildings with direct outside entrances or those constructed with breezeways, but they should not be permitted in buildings with inside corridors. The same is true for boxes that might be used for the storage of boots, rubbers, and umbrellas.

Floor Coverings

The selection of floor-covering materials involves striking a balance between sustaining a sense of the practical and creating a soft, warm feeling. You must understand that the front of a single-entry building gets the heaviest traffic, so the entry's floor-covering material must be chosen to accommodate this extra wear. As residents and visitors go in different directions, use and wear diminishes and softer materials can be introduced.

The use of different materials should be limited: Two are okay; I don't think there should ever be more than three. Many designers insist that a person should never see more than two floor treatments at any given point in the building.

Carpet is the standard choice for most residential applications. Carpet is soft underfoot and helps absorb sounds and reduce the glare of lights. Patterns work well in corridors, and the color tone should be a medium value; usually a tight, cut pile gives the best wear. Designers recommend that a contrasting carpet color be used in high-wear areas such as the lobby, the area in front of elevators, or on the floor of the elevator cabs. The carpeting in these areas will require replacement much more often than the materials installed in less-used space, and matching carpet that shows some wear is impossible.

Stair carpeting receives heavy use, especially where the carpet passes over the nosing of the tread. One way to extend the life of stair carpeting is to have the carpet installer leave enough material at the top of each flight of stairs to allow you to lift the carpet and shift it the length of a tread. This moves the worn portion into the crevice between step and riser where it can't be seen easily—doubling the life of the carpeting. The extra carpet is first placed under the carpeting that covers the landing beyond the top step and is cut off when you shift the length. Stair pads, that fit over the nosing of the tread underneath the carpeting, are another way to extend carpet life.

The building may have a breezeway or outdoor stairs that you may be tempted to cover with indoor-outdoor carpeting. This material looks fine when first installed but quickly loses its appearance because of weathering, stains, and spills. It's better to leave outdoor stairs and landings in their natural condition.

Indoor Lighting

Lighting equipment and efficiency are improving all the time. If the property that you are managing isn't new, there are probably many innovations you can implement to improve its appearance or energy usage. Bulbs using only five or seven watts of power can produce the light level of those that once consumed sixty watts. Bulbs that will last for 20,000 hours are commonly available, and bulbs with an even longer life span can be expected in the future.

Take the necessary time to study your lighting scheme and search for ways to take advantage of the new light systems available. Many complexes do not have the funds to change all their lights, but most can afford to schedule replacements in a breezeway or on one floor every other month.

The most important lighting to change is that which would improve building appearance because this has an impact on marketability. The next most important are lights that burn continually because the payback will be the greatest for these. Stairwells, corridors, and basements are among them. Then, work your way to the lighting that is used only a few hours each day. If lights are used in areas that have little or no activity, consider motion detectors that will quickly turn on the light when needed.

Apartment building corridors tend to be either too bright or so dark that visitors have difficulty finding their way. I recommend investing in a light meter and establishing light levels that you find satisfactory.

Exit Signs

Most localities require exit signs in apartment building corridors. Most of these signs must be illuminated. If your exit signs have incandescent bulbs, replacement with long-life fluorescent bulbs will eliminate frequent and expensive bulb changes. Unfortunately, exit signs have a habit of disappearing from halls and doorways. You then have a problem of finding a replacement that matches the others. This may be difficult to do because of varying sizes. It's best to order a supply of replacement signs all at once and keep them on hand because you certainly will need them.

Fire Extinguishers and Hoses

In the days when water or soda acid fire extinguishers were common, they were seldom stolen because of their bulky size. But the modern, compact, pressurized ABC-type extinguishers can be used in home, car, and boat. This is why they vanish so quickly from apartment buildings and the prospect may notice the absence of fire extinguishers while walking through the halls.

Some local ordinances will permit you to place an extinguisher in a cabinet behind a glass door; this discourages theft. Extinguishers that are simply hung on the wall may be stolen and then must be replaced. I've found that it's a good idea to place each fire extinguisher in a wall recess; this avoids the creation of "shoulder busters" in the hallways. If you follow this advice, make sure each wall recess is kept free of the litter that's almost certain to accumulate.

Fire hoses in corridors or stairwells should be checked to make sure they are hung neatly. Like extinguishers, the brass nozzles on hoses are often stolen. It's up to the manager to replace them immediately.

Numbering

You may wonder why numbering is included in a chapter on product preparation. The reason is that people need a sense of personal identification and status, which the right number can provide and the wrong number may deny. The numbers a prospect sees on the building and the individual apartment doors can be designed to appeal to the prospect's ego.

The building should be identified either by an address or a special name, never by its construction project number or a single letter. Apartments should be identified by numbers that refer to their floor. Consider the difference between a person whose address is Apartment 802 at 415 Park Terrace and the individual who lives at Apartment 14 in building 10. The first person is proud to tell people where he or she resides, the second may feel rather like a convict from a cell block.

The common practice is to have the first part of an apartment number identify the floor and the other part refer to a specific apartment, with numbering starting at the northernmost or easternmost apartment and proceeding clockwise. For example, apartment 302 would refer to the second apartment on the 3rd floor, apartment 2102 would mean the same apartment on the 21st floor.

Numbers should be applied uniformly to apartment doors, or they can be inscribed on the door knocker. Check the numerals on all doors to make sure none are missing. Residents shouldn't be allowed to put anything else on corridor doors; occupants' names, stickers, handlettered names, numbers, and signs detract from corridor appearance.

Odor

In a discussion of property preparation, one cannot ignore the very sensitive subject of odor. The sense of smell (olfactory sense) is the most easily fatigued of all the senses. This means that it is very easy for a property manager to become accustomed to unpleasant odors and, before long, not notice them. But the prospect who notices a bad smell is apt to remember it.

Mildew is one of the most common odors, especially in humid areas. The *odor from backed-up sewers* is another annoyance. These odors are especially common in inexpensively built garden apartments with poor sewer systems and leaky construction. *Cooking odors* are also prevalent, especially in buildings with kitchens that back up to the corridor walls.

Most corridor odors can be removed by opening exterior doors periodically to air out corridors. If necessary, set a window fan in the doorway to speed up the exhaust. If bad odors are a chronic problem, consider installing a ventilation system in each corridor. Don't use deodorants; they add an odor of their own, which is a sure sign to prospects that you're covering up something.

In a permanently enclosed hall, the easiest way to deal with odors is to provide exhaust fans. This advice is not always so easily applied; consider the building with pressurized halls, for example. In such a building, exhaust fans would defeat the system. You are best advised to consult an expert on these matters.

The best approach is to *correct the source of the odor* if you can. Poorly designed sewer systems should be fixed. Seepage around windows, doors, eaves, and overhangs should be eliminated so that building components will not mildew.

The odors caused by fire and decay need special treatment. Local exterminators can usually apply a foam that will absorb the odor in a few days. The smell caused by water-soaked carpet padding can only be corrected by removing and replacing the padding.

Amenities

Product preparation should also cover the amenities of the building (i.e., those features a prospect who becomes a resident will have the opportunity to use). If these areas are maintained properly, they are assets well worth showing. If maintenance is neglected, you will not want to show them and thus lose a chance to impress prospects. In addition, poorly maintained amenities will irritate existing residents, who may move. Check and clean the following areas regularly: the laundry room, storage room, garbage chute room, and all recreational facilities.

SAFETY

The expression "safety first" should always be on the property manager's mind; it is an important aspect of preparing and maintaining an apartment complex. A manager's safety-related responsibilities are substantial; they involve maintaining a safe environment for both employees and residents. To begin with, the manager must make sure basic equipment is provided and maintained (e.g., fire extinguishers, smoke alarms, generators for emergency lighting, safety goggles for appropriate maintenance personnel, etc.). It is also important for the manager to conduct regular safety inspections and develop evacuation plans. To reinforce such a safety scheme, it is a good idea to publish evacuation procedures in employee and resident manuals.

Matters of safety extend beyond the limited responsibilities I've described above—this text is not intended to serve as a safety manual. Before going on to another topic, let's take a closer look at two significant safety concerns that affect the property manager.

Hazardous Substances

Unfortunately, one hears about toxic substances all the time. Such substances become a property manager's concern when they exist on his or her property and present a threat to the health of employees and residents. Asbestos (previously used for fire-proofing and insulation), formaldehyde (used as an additive in some insulation and building materials), polychlorinated biphenyls or PCBs (found in electrical equipment), and radon (a naturally occurring radioactive gas) are examples of substances that exist in residential buildings and are a menace to human health.

The legislative picture is constantly changing in this arena; be aware of new laws (local, state, and federal). While there may be no legal requirements to remove hazardous substances, the Environmental Protection Agency (EPA) and the Occupational Safety and Health Administration (OSHA) have established tolerable limits of exposure—these guides should be taken into consideration. Obviously, there are ethical reasons to recognize the problems presented by hazardous substances. It is also necessary to acknowledge the possibility of incurring future liabilities; the owner faces an obvious liability risk when hazardous substances are found on his or her property and the property manager may inherit some of that liability. Finally, there is the issue of protecting the owner's investment; a property that contains hazardous substances may be impossible to sell (and state or local law may require disclosure of the hazardous substance to the party purchasing the property). Property managers must be aware of the dangers hazardous substances present as well as the requirements for removal or containment. Public concern regarding this subject is surely going to increase and more stringent laws will be enacted.

When hazardous substances are located in an apartment building there are no easy solutions to the problem. It should be noted that the mere presence of a hazardous substance does not have to result in a health threat to residents and employees. Nevertheless, the best plan of action may be to remove or contain the dangerous substance. One thing remains constant: Any kind of action (even the decision to do nothing) requires the advice of specialists. Inspections should be conducted by knowledgeable consultants and removal (or containment) should be carried out by qualified contractors.

Security

Prompted by reports in newspapers and over radio and television of soaring crime rates—assaults, rapes, and increasing numbers of burglaries—many managers have seized upon security as a lure for rental prospects. A quick look at apartment advertisements will prove this point: One building claims to offer regular security patrols, another advertises security entry gates, and a third touts armed, uniformed guards. Each manager attempts to rent apartments with the promise of maximum protection for the life and property of the resident.

The public is concerned for good reason: In a single year's time, one out of every twenty people is the victim of burglary, vandalism, mugging, robbery, or car theft. No wonder managers think they've hit on something special when they promise security. Nevertheless, such a promise—either in the form of a direct claim or an implied commitment—should not be made without knowledge of the consequences. Prospective residents will not take the promise lightly, nor will the public, a judge, or a jury.

To begin with, promoting security may make prospects fearful or aggravate fears that already exist. Prospective residents may dwell on security when they would not normally focus on the subject. Promoting security may even cause the prospects to think that the security protection is not what it should be—and off they'll go, looking for something better. The truth is that no apartment property will ever be 100 percent secure.

Security is a frame of mind. Hotels generally do a superb job of providing security, but they never promote it. Yet try something funny in a hotel lobby and watch how quickly the house detectives materialize. Hotels know that the suggestion of security is disturbing to guests, so they provide security quietly. Apartment managers would be smart to do likewise.

What happens when you promote security? Not only do you raise people's fears, but you may very well incur a liability that you would not normally be exposed to. That liability could materialize if a resident is robbed, injured, or killed, and you are blamed because you did not provide the security that was promised. No matter how good the security system is, an injured party can always claim management could have done more (e.g., doubled or tripled the guards, increased surveillance, trained personnel better). Right now, there are court cases pending and already settled in which this very principle was the deciding factor.

If you are thinking of promoting security to attract prospects, I have one thing to say to you: Don't do it. When I recommend against promoting security, I mean two things: Never install systems that seem to "guarantee" security, and never mention security in your advertising or promotional literature. If you have already "promised" building security, you may face risks (these will be discussed later).

Whatever you provide in the way of security, make sure that it is done correctly at all times. Security patrols (should you choose to use them) must be regular and all security equipment in perfect working order. In my opinion, your guiding principle should be to avoid systems that involve people other than the residents. Gatekeepers should not be dressed like guards and should not carry guns. Canine patrols are unacceptable. Don't give an apartment rent-free to a law enforcement officer in exchange for part-time guard service during his or her off-duty hours. All of these measures imply that management is assuming the responsibility for security. Again, I want to stress the importance of deciding what security you're going to offer and then doing it right.

Do provide residents with security devices they can use themselves. For instance, dead bolts that must be locked by the residents are excellent. Apartment-to-lobby intercommunication and TV systems that allow the residents to screen visitors are acceptable because residents have to use them. In short, anything that can be controlled by the resident is acceptable; anything that involves another party is not.

Security requirements vary from one location to another. For example, some cities require such things as dead bolts on doors and bars on ground-level windows. Beyond such requirements, does the property owner have an implied duty to provide security beyond putting locks on doors? This question is being debated in the courts. As yet, there is no clear answer. One decision that seems to have set a precedent requires owners to meet the standard of protection commonly provided in the community. This would mean that if most of the buildings in the community have round-the-clock guards, your property must have the same; it also suggests that there is no need to provide more than what others are offering. It is important to be aware of any laws or high court decisions that may have an impact on the amount of security you should provide.

There is another important piece of advice I should share: Take immediate steps if you are aware of any criminal activity on your property that implies a breach of security. For example, if a burglar enters a unit by way of a faulty patio door, make sure that all the patio doors in your complex are secure. If a resident is mugged in a dark area of the parking lot, increase the level of illumination immediately. You want to prevent "copycat" crimes that come about because a security weakness has been discovered in your building. If you choose to do nothing and subsequent crimes occur, you and your owner are at a much greater liability risk because you were aware that a problem existed and failed to act to remedy the situation.

Most crimes in apartments occur because of resident carelessness— residents doing such things as holding the lobby door open for strangers, failing to screen callers before pushing the switch unlocking the door, or propping doors open for convenience. People should be warned against such practices. The best way to keep residents informed is to ask the local police department for literature on security and regularly distribute it to all residents. Do not reproduce security advice under your name or the building's name because this may imply liability. Always use police literature; the police department should play the major role in any security situation.

Now that you have avoided any system that implies guaranteed security, the next step is to make sure that security is never mentioned in advertising, sales literature, or by rental personnel. Not only should the word "security" never appear, but you should refrain from describing any feature of the property that implies security. If you deal with an advertising agency, be sure that it adheres to this rule.

You are fortunate if you have avoided security promotion to date. If you are already promoting the building's security system, you'll have to live with a few problems. There is a definite risk in suddenly reducing security because someone may claim you are reneging on your security promise should an incident occur. Even if you maintain the status quo, you run the risk of being accused of providing insufficient security because of your residents' heightened security awareness. The first plan of action should be to increase liability insurance to cover the added exposure.

The whole security issue is a difficult one. Perhaps problems can be avoided if owners and managers refuse to play on residents' fears and instead focus on the positive aspects of their developments.

THE APARTMENT

If you have skipped over everything else in getting your product ready, the one place you should never neglect is the apartment you're going to show the prospect. It should be absolutely perfect. This is the rule: *When there's no further reason to enter the apartment to make any improvements, when the apartment is absolutely market-ready, then and only then, should you show it.* More prospects will be lost through violation of this rule than for any other reason.

Picture this: The manager is showing an apartment to prospects and immediately steps on a stack of literature that has been slipped under the door during the past few days or weeks. The apartment itself is musty, dirty, and either overheated or chilly. The carpet is stained, and the walls are full of holes and marked with dirt where pictures have hung. In the kitchen, the refrigerator has food stains, the stove is encrusted with baked-on debris, the sink is rust-streaked, and powdered insect poison is spread in the cabinets. The bathroom has a tub with dead spiders, a dried-up toilet bowl, and a medicine cabinet with rusty shelves and a de-silvered mirror. To top it all off, bulbs are missing from the light fixtures or the power is off, so the manager has to show the apartment by flashlight.

This may sound like an exaggeration, but a good many of these conditions are present in many vacant apartments that are shown. The standard response of the leasing agent is: "We'll fix it before you move in."

This approach seldom works. Prospects judge by first impressions. You can never get the maximum rent for an inferior product. If you ask for and obtain the rent you want for a product that is not in its best shape, then you automatically know you could have received more if the product had been in perfect condition. *Prospects respond on the basis of what they see, not on what you promise,* and they will predict future service accordingly.

If you don't accept this argument, then ask yourself, "What kind of person is the prospect who will move into an apartment that's not first-rate?" People generally want to move up in status. If a filthy apartment means moving up, just how bad is the prospect's current apartment? Again, do you want this kind of person in your building?

It's vitally important to make the apartment as perfect as possible before you show it. If you do this, you'll get higher rents and attract better residents. What's more, your property will be ahead of the competition. In addition, the closer to perfection your apartment is, the more confident you'll be when you ask for the maximum rent.

Let's state the rule again: *When there's no further reason to enter the apartment to make any improvement—when it is absolutely market-ready—then, and only then, should you show it.*

Market-Ready Check List

There's no need to have all of your vacant apartments ready for showing at the same time. Instead, have an assortment of every type and kind of apartment in what can be called *market-ready condition.* The number of apartments that must be kept in this condition depends on the pace of the market at any particular time and the variety of apartment sizes and floor plans. For your guidance, here is a list of nine items that should be checked to make sure an apartment is market-ready:

1. All walls and ceilings should be freshly painted. Don't overlook closets or shelving.
2. Carpeting should be freshly shampooed. If there are any stains or burns, remove them or else the carpeting should be replaced.
3. All windows should be washed, both inside and out.
4. Windowsills, the tops of double-hung sashes, ledges, and shelves should be wiped clean of dirt and dead insects.
5. Light fixtures and switches should be in working order. Fixtures should be clean and there should be no dead insects inside the globes.
6. The temperature should be set at the level appropriate to the season. On moderate days, open the windows to air out the apartment.
7. The kitchen should be immaculate with all appliances clean and in working order. Make sure the refrigerator has the proper number of ice cube trays and that the cabinets are clean. Pay particular attention to the cabinet under the sink. There should be no stains in the sink and no dripping faucets.
8. Bathrooms should be spotless. Watch for dripping faucets, stains or worn-out enamel in the tub, and stained or dirty toilets. The medicine cabinet should be freshly painted and empty, with no leftover razor blades or other personal items. Tub and tile grout should be tight and clean.
9. Watch out for the typical apartment starter kit (i.e., a few bent hangers in the closet, some half-used soap in the bathroom, and a few sheets of toilet paper left on the roll). Get rid of these.

To help get the apartment ready, you should make a *market-ready check list* of all items that need to be inspected. This check list can be printed on a card that the manager personally signs and posts in the apartment in a prominent position, testifying to its first-rate condition. The card should not be dated; you wouldn't want a prospect who comes in February to see a card dated last November. This would indicate that you're having trouble renting the apartment.

The supervisor should check to see that *only the manager's signature is on the market-ready inspection card* and that the card is never placed in an apartment that is not ready to be shown. This procedure is critical because it forces the manager to inspect each apartment carefully.

Daily inspection of the market-ready apartments is essential to make sure they stay in top shape until they are rented. Every day, before the start of business, the site manager should personally inspect the apartments. The procedure accomplishes several things:

1. To visit the apartment, the manager must first obtain the key. This ensures that the key is available. It's surprising how often the key is missing when the manager or rental agent wants to show an apartment to a prospect.
2. Daily inspection eliminates the possibility of showing an apartment that is not ready.
3. Daily inspection also reveals problems that may have developed since the last inspection, such as leaflets slipped under the door, a dead insect that fell into the sink, or a window leak that has stained the carpet.
4. The manager is reminded to check the function of lights in the apartment and adjust the heating or air conditioning.
5. Finally, this procedure compels the manager to walk the property, during which time he or she may discover other things that need attention.

In summary, getting an apartment ready means inspecting it to make sure it's in the best condition, and then doing a daily follow-up to make sure it remains an apartment to show prospects.

Window Covering

Draperies, venetian blinds, and other window coverings merit special consideration as part of product preparation.

Draperies are frequently included in suburban garden apartments as a marketing aid. Some city apartments provide them, too. Uniform drapes can give the building a neater appearance from the outside. Drapes also are appreciated by residents whose budgets for furnishings are limited.

However, drapes can present a problem. Generally, the drapes that come with an apartment are not of the highest quality and they don't hang well after a while. Discerning residents realize this and prefer their own drapes. Prospects may even resist renting an apartment because drapes are included; this is an example of negative marketing.

Meanwhile, transient residents who like drapes sometimes neglect them. They may leave windows open, exposing the drapes to dirt, soot, and rain. As a result, the drapes need cleaning too often, certainly every time there's a change in tenancy. Because the drapes are usually poor quality to begin with, they seldom last more than a few years.

Nor do drapes accomplish the uniform outside appearance that many managers want. Even with drapes, some residents will place aluminum foil against the windows to reduce heat in the summer, and others will put up newspapers, especially on bedroom windows, to make the room darker. In many garden complexes, the drapes can't be seen from the outside because balconies interfere with the view. So the effect on external appearance is negligible.

Mini-blinds are the preferred choice of many owners as well as apartment renters. They have a neat and uniform appearance and allow light and ventilation, while at the same time they preserve the resident's privacy. Blinds also divert direct sunlight, which helps hide many imperfections and indentations in the finished walls.

Children often bend and crease the metal blinds when they separate the slats to peer out. The vertical blind, which is often made of a more pliable material, seems to take such abuse better. If you opt for the vertical rather than the horizontal blinds, it is recommended that you invest in the more-expensive, double-mount type. Vertical blinds that are mounted only at the top will be blown by wind and can actually become tied in knots and destroyed.

Floor Covering

In most suburban complexes, *wall-to-wall carpeting is standard* in all living areas (living room, dining room, bedrooms, and hall). As mentioned, carpeting is an excellent sound absorber and buffer—but only if it's wall-to-wall. Some apartments are finished with hardwood or tiled floors and managers may require residents to install their own carpeting on at least 80 percent of the floor area. This requirement is hard to enforce, and the practice does not adequately reduce noise caused by vibration and by furniture moving.

Carpet styles change with fashion trends, so what is "in" today will probably be "out" tomorrow. Durable sculptured patterns were replaced by shag carpeting. Subsequently, shag carpeting was replaced by "splush" pile, which was replaced by cut pile, and so on. Carpet manufacturers will continue to come up with other new looks. Don't make the mistake of buying high-priced, long-wearing carpeting for apartments. It will show wear patterns and is just as likely as lower-grade carpet to suffer from stains, burns, and spills. A reasonable life for carpet is five years and rarely more than six.

Carpeting must be shampooed with every resident change and no less often than every two years. If the carpet is badly stained but not worn, consider having it dyed; this usually costs one-half the price of replacing the carpet. Call in a carpet expert before you decide. Be aware that if you have the carpet dyed, the dye may get onto the baseboard woodwork and repainting will be necessary. Dyeing should be done with the carpet in place. If the carpet has to be taken to a plant, it will undoubtedly shrink. Also, the cost of picking up and re-installing the carpet will add to the total cost, possibly eliminating the savings difference between dyeing and replacing the carpet altogether. You should also be aware that dyed carpeting will occasionally change color when exposed to sunlight, and the new hues can be undesirable.

Less common than carpeting, *tiles are a good alternative in buildings with concrete floors*. Some buildings provide asphalt or vinyl tile as standard; others may have resilient sheet flooring.

Hardwood flooring is common in many older buildings and may also be installed in some newer, wood-frame buildings. Oak flooring is expensive to buy and install. Although attractive initially, it can show scratches and stains and must be sanded and varnished to remove these mars. Each sanding removes roughly $1/16$-inch of hardwood floor surface; eventually the flooring nails are exposed, at which point no more sanding is possible. During the life of a hardwood floor, you can expect to be able to sand four to six times. Hence, it is important to avoid unnecessary sanding. Admittedly, a hardwood floor that has been used by a careful resident can last for years and years, but generally carpet is better choice when you compare the cost with that of sanding and eventually replacing hardwood floors.

ESTABLISHING PRIORITIES

Let's talk about establishing an action plan for improvements. When making improvement plans, a property manager may face limitations imposed by the goals, objectives, and financial situation of the owner of the property. In this discussion, however, I want to talk about developing the optimal plan for improvements. Knowing how to develop such a plan will lead to an understanding of what to do when you are faced with limitations.

The best place to start might be with an examination of the components of a new, soon-to-be-opened development. However, at the beginning of a property's life, there are few things that will require our attention (not to mention the fact that the process of decay progresses very slowly at first). The impact of condition is best assessed in a property that is in trouble and approaching the bottom of the condition cycle.

Let's assume that you have been appointed to manage a property that has been allowed to run down. The neighborhood is good and most of the neighboring properties have had much better care over the years. Consequently, the competition enjoys much higher rents. It is up to you to map out a program that will bring this new account up to standard.

When faced with such an assignment, the best place to start is to identify the problems. There are three distinct categories of improvement: *must-do, should-do, and could-do*. The following is an explanation of the three improvement levels.

Must-Do

This category includes the required replacements or repairs to the structure. Examples would be the roof, the facade, mechanical and electrical systems, plumbing and sewer lines, modifications to remedy safety concerns, etc.

Most of the money in an upgrade program will be spent correcting problems in this category. Items like a new roof or boiler or replacement windows have costs that range into the thousands and tens of thousands of dollars.

The unfortunate aspect of a must-do investment is that there is almost never an associated increase in the rent. A renter expects the roof to be watertight and is not willing to pay more because the property had to spend money to ensure that this is the case. The same is true for the plumbing, heating and air-conditioning system. When you put out a "for rent" sign, there is an implication that the major components of the building function normally. This is a disturbing fact for many owners since they traditionally like to measure their return on invested capital, even when it is spent just to bring the property to a livable standard. Owners often ignore the fact that money was not set aside from operations and placed into a reserve fund. If the property was recently purchased, the must-do items are really an addition to the purchase price.

In the final analysis, managers are graded by their ability to achieve better occupancy levels and higher rents by making changes in the property and its operation. Money, usually the limiting factor, often leads us to play down must-do improvements in favor of the should-do and could-do items that have the greatest effect on our scorecard as managers. Usually there is a limit to the money available. If the available dollars are invested in a roof that brings no additional income, there is a proportionate reduction in money for lush landscaping, new carpet, better decorating, and upgraded apartment layouts. While this is certainly true, your reputation will quickly suffer if you direct a turn-around of a property where most of the money is invested in visible upgrades, but your residents live under a leaky roof or with old rusty pipes just waiting to ruin all of the new improvements. Must-do items form a foundation for the rest of the work that you are planning. Don't ignore these critical items even though you can't demonstrate an immediate payback.

After carefully inspecting the entire property and placing each job in one of the three categories, it will be necessary to write specifications. This is certainly essential for the items that fall into the must-do category. As we said, these are invariably big-ticket items and they almost always involve a level of knowledge that requires expert advice.

For example, say that we will need a series of new flat built-up composition roofs. The cost will be in the many-thousand dollar range, and there are almost a dozen different types to choose from. We can choose one of the old standbys or experiment with some of the state-of-the-art roofing methods. In most areas consultants are available to explain the pros and cons of each option and to prepare the specifications that will be sent to selected roofing contractors. The cost of this service is minor when it is compared to the cost and problems that can result from a mistake. After gaining experience from a number of jobs, you may apply what you have learned from your consultant by repeating the process yourself in the future. Always learn carefully with the help of experts first; do not move quickly to try new products until they have really proven themselves. As a manager, you are spending other people's money and if you err, let it be on the conservative side.

Even with a set of well-written specifications, the bids will often vary widely. Never do a job after receiving only one bid. When the bids have too wide a variance or the amounts are much higher than expected, hold a bid conference and identify the items or procedures that are driving up the cost. The contractors will usually inform you of changes in the specifications that will result in a reduction of the final cost. At this point you can judge whether or not to make a change.

Many experienced managers develop a "stable" of dependable contractors who are used for most of the work needed. This is comfortable because the manager knows that he or she can rely on these particular firms; and if something goes wrong the contractors will be there to back-up their work. Unfortunately, this arrangement almost always ends up costing more. If you were to have a conversation with one or two of the premier builders in town, you would learn that they work with a list of at least three subcontractors for each trade. They constantly bid one against the other, and they never rig the bids or give one contractor a *last look*. They know that when they do, the word gets out quickly and the benefit of competitive bidding is lost. After you solicit bids from numerous subcontractors for a while, you will witness the variance in the bids and be able to calculate the savings from following this method.

When you receive widely differing opinions from a number of contractors and are confused about identifying the better solution, seek out an expert who has dealt extensively with that problem. If your problem has to do with resilient flooring, talk to a facilities manager for a school or hospital where a lot of that type of floor product has been used. Rarely will you receive the objective opinion you need from the person who is attempting to sell you a particular product. A phone call to another manager or someone who has considerable experience in a given area can save the property a great deal of money and save you the embarrassment of making the wrong selection.

A must-do item is purchased to provide trouble-free service over its life expectancy. You should be more concerned with the quality of its performance than with its appearance.

Should-Do

In preparing our should-do list, we should include items that will help the property meet current modern standards. Included in this list are carpeting and appliances in the apartment units; upgrading of entries, stairways, or corridors; resurfacing of parking lots; and a general renewal of the landscaping.

Should-do items will help keep existing residents and attract qualified new ones. The money spent in this category can be meaningful, but the return on investment is often considerably less than the amount the owner might earn in alternative investments. Money spent on these improvements simply protects the money already invested. However, without this periodic reinvestment, the property would begin a decline in the quality of its residents and thus in its value.

Most of us have witnessed the need for should-do items in hotels or motels. The lobby begins to look seedy and so do the corridors. The carpeting in the guest rooms is matted and stained. The furniture shows signs of hard wear. The bathrooms are out of date. If you are a regular traveler, you know that this is about the time that you begin searching for new accommodations. Money must constantly be funneled back into the property if it is to maintain its position in the market. If this doesn't happen, you can see the beginning of the end. As a property manager, you will consume considerable energy explaining this transition process to the individuals who own the properties you manage.

If you are considering the purchase of new appliances for certain kitchens, you might examine the feasibility of buying refrigerators with one or more special features rather than the stripped down models. You need to ask yourself if the more expensive refrigerators will give you an edge in the market, and you need to know if you can charge additional rent for it. If the answer to either question is yes, the best advice usually is to opt for the fancier product. This advice runs contrary to some past practices. In the past, owners and managers often opted for stripped-down equipment because it had the fewest parts and the lowest price. This strategy led to the continued downgrading of the rental unit and drove many families to seek homeownership when they might otherwise rent. Renters are very aware of the modern conveniences available in the market, and they would like to enjoy these conveniences, too. This recommendation is not intended as a license to go overboard and purchase ovens and dishwashers with every conceivable button and function. Increased purchase costs and service costs are still considerations. This is just a recommendation that we as property managers should strive to provide the conveniences that are commonplace in a modern lifestyle.

Light fixtures, faucets, shower heads, medicine cabinets, mirrors, woodwork, hardware, windows and windowsills, paint, floor coverings, even bathtubs and vanities in an apartment complex, have often been the cheapest type available. That fact does not go unnoticed by prospective residents. When one of these components fails or requires replacement, don't search out one of equal quality. Spend the extra money necessary to begin a systematic upgrade program. Investigate better alternatives and begin to replace these poor-quality components with the latest and most durable designs.

Now, for our purposes, let's assume that we have carefully detailed the must-do items, solicited the professional help needed to write the specifications and supervise the work, and set aside an adequate budget for implementation. We've also addressed the should-do items on our list; we've done some landscaping, repaved the parking area, and improved the development's lighting. Now we're ready to turn our attention to an even more subjective category of improvements.

Could-Do

The final column on your inventory sheet contains those items that are truly optional. This work might include enlarging a small bathroom, converting a bedroom to a "get-away-room," or adding a private patio off the living room of one or more of the units. Adding wallpaper, changing wall colors, installing new hardware, and revamping the bath or kitchen layout are just a few more possibilities in the category of could-do.

Unlike the first two categories, money spent on could-do items brings substantial rewards. Returns on invested capital can range as high as 30 percent. Anything that is done to set an apartment apart from the run-of-the-mill or gives a unit a special personality pays quick rewards in both added profits and a better clientele. Unfortunately, we cannot address could-do issues first, as there is a built-in assumption that you have already taken care of the problems identified in the must-do and should-do categories.

Variety and Change.   In the could-do category, variety is one of the most important ways to increase the property's appeal as well as its rental level. A formula that does not work today could be described as "a lot of the same," and that happens to be exactly what most apartment complexes offer. Apartments with routine layouts and everyday appointments cannot attract and keep good residents. Rental housing will simply become the temporary housing for those people who are saving for down payments.

Take a ride down a street with rows of single-family homes and you'll understand that people have different needs and the desire to establish their own identity. Even though many of these homes began as "cookie cutter" versions of the same plan, the owners have made their own special modifications. In the rental world, the job of beginning an individualizing process belongs to us.

Starting with the structures themselves, don't end up with fifteen identical buildings: Vary the color schemes, alter the landscaping, add different treatments to the stairways or corridors. When striving to achieve vari-

Must-Do	Should-Do	Could-Do
• Roof repairs • Boiler work • Hot water heater replacement • Electrical switchgear	• Repave parking lot • Upgrade landscaping • Replace worn carpeting • Redecorate hallways • Update appliances	• Add new features and equipment (e.g., ceiling fans, ice-maker kits) • Change some apartment layouts • Add customized decorating schemes
Amount of expenditure, $60,000	Amount of expenditure, $195,000	Amount of expenditure, $45,000
Percentage of total spent, 20%	Percentage of total spent, 65%	Percentage of total spent, 15%
Return on money spent, 0%	Return on money spent, 4%	Return on money spent, 30%
Total budget, $300,000		Overall Yield, 7%

ety, exercise caution in the addition of new materials and textures. It doesn't take long to create a circus atmosphere. Vary the combination of colors, but maintain a common thread that ties the separate buildings together.

In the individual units, find ways to get away from the standards (i.e., one-bedroom, two-bedroom). You will always have enough of them. Remove a wall, if you can, to create one great room. Perhaps you could expand the kitchen and eliminate the dining area, or, double the size of the bathroom. A bedroom without an accompanying bathroom can be transformed into a den, library, or get-away room. End units offer opportunities to add bay or bow windows. These alterations will change the exterior appearance of the building and can improve the look and use of the apartment. (Obviously you must keep the exterior design of the building in mind when making such structural changes.) Even though a building was originally constructed with sliding glass doors, you shouldn't restrict yourself to them. Sliding glass doors dictate furniture arrangements in the living rooms. The addition of a large wooden deck to connect an apartment's living, eating, and sleeping areas will pay for itself in just months. You'll also reap the benefit of attracting top residents. Many two- or three-story apartment buildings can be modified to include skylights. Converting three so-so units into two dynamite units will pay dividends for years to come. Connecting a first- and second-story unit together into one with its own staircase is another way of adding variety and value.

Many of us have had the opportunity to visit major rehab projects where very creative architects and designers have taken old factory buildings and converted them into very special apartments. That's what should be done with "cookie cutter" apartments. Break away from the routine. Give your apartments a different look and layout. You should start slowly and become more creative and aggressive as you develop a feel for the market. Most of us do not have the training or the skills to conceive major changes on our own. Seek help from people with training and talent. It's usually best to begin with a progressive professor and his or her class of architectural or design students. They are not intimidated by the past, and their minds bubble with fresh ideas and approaches. Tell them what people want today in the way of living spaces, bathrooms and kitchens. Visit something like "The Parade of Homes" to understand the lifestyle changes taking place and the things people perceive as desirable. Once you take the time to understand what people want, it is fairly easy to scale down a version to fit the space and pocketbook of an apartment complex.

You shouldn't serve up the same old tired apartment layout month after month. Take each apartment as it becomes available, study it, and then begin to make changes. Soon, you will have the variety of housing stock necessary to compete successfully today.

Up to this point, I have unequivocally recommended that you seek opportunities to implement could-do improvements and changes. Now a word of caution is appropriate. Few will argue with the premise that most people would enjoy a better lifestyle and improved living conditions; but you as manager cannot ignore the issue of affordability. Unfortunately, those residents who constitute the low- and limited-income groups are not in a position to pay the additional money to cover the cost of could-do improvements. Owners and managers of low- and limited-income housing should work to slow down the constant decay process and extend the life of the property. These same owners and managers must also recognize that their residents may be unable to pay for a better lifestyle.

This is not an issue for the segment of rental housing that caters to people of the adequate- or ample-income groups. In these cases, the obstacles are surmountable: First, you must obtain the funds for could-do improvements and second, you must have the imagination to conceive a constant flow of new ideas.

Ongoing General Maintenance

Getting your product ready is half the job. Keeping it ready is the other half. In an existing apartment complex, you are constantly in the process of showing and renting units. Current residents are prospects for the next lease renewal period. You can't afford to let the property run down once it's in shape. You must work at upkeep continuously. So far the discussion has focused on the challenge of getting the property in market-ready condition. Now let's turn our attention to keeping it that way.

Most properties suffer physically and economically as a result of *crisis maintenance,* the kind performed only after something goes wrong. The manager delays acting until conditions are really bad or a piece of equipment breaks down. For example, a lamppost begins to lean; it will never right itself and very likely will lean more until it topples over completely. At that point, a major repair or replacement is in order; whereas, if the pole had been straightened earlier, the cost would have been less. On the other hand, the manager may simply neglect to maintain a piece of equipment with a predictable life span. Tending to it at regular intervals involves a small cost; replacing a broken or burned-out piece of machinery can be a major expense.

Many breakdowns occur because the manager fails to maintain equipment according to the manufacturer's instructions. Fans and motors may have to be oiled regularly. Pumps may have to be dismantled and cleaned periodically. Perhaps the manager doesn't know what's required because the instruction booklets have long since been lost. If this is your predicament, write to the manufacturers for replacement booklets and set up a permanent library of these manuals. Most manufacturers will gladly send extra booklets because they're anxious for their equipment to operate properly. Some manufacturers will even offer to train your staff in proper maintenance procedures.

You can be sure that maintenance is a constant. While a building's mechanical equipment must have frequent maintenance, the property's many structural components also require attention. Wear and tear on these items usually occurs so gradually that it is hardly noticed, but it does take place.

If you haven't taken the time to prepare a schedule and assign various maintenance responsibilities, the property will suffer, as will your nerves when you follow up and find conditions deteriorating.

Identify problem areas, establish a schedule, and allocate the time. Make a sample chart to describe some of the areas of greatest concern and include a schedule of maintenance frequency. Take the time to prepare such a chart for each of your properties and continually check to see that the assigned personnel are performing these tasks. The manager is directly accountable when conditions begin to slip.

MAINTAINING THE PROPERTY

In the sections that follow, I'll outline a program of *planned maintenance* that can be used to avoid a continuing stream of crises and keep your property looking as sharp as possible. You'll discover that planned maintenance can be done with fewer people, and this inevitably leads to lower operating and maintenance costs. Again, the payoff is more net operating income for the owner.

Maintenance and Equipment Rooms

If you are ever hired to judge the caliber of the maintenance in a particular complex and your time is limited to just a few minutes, you should ask to see the maintenance and equipment rooms. They will reveal the level of organization and cleanliness in the property. A messy, poorly organized maintenance shop is almost always indicative of the condition of the property's equipment. When there is a chaotic accumulation of questionably useful things, there is little hope of ever locating a specific item when it's needed. Also, this practice can create a fire hazard.

Bins and shelving are certainly affordable items, and there is no excuse for not having a specific place for all of the property's tools, equipment, supplies, and replacement parts. The time and money spent setting up a proper maintenance operation will pay dividends for years to come.

Mechanical Equipment Inventory

Every piece of mechanical equipment in the building should be located, identified, and inventoried. As manager, you should know what equipment is on the property and where it is. The way to get this information is to walk through each building looking for the equipment and making a list as you go along. Your custodial engineer may accompany you. In a larger structure, you may want to hire a mechanical engineer, preferably the one who was involved in the design of the building, to help you locate the equipment. Still, you must know where all equipment is.

The equipment you're seeking includes fans, motors, pumps, ventilators, and valves. You should note anything that has moving parts or needs even occasional maintenance. As you go through each building, make a list of what you discover, *identifying items by their general name, manufacturer, and model number.* Generally, you'll find this information stamped, printed, or engraved right on the equipment. You may discover maintenance instructions on the equipment, too.

Back in your office, draw up a *maintenance schedule* listing each piece of equipment and when it needs attention. The manufacturer's instruction manuals will help you with this job. When all of this is written down, you can determine who will maintain each item: your own people, a factory representative, or a service contractor.

Now *assign each piece of equipment a code number* and place a large, legible sticker or tag on each item so that the code number shows clearly. You can then refer to items by their code numbers on a maintenance and inspection check list. The item's sticker or tag should be large enough so maintenance workers can write on it to indicate the last date of maintenance.

Warranties

In setting up a maintenance program, find out which items are protected by warranties. This may be indicated by labels on the equipment, in the manufacturer's instruction booklets, by separate warranty certificates, and possibly on invoices. Generally, the roof, heating and air-conditioning equipment, pumps, and apartment appliances are protected by warranties.

You need warranties for two reasons: First, a warranty may provide service coverage for an item if it needs repair or replacement; there's no sense in paying for work if the warranty covers it. Second, many warranties are valid only if service is performed by the manufacturer or an authorized agent. If you tinker with the item yourself or have someone unqualified do it, the warranty may no longer apply.

Apartment Maintenance

The maintenance schedule should also take into account a number of items that are found in the individual apartments. Some of the more important considerations are:

- *Plumbing.* Without waiting for leaks to develop, arrange to have faucet washers and valve seats replaced periodically. Inspect the ball cock or flap valve in each toilet tank. Have spare parts on hand to make quick replacements. The quickest and best way to make plumbing repairs is before a crisis develops, when you can select a time that's convenient for you and the residents. It's better to shut down an entire building for one day to replace all worn plumbing parts, than it is to shut down repeatedly for short intervals to handle emergencies. Repairs never get cheaper if you wait; in fact, waiting increases the risk of higher costs and greater damage later.

- *Tub and shower caulking.* As a building settles, the grout between tiles and the caulking at the joint between the tile and the tub or shower floor will work loose. Unless these joints are kept tight, water eventually will seep into the cracks and damage the walls. Replace caulking or grout as soon as cracks are noticed.

- *Fans.* Many apartments have ventilator fans in kitchens and bathrooms. Unless these are permanently lubricated, they will need oiling periodically.

- *Filters.* There is no excuse for not changing the filters in heating or air ducts several times a year. A dirty filter causes the furnace and air conditioner to work harder, and this increases the fuel bill unnecessarily. If the owner is paying the bill, you're losing money. If residents are paying the bill, they undoubtedly are disgruntled about paying too much.

- *Cannibalization.* Sometimes parts are taken from one apartment to make repairs in another. This practice is harmful. First, it doubles the work because both the working part and the defective part must be removed. Sooner or later, the working item that was cannibalized will have to be replaced. Second, a resident feels shortchanged when used parts are installed. Once you allow cannibalizing, it will be difficult to stop. First, a switch plate is removed from a unit, then the toilet seat; and before long a major overhaul is needed to restore the cannibalized apartment. When the situation becomes extreme, it's not unusual for a cannibalized apartment to become a storeroom, or for workers to strip other parts and take them home. All of this reduces the chances of that apartment ever being restored to income-producing condition. Cannibalization should never be permitted. You should maintain an ample stock of frequently used parts or know where they can be obtained quickly.

Performing scheduled preventive maintenance may require entering a resident's unit. If the resident is a pet owner, he or she should be instructed to confine the pet to a separate room. Be sure to give all residents several days advance notice before any inspections are done or work is performed.

If the crew enters the apartment while the resident is out, make sure they (1) post a sign on the door to alert the resident who may return while the crew is still inside and (2) leave a notice saying that maintenance work was done. This will keep the resident from becoming upset if the crew has left anything behind. Naturally, this should not ordinarily happen.

Complaints may stem from a resident's misuse of the apartment or equipment. If it appears that this has happened, your maintenance worker should suspend work and notify you. You, in turn, should obtain payment from the resident *before* proceeding, unless you are required to make the repair for health or safety reasons.

Maintenance Staff Communications

We promise fast service; and in our efforts to deliver, we find ourselves searching for effective ways to communicate quickly with our maintenance personnel. The beeper is the most popular device, but it has its limitations. Some services can delay sending the message for a considerable period of time. Many services only flash a telephone number requiring the message recipient to find a place to call or to report to the office. Obviously, such interruptions can be very inconvenient. While beepers are commonplace in large apartment complexes, they may cause more problems and inefficiencies than they were intended to cure. The office staff, eager to respond quickly to a problem, will frequently beep maintenance personnel throughout the day. The person doing the beeping does not have any idea of what the other person is doing. The assumption that maintenance personnel are just idly waiting for the next assignment is rarely true.

Many times tasks are interrupted and dropped for another assignment. After a while the frustration may lead to employees choosing not to respond to their beepers. When we tracked the beeper calls made to a staff of two maintenance people over a period of a week, we found that only 30 percent of the calls were really necessary; and many, many work hours were wasted responding to calls that could have waited or could have been handled without taking the worker away from the job at hand.

Portable telephones are instantaneous and provide two-way communication, but their use can generate a substantial bill every month. Portable phones have their place, but they can make communication too easy. Employees can be tempted to sit outside of the office and make calls on a portable phone rather than use the less-expensive stationary phone inside.

The two-way radio is an effective, economical way to keep in touch with the office. It is instantaneous and provides the two-way conversation capability that is often needed. As is true with many technologies, the quality and dependability of these units continually increases while the size and cost per unit shrinks. Granted, two-way radios have limited range, but this does not often create a problem within the confines of a single complex.

Painting

The subject of painting deserves some discussion because it's an operation the manager will deal with constantly. *Every vacant apartment should be painted before it's placed on the market.* In addition, occupied apartments will need redecorating as determined by your policy or the lease renewal terms.

Whether your own staff does the painting or you hire an outside contractor, experience will help to *establish a painting norm* for each apartment. This will let you know how much paint is required and how much time is needed. A full-time "house" painter would only be appropriate in unusually large developments. Typically, contract painters can answer our needs given short notice and tend to be more efficient.

A number of suggestions follow to help you get the best possible results.

- The manager, rather than the painter, should buy the paint or at least supervise the purchase, so color and quality can be controlled.
- Latex paint is used almost universally. It wears as well as other paints, is easier to clean up, and doesn't produce odors that annoy residents in the building.
- Don't use spray paint; use only rollers or brushes. Spray paint is messy, and you risk overspraying and damaging apartment components (e.g., carpeting, appliances).
- Have the painters use drop cloths and make them responsible for all spills. Painters should also be responsible for unclogging drains if they clean their brushes and rollers in a sink or tub.
- Use semigloss paint in kitchens and bathrooms and on painted doors and woodwork, including window frames. Semigloss is more resistant than flat paint to water, dirt and stains. It is also easier to clean and wears longer.
- Don't paint any baked enamel surfaces in the apartment, such as

grilles, ventilators, or convectors. These surfaces attract dirt, and, once painted, they can't be washed as easily. Leave them the way they are.

• Don't paint ceilings that have been sprayed with acoustical coating. These surfaces not only soak up vast quantities of paint but, more important, they lose their acoustical properties once painted. If there are stains on the ceiling, it's better to reapply the acoustical material than it is to paint it.

• Painters should not paint any electric outlets, telephone jacks, switches, master antenna outlets, window or door hardware, tile, laminated plastic surfaces, or plumbing fixtures. Insist that all switch and outlet plates and window and door hardware be removed before painting and then replaced afterwards.

• Natural-finish doors, windows, cabinets, and other woodwork should be oiled or varnished, not painted. You will not need to varnish as often as you paint.

• Remember to paint all closet walls and shelving, the inside of the bathroom vanity, and the bottom of the medicine cabinet (areas that are easy to forget and sure to be noticed by prospects). The medicine cabinet may have a baked enamel interior surface, but if necessary, it should be painted nonetheless. Today, there are many epoxy paints that will simulate the cabinet's original finish.

The popularity of paint colors changes with almost the same rapidity as that of carpet colors and patterns. There was a time when the industry standard was clearly off-white and nothing more. That is no longer the case, particularly in the middle to upper-middle rent levels. Just about every conceivable color and even combinations of colors are being offered. Wall coverings in kitchens and bathrooms are also very popular.

There are still some apartment managers who insist on limiting the color and decorating choices to off-white. They hang on to the old ways hoping for a greater profit based on the savings they think they will achieve in labor and paint costs. Sticking to such habits means missing some of the very best residents who are searching for an apartment that can really be made into a home.

Owners complain that they could make a mistake in the color combination and lose an otherwise acceptable resident, because the decor didn't suit the prospect's furnishings. The risk exists: You can lose a few prospects when you depart from sterile white. The fact that colors and patterns follow fashion trends allows you to predict resident preferences with some degree of accuracy. Also, one prospect may adore the same apartment that another prospect disliked. Imagine, if all clothes or automobiles had to meet an exact set of specifications. We are interested in finding the discerning resident, who will stay and join our family of stable residents. These discerning residents are preferable to those who take little care in their moving decisions and will soon move their few possessions to the next complex in search of a new round of move-in enticements.

Experiment with color and textures. When you find a combination that works, don't repeat it. Instead, look for an even better solution. This way you will be constantly improving the property's image and, ultimately, resident quality—which will increase the value of the property.

Pest Control

Insects and other vermin are objectionable to prospects and residents alike, and justifiably so. Roaches and rodents are among the most common invaders and are difficult to eliminate. Roaches are rarely in the building to begin with and often enter via grocery bags and food products. Rodents need food to survive and prefer darkness. You must take steps to provide a pest-free environment.

When you exterminate, do the whole building, not just one apartment. Otherwise, you simply drive the pests from one apartment to another.

It is usually advisable to contract for pest control; hire a licensed exterminator to do this work.

Grounds Keeping

How the grounds and particularly the landscaping are maintained will depend largely on the region of the country the building is in, the climate and season of the year, and the type of landscaping. Obviously, a *regular schedule for fertilizing, weeding, spraying for insects, and disease control* is needed.

The county extension agent is the right person to ask for assistance in planning this schedule. Often, the state agricultural service will analyze soil samples and recommend ways to improve soil quality. In addition, you should work with local landscape contractors in developing a program.

Seasonal Maintenance

Snow and ice control are major maintenance problems in many areas of the country. You need to determine who is going to do the work—your own crew or an outside service—and where to pile the shoveled and plowed snow.

Most apartment complexes aren't large enough to justify the cost of a large snowplow. Trying to do the job with plows mounted on smaller vehicles leads to early transmission burn-outs. Generally, it is better to contract for plowing service and have the building staff take care of walks and stoops. Planning a program during the summer means you'll be prepared for the first snowfall.

Be careful in your use of snow-melting materials. Rock salt is the cheapest and most commonly used; but it can damage pavements and plants severely, and it won't work at all if the temperature is too low. Also, rock salt can damage carpeting if it's tracked inside. You should be aware, too, that some localities prohibit the use of rock salt.

Chemical snow-melting pellets cost more than rock salt but cause less damage and continue to work at very low temperatures. However, these pellets cannot be stored for long periods or they may solidify or lose their effectiveness. So if pellets are used, buy only what can be consumed in a short time.

Shoveling is better than using salt or snow-melting chemicals. Usually, sand can be used to provide traction on slippery ice.

Your Check List

Many of the foregoing points are contained in standard maintenance check lists available from the Institute of Real Estate Management, local apartment associations, or local real estate boards. These check lists are adequate guides, but, since every building is unique, you are advised to *develop a custom check list* that contains everything you need to know about your property.

There are only two acceptable answers on an inspection and maintenance check list: "okay" and "not okay." If an item is "okay," then it's in the best possible condition and needs no further explanation. If it's "not okay," then an explanation is required. Leave room on the check list for a description of items that are "not okay." The person who performs the inspection should write down whatever is wrong; the inspection should be done by the manager in most cases. Don't use terms such as "good," "fair," or "poor." They tell you nothing. The narrative explanation, on the other hand, clearly states what is wrong and what needs to be done about it.

DEFERRED MAINTENANCE

If you set up a program carefully, most maintenance will be routine and emergency maintenance will be minimal. There is a third category, *deferred maintenance,* that takes into account items that will need care sooner or later but have not received immediate attention.

In a sense, all properties are in a constant state of decay. The property manager has to keep maintenance expenses within the budget and the property looking well. Those things that should be done, but have not yet been addressed, qualify as deferred maintenance. Actually, almost everyone has some deferred maintenance on their property—the key is to keep it in control.

You must keep a sharp eye out for deferred maintenance items, because they have a tendency to build up and then cause sudden, serious breakdowns. For example, if six water heaters fail in one year, you can expect that the other twenty-two installed at the same time will fail very shortly. Be prepared for this eventuality and have enough money in reserve to pay for replacements.

Maintenance that has been deferred may be noticed by prospects whose favorable opinion of the property will diminish. Most apartment complexes have long lists of deferred maintenance items such as cracked concrete sidewalks or curbing, dead shrubs, worn patches in the parking lot, and clogged water drains. Some of these items—for example, the dead shrubs and the holes in the pavement—should have been corrected by routine maintenance.

The purpose of planned maintenance is to avoid surprising the owner with expenses. You do this by constantly allocating money for necessary repairs and by replacement of aging equipment and components on a rotating basis.

Practically every piece of equipment in an apartment building has a predictable life span. Knowing this, plans can be made for replacements, and cash reserves can be set aside to cover the costs. Sometimes it is even possible to extend the life of one of the components of your equipment. For instance, recoating a built-up composition roof in its sixth or seventh year, can extend the life of that roof another seven years. If you wait until the ninth year before recoating, the impregnated or fiberglass felt may have disintegrated and a completely new roof will be necessary. Water heaters are another example. Sometimes it is possible to prolong their lives and cut replacement costs by installing a water-treatment facility.

At least once a year, right after an inspection, make a list of all of the items that can be classified as deferred maintenance. This is when a narrative inspection report is invaluable. If you find that the roof needs repair, the inspection report should indicate its condition and provide an estimate of its remaining life. Make similar notes for every item on the check list. Then, take whatever action is appropriate to prevent matters from getting worse, and advise the owner how much money must be set aside to cover eventual replacement or major repair.

STAFF REQUIREMENTS

By following the recommendation for programmed maintenance presented here, it should be possible to reduce both the size of your maintenance staff and your maintenance costs. Two people performing jobs that are planned and programmed usually can accomplish as much as three people working in a crisis situation. As a rule of thumb, one full-time maintenance employee will be needed for each fifty apartment units. The chart below, developed by my firm after many years of apartment management experience, shows how large a supervisory and maintenance staff is needed for various sizes of developments.

Employee Classification	Number of Units					
	50–100	100–150	150–200	200–250	250–350	350–450
Maintenance Supervisor				1	1	1
Maintenance Personnel	1	1	2	2	3	4
Custodians/ Groundskeepers	1	2	2	3	3	4

Note: Covers all normal repairs and maintenance performed by staff personnel, including apartment cleaning and grounds maintenance. Seasonal work has been adjusted: 2,080 hours of work = one employee's working year. Apartment and common area painting is not included.

In-house or Outside Personnel

Once inspections have been made and the maintenance schedule is prepared, you still need to decide who will do the work. Should you use your own maintenance people or outside organizations? This question is hotly debated at practically every gathering of management people. Contracting maintenance work to outsiders has certain advantages. For instance, at peak periods, you can get extra help without adding permanently to your payroll. Employee record keeping can be minimized, and often expenses can be kept low. You may acquire access to some specialized skills that members of your staff do not have. Also, you may minimize union pressures by dealing with an outside firm.

The disadvantages are (1) it often costs more, and (2) you lose control. Given two equally able crews, one your own and the other belonging to an outside contractor, your crew will do the job for less. Also, an outside organization's reaction time is slower; you can't give direct orders because you must work through a designated supervisor. Most contracts provide for specific services to be performed under specific terms, with no provision for extra duties. Finally, although using an outside service is an easy way to avoid training a crew, it results in spending more of the owner's money instead of maximizing net operating income.

In general, you probably are better off doing the work with your own labor. There is more control this way and, if proper supervision is provided, it's considerably less expensive.

However, there are certain maintenance tasks in an apartment operation for which outside service is advisable. I have already discussed the desirability of hiring contract painters. Other examples include:

- *Central air conditioning.* At the very least, an expert is needed to start the system at the beginning of the season and shut it down properly at the end. Failure to do this correctly can mean interruptions and costly repairs during the cooling season. Generally, the building crew can take care of individual apartment air conditioners.
- *Elevators.* Authorized service organizations have the training and equipment to provide the constant maintenance necessary to keep building elevators functioning properly. Never attempt repairs or adjustments yourself; the risk to human life and safety is too great. Managers often disagree when discussing the advantages of full-service contracts as opposed to limited service "grease and oil" contracts. Full-service contracts probably have a slight edge, but they can cost considerably more. Even a full-service contract can involve overtime charges for off-hour emergency calls.
- *Swimming pools.* Like central air-conditioning systems, swimming pools need experts to get them in operating condition at the beginning of the season and close them down at the end. Routine pool maintenance between these two times can usually be performed by your own crew, except when special licensing is required.
- *Master antennas.* With the advent of cable television, these are increasingly rare. Most antenna systems are solid-state and virtually maintenance-free. If the building has an old antenna system, a specialist will probably be needed for maintenance and repairs.
- *Pest control.* Check local laws to find out if this job must by done by a licensed exterminator. Some states prohibit the sale and application of exterminating chemicals to anyone who is not licensed.
- *Recharging fire extinguishers.* Virtually all municipalities require annual fire extinguisher tagging. Licensed services can recharge and retag these units for a nominal fee.
- *Sewer rodding.* Generally, the site crew can be trained to rod as much as 500 feet of sewer length. Anything beyond this requires professionals with special equipment and training.
- *Window-washing.* Windows in tall buildings or in places that require special equipment are better served by outside contractors. Most garden apartment windows can be cleaned by your own staff.
- *Landscaping and snow removal.* As already mentioned, outside contractors can be employed to reduce seasonal peak demands on staffing and large capital outlays to purchase major equipment.

In summary, outside service is often dictated on the basis of licensing requirements, the complexity of the machinery to be serviced, and the need for specialized equipment or skills.

Service Contracts

Whether you purchase outside services on an as-needed basis or contract for them on a regular basis will depend on your analysis of the property's requirements. A good contract that provides for preventive maintenance can help you avoid big expenses later.

Before hiring outside services, shop for a reliable firm and examine the contract to see what is included. Does the fee cover everything, or is there a deductible amount? Does it cover parts and labor? Are overtime emergency calls included? Not surprisingly, the more the contract includes, the more it will cost.

You also have to determine whether to deal with a manufacturer's service organization or an independent contractor. Service from the manufacturer may cost more, but the manufacturer's organization understands the equipment better and has easier access to parts.

SUPPLIES AND PARTS

Having the right parts and supplies on hand is essential to a maintenance program. If you run out of 100-watt bulbs and start using 150-watt replacements, you'll create spotty lighting, and bulbs will have to be replaced more often because of heat buildup. Not having the right parts and supplies means the building maintenance program will not be effective.

The supplies you need will be determined by the property itself. A walk-through inspection of the property, as previously recommended, along with market-ready preparation of apartments will help you to compile a list of what should be on hand.

The following recommendations may be useful:

- Keep supplies and parts in a central place, not scattered. This will enable you to monitor what's available, what should be ordered, and what may be disappearing because of pilferage.
- Balance the inventory to take advantage of quantity discounts and, at the same time, avoid having too much on hand. Some chemical supplies may deteriorate with time, so it doesn't always pay to buy in large quantities.
- Buying in bulk lots discourages theft. Paint in small containers disappears especially fast. Instead of buying it in one-gallon cans, buy it in containers of five gallons or more. Long-lasting chemicals can be purchased in bulk quantities and dispensed into smaller containers.
- Avoid aerosol sprays. Apart from environmental considerations they're expensive and easy to steal. You can usually buy the same chemicals less expensively in other forms.

- Anticipate needs and schedule purchases so that orders are placed as seldom as possible. Group orders and arrange for a single delivery instead of having your staff waste time making individual trips to the hardware store. If such trips are necessary, limit them to twice a month.
- All orders should be authorized and signed only by the manager or assistant manager. This reduces the chances of the staff buying too much, buying what isn't needed, buying personal items, and getting kickbacks from suppliers.

Maintenance Equipment and Major Tool Inventory

A complete inventory should be made of all maintenance tools owned by the property, noting the specific location for each item. If an article is assigned to a particular person, list this, too. Tools and equipment also require regular maintenance; this should be scheduled during the off-season when they are not in heavy use and when you can get good service at fair prices.

To reduce pilferage, consider painting equipment a special color or applying a distinctive marking so it can be identified readily and is no longer salable or worth stealing. Proper storage under lock and key will reduce theft, if not eliminate it. Only the manager and the head of maintenance should have these keys.

GETTING THE RIGHT START

Many managers who attend seminars on property maintenance come away fired up with enthusiasm and the determination to set things right at their properties, but their enthusiasm soon wanes and the maintenance program bogs down. Why? Because in most cases, the manager attacks problems all at once. This seldom works. There are just too many tasks for the staff to accomplish at one time. Resistance builds up, discouragement sets in, and it's back to business as usual.

Programmed maintenance can work, *if each task is divided into manageable segments* and each is finished completely before proceeding to the next. Consider this approach: Take a site plan of your property (or a building plan if you have only a single building) and divide it into areas or zones. Label them A,B,C, etc.

First consider area A. List everything that needs to be done to make area A first-rate. Determine the equipment and staff needed. Gather the staff together and explain what needs to be done in area A. Give each person a calendar and a list of specific tasks. Don't simply say, "Maintain it."

Instead, give detailed instructions: "Once every two weeks the grille must be removed; the filter taken out, washed and replaced; and the grille replaced." That's an instruction few could misunderstand. Then put the crew to work on area A. Watch them as they work. When they do something right, tell them so. If they do something wrong, correct them. Evaluate the work as they go along. While there may be a supervisor in charge, you must be involved so the supervisor knows what is expected. Work together to set standards of quality, establish schedules, and determine if other tools are needed.

When area A is in first-class condition, then, and only then, proceed to area B. Meanwhile, set up a continuing maintenance program for area A so it won't slip again. Proceed through the entire building or development in this way, item by item. By the time you are finished, the entire property will be in top condition, and you will have a self-sustaining maintenance program.

This kind of program is only possible if you, the manager, do a thorough job of scheduling, supervising, and evaluating. By doing your homework, you know what has to be done and when, how many people are needed, what kind of supervision is required, and what tools and equipment must be provided. Finally, regular inspections provide the feedback needed to evaluate your system and make corrections.

If you think all of this will cost extra money, think again. As we've noted, an ongoing product preparation and maintenance program costs less than one based on crisis management. Experience proves there is little or no difference between the cost of operating a first-class development and a run-of-the-mill one. The difference is in daily attention and supervision.

There is also a significant difference in occupancy and turnover rates. A better-maintained property will attract desirable residents faster and keep them longer than a run-down property will. A difference like this makes a lot of sense to the manager who wants to see net operating income at its maximum level.

6

Leasing, THE Bottom Line

Residents are very much a part of property management. They are the source of the property's income, and consequently they must be regarded by the property manager as an important responsibility, perhaps *the* most important responsibility.

In the past, residents primarily leased apartments and paid rent; if they didn't like things, they either moved out or were told to move by the owner. No one believed that residents had any rights other than the right to live in their apartments as long the rent was paid and they behaved themselves. All of this has changed because of the impact of consumerism. Renters have demanded their rights, and these rights are being granted through legislation and the courts. When rights are slow to be granted, renters take matters into their own hands by forming unions, staging rent strikes, and setting up picket lines. Renters have become adept at confrontation. They have learned how to use the press to make their grievances known. All of this can exert extreme pressure on the property manager.

Just how far apartment residents have come in the fight for their rights is seen in the landlord and tenant legislation that has been enacted on the state and local level. These landlord and tenant bills may state that the owner must deliver and keep apartments in habitable condition; that security deposits must be put in escrow and interest paid to the renters; that the owner who does not intend to renew a lease must give specific notice; that a renter may make necessary repairs to an apartment and deduct these expenses from the rent; that residents may withhold rent in certain cases; that owners may not take retaliatory action against renters who complain; or that a system of housing courts should be set up to handle complaints. This kind of legislation signals a major change in the balance of power between owner and resident. It is crucial to know the landlord and tenant code that exists in your municipality. Be aware that some states also appoint landlord and tenant commissions to monitor or interpret these laws.

Leases traditionally were written to protect the property owner and showed little regard for habitability. This practice was established in a bygone era under conditions that no longer exist. The world has changed. The old saying, "Let the buyer beware," has changed to "Let the seller or, in our case, let the owner beware!" Property managers must recognize the resident as an equal partner in the relationship between the owner and those who live at the property. A manager who persists in the old ways will very likely weaken his or her property's market appeal, antagonize residents to the point of high turnover, and reduce the property's income.

RESIDENT SELECTION

By renting to the best qualified applicants at the beginning, half of all management problems can be avoided. A thorough job of screening applicants—encouraging the desirable ones, discouraging the less-desirable ones, and educating people about your property—results in a much higher percentage of residents who pay their rent on time, observe rules and regulations, and remain in your building year after year. At the start, it is wise to anticipate all of the key questions that sound rental policies should answer: What about pets? How many people can live in an apartment? What kind of security deposit will be required?

It should be emphasized that the law leaves few areas untouched when it comes to resident selection. Fair Housing Laws at all levels—federal, state, and local—exist to prevent discrimination. These laws are very clear and so are the penalties for establishing or following policies that effectively discriminate against people for such reasons as race, nationality, sex, religion, age, family status, or any physical or mental disability they might have. Local laws vary; some exist to prevent the discrimination of classifications of people other than those stated earlier (homosexual couples may be protected, for example) and these laws may also provide unique policies and penalties. Because these laws are constantly being expanded, it is extremely important to know what applies currently. Bear in mind that the Department of Housing and Urban Development tests to ensure that Fair Housing Laws are enforced. Trying to get around them will surely shorten your career in the rental business.

The color of a person's skin or his or her choice of worship is not and should not be the determining factor in deciding whether that person will be a good resident. A number of other indicators will forecast the future of a prospective renter.

The Home Visit

The home visit is probably the least used and the most effective method of avoiding bad residents. The program involves hiring an interviewer to make an appointment to meet with the applicant in the applicant's home. This process slows down the acceptance or rejection process and it certainly adds to the operating costs. Regardless, the benefits are many. Most of us have experienced the multiple problems generated by the "disaster resident," including the cost of repairing damages, loss of other residents, and hours of frustration dealing with these cases.

The best person to do your home visits is someone who knows about our business. My company uses resident managers or assistant managers referred by our local Apartment Association. These people know a good resident from a bad one. If a manager hires an interviewer who is not a regular employee as an independent contractor, the interviewer can provide a more objective report. This may be helpful if the manager is challenged for not accepting a particular individual. As a rule you'll need to allow some time for the completion of the interview. Usually they are handled on weekends when it is easier to find the applicant at home. It is best to avoid evening visits during those months when early evening darkness makes address hunting more difficult.

Be somewhat generous in the fee for such a service, and you will have a willing pool of interviewers ready to handle assignments. This is important because time will be a factor. The cost typically approaches 8 percent of the monthly rent, rounded to a convenient increment. It is not recommended that this cost be passed on to the applicant.

A policy to visit the homes of prospective renters cannot be a selective one. I cannot emphasize this enough: Once you choose to do this, every applicant must go through the same procedure. You cannot restrict your home visits to applicants for your low-rent units only, nor can you visit just those you suspect of living below your standards. You can make overall exceptions however. For example, you could decide that you will not arrange home visits for applicants who live more than thirty-five miles from your office or the apartment development.

The home visit answers more questions than any other method of screening. It provides a look at the care prospects are giving to their current unit. Frequently you'll also witness the way prospects relate to their children and whether or not these children are under control.

Are you questioning this plan's effectiveness? Perhaps you would guess that applicants would clean up their living space, knowing that someone is coming for a visit. In fact, most people do clean up in preparation for the visit. It's interesting to note that the really bad residents do not or cannot make the effort. Some people do not know good from bad and others are living without normal furniture or in double or triple occupancy situations. You will witness conditions that are exactly like those that managers find when a less-desirable resident vacates and leaves a disaster.

The home visit is a way to identify those applicants who could create problems as residents in your complex *before* they occupy your property. It is important to establish guidelines to define what you are looking for; this is not a method that should result in the rejection of those prospects who have less money. *Order and cleanliness are at issue here, not wealth and style.* Here is a good rule of thumb: When conditions that would constitute grounds for eviction are observed on the home visit, then the application should be rejected.

Yes, some applicants withdraw their applications when they learn they must have a home visit. On the other hand, the most responsible prospects may at first object to such an invasion only to become very pleased when they understand the purpose of your extra effort. Virtually everyone has had an experience with bad neighbors. If you ever find yourself saying "I wish I had known," the chances are good that you would have known after a home visit.

Automobile Insurance

One of the quickest ways to separate people who are living on the edge from those who are abiding by the law is to investigate whether they have purchased automobile insurance. Let's assume that most of the unsightly, derelict cars parked in an apartment complex are uninsured. The same people who observe the rules of normal civilized conduct will continue to do so when it comes to maintaining insurance coverage. This inquiry should probably be limited to general liability coverage, but that alone is an excellent indicator. If these autos are going to be driven on the grounds of the apartment development, a risk is present. It is not unreasonable to require proof of insurance.

Shaping Resident Mix

Unfurnished versus Furnished. Whenever there are prolonged downturns in the economy and unusual numbers of vacancies appear, managers begin considering the advisability of furnishing their apartment units. They do this in an effort to maximize the potential market, hoping to attract couples and families who lack the money to buy furniture and residents such as corporate trainees or transferees. Unquestionably, furnishing apartments brings an additional dimension to the market.

Nevertheless, renting furnished apartments can be a management burden and a drag on net operating income. Those who rent furnished apartments may have little commitment to their residences. Even when paying larger security deposits, people are not likely to care for somebody else's furniture as if it were their own. Consequently, furnished apartments need constant refurbishing. At the end of three years, a complex that had every unit furnished when it was new, might only have enough furniture to fill half of the units because of breakage, abuse, wear, and theft. Moreover, furnishing requires a substantial capital outlay, a cost that is seldom recovered through higher rent.

Under special market conditions, renting furnished apartments makes some sense. Student housing and residences for seasonal occupants in vacation areas are two such situations. Otherwise, people who want furnished apartments can easily satisfy their needs by renting furniture. The furnishings suit their tastes, and the burden of paying for and taking care of the furnishings is on them. If you're managing a building that already has furnished apartments, you may want to consider selling the furniture. The best potential buyers usually are the current occupants of the apartments.

Corporate Units.   Closely allied to furnished apartments are those units outfitted to serve the employees and visitors of corporate clients. There are countless situations in which businesses move their employees for a temporary assignment or a training session and decide against housing those employees in a hotel or motel. This may be a method of economizing or simply making life more homey than staying in a hotel room. Proximity to the business is an important criterion in selecting such housing, as is the unit's actual size and layout.

These apartments are almost always furnished by the apartment development, and the furnishings often include cooking utensils and linens. Providing maid service a few days each week is also common. Rent for a fully equipped apartment with service is frequently twice that of the same apartment if it were unfurnished. Even at that doubled rent, the client company saves a great deal over the daily or weekly rate at a hotel or motel.

The quality of residents who use these units is generally good. Most long-term stays involve the company's top talent, and these people rarely cause problems that would prompt complaints from other residents.

A final note: Hotel chains are going after this niche of the market with the increasingly popular "residence inn" concept. If apartment managers wish to remain in this arena, apartment complexes must offer better service or more economical accommodations.

Pets. Pets have long been a source of contention between property managers and residents. With the pet population booming, the situation could become more troublesome.

Estimates place the pet dog and cat population at 110 million—and that doesn't even include other types of pets (rodents, fish, birds, reptiles, etc.). An estimated 52 percent of the nation's households, or 47 million, have a dog or a cat (or both).

While homeowners own more pets than renters, an estimated 35 to 40 percent of renters have pets. This means that if you have and enforce a "no pet" policy, you're effectively cutting off more than one third of your rental market.

The wrong answer to the question of pets can slow a rental program and damage resident relations. So, establishing a workable pet policy is important for the smooth management of a residential rental property. The key word here is "workable."

Do not make the mistake of thinking you can avoid the issue by not having a pet policy. That's worse than having a policy that forbids pets. The absence of a policy is an invitation for pets to come in without control. The damage is done when the first dog or cat arrives. Decide on a policy early, ideally before the property opens. Even if the building has been in existence for a while, a workable pet policy still can be implemented.

Begin early by separating the *dedicated pet owner* from the *casual owner*. Dedicated pet owners consider pets a part of the household and will make sacrifices to meet the pet's needs. The casual owner does not look upon the pet with as much seriousness and usually is not willing to sacrifice personal comfort and convenience for the pet. In these cases, the pet is a whim.

One way to separate the dedicated pet owner from the casual one is to charge the pet owner more. Some property managers charge a monthly pet rent of $10, $15, or $25, while others require a nonrefundable pet deposit of, say, $100 to $300. Both of these methods are ineffectual because once owners pay the surcharge, they think they have paid for whatever damage their pets may cause. They no longer are concerned with the harm their pets do to doors, carpets, and plants.

A better approach is to ask each pet owner for an additional amount to be *held as a refundable pet deposit.* This way, the pet owner has some hope of recouping the money if the pet behaves. If the pet causes damage, this additional deposit will probably cover it. It is even acceptable to make a portion of the pet deposit nonrefundable. For example, you might establish an additional deposit for pet owners of $200, of which $75 is nonrefundable and is earmarked for charges to rid the apartment of fleas and pet odors when the resident leaves. Asking for the extra money is a good way of discouraging casual pet owners, who may decide that their pets are not worth the added cost. Those who do decide to keep their pets will probably be more careful with them.

Another way to distinguish the dedicated pet owner from the casual one is to ask who will take care of the pet when the owner is out of the apartment. This is especially important when dealing with working people. The dedicated pet owner will provide for the animal; the casual owner may not have thought about this problem nor care that a barking dog left alone can be a nuisance.

You can also set the dedicated pet owner apart from the casual owner by designating certain areas of the property for pets only. If there are several buildings on your property, take no more than 25 percent of them and reserve these buildings for pet-owning residents. The rest of the buildings are then pet-free.

This kind of physical separation is easiest to set up in a new property before the rental program starts. In existing buildings, you may not want to risk antagonizing long-standing, pet-owning residents; but over a period of time, you can restrict new residents who are pet owners to certain parts of the property. You can also tell present residents who are pet owners that when their pets die, they may not replace them unless they agree to move to the part of the property designated for pets. Practically speaking, it is most difficult to prevent a resident from replacing a dead pet (and Spot II may look exactly like Spot I). Converting a building with pets to a building that's pet-free is a long slow process. You have to depend upon the residents' honesty and the eventual turnover of residents who have pets.

Whether or not you establish this kind of separation, you should make the pet policy and rules known when a prospect applies for an apartment. By making the policy known early in the rental process and having the policy in writing, there can be no misunderstanding. These are some of the items that should be in the pet policy:

- Residents may have no more than one dog or cat; or two lovebirds, canaries, or parakeets; or one myna bird. No pet offspring are allowed.
- Dogs must be no taller than 14 inches and cannot weigh more than 25 pounds fully grown.
- Tropical fish limited to a 20-gallon tank are permitted.
- No other mammals, birds, fish, or reptiles are permitted (including monkeys, snakes, turtles, zoo animals, and rodents).
- When outside the apartment, dogs and cats must be kept on leashes at all times. They cannot be staked out or allowed to run loose. Birds must be caged at all times.
- Animals must be walked in designated areas only. If the pet leaves droppings in other areas, the owner is responsible for removal.

Although difficult to enforce, these rules are needed and should be spelled out along with any others in a *pet agreement* that the prospect signs along with the lease. The agreement amounts to a revocable license that applies to a specific pet. Ask the prospect to bring in the pet so you can see it and make sure it meets the limitations imposed. It's also wise to keep a picture of the pet on file with the prospect's application.

Besides giving the resident permission to keep the pet, the agreement should also state that: (1) the resident agrees to pay for all damages caused by the pet, and (2) if the agreement is violated or if the animal becomes objectionable, the manager may demand the removal of the pet without affecting the validity of the lease or the resident's responsibility under it. A pet agreement is an important psychological tool in impressing pet owners with management's seriousness. The pet owners will know what the rules are and that they will pay a penalty if the rules are broken. At the same time, pet owners are not ruled out of the rental market.

People without pets appreciate this kind of policy too, because they know they won't come home one day to discover that their new neighbors have a Great Dane or a monkey. This protection is an incentive for them to rent in your building.

In short, you have the best of both worlds: A maximized market for your apartments and peaceful relations among your residents.

Policies Relating to Possessions.   Pets are not the only potential disruption to the peaceful and orderly operation of an apartment building. Without being negative, the rental agent must try to learn if the prospect has any troublesome possessions, and the manager should have policies to deal with them. Here are some policies that may be considered:

- *Waterbeds* violate most floor-loading regulations. They're messy to fill and empty. If they rupture, waterbeds can damage the residents' apartment and the one below. And even if they remain intact, the chemicals added to the water to keep it from souring can leach through in gaseous form and ruin the carpet. It should be noted that waterbed insurance is available, and you could consider making it a requirement.
- *Electronic equipment* such as ham and citizens' band (CB) radios requiring special outdoor aerials should be discouraged. The resident who puts up an antenna on the roof may punch a hole in the flashing and break the water seal in the roof. Furthermore, a poorly installed antenna could blow off the roof, presenting a danger to people below. Individual television antennas are much less of a problem now that cable is widely available.
- *Noisy equipment* includes drums, stereos played too loudly, hobby tools, and the like. Other residents will object to hearing these sounds through walls and floors.
- *Flammable articles* such as torches for glass blowing and welding

equipment for metal sculpture are obvious dangers and should not be allowed.

Lifestyle Choices

Whether you will rent to unmarried couples or to those with unconventional lifestyles is generally a matter of choice, and such issues may be more pressing in some communities than in others. Individual owners—and some residents—also may have keen feelings about them. Unless local laws forbid such arrangements, you are refusing potential income if you decide against renting to such people in today's liberated society, and it could be interpreted as discrimination. As I mentioned earlier in this chapter, some localities may have laws protecting these people.

It's a fact of life that unmarried men and women will live together. Even if you establish a policy prohibiting unmarried couples, you will undoubtedly end up with them living in your complex. One party will apply for and lease the apartment; in a short time, the second party will arrive. You now have two people in residence with only one person responsible under the lease. You would be better advised to rent to the couple and have both parties responsible. The rental policy should not be to judge morality but to determine whether nontraditional residents can peacefully coexist with other residents and pay the rent.

Application Deposit

As you will learn in chapter 8, a completed application form without an application deposit accomplishes very little. With the deposit comes a decision and a commitment; without a deposit, there's a high probability of the manager expending a lot of effort and expense with no result.

An effective application deposit can be as small as $25, but it should not exceed $100. A larger deposit will discourage many prospects. Here are three recommended conditions for the deposit:

1. If the application is accepted and the prospect takes the apartment, the deposit is applied toward the security deposit. It is important to first apply money received toward the security deposit and then to the first month's rent. The lease agreement will give you rights and remedies to collect rent but seldom provides for collection of a security deposit that was agreed to but not paid.
2. If the application is not accepted, the entire deposit is refunded to the prospect.
3. If the application is accepted but the prospect withdraws, the deposit is retained to cover the administrative and processing costs. Avoid terms like "forfeit." People can accept paying a fee for a ser-

vice, but they don't like forfeiture. The result is the same; the terminology is easier to accept.

Application Form

A rental application form focuses on two types of information: details concerning the prospect and details concerning his or her impending occupancy. The form can be completed by either the applicant or the rental agent; although it is recommended that the rental agent fill out the application form and then have the prospect sign it. By asking a prospect the form questions and listening to the answers, the agent can gain valuable insight. Also, the manner in which a prospect responds can indicate more than the answers themselves.

The document itself can take many forms, but certain information must be provided if a prospect is to be evaluated properly. Consider the needs and uses of this information:

1. *The name of the applicant,* spouse and all others who will reside in the apartment. All adults who will occupy the particular apartment must be identified to ensure responsibility for the lease. You need to know the total number of prospective occupants in order to prevent overcrowding. Overcrowding is hard on an apartment; too many overcrowded apartments are hard on a building. This condition creates problems in keeping the property clean and providing essential maintenance services. When move-out time arrives, damage to the apartment may be extensive.

   In addition, overcrowding is usually objectionable to other residents. Nevertheless, this varies: There may be no objections if a single person living in a studio takes in a roommate but expect complaints from neighbors if a family of six is crowded into a two-bedroom apartment.

   It's important to establish occupancy standards and adhere to them consistently—otherwise you may run the risk of being perceived as discriminatory. It is also critical to monitor the interpretations of the Fair Housing Amendments Act of 1988 that protects families with children because this may affect acceptable occupancy guidelines.

2. *The prospect's age.* Check your state law to determine whether age is a protected classification and how old a person must be to sign a nonrescindable contract. If the prospect is underage, get a parent or guardian to sign. A minor can rescind a contract that does not involve one of the primary necessities of life; a person of majority cannot. A minor who is married or orphaned or for

whom housing is a necessity is frequently emancipated from the restriction against minors and can execute a binding contract.

3. *The prospect's driver's license number.* This will help confirm identity. Most people don't know their driver's license number. When the prospect takes out the license to look at it, the rental agent can see if the name and address on the license are the same as the ones on the application. Also, the agent can check the birth date on the license to make certain the applicant is of age. The driver's license number may be valuable later in tracking down an individual who leaves without paying rent.

4. *The prospect's social security number.* The social security number is useful in assisting the credit bureau, should one be used, in its check of a prospect's background. Credit bureaus maintain records of people by their social security numbers, so having a prospect's social security number makes it easier for the bureau to look up information in their files.

    Contrary to many managers' beliefs, however, social security numbers have little value in tracking down residents who skip out. One reason is that people who do not receive benefit checks rarely report changes of address to the Social Security Administration because they're not required to. In addition, the Social Security Administration will not reveal any information it may have about the person. So don't expect any help from this source.

5. *The applicant's nearest living relative.* Be sure to get this individual's name, address, and telephone number. Not only is it helpful in emergency situations, the information can be invaluable when you're tracking down a resident who skips out on you.

6. *The prospect's housing record.* You need the name, address, and telephone number of the prospect's present landlord or managing agent, together with the size of the apartment, rent paid, and length of stay. If the stay has been less than two years, you should obtain information on previous places of residence. Be wary of the applicant who has resided at more than three addresses in the past two years. You don't need a new resident who will move in and then out in a matter of months. However, there may be good reasons for those housing changes, so take the time to ask. Also, when the rent being applied for is substantially more than the rent currently being paid, it might be an indicator of potential problems ahead. The applicants should be able to explain how they can handle a large jump in rent.

7. *Information on the applicant's employment record.* The name, address, and telephone number of the prospect's employer, together with the name of his or her immediate supervisor, should

be included. You also want to know the applicant's income, occupation, and number of years on the job. As in the case of resi-
dency, you need to know the prospect's employment history for
at least two years. If this includes more than three jobs in the past
two years, be alert. Determine the reason, it could be quite legitimate. A highly skilled trim carpenter could very well have two or
three employers in one year; skilled craftsmen often move from
job to job with little or no loss of time. If the applicant doesn't
have this kind of job, you may wish to pass on the applicant rather
than risk problems in collecting rent or regaining possession of
the apartment.

The ratio of rent to gross monthly income is a very important
factor in determining an applicant's ability to meet rent obligations. Chances of rent collection problems increase proportion-
ately when the rent exceeds 33 percent of the prospect's gross
monthly income. Only regular salary should be considered in this
test and by law, you must take into account the full gross income
of working couples. Do not include overtime pay—even though
it may be very consistent—or income received from a second job.
An applicant who needs such income to qualify for an apartment
is stretching things and may become a collection problem.

When the total of rent plus monthly payments on installment
purchases is greater than 50 percent of the applicants' monthly
gross income, do not rent to them. There simply will not be
enough money left over to meet all normal living expenses.

8. *Information on checking and savings accounts,* including ac-
    count numbers. This can be useful in judging the applicant's fi-
    nancial situation and sense of responsibility.

9. *Information on both open and closed loans or charge accounts*
    completes the important credit information on your application.

The application should also provide information concerning
the particular unit for which the prospect is applying and any
policies that may be applicable. Commonly, the information contained in the application that is needed to draw up the lease document includes:

- Address and apartment number.
- Term of the lease, with beginning and ending dates.
- Monthly rent.
- Security deposit.
- Information on pets.
- List of any optional features or services.
- Special conditions, including promises of additional improve-
  ments, free rent, or special lease provisions.

All of these special conditions should be not only stated on the application but also explained to the prospect to avoid later misunderstandings. A prospect becomes wary when these additional items are not stated in writing.

10. *Other items to consider.* You may want to ask the applicant for references even though the people listed as references will invariably be primed to give you a positive report. You should also make sure that you know the name, address, and phone number of the person who should be contacted in case of an emergency because that individual will not necessarily be the nearest living relative. Finally, you may want to seek information about the applicant's car(s); asking the year, make, and license number of every vehicle that will be routinely driven or parked on the property is a good place to start.

A great many problems arise from a resident's failure to insure personal belongings. Many people believe that the building's insurance covers resident possessions. It doesn't, of course. Including a space in the application form for prospects to indicate whether they have coverage for their personal belongings is one way to avoid this confusion. If the prospect is without insurance, you may wish to provide the names of two or three reliable agencies who can write renters' policies. In any event, the applicant must understand that personal belongings are not covered by the building's insurance.

The final step in the application process is to have the applicant(s) sign the form. Now, you can begin checking out the listed information in order to decide whether to accept the prospect as a resident.

The Credit Check

The credit of every applicant should be checked thoroughly. It's foolish not to. Otherwise, you risk rent loss and costly eviction and collection procedures. Even the best-appearing applicant can turn out to be a poor credit risk, while the seediest-looking person can be as good as gold. A credit check will help tell the tale.

A credit check isn't foolproof. It's difficult to outsmart a professional who can rig credit references so you don't find out until it is too late. You want protection against the casual poor credit risk, the person who isn't deliberately seeking to bilk you but whose careless financial habits will make rent collection difficult.

The best way to run a credit check is to do it yourself. Don't use a credit bureau at the start. It rarely will do more than ask the same questions you've already asked on the application form, checking for inconsistencies. Besides, federal laws govern the information that credit bureaus can provide.

The first step is to call the owner or agent of the property where the prospect currently lives; if you're dealing with a first-time renter, obviously you'll have to skip this. Warning: Owners and agents who are trying to evict a resident may give him or her a good send-off. This is a risk you take and it is to be hoped that honesty will prevail.

Next, try to verify the applicant's employment record and salary by telephone rather than in writing (correspondence can be slow). Be aware that an applicant may give you the name of a fellow worker and set things up so that this friend will give you a positive recommendation. This is a possibility, but often you can detect a problem by the person's hesitant manner. If you are really suspicious, hang up and try again, only this time check with the personnel department. In any event, using the phone is better than writing to the personnel department because getting an answer may take weeks.

As an extra step, you might have a credit bureau check the public record for any evidence of bankruptcies, judgments, convictions, divorces, and so on, which can bear on an applicant's ability to pay the rent. This limited service is generally very inexpensive and well worthwhile.

Many local apartment associations or groups of apartment owners and managers maintain a list of people who have given them problems. These difficulties may include a history of slow payments or evictions, troublesome living patterns, or a tendency to cause damage. Joining such a professional organization and sharing information about residents who have problems conforming to accepted lifestyle standards will surely pay dividends. One caveat is necessary: Make sure any exchange of information that you participate in is within the law. The legal ramifications of credit checks usually do not involve obtaining information; the distribution of information is of much greater concern.

Further investigation of an applicant's background may be required, depending on the responses obtained by this limited checking. No matter how careful you are, you will occasionally make mistakes in judgment. Your best tactic is to pay close attention to both the renter's living and payment habits and to act quickly when something goes awry.

Security Deposits

Owners used to ask prospects to pay the first and the last months' rent in advance. This was done to increase a prospect's commitment to an apartment, weed out people with minimum cash, and provide a cushion in case a resident skipped out or left without paying the last month's rent. However, the Internal Revenue Service has ruled that money collected as the last month's rent is prepaid rent and, therefore, taxable as income in the year collected.

To avoid this tax, owners began to consider this payment as a security or escrow deposit to be held as a guarantee of faithful performance of the lease. In current practice, this means that if a renter leaves his or her apartment in good condition after fulfilling the lease requirements, the security deposit is returned. If there is damage, the owner deducts an amount from the security deposit to cover repairs. Meanwhile, for the period of the renter's stay, the owner has had the free use of those funds to spend or invest.

The subject of security deposits invites opposing reactions. Owners usually regard a full month's security deposit as a sacred right. Without it, they say, there is no protection against the resident who damages the apartment or violates a provision of the lease. The prospect, on the other hand, objects to the security deposit on the grounds that the owner has free use of a month's rent for the full period of tenancy.

When a security deposit is requested from a prospect, fears are triggered about the fate of this deposit in the hands of an owner or agent. The prospect has doubts of ever seeing it again. Either from stories heard or through actual experience, residents expect a struggle when they leave the property and ask that the deposit be returned. The defense used by most residents is simply not to pay the last month's rent. In doing this, they avoid the risk of their money being withheld, and, at the same time, they have the money for the advance payments required at their new apartment. A full month's security deposit provokes residents and doesn't provide the protection the owner or manager seeks. The resident who has breached the lease, damaged the property, or expects problems in getting the deposit back can simply withhold the last month's rent and tell the manager to use the security deposit.

If the manager agrees to this arrangement, there may be a deficit. Say, for example, the apartment was rented when the monthly rent was $525 and the rent has gone up to $550. The $525 security deposit originally required will leave the manager $25 short on the rent, in addition to having nothing to cover any damage to the apartment.

Of course, the manager may not agree to apply the security deposit to the last month's rent. Pressure may be exerted on the resident to pay or risk court action. Court action is expensive and takes time. The tenant probably will have vacated the apartment before the case comes to court. When it does, the manager will usually find that the court will order the security deposit applied as an offset to any rent owed, leaving the property in the same spot, without any money to cover damages.

Security deposits are in disfavor for another reason: Many states now have laws that require owners to pay interest on security deposits and to give an accounting to residents whose deposits they hold. Methods of accounting and the rates and frequency of interest payments vary among states. Some states forbid the property owner from using this money, requiring that it be held in escrow for its eventual return to the renter. Owners of property insured under various FHA titles are required to invest security deposits in government bonds or with institutions insured by the United States government. The laws of some states exempt interest payments on security deposits if the deposits are under a certain amount— usually $100 and others exempt interest payments on security deposits collected for student-occupied housing and furnished apartments. Security deposit laws vary from state to state and even city to city, but renters' feelings on the subject don't. Security deposit policies remain a sharp thorn in relationships between owners and residents. In fact, many surveys of resident opinion indicate that the security deposit is a major grievance.

The biggest reason security deposits are not what they used to be is that they place the property at a marketing disadvantage, particularly when a competing property is being rented without a deposit. If all competing properties require a one-month security deposit, you can gain a marketing advantage by reducing or eliminating yours. As an alternative, you might want to ask for a deposit of $100 or a figure substantially below one month's rent.

Given the option, most people would actually prefer to pay more rent and a lower security deposit. We can interpret that as an extension of the American buying principle: How much down? How much a month? Take the example of a group of prospects given a choice of paying $500 monthly rent plus a $500 security deposit or $525 monthly rent plus a $100 security deposit. The prospects would probably compare the $1000 entry fee to the $625 entry fee and choose the latter, even though it would mean an annual increase in rent of $300 (the $25 per month difference in rent for 12 months). Obviously, this is preferred by the manager as well. The additional rent increases the property's income, while a larger security deposit has little or no financial impact.

Most prospects, when they sign a lease for a new apartment, are also paying rent on their present one. In addition, they are now required to pay a full month's advance rent on the new apartment plus a security deposit equal to another month's rent. While people may be able to afford high monthly rents, not many have savings that will permit them to pay two months' rent in advance in addition to all the other costs of moving. So, given a choice of two apartments with the same features and amenities, most people will take the apartment with the lower security deposit requirement—even if it has higher rent.

Resident ill-will, administrative costs, and marketing disadvantages render the traditional security deposit no longer useful. However, the reasons for requiring a security deposit—to assure the prospect's commitment and to establish a reserve fund to pay for damages—are still valid. To resolve this issue, you may find it useful to adopt a policy of asking for *a deposit of substantially less than one month's rent.* This accomplishes three things:

- It provides a marketing advantage over properties that continue to ask for a deposit equal to one month's rent.
- If the rent and the deposit are not equal, prospects are less likely to consider the deposit as an advance payment of the last month's rent. Properties with this policy have reported a sharp improvement in the number of vacating residents who voluntarily pay their last month's rent.
- If the deposit is minimal, it may be exempted from controls required by current legislation.

These advantages deserve consideration when you establish your security deposit policy, but we should make one qualification. The exception applies to the rental of single-family homes. In a building with many occupants, there are people close at hand to report disturbances, undue noise, or situations that appear out of the ordinary. This benefit does not exist in a single-family home and a great deal of damage can be done before you become aware of trouble. A security deposit of two months' rent is recommended when you lease a single-family residence.

The issue of returning the deposit when the resident vacates also is important, but this will be discussed in chapter 7, Resident Relations.

THE LEASE AGREEMENT

Leases traditionally have been written to favor property owners. They are couched in language that is not only hard to understand, but also intimidating. Because many of their provisions are outmoded, leases are becoming harder and harder to enforce in the courts.

Nevertheless, leases are necessary. A written document is needed to serve as a contract and spell out terms and conditions. Owners and residents alike need the psychological value gained from the act of signing a formal agreement.

The lease document can be revised into a more acceptable and workable form, however. For one thing, it doesn't have to be called a lease. The term *occupancy agreement* can be used. This lacks the sting of the word "lease," conveys a more up-to-date approach, and is equally binding. You would be well-advised to work with your attorney on the development of a modern-day version of a lease or occupancy agreement for use in your properties. By eliminating provisions that are no longer applicable or enforceable and lightening the legal terminology, you can provide a more workable document; it will be valuable in resident relations and as a marketing tool.

Terms of Occupancy

Certain provisions are more or less standard. A brief outline of the important provisions is provided here for a better understanding.

Parties to the Agreement. An occupancy agreement should identify the name of the legal owner of the property; however, when the property is managed by an agent, it should identify the *agent* of the owner. This establishes that the manager is acting in the capacity of an agent. The owner can be referred to as the owner, lessor, or landlord. Whatever you choose, use it consistently to avoid confusion.

All adults and emancipated minors who are to occupy the apartment should be listed by name on the occupancy agreement and should sign it, so that all are held responsible for the performance of the agreement. The law generally holds that there is no such person as "Mrs. John Smith." So, in the case of a married woman who uses her husband's surname, have her sign using her given first name (e.g., Mary Smith).

If you rent an apartment to two or more people and only one person signs the occupancy agreement and that person later leaves, you may have a hard time collecting from the remaining occupants. This problem can be minimized if you list all adult occupants on the agreement and obtain their signatures. This policy will also protect you in the event of the death of one of the occupants. If a husband and wife occupy the apartment, have them both sign the lease. If one of them dies, the other is still obligated to the occupancy agreement terms. If the remaining resident doesn't pay, you can pursue the remedies provided in the agreement. If the surviving spouse has not signed the occupancy agreement, you'll certainly have more difficulty proving your rights.

If you require a *guarantor* or *cosigner,* this person should execute a guarantee that is either part of the occupancy agreement or on a separate form attached to and made a part of the document.

Identification of Premises. While many apartments are known by name, the occupancy agreement should identify the premises being rented by apartment number, common postal address, city and state.

Rent. For the most part, rent is in the form of a monthly charge. This is particularly true in unfurnished apartment buildings. Rents are generally due and payable, in advance, on the first day of each month. The occupancy agreement should state when and where rent is to be paid and require that the first month's rent be paid when the occupancy agreement is executed and before the apartment is occupied. A few owners make the mistake of dividing the year into 12 periods of 30 days each and charging rent beginning on the day that occupancy takes place. This practice is confusing, and complicates bookkeeping. If occupancy begins on any other date, prorate the rent for the first month, and be sure the lease term ends on the last day of a month to avoid difficulty and confusion at renewal time.

Other methods of rent payment are also used under certain circumstances. In some furnished units, rents are stated as monthly, weekly, or sometimes semimonthly rates. A discussion of additional types of rent follows.

- *Aggregate rent.* Many office and commercial lease agreements provide for an aggregate or gross term rent that is payable in monthly installments. For a time, this practice extended to residential units, but it has lost favor with both owners and residents. Its purpose is to obligate the renter for the rent amount for the entire lease term rather than for each monthly period only as it came due. This provision permits monthly installments of the rent payments as long as the tenant is not in default. The lease usually contains an acceleration clause that makes the entire sum due if any installment is late or missed. This arrangement saves the manager from having to sue each month as another rent payment becomes due.

  Courts take varying stands on such provisions. For apartment leases, the courts tend to disclaim the acceleration provision and to rule on rent claims as if a standard lease with a fixed monthly rent were in effect.

  If you use an aggregate rent lease, extra care should be exercised in its preparation. For example, if a lease is written for a two-year term, and an aggregate rent amount for only one year is inadvertently inserted, you have granted two years of occupancy in return for only one year's payment of rent. It's doubtful that the court will give you or the owner much sympathy.
- *Graduated rent.* Use of a graduated rent provision is common in leases, particularly when the term is longer than one year. To avoid confusion and possible later argument, make certain that the beginning and ending dates for each rent rate are stated clearly.

  It is generally easy to negotiate a lease with a rent that steps up periodically. People are usually more concerned with the immediate future and will agree to higher charges at some distant date.

  A different form of graduated rent is often found in apartments in college towns. Student housing frequently has two rates: one for the ten-month school term, and a much lower one for the two-month summer term. The two-rate system works better than averaging the rent for the entire twelve months. A resident is required to pay the first ten months' rent at a higher rate, and then if he or she remains for the summer, those two months are discounted.

- *Head rent.* In college towns and in developments trying to attract young single people, you may find rent being charged by the "head" rather than by the dwelling unit. This is used more frequently for furnished than for unfurnished units. In this type of housing, the owner or manager establishes a rent by first determining the number of people who could comfortably occupy the apartment. For example, a two-bedroom, two-bath apartment might accommodate four adults. The apartment is then offered to four adults individually, each of whom would pay, say, $180 per month and sign his or her own occupancy agreement. The unit can then be rented to four persons unrelated or unknown to each other at that $180 per month head rent. One of the roommates can leave without affecting the rent of the remaining three. While these renters enjoy the benefit of low individual rents, they also face the prospect of not knowing their new roommates. There is one thing to remember if you are developing policies for head rent: Don't plan to have three occupants in a single unit, although units accommodating four or more may occasionally have only three residents. In my opinion, groups of three people are notorious for difficulties; invariably two people conspire against the third, who in turn leaves. Groups of five or seven are acceptable for a suitable space because additional people seem to defuse the problems of "odd man out."

  Generally, when this type of rent program is in effect, the owner may agree to lease the unit to a family or smaller group of people who will accept responsibility for the entire rent payment for an amount that is less than the four individual rents.

  This method of charging rent is unique and is not recommended unless you find yourself in a very difficult or specialized market condition. Bookkeeping and collection problems increase dramatically when head rent is used instead of the standard unit rent.

- *Seasonal rent.* Seasonal rents are common in vacation areas, with the highest rents charged during the period of greatest demand. If you manage an apartment building in Aspen, Colorado, or Palm Beach, Florida, it will be necessary to collect about 80 percent of all rent dollars during a three- or four-month period of the year. During the off-season, demand for these rental units decreases substantially due to the much smaller number of year-round residents.

  Seasonal rents are, for the most part, paid in advance. For example, a person who rents housing for a season that normally lasts six months can be expected to pay as much as 50 percent of the total season's rent before taking occupancy. The resident then would be expected to pay the remaining rent on the first of each month for the first three months, with the advance payments applied to the last three payments. There are a variety of systems for collecting seasonal rents, but most involve substantial advance payments.

For both seasonal and student housing, owners adjust rental rates to produce the required gross rental income. Most operating costs go on whether residents are present or not, so rents are adjusted to recover these costs during times of heaviest market demand. In addition, the rent must reflect the higher incidence of turnover which of course increases the operating costs overall. Turnover is high in seasonal and student housing, perhaps twice that found in normal unfurnished apartments. The level of apartment abuse by transient residents is also higher than normal.

- *Other rent.* If rent covers more than just the apartment—let's say a garage is included—the lease should separate the rent for the apartment from the rent for the garage. Defining what the rent does not cover—for example, cable TV, use of recreational facilities, or whatever is paid by special fees—is critical, too.

Escalator Clause.   Leases can be modified so that the rent will increase as the cost of living rises or operating expenses increase. This is accomplished with escalator clauses like those used widely in office buildings. Office buildings typically establish a base year for both real estate taxes and operating expenses. As these costs increase, they are billed to the tenant as additional rent. Because office leases are written for longer terms (three to ten years), the rent adjustment protection provided by escalator clauses is necessary.

The same strategy can be applied to apartment rentals, even though their leases are written for only one- or two-year terms at most. The problem is one of applying an automatic device that will let the apartment manager and resident know that a rent adjustment is necessary to keep pace with changing costs. We need an index that reflects price increases, is readily available, and is accepted as reliable. Utility charges and real estate taxes come to mind because of their alarming increases in recent years, but they probably are too erratic and too political to meet the test of sustained reliability. Both of these expense items, as well as all other expenses incurred in the operation of multifamily housing, are incorporated in one index—the Consumer Price Index (CPI). This index is published monthly by the U.S. Department of Labor, Bureau of Labor Statistics. It reflects changes in the cost of living not only nationally but in most major cities as well. The CPI receives front-page attention in most newspapers every month. Property owners and residents can receive these statistics through a monthly subscription that's free for the asking.

Adopting this type of lease provision will allow the owner to preserve a margin of profit in an inflationary economy. Its purpose is not to turn a losing investment into a winner, but simply to maintain the status quo.

At first glance, you may think that the concept of a clause providing for automatic rent adjustments would have a negative marketing appeal and people would resist. Just the opposite can be expected. Because rent increases are tied to an impartial, well-known government index, apartment renters are likely to accept the escalator clause and complain less about so-called rent gouging.

It is important, though, that renters be told about the escalator clause at the outset. Managers and owners cannot assume that the clause has been read and understood just because a resident has signed a lease containing it. Courts no longer assume that everyone reads and understands lease provisions, so you must call the escalator clause to the prospect's attention. One way to do this is to include a legend on the title page of the lease: "This lease contains a rent escalator clause; please read it carefully." Another way is to affix a sticker with similar wording on the lease. It also helps if you personally inform the prospect of the escalator clause. In other words, do all you can to assure that the renter cannot complain later that he or she didn't know about the clause and assumed the lease form was conventional.

Lease Term.   Set down the specific dates on which the lease begins and ends. The lease period can be any term acceptable to you and the resident. You can set a term that benefits your rerental needs. In most areas of the country, any month-ending date from March 31 to October 31 is a good expiration time. Should you have to rerent, the market is active in these months. Some managers believe that it is usually best to avoid leases that terminate in cold weather months because fewer replacement residents will be out looking for apartments at those times.

In a new property, set up your leases so they expire at staggered times rather than all at once. This will minimize rerenting problems. If you're managing an existing complex with a tradition of having all the leases come up for renewal at once, begin staggering their expiration dates gradually as they are renewed.

Normally, you are under no obligation to renew a lease. You can renew by including the terms of renewal in the current lease or by submitting a new lease document or a lease extension rider.

Be aware of the *holdover tenant.* Suppose you don't renew the lease. The resident remains and remits another month's rent. If you accept this rent, he or she may become a holdover and be entitled to remain in the apartment at the same rent for another year! Local laws vary on this point. You can avoid a lot of trouble and guard against the possibility of holdovers by having your leases run for a specific period "and month-to-month thereafter." Then, if a new lease is not signed and the resident remains on a monthly basis, you can terminate occupancy at the end of any month with thirty days' notice.

Security Deposit.   In the body of the lease document, it is advisable to acknowledge receipt of the security deposit and to provide for its escrow, use, and return. This not only helps avoid misunderstandings, but also alerts a prospective buyer of the property that security deposits exist and should be credited to his or her account in any sale prorations. When purchasing an apartment building, an investor is buying both the benefits and burdens accruing from the existing leases—as well as the property itself—and is responsible for performing the landlord's part of all lease obligations. This includes returning security deposits. Unless the security deposit is noted in each lease, a new owner may be unaware of this obligation or its extent.

Special Provisions.   Up to now, all of the information given in the lease sets out the terms as stated in the application form. In addition, you should include any special provisions appropriate to the circumstances. These include escape clauses; some examples follow.

- *Transfer clauses* permit residents to cancel leases when they produce written evidence from their employers that they are being transferred to other cities. Anyone can get a letter from a supervisor; it could even be forged. Permitting cancellation this easily is foolish. The resident cancels at no cost, and you're stuck with an empty apartment.
- *Home purchase clauses* should be excluded in general. They fall into the same category as transfer clauses. It's easy to get a cooperative real estate broker to write a letter saying that the renter has purchased a home. But why should you be penalized?
- *Death clauses* may be written for older people who are concerned that leases may be involved in the settlement of their estates. This clause provides for cancellation, generally thirty to sixty days after the resident's death, allowing time to settle estate matters and vacate the premises. If you refuse to grant this cancellation privilege, most prospects won't press the matter.

Of course, you can write a lease with no escape clauses and then try to enforce it. That means if the resident moves out before the lease is up, you can go to court to collect rent as it becomes due. However, the law in most jurisdictions requires you to mitigate or reduce the resident's liability. You can't just let the apartment remain vacant and sue for what the original resident owes. You must try to rent the apartment to someone else. If you incur expenses in renting it again, usually you can include these costs along with what the resident owes you.

Trying to collect on broken leases in court is time consuming and costly. You need a policy that will be fair to all residents, give residents the flexibility to move if relocation is required, and at the same time protect you and the owner against rent loss and extra expense.

We recommend that you and the resident cancel the lease by *mutual agreement* according to one of the following two sets of terms:

1. You both agree to look for a suitable replacement. When one is found and approved by the manager, a new lease is issued, the old one canceled, and the former resident pays a fee for administration and advertising.
2. The resident agrees to pay a set amount, upon receipt of which the manager cancels the old lease and seeks a new resident on his or her own. The set amount could include a forfeit of part or all of the security deposit.

Other possible special lease provisions include these:

• *Renewal options.* Granting a renewal option gives a tenant the right to continue occupancy for one or more periods at rent level(s) that are usually preset. As an example, someone might be offered a one-year lease at $675 per month with the right to extend that term for an additional year at $700, followed by another one-year extension at $725 per month. The resident will take advantage of this provision if it represents a good value at the time the option must be exercised. If the market has softened, however, and the resident believes that a better deal can be negotiated, the resident will probably forego the option. In contracts, terms and conditions should enjoy mutuality. There is little mutuality in an option, and therefore owners and managers should resist including them in leases.

Renewal options make sense when market conditions give the landlord few alternatives or when the tenant is making a considerable investment and the option provision helps ensure the tenant's ability to continue in occupancy. If the option period extends much beyond one year, it is recommended that the rent be tied to the market rent being charged at the time the option is exercised. This way the rent increase does not trail the market in times of high inflation.

• *Promises of improvements.* If you made any promises in the application, they should be inserted in the lease document to reassure residents and to avoid future misunderstandings.

• *Pet clauses.* These might be included as special lease provisions. As stated earlier, however, a separate pet agreement or license is preferred.

• *Condition of the premises.* Some printed lease forms state that by signing the lease the prospect acknowledges that the apartment is in a clean and safe condition, even when it may not be; but things are changing. In many localities, there are ordinances stipulating that the execution of a lease by the owner is a form of guarantee that the apartment is in a clean and safe condition and that it conforms to all local codes. An owner can be held liable if an apartment does not conform to these standards.

• *Limitations.* A good lease will specify certain restrictions regarding the apartment's use and occupancy. It should *list all the people who will live there,* with a provision for additions only through birth and adoption. This permits the agent to take action against violators, such as a single person who rents an apartment and then has three or four friends move in later.

The lease should specify who is responsible for *repairs and breakdowns.* If damage is caused by resident neglect, the lease should explain how the owner will recover damages. The lease should also state *how the premises can be used.* Apartments are for private residential use, not for commercial or illegal purposes.

• *Right of re-entry.* The lease should provide for the owner's right of access and entry. The owner or manager should be permitted to enter an apartment for periodic inspections, repairs, and modernization. The owner should also have the right to show an apartment for rerental during the last sixty days of the lease term, at reasonable hours—which have generally been established to be between 9:00 A.M. and 6:00 P.M. Similarly, the owner should have the right to exhibit the units in the event the building is offered for sale.

Again, your familiarity with local laws is a necessity. Some laws specify that residents must be provided with a *written notice* before anyone enters the apartment. The period of notice is also prescribed in such laws.

• *Repossession.* Included in the lease should be a provision that the owner has the right to repossess the apartment, that the resident loses the right to possession when he or she fails to pay rent, abandons the apartment, or violates the lease terms. According to the law there is a significant difference between the resident's losing his or her *right to possession* and your right to seize the possession. Awareness of state and local laws on these issues is imperative.

• *Abandonment.* Be careful about this one. Each jurisdiction has its own definition of abandonment. If you violate it, you may be trespassing.

Check the local law with an attorney, then specify what constitutes abandonment in each lease. Generally, if a resident has paid the rent, the apartment is not abandoned—even if the renter does not live there. Payment of rent usually gives someone the right to use the apartment; nonpayment of rent is often part of the test for abandonment.

Formal abandonment may have to be declared before you can do anything about any personal property that may be left in the apartment. Know your local laws before invoking your rights in the case of an apparent abandonment.

If you decide to enter the apartment and remove possessions that have been left there, it is advisable to document the appearance of the apartment and to inventory all of its contents in detail. Many managers photograph or videotape the entire apartment to show its condition and contents before removing any articles. Items of value should be stored for a period of time. The length of time depends on the value of the articles and, in many jurisdictions, the law. The risk of a claim is great and the advice of the owner's attorney is highly recommended.

Finally, it is critical that staff members do not take items left in an apartment. If such a practice is permitted (or not expressly prohibited), the staff may begin to take items that may later be claimed for possession. If left with apartment contents, the manager might decide to donate them to a charitable organization that will provide a receipt and perhaps even indicate a value of the items donated. If the residents do return sometime later to claim their possessions, give them the receipt and description of the donated items to use for tax purposes. People are often more understanding when they learn that the items were donated to a charity.

- *Fire and casualty.* The lease should state what happens if the apartment becomes uninhabitable as a result of fire, flood, or other disaster. As a rule, the rent stops at that point, and the resident is credited or refunded any unused rent for that month. The owner then has a period of time—90 to 180 days is customary, but the lease should be specific on this—to decide whether to restore the apartment and continue the lease or cancel it.

- *Assignment.* Most leases should and do forbid the resident from assigning the lease to someone else without the property owner's written consent. The reason is obvious: The owner or agent must know and approve of the occupants in the property. When this control is lost, serious problems will result.

- *Waivers and exculpation.* Most leases state that the residents will hold the owner harmless in the event of any property damage and personal injury occurring on the premises. A great many courts have held these clauses null and void (or at least as they apply to bodily injury). A resident can sue—and generally collect—for damages arising from a personal injury that occurs on the property. While you may want to include this kind of exculpatory clause for it psychological value, be aware that it may not hold up in court.

  Also common are clauses in which residents waive their rights concerning legal notices, remedies, and procedures. The legality of contract provisions in which the parties waive or lose some of their rights is being questioned and challenged. Remember, you can't enforce contract provisions that are against the law.

- *Subordination.* This is a common feature in many commercial leases but is much less common in residential leases. A lease gives a tenant a leasehold interest in the property. The subordination clause simply states that the owner can sign on behalf of the renters and handle certain legal formalities without seeking their approval or acquiescence, so long as these actions do not affect the renter's right to possession.

- *Condemnation or eminent domain.* This clause generally provides that if an empowered authority takes the property through condemnation proceedings, the lease is automatically cancelled without any compensation to the renter (who is required to leave), but with adequate notice (usually sixty to ninety days).
- *Bankruptcy.* The lease should provide for the eventualities of resident bankruptcy, insolvency, assignment for the benefit of creditors, reorganization, and even insanity. If any of these problems occur, you may be restrained from pursuing financial claims for monies due prior to the filing date. Your claim might have to wait for a settlement with all of the other creditors.

  Bankruptcy law grants the debtor the right to choose whether to reconfirm the lease. The decision, as the law stands now, belongs to the renter and not to the property owner. This is contrary to the language of many residential leases which read that the owner has the right to terminate the lease in the event of a bankruptcy. This clause should be drafted by an attorney familiar with bankruptcy law.
- *Rules and regulations.* The property's most important rules and regulations should be listed, along with your rights to change them. The more reasonable and up-to-date these rules are, the better chance you have to enforce them.
- *Signatures and delivery.* Finally, the lease must be signed by all the parties and copies delivered to them. The validity of a lease is questionable if a resident does not receive a copy even though all parties have signed it. The lease endorsement should include the ownership title as first indicated on the lease and the capacity of the person executing the lease on behalf of the owner.

With the lease signed, copies delivered, and the first month's rent and security deposit paid, the new renter is ready to take possession. The next section will discuss the policies that should be considered to help govern the resident's stay.

RENT PAYMENT

Establishing rent payment policies encompasses aspects of apartment management that should be carefully thought out and thoroughly understood. The main issues concern where, when, and how rents are to be paid.

A Matter of Habit

Traditionally, and by contract, rent is due on the first day of each month. Payment of rent is a matter of training and habit. If you don't establish this policy, you will not enjoy prompt or complete payment. Count on some residents testing you and delaying payments as long as they can.

Many renters spend what they have each month. Most workers are paid twice a month on average, and the average renter uses most of one paycheck to pay his or her rent obligation.

Once a resident falls behind in paying rent, it is most difficult to catch up. Skilled managers know this and constantly apply pressure to keep each rent account current. They know that the best catch-up months are May and June because expected income tax refunds usually arrive about then. Most rent collection problems begin because the manager was slow to act.

Make the Policy Known

Your policy on rent collection should be spelled out when the prospect first completes the lease application. It will not affect your sales presentation, because people expect rent to be due on the first. This policy should be stated again when the renter signs the lease. In doing this, you firmly establish the collection policy and eliminate many future problems.

Rent Bills

Should a resident be billed for rent each month? This is a commonly asked question, and the answer is "no." Rent is usually a fixed amount. The precise amount is known by the resident, who also knows that it is due on or before the first of each month. What, then, is the reason for billing? In a luxury building with variable charges added to the rent, or in a condominium with owners, not renters, a monthly billing might be useful. For the most part, however, rental property does not need the extra cost and problems associated with the billing of rent. If the mails are delayed or there is an error in your billing, you have provided an easy excuse for the resident to be late.

Paying at the Site Office

You gain maximum control over rent payments when they are collected at an on-site office. Granted, from an efficiency standpoint, more rents can be collected and posted in a single day when they are received by mail at a central location. The loss of control that mailing rather than hand-delivering payments will cause, however, is more than enough to offset this advantage. Convenience to the resident and the benefit of personal contact each month are additional advantages that result from on-site collections.

Lock-boxes

Some companies and complexes have incorporated a central cashier or bank lock box system for the collection of rent. These systems often provide the resident with an excuse. The delay in processing information back to the manager is called the "blackout period." During this time, site personnel do not have an up-to-the-minute listing of residents who have and have not paid. Depending on the system, this period can extend to as long as fifteen days. The renter, when approached about overdue rent, learns to reply: "I have sent in my rent payment."

Direct Transfer

Some banks offer an arrangement in which they automatically deduct the resident's rent payment from his or her checking account on the first of each month. The benefits to the user are simplified bookkeeping and one less check to write each month. The benefit to the property manager is punctual receipt of rent.

My company experimented with such a program and in fact offered our residents free checking accounts at a local bank that included the direct transfer feature. The problems were numerous. Many people write checks knowing that the check clearing process allows some time that amounts to a short grace period. Checks sent through the mail clear more slowly compared to automatic transfers which are instantaneous. Our residents did not like the program once they found their accounts overdrawn; in fact, more than half of the people in the program withdrew within one year.

Forms of Payment

Rent payments can take many forms: money orders, cash, personal checks, and even third-party checks. You need a firm policy with regard to the form in which rent is paid.

- *Money orders and cashier's checks* are the best method of payment from an owner's and manager's standpoint. They are convenient to process, recoverable if lost or stolen, and safe in terms of cashability. To a resident, they lack convenience and involve additional expense because they must be purchased. Your policy should be to accept them gladly but not to require them.

- *Cash* should be, but isn't, a welcome form of payment. Managers are often reluctant to accept cash. When large amounts of cash are known to be kept on the premises, you run a risk of theft that can compromise the safety of your site staff. Many managers either discourage cash or refuse to accept cash rent payments (even HUD's policy endorses this). Cash collections require frequent trips to the bank or a cash station; checks, on the other hand, can be deposited through the mail. Use caution in establishing a "no cash" policy. Cash is legal tender in this country. Refusal to accept cash payments of rent may void your right to collection. You certainly can ask residents to pay by check or money order, and most will accommodate you. Most major thefts of rent money result from a failure to make daily bank deposits. With the extra work volume around the first of the month, several days' build-up of deposits makes a robbery an even greater loss. The solution is to make bank deposits daily.
- *Personal checks* account for the vast majority of monthly rent payments. They offer convenience to both the resident and manager and generally can be replaced if lost or stolen. The problem arises with NSF (not sufficient funds) checks, which frequently are delayed several weeks in being returned.

  In my experience, people who write checks when there are not sufficient funds in the bank to cover the amount do not seem to be affected by the charge that the bank levies or the service charge that we impose. Limit your residents to two NSF checks. After that, you should insist on money orders or cashier's checks.

  Postdated checks are another favorite of people with money problems. The best advice is to refuse a postdated check. We'll address this issue in more detail during our discussion of The Fair Debt Collection Act.
- *Third-party checks* should be avoided. Even though these may be company payroll or social security checks and can be termed "good as gold," they present problems. To cash these checks, you may need to make change for the resident if the check exceeds the rent amount. Also, when a third-party check is returned as NSF, it causes enormous problems in identifying the resident, making bookkeeping adjustments, and obtaining a replacement check.

Advance Payments

Occasionally, a resident will offer to pay rent for a number of months or even a year in advance in return for a discount on the rent. Advance payments may be fine; discounts are not. Even though the additional cash would be helpful in meeting current bills, you would be ill-advised to accept this money if it means discounting the rent.

RENT COLLECTION

Collecting rent is almost as painful as raising rents. We are not speaking of rents that show up in your office voluntarily, but rather the ones that don't. A manager's ability to collect all rent that is due is an important measure of job performance. A poor manager rarely will have a good collection record. Long, hard experience suggests that your rent collection policy should contain very little flexibility.

Many managers prefer a more liberal policy regarding rent collections. They quickly point out special circumstances that might be involved along with the fact that most local laws require a lengthy procedure to dispossess a renter from a unit. Most managers, however, when asked to name the residents whose rent payment will be outstanding on the tenth of the following month can do so with uncanny accuracy. The point is this: If those residents are so well known, why isn't the manager doing something about them?

Enforce on the First

If the rent fails to arrive in your office during the very first few days of the month, you must begin enforcement, preferably in person. A telephone call or even a hard-hitting letter is not as effective as a personal visit. Reminder notices and final notices are not worth their paper value, much less the stamp required to mail them. It doesn't take residents long to discover your complete rent-collecting procedure. They quickly learn the steps you follow: reminder notice, final notice, five-day notice, letter, phone call, attorney. They will make their payments just before the nasty personal letter or phone call. Knowing this, why waste time with the preliminaries?

One thing you have to be mindful of is the Fair Debt Collection Act. This federal law that has been on the books for some time, is beginning to find enforcement in rental housing. Challenges and varying interpretations can be expected to go on for years. The primary points of the law that affect those in the apartment rental business are:

- *Direct collection efforts to the debtor.* Collection techniques in the past have included advising the employer or the parents of a late-paying resident. While this practice often brought quick results, the rights of the particular consumer were probably violated.
- *Announce the purpose of communications.* The Fair Debt Collection Act would have you clearly announce that the purpose of a telephone call or letter was primarily for the purpose of collecting a debt. This allows the debtor the option to continue listening or reading once you have stated your purpose. Most landlord communiques

are very direct, so this provision should not change your typical collection method.

- *Always notify the resident when a postdated check is cashed.* The way
  to eliminate this step is to not accept postdated checks. Most apartment operators insist that all checks carry the current date. In certain situations you may agree to hold the check for a few days before
  depositing it, but be sure the check carries the date it was written so
  that it can't be construed as postdated.
- *The debtor has a thirty-day period in which to disclaim the debt.* This
  provision is subject to a number of varying interpretations. Some say
  that landlord-tenant law effectively provides the debtor with an opportunity to object. Others argue that the contractual agreement of
  an ongoing lease is different from a consumer debt obligation, and
  that this provision in the law gives a resident an automatic one-
  month grace period. Property managers should be familiar with this
  law and with its interpretations locally.

Spotting Trouble

Some simple rules will help in spotting potential rent collection problems. When the rent exceeds 33 percent of a renter's gross income, pay
attention. The risk of having a collection problem increases dramatically
with each rental dollar over that 33 percent mark. Another warning signal
should go off when the combination of the rent plus monthly installment
payments reaches 50 percent of the renter's gross income. When these
two situations occur, there won't be enough income to go around, and
somebody will come up short—probably you.

Another early sign of trouble is the NSF (not sufficient funds) check
that has been returned. When the first check comes back, that is the time
for a personal visit. Have the resident replace the NSF check with either
cash or a certified check. Make it clear that after two NSF checks, all payment will have to be in the form of money orders or cashier's checks.

Penalty Charges

When residents become delinquent in rent payments, some managers like
to impose a late or penalty charge. This is a poor practice. First, it implies
that rent can be late as long as a late fee is paid. Residents who pay their
rent late and accept the penalty assume they have paid for the privilege of
paying as late as the last day of that month. Such a policy bends what
should be an inflexible rule—that rent is due on the first. Second, courts
usually do not lend a hand enforcing penalties. However, by calling the
late charge a "service charge," you may be able to collect it; but you will
be required to demonstrate how your costs increased because a particular

renter was late. While this is preferable to a "penalty," you should not regard it as an alternative to prompt payment.

Discounts

If you insist on providing flexibility in your rent payment policy, consider this suggestion: Increase rents by the amount you would set as a late or service charge, then allow a discount of that same amount on rents paid *before* the first of the month. Your claim will be for the gross rent once the new month begins. This is both acceptable and enforceable. The advantage of using this system is that you appear to be rewarding residents for doing something above and beyond what they have already agreed to do—paying the rent on the first day of each and every month.

Contests

Some managers dream up contests or incentives to entice residents to live up to their commitment to pay rent on the first of each month. Don't do it! When you offer a prize drawing to residents who have paid their rent promptly, or some other incentive, you are effectively saying that a considerable number of residents are late with their rent. That admission gives support to the late-paying residents and signals to them that they are not alone—and makes the job of collecting rent even more difficult.

Excuses

When a resident who is behind in rent is confronted by management, he or she usually has a variety of excuses. Seldom will you hear the real reason: "I don't have the money." You will often be told about the deficiencies in the apartment with the explanation that payment is being withheld until the defects are corrected. Never trade repairs or improvements for rent. If repairs are needed, they should be made in the normal manner, and you can reiterate your standard procedures for requesting such work. The resident is using this ploy to buy time and save face. After a year or two, most managers have heard many of these resident tales and realize that they are merely flimsy excuses.

Payment Plan

Once residents admit to being short of the money needed to pay the rent, they may try to negotiate a payment plan. This is something else to avoid. The great majority of these plans fail. The very reason residents are behind is because their expenses exceed their income. If this is true, how can they get ahead again? Usually, they report the promise of a Christmas bonus or an expected tax refund. The question is, how many more creditors are waiting for that same check? Remember, there is a new rent charge each month. There are also businesses whose existence depends on people who need money temporarily. They are called banks and loan companies. Property managers are not in the business of lending money, and, therefore, should not.

Some will argue that it is better to receive a partial payment than to have an empty unit and no rental income. That theory is totally wrong. You are far better advised to enforce your policy on rent payments rigidly. A vacant apartment is far superior to one occupied by someone who hasn't paid for it. At least you have the potential of leasing it to someone who can and will pay the rent on time. If word gets out that you are "soft" about collecting rent, your problems will increase with each passing month. The weaker the market, the stronger your policy on rent collection should be.

Settle in Court

It is interesting that some residents will not pay their rent even when threatened with eviction notices, subpoenas, a court date in front of a judge, and the final humiliation of the eviction process. Then, on the court date, sometimes even after the judge has ordered their eviction, they will decide that they want to stay and are willing to pay all back rent plus your legal fees and all court costs. You might be tempted to accept, especially if the market is weak and one additional resident can make the difference between profit and loss. The advice of this writer is: "pass up the offer." Let them go. My years of experience have shown that you can almost guarantee a recurrence within the year. Use your energy to find a renter who will pay; let some other landlord waste time chasing the chronic delinquent every month.

Throughout this book, many policies and procedures are recommended. Of all of these, *the rent collection policy should be the most inflexible.* Failure to adhere to this principle can cost thousands of dollars each year.

Damage Deductions

Occasionally, a resident may send in the rent, minus deductions for so-called damages: the oven is unreliable, the refrigerator broke and $100 worth of food spoiled, the air conditioner didn't work and the family slept in a hotel. Don't allow such deductions. Your policies should insist that payments for damages are a separate matter and rent is always to be paid in full. If you are responsible for a delay in repairing the stove or refrigerator, pay for the damages separately—not as an offset against the rent. Of course, if repairs are made promptly, such situations will not occur often.

Gauging Delinquencies

In the apartment rental business, you will inevitably lose some money due to delinquencies. People lose jobs; the economy can falter; families get into trouble; and you can misjudge applicants. Just how much rent loss is too much? According to the accepted standard, you are within bounds if you have less than 1 percent of your total monthly rent outstanding at the end of the month. That is not to say that you should accept 1 percent as a goal. Many managers achieve a 100 percent rate of collection. We're saying that if your total rent roll is $40,000 per month, you might have as much as $400 remaining to be collected. Outstanding rent between 1 and 2 percent signals trouble. The problem may be a softening economy and shorter work hours or layoffs, or it could be the result of a softening rental market. When delinquencies go over the 2 percent mark at the end of the month, major problems exist; and this indicates the need for an immediate change in management.

Resident Relations

Harmonious resident relations begin even before anyone moves in—in fact, even before the leases are signed. They begin in the rental office when a prospect inquires about an apartment. If you have established fair and reasonable policies for dealing with prospects, you can prevent many of the problems that may arise after prospects become residents.

GENERAL RESIDENT POLICIES

It is crucial to establish and use resident policies. The manager must make residents aware of policies that affect them. After a resident understands policies relating to leasing and the payment of rent, he or she should learn the general policies that guide and influence behavior on the property.

Resident Guidebook

A good way to set the tone of your property and let residents know what you expect of them is to publish a resident guidebook. It's a smart idea to give each incoming renter this guidebook before the move-in date and certainly by the first day of occupancy.

The guidebook should be a simple explanation of all the rules, regulations, and policies of the management, along with some practical and useful information. It should be written in understandable language; a good free-lance writer, advertising copywriter, or publicist can write it for you. It is wise to avoid a list of negative dictates: "you can't to this" or "don't do that." If possible, illustrate the guidebook with professional drawings. If the booklet is lively and interesting, people will want to read it. Don't mail the guidebook or leave it inside the new apartment; hand it to the resident personally with the suggestion to look it over as soon as possible.

Some of the subjects a resident guidebook should cover are listed below; managers should include any additional topics that are pertinent to their properties.

Rent payments	Parking
Renewals	Motorcycles, campers
Recreational facilities	Bicycles, buggies
Waterbeds	Auto repairs
Stereo, musical instruments	Laundry room
Security deposit	Deliveries
Decorating	Keys and lockouts
Resident improvements	Emergencies
Occupancy limits	Disturbances
Children	Complaints
Pets	Storage

To assist new residents, you may also want to provide some practical information about the neighborhood, such as:

Utility companies' names, addresses, phone numbers
Churches and synagogues
Schools, both public and private
Public library
Public transportation stops
Shopping districts
Nearest post office
Telephone numbers of police and fire department
Voting precinct number and local polling place
Names of government representatives—federal, state and local

Guidebooks also help your rental personnel because they contain useful information for talking with prospects. A guidebook's main purpose is to make residents aware of the property's policies and procedures. The next few topics are subject areas that should be addressed in your resident guidebook.

Keys and Lockouts

Policies on keys and lockouts are needed for several reasons: to reduce replacement costs, to prevent wasted time, and to maintain security.

The renter moving in should receive a fixed number of keys. Charge a fee for extra keys or for replacement of lost ones. If the resident wants extra locks on the door or asks to have the lock changed because of a lost key, have this done at the resident's expense; but use your own personnel or an approved locksmith so that you can have the new lock fitted to the master key, as well as providing uniform and professional installation.

Lockouts can be a nuisance. You may have a working parent whose child is locked out of the apartment after school and comes to the management office for the key. There are always occasional adults who lock themselves out and need keys—often at one o'clock in the morning.

To discourage lockouts have a policy of charging a small fee (say $8) to let residents in during the day, $25 or more if it happens after 10 P.M. Another approach is to render no help. This forces residents to gain access on their own and pay for any damages.

One important precaution: *Never lend master keys.* With this practice you run the risks of having the master key lost, stolen, or duplicated, and breach the security of the entire property. A building should have only a limited number of master keys. No keys should be identified as masters; they should be numbered and assigned to a few designated people such as the manager and the head of maintenance. It may be a good idea to have the keys returned to the office each night. If a master key is stolen, the manager should have all of the locks rekeyed to a new master. Although this is expensive, it is a necessary precaution.

Politics and Voting

Common sense suggests that your property and management staff should remain politically neutral, but meeting facilities may be made available for political purposes provided they are made available to all political parties on the same terms.

That's where political cooperation should end. Political signs in resident windows or anywhere else on the premises should be forbidden for reasons of appearance. Displays on bulletin boards should be allowed on an equal basis. Political canvassing or distribution of political literature on the premises should be discouraged.

Some complexes are large enough to constitute one or more voting precincts, and the local election board may ask to rent polling space in your building. This generally is an excellent idea. An on-site polling place is a convenience to residents and encourages their participation in the democratic process.

Door-to-Door Sales, Canvassing, Etc.

Rules on these matters pose special problems. Many communities have laws governing soliciting. Ideally, you should prohibit commercial salesmen in order to avoid disturbing your residents. There is, however, the question of your own residents doing the soliciting. A good policy is to permit them to invite contributions on behalf of a recognized nonprofit organization but to forbid door-to-door sales.

Move-In

A move-in policy is necessary to ensure that an orderly procedure will be followed. This is especially important if a number of moves occur in the same building on the same day. A smooth move-in procedure will create a good impression for new residents and guarantee fewer management problems later on.

The move-in policy should require each new renter to let you know the date and approximate time of move-in so that you can be on hand to welcome him or her. This notice is also necessary in order to coordinate the use of elevators in high-rise buildings. People moving in become irritated quickly if they arrive to discover another party using the elevator; meanwhile, they are faced with mounting hourly charges as the moving crew stands idle.

Occasionally things do not go according to plan. If the old resident hasn't moved out when moving day arrives, get in touch with the new residents right away and tell them to remain where they are. That's the only thing you can do. If the new renters are already on their way, this can be a real problem. If it seems the delay will be a day or more, suggest that they move into a motel. You will have to work out some means of pacifying and compensating these people, even though you may not be at fault.

Someone may ask about moving in one or two days early if the apartment is already vacant. Although the resident technically is not on the lease for those few days, it makes some sense to permit an early move-in. Earlier occupancy may allow for easier scheduling and you will gain some goodwill at little or no cost.

Finally, the manager or a staff member should be present when the renter moves in to give whatever assistance is needed, explain procedures and answer questions, arrange for a tour of the premises, make note of any necessary adjustments or shortcomings, and explain to the new resident how and when corrections will be made. Before the move-in itself, a check list should be followed to ensure that everything is ready for the incoming occupant. The apartment should be given a final inspection; the temperature should be set at a comfortable level; the refrigerator should be turned on; keys, including the mailbox key, should be ready; the resident's name should be on the mailbox; and the storage locker should be clean and secured. You may also find it worthwhile to inspect the unit with the new occupant on move-in day. After completing the move-in inspection, have the new resident review the inspection report and sign it; you should also sign the report. This way you have a document on file that verifies your mutual acknowledgement of the condition of the premises.

Resident Improvements

Some residents may want to improve their apartments by painting, installing paneling, putting up wallpaper, or laying new floor coverings. They may ask you first or just go ahead and do it, creating a surprise for you later.

As a rule, it's a good idea to encourage residents to invest their own time, money, and energy in upgrading their apartments. By doing this, the resident's sense of commitment to the apartment increases; this adds to the likelihood of developing long-term residents.

To understand how this sense of commitment is created, think about your purchase of an automobile. You don't really regard it as your own until you wax it or add some bit of your personality to it. If you buy an antique ring, it doesn't really feel like yours until you've cleaned and polished it. In the same way, an apartment isn't really the renter's home until he or she invests some extra money or special effort in it. Your job is to look for ways to help the resident make that all-important commitment.

Assume you are facing a series of move-outs to newer buildings with more modern kitchen appliances, yet you cannot afford to make mass replacements. Rather than lose residents who want new appliances, allow them to select a new appliance for their apartments. Let them pick out something from a catalog or display—a stove with a self-cleaning oven, a self-defrosting refrigerator—and then go fifty-fifty on the purchase (the appliance then becomes the property of the building owner). Because residents pay half, they will take better care of the new appliances; at the same time their commitment to the property is heightened. Residents are often more financially equipped to participate in the purchase of a desired appliance or improvement than they are to incur the greater cost of moving and perhaps higher rent payments. If residents approach you, offer each of them the same deal. In doing this, you retain your residents while improving the property.

You have to protect against poor workmanship and the cost of restoring apartments at a later date, so consider a policy that tells the renter you favor improvements but with certain restrictions: (1) the resident must use materials that are removable during restoration (strippable wallpaper, and light-colored paint); (2) the improvements cannot be a danger to others (flowerboxes insecurely attached to balcony railings); and (3) the work can be done only after securing the approval of the management.

Some improvements should be prohibited outright. These include painting entry doors or those with a natural or stained finish; using adhesive-backed paper anywhere in the apartment (it is difficult to remove and leaves a coating that cannot be painted over easily); installing permanent, nonslip materials in tubs and on shower floors; and attaching any signs to the property.

Screw and nail holes of one-half-inch or less in diameter are "damages" created by an acceptable installation and must be tolerated.

The resident may want to install his or her own refrigerator or add other appliances and fixtures. Let's consider these:

- *Refrigerator.* The resident wants to use his or her own refrigerator and asks you to store yours. This leads to problems, because a stored refrigerator will deteriorate quickly. You may decide to permit such an installation if the appliance can be utilized in another unit. If you do permit a resident to install and use a privately owned appliance, mark your records so there is no misunderstanding.
- *Plumbing equipment.* Residents should not be allowed to install dishwashers, disposals, washing machines, or dryers in their apartments unless your building is designed to accommodate such equipment. The existence of these appliances can lead to problems with vibration, flooding, noise, and plumbing back-ups. Also, some have special power requirements.
- *Lighting fixtures.* If the residents want to take down your lighting fixtures and put up their own, let them know they must restore the original lighting fixtures at move-out or pay for replacements and installation.

These are just some of the improvements that residents may request. Think about others that may occur on your property and formulate policies to deal with them.

Service

In my experience, declining maintenance and service levels are responsible for more move-outs than any other category of complaints. The first step toward change and improvements requires an honest recognition that when maintenance and service decline, residents begin to look elsewhere for housing. Residents need a constant show of appreciation. The best way to demonstrate appreciation for residents is to provide them with a well-maintained and improving property, together with a high level of personalized resident service.

PROBLEM-SOLVING

The property manager must confront resident-related problems. Having contingency plans for these situations may mean the difference between taking care of a minor difficulty and creating a huge dilemma. Let's examine a few of the most frequently encountered problems.

Complaints

A complaint that is handled slowly is almost as bad as a complaint that isn't handled at all. As a worst-case scenario you would handle a resident complaint within twenty-four hours. Most top-quality management companies respond to service requests filed in the morning during the afternoon of that same day. Problems that develop in the afternoon are taken care of the next morning.

It's important to *keep track of complaints.* Don't try to do it by memory. Every complaint should be written down. If a complaint is made by telephone, write everything down and then repeat it so the resident knows you understand the problem. The very fact that the complaint has been acknowledged will help satisfy the resident.

Complaints usually concern three subjects: (1) other residents, (2) the apartment, and (3) the property.

1. *Complaints about others.* "My neighbors play their stereo too loudly." "They're fighting next door." "I think the people down the hall are drug dealers." These are the types of complaints you may get from some residents about others. Some of these are frivolous, others are serious.

   If a complaint deals with an *emergency or civil disturbance* involving others, find out if the resident has already called the police or fire department. If not, ask him or her to do so immediately. If the resident balks, place the call yourself. Be quick to act if life or property is threatened. Be careful about trying to deal with civil disturbances yourself, particularly fights resulting from domestic quarrels. These are best handled by the police.

   If there is a complaint about a nonemergency situation pertaining to others, tell the resident you'd like to see his or her experiences presented to you in writing. For every ten telephone calls of this nature, you'll get only two or three letters. When you get the letter, visit the offending resident and tell him or her about the complaint, but *do not identify the individual who filed it.* After settling the matter, contact the person who made the complaint and explain what action you've taken. This can be done in person or by telephone.

2. *Complaints about the apartment.* Requests for repairs and maintenance should certainly be handled within twenty-four hours. If you need access to an apartment, let the resident know you'll have to enter the apartment during normal business hours, assuming it's not an emergency.

3. *Complaints about the property.* If residents complain about the way the property is maintained ("too much litter," "the grass isn't cut,"

"the laundry room smells," "recreation hours are too short"), pay careful attention. These criticisms of the property are warning signs of resident dissatisfaction. They likely extend to many more people than those who actually complain. In fact, your very best residents may be equally bothered but say nothing; then one day they simply move out. So, if you start hearing general complaints, acknowledge them and begin a prompt investigation.

Emergencies

Life in an apartment complex goes on twenty-four hours a day, seven days a week, 365 days a year. While your office hours are established to take care of routine business, you need a policy to provide for emergencies in an orderly manner. The first recommendation is that you have a listed *twenty-four-hour emergency telephone-answering service.* It should be listed as an emergency number to distinguish it from the regular office number that might be used by prospects calling with questions. You may want to have the number printed on a sticker for residents to put on or near their telephones. Include the emergency number in the resident guidebook and post the number on bulletin boards. The answering service should know whom to call for various emergencies. This might be the site manager, although most developments rotate "on days" among several staff members.

The next recommendation is to *let residents know what constitutes a real emergency.* If a resident needs a replacement light bulb, that can wait; but if a water line breaks in an apartment, that's a real emergency. There are six types of real emergencies:

1. *Flooding caused by a plumbing breakdown.* This must be corrected instantly. The longer repairs are delayed, the more extensive the damage will be.
2. *Lack of heat in winter or air conditioning in summer.*
3. *Damage caused by wind, storm, or fire.* In a disaster, you have to take instant steps to minimize the damage. Residents should call the fire department first in case of fire; if they haven't, the answering service should do so immediately before relaying the message to building personnel.
4. *When security has been breached or is threatened by burglary, vandalism, or other disturbances.* Again, residents should call the police first, and the answering service should notify the appropriate staff member.
5. *Back-up of a sewer or other sanitary facility.* This is a health hazard and must be corrected immediately.
6. *Electrical failures or short circuits.* These can threaten the safety of the building and the lives of residents.

You should make residents aware of what constitutes emergencies and whom to call about them by publishing a separate information sheet or by incorporating the information into the resident guidebook. You also should make sure that your answering service knows whom to call for each type of emergency. The answering service should also ask residents with nonemergency requests to call back during office hours.

Disasters are a period of extreme tension for a manager. After the initial shock of the disaster itself, there are physical and emotional pressures caused by injuries, deaths, or loss of possessions. Later, in chapter 10 on Insurance, we'll discuss the manager's obligations and responsibilities after a disaster.

At present, we will limit this discussion to the issue of rent. It's a good policy to *discontinue rent charges* if an apartment is uninhabitable and to refund or give credit for any unused portion of that month's rent. Then, depending on the terms of the lease, the owner usually has a period of time to determine whether to restore the apartment and continue the lease or to cancel the lease.

Remember, once you have established your policies for dealing with disasters, put them in the resident guidebook so everyone knows what to expect.

Illegal and Immoral Uses

How do you deal with a resident who engages in drug abuse, gambling, or prostitution in the apartment? Most leases state that the use of the apartment for illegal or immoral purposes is grounds for eviction, but eviction is a court procedure that is slow, expensive, and open to question. It's better to meet with the resident, cite the objectionable behavior, and offer to cancel the lease and return the security deposit.

Before you take any action, consider whether you want to act against the offender at all. He or she rented the apartment for personal use. If what is done within the apartment is not offensive to others or damaging to the property, you may be better off ignoring it.

If you decide to take action, confront the resident by going to the apartment or asking him or her to your office. Do not write a letter stating the complaint. If the complaint turns out to be unjustified, the resident might use the letter against you in a court action. When you confront the resident, you can simply say, "I know what's going on here, and I think it would be best for all concerned if you moved."

In most cases, the offending resident will leave, not because of a legal requirement but because most people will do what they're asked to do. Have the departing resident sign a mutual cancellation agreement, and return any prepaid rent or security deposit money you may be holding when the apartment is vacated. If the resident is suspicious that you won't refund the money once he or she leaves, offer to put it in escrow.

Resident Abuses

Resident abuses (i.e., disregard for fellow residents or the property) are a source of many complaints and problems for managers. One resident uses the balcony for storage; another leaves wet clothing in the coin-operated washers. There may be a family that is extremely noisy or a working resident whose children continually have to be let in after school.

The offending resident may not realize the problems being caused. The best way to deal with the situation is simply to show up at the apartment door and discuss it. Most people will agree to correct their ways. Here again, don't write a letter because it will probably be ignored, or the resident might over-react, exacerbating the problem. The resident can't ignore a face-to-face meeting.

If the offending activity continues, make a second visit. On this occasion, suggest that perhaps the resident should live elsewhere and offer to cancel the lease by mutual agreement. This tactic demonstrates your seriousness, and the individual is likely to reform. If the offer of cancellation is accepted, the problem is solved then and there.

Of course, the resident may reject your offer and continue the offense. In that case, court action is your next recourse. Be aware that going to court is a long, uncertain process, and the lease will probably expire before the action is resolved. You may be better off to put up with the nuisance until the end of the lease term, or you can begin the lawsuit in the hope that it will encourage the resident either to change his or her habits or to accept your cancellation offer.

Resident Damage

The best protection you have against damage to the apartment caused by the resident is the security deposit. It is very difficult to collect in court for damages that exceed this amount. Your policy should be to try to collect damages at the time of the occurrence, thus preserving the security deposit amount to cover damages revealed when the occupant moves out.

For example, if the toilet overflows because someone has dropped a soap dish or rubber ball into it, let the resident know that this is not a normal malfunction and that payment for the repair is expected. Most reasonable people will accept this; if the resident refuses, you still must make the repair for health reasons.

Suppose a resident uses an ice pick to defrost the apartment refrigerator and in the process punctures the refrigerant tubing. In many jurisdictions, you're under no obligation to repair or replace an appliance damaged by a tenant's gross misuse. Point this out to the resident and request payment for the damage. (By the way, if the refrigerator in this particular example is more than a few years old, you are probably better off purchasing a new refrigerator and applying the resident's damage money toward that purchase. The new refrigerator should then be installed in the apartment of one of your best residents. Move their old unit to the apartment where the damage occurred.)

As for damage caused by resident neglect (e.g., water damage from a bathtub overflow or a window left open during a rainstorm), you should always try to collect—even though you may not succeed. Rarely will you be able to collect anything beyond the security deposit. If a fire is caused by resident negligence, you'll have to rely on the property's insurance for coverage. The insurance company probably won't pursue the resident for payment, nor will a court generally rule against a resident in favor of the owner.

There are several other possibilities to be considered in setting a damage policy. Broken windows, for instance, are generally an ongoing maintenance problem; replacing them is a cost of business you should absorb. Property damage caused by a resident's car may be collectible through a claim against the resident's auto insurance carrier.

If you rent furnished apartments, it's advisable to increase the security deposit to cover the added risk of damage. Also, inventory all the furnishings and indicate their condition before anyone moves in so you can use the security deposit to pay for any loss or damage. Photographs and video tape are an easy way to inventory furnishings and document their condition at the time of move-in.

Tenant Organizations

Tenant organizations are one outcome of the impact of consumerism on rental housing. They are often the result of both owner and management insensitivity to resident requirements. I believe that the kind of sensitivity needed to provide the products and services residents want should come from management's awareness of existing problems—not from collective bargaining. It's difficult to manage real estate effectively by committee. If you attempt to satisfy every resident through a tenant organization, you may wind up satisfying no one.

Not content to act individually, some renters have realized the power of group action. They have seen what labor unions have accomplished and what civil rights groups have won. They have taken a cue from condominium associations that manage the affairs of buildings. Residents often band together in the belief that "the landlord can't throw us all out."

Many tenant organizations are started in response to nonspecific issues. The residents have a general but undefined feeling that it's unsafe to live in the property or they don't like the way the place is run. Seldom do they focus on specific grievances such as loose carpeting in the second floor corridor. Because tenant organizations do not understand—and often have no wish to understand—the need for good business practices, they can make decisions solely on the basis of collective emotion and pressure.

Another factor leading to the formation of tenant groups is the idea that democratic principles should rule a community of residents. Participation is the watchword, an idea promoted by the U.S. Department of Housing and Urban Development in the housing that it sponsors or assists. HUD in fact requires the managers of federally assisted housing to support resident organizations.

Once owners or managers allow tenant organizations to tell them how to run their properties, they forfeit their rights to control and their expectations of maximum net operating income. A manager who becomes too involved with a tenant organization has to deal with the same kinds of problems faced by the manager who socializes with tenants; this softening of the relationship between resident and manager can easily create difficulties.

What should the manager's policy be? You rent to tenants as individuals, and you should try to deal with them as individuals. This means you should not encourage or assist them in the formation of any kind of organization. Don't even help them form a ski club, bridge club, or resident newsletter, as any of these can backfire. When a meeting is necessary you should call it, run it, and adjourn it yourself.

Residents are less likely to feel the need to organize when you adopt the following principles of action:

- *Fair and reasonable policies, uniformly applied.* All of your policies should be founded on sound reasoning, consideration of the residents, and fair and uniform enforcement.
- *Good communication.* If a problem exists, tell residents that you know about it and that you are seeking a solution. Don't be mute or try to ignore a problem. You can communicate with residents through letters or personal visits. Incidentally, management newsletters are not effective for this purpose.
- *Prompt response to service requests and complaints.* Satisfied residents have no reason to band together. By taking care of their individual complaints, you will eliminate most of the problems.

Tenant organizations do exist, however. The smart manager turns a bad situation into a good one by using the tenant organization to his or her advantage. You could, for example, use the tenant organization to encourage residents to report specific problems when they are small and controllable. It's not necessary for an owner or a manager to relinquish control of the property to the resident organization any more than it is necessary for a fifth grade teacher to lose control of his or her class. Your written policies come in handy here, because you have established your position as the maker and enforcer of the rules.

Arbitration

Arbitration is a viable way to settle disputes. By including an arbitration clause in your lease, you and the resident can agree to submit any dispute to arbitration. Whatever the arbitrator decides is binding on both of you.

The usual procedure in settling a dispute is to contact one of the 55,000 arbitrators recognized by the American Arbitration Association. The arbitrator hears both sides and then makes a judgment for one or the other of the parties. The fee, about $500, is usually divided between the two parties. If residents know their complaints will be settled fairly, they are less likely to resort to group action for satisfaction.

AFTER THE FIRST LEASE

There are ways to retain good residents. Naturally, the apartment manager would like these people to renew their leases continually. When this doesn't occur, the move-out becomes an important part of satisfying residents. Maintaining good resident relations begins before any lease is signed and continues through move-out day.

Apartment Transfers

A resident may ask to transfer to a different apartment during the lease term to accommodate a change in circumstances. Policies covering apartment transfers should take some variables into account. Generally, you should discourage apartment transfers because they create added administrative work and cause premature wear and tear on apartments, but you should also be flexible. A resident who is not satisfied with his or her particular accommodations and seeks a change will probably go elsewhere when the lease is up—and you've lost a resident. This is especially true if there are just a few months left on the lease.

In determining whether a transfer is a good idea, consider market conditions. For instance, if a resident loses a roommate and wants to move from a two-bedroom unit to a one-bedroom unit, you might have the resident agree to pay a prorated share of redecorating the old apartment in order to facilitate the transfer. This is certainly a good idea if two-bedroom apartments are in tight supply and one-bedroom units are plentiful. You've just rented a one-bedroom unit, and you should have no trouble re-renting the two-bedroom apartment.

Lease Renewals

It's common practice to offer the resident a renewal lease prior to the expiration of the current one. Frequently, the new term would be for one year. I am learning that such a practice actually increases tenant turnover. Presenting existing residents with renewal leases has the effect of forcing them to decide what they want to do with their lives for that period of time. There are many people currently renting their accommodations who have long-range plans to own their own home. By presenting a lease to them, the decision is placed squarely on the table. It's common for a couple to receive their renewal lease in the mail and to set aside the next few weekends to explore new housing developments and the possibility of making a move. Bypassing the formality of a renewal lease does not eliminate the thought of moving, but neither does it force people to action.

At the properties my company manages, we experience the least resident turnover if we first lease to a resident for a given period—say six months or a year—and follow that by an invitation to continue on a month-to-month basis, with the assurance that future rent increases will be limited to once-a-year on the anniversary date of the original lease.

Some building owners fear that residents will opt to move during off-season (when there are few replacements available), or they may be concerned that their lender will prefer the security of having annual leases in the file. Nevertheless, people typically avoid off-season moves. So, while the risk is there, it is not a great one. Also, lenders are coming to the realization that signed residential leases in a file cabinet do not offer the same security as major commercial credit tenant leases. Hence, they are not as troubled by month-to-month tenancies as they have been in the past.

Renewal Rewards

One of the most important policy considerations that you will have in the management of rental apartments is the way you plan to encourage a resident to renew a lease or stay another year. Existing residents will certainly notice that their new neighbors move into freshly prepared apartments (often with new carpet or appliances). Unless there is a specific policy to reward the existing resident with an apartment improvement for each lease renewal, the property will face a constant procession of move-outs, and operating costs will be driven to a point where all hope for profit is gone.

Many apartment operators provide a display showing the various apartment upgrades and improvement packages that can be selected by a resident who renews the lease. For example, if the person is just completing one year, the renewal reward might be a fairly inexpensive improvement such as wallpaper for the kitchen or bath, a ceiling fan, new hardware or a new light fixture. On the second anniversary, the improvements should have more value. Examples might be a large bathroom mirror, new medicine cabinet, new kitchen floor covering, decorative chair rail, etc. Four- or five-year anniversaries might be rewarded with a new major appliance, new carpeting or a new tile job in the bathroom.

As you will soon see, the cost of turnover is the highest single expense in the operation of an apartment property. A great deal can be spent making existing residents more comfortable before you begin to approach the cost of replacing them.

Security Deposit Reduction

One of the best ways of showing confidence in your residents and expressing appreciation for their tenancy is to return some of the security deposit at given lease anniversary points. If the full security deposit was $150, you might have a policy to return $50 after one year, another $50 the following year and the remainder after three years. This process certainly acts as a reward and is welcomed by the residents. As time goes on, haven't we really amortized many of our costs?

Such a policy has an additional benefit: It affects the resident's cash outlay if he or she decides to move to another property. Let's assume you decide to hold a resident's full security deposit for the duration of tenancy. When that resident moves, he or she effectively transfers the security deposit from you to the next landlord and the out-of-pocket expense is only the rent on the new apartment. If you had given that same resident a security deposit refund the cash outlay for a new apartment would have been the security deposit plus the rent. Remember, one of the deciding factors in moving is cost. With this in mind, we can adjust our thinking to make it more cost effective for the resident to stay.

Turnover

Frequent tenant turnover is very expensive. In fact, it ranked right up with utilities and real estate taxes in a study of annual operating costs. Over a period of twenty years, national average turnover rates rose from 30 percent to greater than 50 percent. In some communities, especially in the southwestern part of the United States, turnover rates regularly approach 100 percent each year.

44 Days Between Tenants

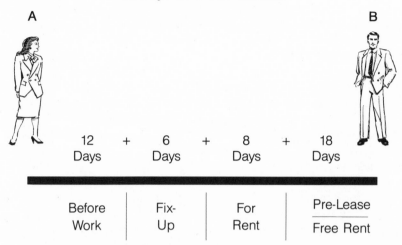

A

B

| 12 Days | + | 6 Days | + | 8 Days | + | 18 Days |

| Before Work | Fix- Up | For Rent | Pre-Lease / Free Rent |

A property's *turnover rate* is the number of new renters moving in during a one-year period as compared with the total number of units in the property. For example, if forty-five new residents moved into a 100-unit property in one year, its turnover rate would be 45 percent.

There are two general types of resident turnover. The first is called economic turnover. It involves residents moving out of apartments because they have purchased a single-family home, townhouse, or condominium, or they are required to live in another part of the city or country as a result of a job transfer or relocation. This is much more prevalent in higher-rent strata than in middle- and lower-rent brackets. The continued appeal of homeownership (including condominiums) is due in part to a desire to hedge against inflation and acquire tax advantages. There is also a tendency to underestimate the costs of homeownership. Economic turnover will always occur to some degree in the better quality, higher-rent apartment complexes. Better service will help minimize such resident losses, but there will always be attrition.

Many apartment building owners and managers attempt to avoid economic turnover by intentionally keeping rent levels at the financial break-even point. By maintaining unrealistically low rents, they hope to cut operating expenses attributable to resident move-outs while still producing a high net operating income. The effect of this practice on a property's economic turnover rate may be minor, but its effect on the economic viability of the property is almost invariably significant.

The turnover you can and should slow down, however, is *lateral turnover*. This type of turnover includes residents moving across the street or down the road because another apartment complex looks nicer, has better service, or offers more amenities. Whenever the supply of apartments out-strips demand, or conditions or service levels start deteriorating, this type of turnover will increase. The largest proportion of tenant turnover—about 70 percent overall—falls into this class. First-class conditions and top-flight service can affect dramatic reductions in both the rate of lateral turnover and its corresponding costs.

It is truly impossible to eliminate turnover in an apartment complex. Renters, even homeowners, come and go. We must minimize the rate of turnover, however, through careful screening and selection, fair rent pricing, constant product updates, and cheerful service and follow-through.

Controlled studies have shown that an apartment complex spends about three times the amount of the monthly rent every time a unit turns over. This figure includes cleanup expenses, decorating and carpet care, window coverings, repairs and replacements, advertising and promotion costs, and utilities and lost rent, as well as concessions and administrative charges. The average time between resident move-out and replacement move-in is over forty days. This includes periods of free rent that may be allowed or taken. In money terms, if the rent were $500 per month, the cost would be about $1,500. Put another way, you could spend up to that amount improving a particular unit if it would make the difference between keeping or losing the occupant. While these figures are averages, they do represent a realistic cost of finding a replacement resident.

Many firms have changed their chart of accounts or have added a special control category so that they can keep all the costs associated with turnover in one place. In doing this, they create a constant reminder of the importance of rewarding the existing resident so that the average stay is prolonged.

If you were to reduce the turnover rate in the property that you control by 10 percent, you would certainly increase operating profits. Or, you could charge less rent and deliver the same bottom line. Using typical numbers, each 10 percent reduction in the annual turnover rate, say from 50 to 40 percent, would allow you the benefit of charging around 3 percent less rent while maintaining the same net operating income. A 20 percent improvement in turnover rate, from 50 to 30 percent would double the 3 percent possible monthly reduction. I certainly do not recommend chasing a rent reduction. I just want to point out that the high cost of turnover is a definite portion of each month's rent. Reduce turnover and you lower the need for higher rent because costs will drop. Every move-out you prevent is one less apartment that you have to rent.

Move-Out

When residents advise you that they intend to move from their apartments, spend some time with them reviewing the different procedures so they will know what to expect. It's crucial that the residents provide you with their moving date so you know when to begin searching for replacement residents. You also should remind the residents of move-out inspection procedures and arrange to inspect the premises on the day of move-out after the furniture and other belongings have been removed so that you can determine their security deposit refund. Finally, you should be interested in the resident's reasons for moving in order to learn about any deficiencies in your property or your performance.

Security Deposit Return

A resident who is moving out may suspect you of trying to keep the deposit by finding as much damage as possible. Your policy should be to minimize these fears by establishing a procedure that will be completely objective and fair.

It's to your advantage to have the occupant leave the premises in the best possible condition so that you can return the security deposit in full and not get into heated discussions about deductions. A well-planned policy will help you meet this goal.

Let the resident know what the *move-out inspection* will consist of, and also explain that a check will be issued promptly. You should always mail the security deposit refund check to the resident within fourteen days—and certainly no more than twenty-one days—after move-out. There is no excuse for taking longer. If you do take longer, you deserve the extra work and aggravation that result from following such a policy.

You should also be aware that local laws can dictate the amount of time you have to return a security deposit. Each year, politicians propose new and more stringent laws to rescue renters who experience difficulty with the return of their security deposits. Penalty amounts of two and three times the money on deposit are common. Your system should allow for a speedy return of security deposit money as well as a lenient evaluation of damages and corresponding charges.

Knowing that their apartments will be inspected on the day they move, renters are likely to take extra care that the premises are in good condition. Without such an inspection, renters may be less careful about the way they leave the apartment. You'll find that your costs will be sharply reduced if these inspections occur in the last minutes of the move-out activity.

Another good reason for move-out inspections is that they enable residents to straighten out any misunderstandings about who did what. For instance, you may claim a renter chipped a washbasin. The resident may reply that the washbasin was chipped before he or she moved in, and it has been the same ever since. If you made an inspection when the previous occupant moved out or if you inspected the apartment with the resident when he or she moved in, you'd have a record of this. If the current occupants are right, then you'll avoid the unpleasantness of arguing over damage they didn't do.

An inspection may also reveal deficiencies the resident can fix on the spot. You may find the oven is dirty and say you'll have to charge $20 for the cleanup. Rather than pay that, the resident may volunteer to clean it immediately.

When you make the inspection, be prepared to make allowances for *normal wear and tear,* such as nail and screw holes and other signs of occupancy. An apartment is a consumable commodity; it wears out like anything else. You shouldn't expect a resident to return it in the exact original condition; nor should you expect a security deposit to pay for whatever you'd normally spend to prepare the apartment for the next occupant.

Remember, the way you deal with any one person quickly becomes common knowledge throughout your property and in the community. Fairness is absolutely essential if you're to preserve good resident relations.

After the inspection is completed, make note of what has to be done, indicate the necessary deductions, and give the resident a copy of your worksheet. This will avoid disputes over what has to be done, and it also acts as a receipt to assure the resident that the remaining portion of the security deposit will be returned.

Your last step in dealing with the resident is to get all the keys to the apartment and mailbox and obtain a forwarding address so you can mail the refund check. Knowing the forwarding address is a big help if you need to contact this individual later and is very useful information for your marketing people.

You should always strive to have the resident leave in the best possible frame of mind.

8

Marketing Strategies

There is a recurring cycle in the relationship between those who manufacture a product and those who market it. In the property management business, if an apartment is not prepared well, the marketing people have a difficult and sometimes impossible job. On the other hand, if the marketing people are not effective in their presentation, there will be few new residents.

The best leasing agent in the world can't overcome a product that is substandard. No one can maintain a replacement rental pace that will match move-outs prompted by poor service and unfair policies. The marketing process must be interwoven with everything that has been discussed to this point. It cannot end when a lease is signed. Time goes by very quickly, and the renewal process is back again before you know it.

Most people work to support themselves, and as they earn more the quality of their lifestyles should improve. The secret to earning more money is acquiring a skill that is relatively rare and in high demand. In the rental apartment business, those who earn the most and who are in the most demand are the ones who have demonstrated exceptional skill in marketing units. Yes, you need to know how to develop a good set of policies, and you certainly must understand the importance of preparing a complex for occupancy; but the brass ring goes to the person who designs the program that results in the most new customers. In this section, I will explore the necessary ingredients for a marketing program.

THE BIG PICTURE

Before I start to identify the specific marketing tools you might use, it's important to step back and consider a few general issues.

Market Identification

Few other marketing people have the advantage of the apartment manager when it comes to identifying the marketplace. While this benefit is clearly available, few people make use of it. The best road to future customers can be found by understanding how you gained the customers you have.

Unfortunately, most marketing efforts begin with a full-scale effort to fill a certain number of vacancies. Even though that is the ultimate marketing goal, dwelling on the vacancy situation will only produce negative results and erode confidence levels. Marketing people using vacancies as a starting point are often the very same people who begin chasing promotional schemes that detract from the property's image. Concentrating on vacancies will produce limited results and make it difficult to stay ahead of the "ten move-in, ten move-out" cycle that plagues so many developments.

A complex with 150 units and twenty-five vacancies has an unacceptable vacancy level, and the property is most likely in financial jeopardy. Given the expense and debt loads of many apartment properties, this vacancy rate (nearly 17 percent) would be near a crisis point. The apartment manager is best advised to ignore this problem in the early stages of creating a marketing program and look to the 125 units with rent-paying customers to find the answers. There are already 125 families who like what is being offered in terms of location and product, and they feel that it represents good value. Why did these people perceive this location as more advantageous than that of the competition? When these people were prospects, what features and appointments attracted them? Were they lured by a special concession that could not be beaten by neighboring developments? Obviously something clicked, because the manager succeeded in attracting the current residents. Discovering the pattern that delivered success and repeating it should produce the needed extra residents.

In my experience, creating a sort of visual matrix is the best way to identify patterns in the relationship between your residents' home (i.e., your property) and their place of employment. You can do the same. Begin with a detailed and rather large-scale map of the township that includes your property. You may also need maps of adjoining townships to complete the assignment. Next, place a colored dot to mark the approximate location of the place of employment of each of the working adults occupying the rented units. This process is slow because it means looking up each resident's application and then pinpointing one or more job locations on the map. Experience dictates certain procedures. If a number of people work at or near the same location, place the dots close together to display the concentration, but leave enough "air" around the dots so they can be counted. If your property is located away from the downtown area and your residents commute to work, try to find an open area on the map (e.g., a forest preserve area, large park, or lake). Draw a box around this area and label it "downtown." This is done to avoid adding a number of extra maps to the display when the downtown area is far removed from the rest of the market. Place a dot in that box for each current resident who works in the general downtown area. If a few residents travel considerable distances to their workplaces, you can simply exclude them. You're interested in finding a pattern; chasing a few stray dots will only distract you when you are ready to begin interpreting the results. If many of your residents are retired, you will need another box, similar to the one created for those who work downtown. The placement of the retirement box should be as close to the subject property as possible, without conflicting with the employment dots. When the number of retired people is meaningful, you may want to select a different color dot to indicate where these people lived prior to moving to your complex. In this case, you're looking for a pattern that signals areas to target a direct mail campaign.

When you have completed the first step—placing the dots—you can sit back and evaluate. The matrix you have created is a tremendous source of information: It establishes market boundaries, illustrates drive patterns, identifies your residents' places of employment, reveals competition, shows public transportation routes, initiates conversations with prospects, helps prospects who are new to town, and reinforces the decision to move to your development.

Market Boundaries.   Those of us in the apartment rental business have an advantage over people in many other industries—we can establish the principal boundaries of our marketplace with ease and considerable accuracy. Location is a key ingredient in the decision-making process of most renters. Locations are perceived as desirable because of such things as prestige or proximity to a school or workplace. As soon as you have 50 percent occupancy, you have enough data to identify your market boundaries. Most renters work, and a travel pattern between their places of employment and your rental complex will develop. When looking for new residents, direct your marketing efforts within the boundaries established by your existing residents. This will usually deliver much better results and will conserve your energy and the expense of blanketing a market area that is simply too broad.

Drive Pattern.   When you complete your map, you will see a pattern that indicates the direction most of your existing residents travel to work and what major streets and intersections are most commonly used. It is a

Marketing Map

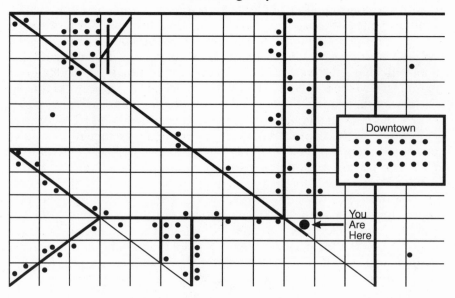

simple matter to measure the distance in both miles and minutes to drive. One of the most important ingredients in the decision to move is the proximity to one's place of employment. Preparing this marketing matrix will help the rental personnel become more conscious of this concern and equip them with the knowledge to discuss travel times, favored directions, and short cuts with prospects.

Places of Employment.   As the colored dots are placed on your marketing map, the sources of employment become apparent rather quickly (e.g., shopping centers, office complexes, factories, service outlets, eating establishments, schools, airports, etc.). Driving the area will reveal those facilities. Also, you will be able to assess the income level of the people who are employed in these work centers—you can often determine the business climate by noting signs advertising for more workers. Generally, you will add to your list of area employers who can be contacted in the continuing search for qualified residents.

Competition.   *Home to work . . . work to home.* This is the driving pattern of most people five or six days a week. People want the nicest place they can comfortably afford within a reasonable travel distance of their place of employment. Assuming that the workplace is established first, how many apartment complexes in the community offer the same basic level of quality with equally acceptable drive patterns and time requirements? If you determine that the majority of your existing residents travel north or south from your development and that a twenty minute drive time appears to be the norm, you can readily identify your competition because their residents will follow a similar driving pattern.

Public Transportation.   In many households, one or more people do not have access to an automobile and rely on public transportation to get to work, school, or shopping. The marketing matrix will point out the major routes used for such travel. It is then up to the apartment manager to learn about the bus routes, train schedules, and fare levels. Unfortunately, many apartment employees either live on-site or depend on automobiles for their sole means of transportation. Hence, they never have the need to learn about public transportation routes—and may not take the time to do so. The marketing map will demonstrate the important public transportation routes that should be investigated by staff members.

Conversations with Prospects.   The marketing map should enjoy a prominent location on one of the walls in the rental center. It is packed with valuable information for the renting process. For example, it is one of the best ways to initiate a conversation with a prospective renter. Remember that *home to work . . . work to home* pattern I discussed. You can pinpoint the property's location and ask the prospect to help you find his or her place of employment on the map. That is a lot better than filling out a guest card. By the time you have finished preparing the marketing matrix, you will be familiar with many of the major employers in the area and the favored routes from your complex to their places of business. You can give estimates of drive times or mention the short cuts that people use to avoid areas of heavy congestion. You may very well learn that the prospect's principal reason for moving is to be closer to his or her workplace. This will be helpful when you summarize your benefits at decision time. The matrix provides you with a highly visible tool that depicts a significant aspect of a leasing agent's daily life: *awareness of the importance of the proximity of home to work.*

People Moving to Town.   About 20 percent of rental prospects are new to town. The marketing map is even more important to new people than it is to those who have lived in the area for some time. The out-of-towner can easily make a mistake in choosing his or her place of residence. As a rental consultant, you can be very helpful in explaining the driving distances and patterns that will work the best. Again, your map is a focal point and helps the customer who is new to town to understand the relative distances between work and home.

The Final Decision.   Even if you have twenty-five vacancies in a 150-unit apartment complex, you will most likely have more than two hundred dots on your completed marketing map. This happens because many households have more than one person who works. The impact of hundreds of dots on the map announces that you have lots of residents. Many people choose a restaurant on this same premise—the restaurant crowded with customers is more likely to be good. The array of dots on your map has the same reassuring effect. Say, for example, that the prospect works at or near the airport, and your map shows that many of your residents also work in that area. This tells the prospect that others who have to make the same basic trip each work day have found this apartment community to fit their needs. It also appears possible that car pools or an occasional ride can be arranged. It is especially helpful in the rental process when the prospect learns that a number of current residents also work at the same place. This reinforcement may be all you need to close the deal.

Competition

Many managers view a competing rental property as a kind of enemy. Because of this, they avoid all but the most essential contact with competitors. This is unwise. Yes, it is true that if the property next door didn't exist, the job of capturing new residents would be easier; but the competition does exist and is likely to continue to exist—even if you could succeed in attracting all prospects. If this were to happen, the existing operator of the competing property would probably lose the investment; but the lender or a new owner would surely arrive on the scene armed with an aggressive marketing campaign (and probably take some of your residents). Apartments are different from other types of businesses. If a shoe store or a grocery store is forced to close because it cannot compete, a different type of business that may have a better chance will probably replace it. An apartment building, however, almost always remains just that. Once competition arrives, it's usually there to stay. So, it's important to learn to coexist.

Most managers have very little first-hand knowledge about their competitors. Typically, the manager will be required to perform a periodic market study, so he or she will call a few neighboring developments to gather information about rent levels and vacancies. Other than that contact, the only information about the competition is derived from ads and through conversations with prospective renters who have visited other properties.

Your job as a marketer depends on timely and accurate information about your competition. It is critical that you take time each week to update your information about the community in which your property is located. This certainly includes first-hand knowledge of your competition. Don't ever trust this job to others; it must be performed by the person who will be doing the future market plan.

It's best to reserve *some* time every week—whether it's an hour or an afternoon—for visiting competing properties. Adhere to this practice with absolute regularity; managers who restrict themselves to their own complexes because of a never-ending workload are usually the individuals with the poorest marketing results. These people are also the best candidates for burnout. Visiting other properties and discussing common problems with your fellow managers will do more than a year's worth of seminars to help you come up with new ideas and approaches. Property management is a small business, and most managers share a camaraderie that is rarely found in other industries. Take advantage of it.

Choose one of your slow days for visiting (chances are it will also be slow for your competitors). Bring each competitor a copy of your complete brochure with all of the inserts and price information, and ask for a copy of their materials in return. Don't make the visit an interrogation: It should be two rental professionals sharing their experiences. Learn what units are renting best, the hours of operation, the best days of the week, and how recreational facilities are scheduled. You shouldn't write anything down; this often worries the other manager, who might think that an evaluation is taking place.

A visit might take as much as an hour; in one afternoon you could meet and talk with up to four managers. Don't restrict yourself to complexes running big ads or buildings that are open every day. In virtually every market (even those suffering high vacancy rates), there are properties that are fully rented and do very little in the way of marketing. While it may prove more difficult to meet the managers or owners of these properties, it is essential that you do. After all, they are doing something right and you need to learn what that is. Another warning: Don't be influenced by the negative attitudes of some managers (often a problem in a difficult market). Ideally, by witnessing a negative attitude and recognizing that it would assure failure, you can avoid developing the same problem.

Your visits will accomplish at least three things. First, you will learn exactly what you face in terms of competition, and this will be invaluable in preparing your market strategy. Second, witnessing the outcome of other people's ideas and solutions will help you prepare and present a superior product. Finally, you will build a file of competitor brochures that will come in handy later in your rental activity.

Have you ever seen a school or scout program in which everyone was given the same materials and guidelines, but it was up to the individual to develop the best plan? Managers of apartment complexes have very much the same challenge. Most start with dull architecture and rooms like sterile white boxes. To these ingredients, the manager adds his or her skills in creating a property personality and the loyal staff to make a difference. Your visits to competitors will uncover many different potential solutions. You will view something that resembles the results of the school project previously discusssed: There will be far more routine solutions than imaginative ones. After you have seen many developments, you will be in an excellent position to judge the differences and to create changes that will set your complex apart.

The benefits of visiting the competition coincide with a great many of the benefits of belonging to a professional association for property managers. The savvy professional always seeks opportunities to meet with others in the industry and share ideas because he or she knows that the best ideas are never created in a vacuum.

I'll explain how a property manager's relationship with the managers of competing developments will play a major role in new rental referrals later in this chapter.

Learn from the Pros

Before you get down to the specifics of a marketing program, you should put yourself through one more learning process. In the property management business, losses are suffered at times and it's possible to learn from these losses. As first-time buyers, many renters select a home, coach house, or townhouse in a new development rather than a used home offered through a local listing service. When one of your residents gives notice after purchasing a new home, ask him or her about it. Learn the name of the development, the size of the home, the resident's reasons for choosing it over others, and any other pertinent facts such as the cost and the source of financing. You should be naturally curious about what appealed to your departing resident, and he or she will likely be delighted to discuss this new venture with you.

Your next step is to call that development and inquire about the homes they have for sale. Pay particular attention to the technique that the salesperson uses to get you to commit to an appointment. Make an appointment and go visit the development with another person so that the two of you appear as a couple. You might even spend some time preparing so that you look and act like potential buyers. This will enable you to view the complete sales technique. When you arrive for your appointment, pay particular attention to every detail. You are about to receive an important lesson in selling. People who sell homes for a living are almost always commission brokers. These people must sell or they will soon be out of the business (unlike leasing people who may be paid a salary). Pay attention to the way the salesperson qualifies you according to your needs and the degree of urgency involved with your potential purchase. How are you registered? What did the sales center look like? Were you given a brochure, and when? What did their models look like? Did the salesperson try to match purchase benefits with your needs? Was there an effort made to close the sale? When you said no, did the salesperson try another sales approach?

The selling process, whether for a home or a rental apartment, does not change. The answers to the questions posed above will help you understand how to be a more effective marketer. One of the most common questions asked by people trying to improve their marketing skills is: "What do I say, and when, to receive the best results?" The answers and techniques are available in a living workshop; just pretend to be a buyer and study the information you collect. You will need to do this at least six to eight times to gain enough experience to differentiate between good and bad techniques. At that point, all presentations, both good and bad, will contain a valuable lesson for you.

MARKETING TOOLS

Now I'm ready to address some of the elements you can draw upon to promote your property and develop a solid merchandising program.

Selection of a Theme

If an apartment complex is new or undergoing a major change, take this opportunity to *establish a theme to be carried through the entire presentation.* If the apartment development is well-established, the theme may be difficult to change, but don't regard an established theme as irrevocable. If it is out of character with the development, it may need changing.

What is a theme? It is a *name and symbol* that represent the development and help to attract the public. Many times a theme is suggested by the architecture or surroundings of the property. Perhaps the architecture is Spanish or Western and suggests a relaxed way of life. A traditional style suggests a more refined lifestyle. There are also nondescript architectural styles that lend themselves to almost any theme.

The presence of lakes, streams, groves of trees, or surrounding farmland provides thematic material. The kinds of amenities on the grounds may suggest ideas, too. If there are swimming pools, tennis courts, playgrounds, sailing, fishing, ice-skating—all of these activities point to possible themes.

In considering a theme, it might be helpful to consult with the owner and architect who perhaps had a theme in mind when the place was built. Also, you should certainly consider the market you are trying to reach. It would be inappropriate to create a relaxed and informal theme for a luxury high-rise apartment in the most exclusive part of town.

Names and Symbols

Themes are evident in the names of developments and in the symbols chosen to represent them. Most garden-apartment complexes are identified by distinctive names (e.g., Knollwood, Glenfield, Versailles) whereas in-city apartments are commonly identified by street numbers (e.g., One City Center, 1000 Lake Shore Drive).

It's very important that the name and symbol be presented in a unified manner. Too often a name will be used one way in a newspaper advertisement, another way on a building sign, and still a third way on a brochure. All of this is self-defeating because you're not building a consistent image in the minds of the prospects.

Consistency is a key element in marketing and particularly in using a theme. It conveys a sense of order that is very reassuring to prospects. When they see a clear and uniform theme, prospects gain respect for your operation. Consistency is important for another reason: It helps to reinforce your development's name in the customer's mind.

If prospects see many variations of a development's name, (through changes of color, style, placement, etc.), they may not recognize it as the same development. The name is the same but the impression is different. If the name and symbol are always the same, the repeated impressions will leave their imprint.

It's important to *develop a unified name and symbol very early* so you will be able to use them consistently throughout your presentation. To do this most effectively, work with a competent graphic designer, either an independent studio or someone on the staff of an advertising agency. Select a qualified designer because you'll have to live with the results for years.

The significance of a professional design cannot be overstated. Corporations spend millions of dollars to develop trademarks and logos to help identify their products and promote them in the marketplace. Fortunately with apartments, the task is smaller; costs are much less, and these costs are incurred only once.

In developing a graphic treatment of the name and symbol, keep things simple. The name will be used in a variety of applications: signs, letterheads, brochures, etc. The simpler the design, the more useful it will be.

Unified Graphics System

A professionally designed treatment of the development's name and symbol is just the first step. Also needed is a *unified graphics system* that spells out the ways the name and symbol are to be used and how you should handle everything else that relates to your property and appears in print. Ask the graphic designer to prepare a graphics manual that shows exactly what is permitted and what is not. The following are items that should be included in this manual.

   • *Name and symbol.* Type size and style (typeface), exact ink color.
   • *Stationery.* Exact placement of development name, symbol, address,

Directional Billboards
These signs are intended to direct, not to sell. The sign illustrated at the top is an example of an off-site directional billboard that might be used on a limited-access highway. The directions are clear but brief. Arrows or additional instructions are not always necessary if the way to proceed is clear.

and telephone and Fax numbers; specific color of paper and ink; type of paper. (This includes letterheads, envelopes, statements, labels, and so on.)

- *Business cards.* Placement of the development name and symbol, address, telephone number, and person's name and title (if any).
- *Signage.* Type size and style, placement of development name and symbol, background and other colors.
- *Brochures.* Type size and style, placement of development name and symbol, ink and paper colors.
- *Advertisements.* Format of ads, type sizes and styles to be used, placement of development name and symbol, margins, use of abbreviations and other constant elements.
- *Vehicles.* Color, placement of development name and symbol. (This would pertain to company cars and trucks.)

These are just starting points. The graphic designer should examine everything that will bear the name or symbol of the development and include these in the graphics manual. Then make sure that everyone in the

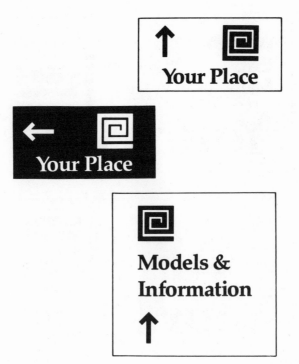

Directional Signs
The two signs at the top are examples of reassurance signs, sometimes called trailblazers. They are usually small, inexpensive, and placed on poles along the route. Note the use of reverse colors. This attracts more attention and is easier to read. The model and information sign at the bottom is an on-site, lead-in sign used to direct prospects. These signs should be used sparingly but enough to avoid confusion.

organization who has anything to do with ordering signs, ads, printed materials, or similar items has a copy of the manual and follows it. It also is a good idea to give copies to your sign painter, printer, newspaper account executive, and advertising agency and insist that they, too, follow the instructions.

Signage

Once a theme and name have been selected, a symbol designed, and a graphics manual prepared, you're ready to tackle the all-important challenge of signage. As a general observation, signs are often badly designed and grossly overdone. The average American is exposed to thousands of signs every day; most are totally ignored. When designing signage, you should be mindful of any sign ordinances that may affect the type of sign you are allowed to post or the manner of its display. If signs are going to have any effect at all, they must always be consistent with your graphics system and they must meet these minimum standards.

1. Signs must always look fresh and clean—as if they had been put up that day. Otherwise, they will present a poor image of your development, and people will ignore them.
2. Signs must be at right angles to traffic, not parallel. Otherwise, they will be hard to notice and read. People should be able to read the sign's message through the windshield of a car traveling at the posted speed limit at least 150 feet from the sign.
3. Signs should have no more than eight words. If there are too many words, people riding by in autos won't be able to read and interpret the message.

Signs serve four basic purposes: promotion, direction, identification, and information.

Promotional Signs.   Signs in this category are primarily off-site billboards (discussed later in this chapter).

Directional Signs.   These signs direct prospects to the complex and, once inside the complex, to the rental information center. The number of directional signs needed and where they should be placed depends on how difficult it is to find the property. Generally, if the project is on a well-traveled road in the midst of competing developments, a good entry sign is sufficient. If the property is in a remote location, directional signs can be helpful. Remember: The sign is meant only to give directions—not to sell.

Another form of directional signage is a *reassurance sign,* sometimes called a *trailblazer.* It reassures prospects that they have indeed made the proper turn and are on the right track. If you've ever been to a company picnic in a rural location, you've probably seen homemade signs on telephone poles to help lead the way. These were reassurance signs. Reassurance signs should not be homemade, but they should be inexpensive because their life span is usually quite short.

As prospects turn into the driveway, they should see a sign directing them to the rental information center. As they proceed along this drive, there should be similar signs at turns or intersections so drivers know exactly how to proceed. Once prospects reach the parking lot, one or more signs should direct them to visitor parking spaces. Signs in the parking area should guide the visitor to the rental information center. If necessary, directional signage should continue into the building so prospects know exactly where to go. All of these signs should conform to the specifications in the graphics manual to reinforce the image you are trying to convey.

Identification Signs.   This category includes the most useful signs. The most important sign of this type is called the *permanent identification* or *keystone entry sign.* This is a permanent sign that establishes the character of the development and is both substantial in construction and architectural in design. It usually displays little more than the development's name.

When designed correctly, a permanent identification sign is usually expensive. It should be lighted and made part of a landscaped setting designed for change of seasons or year-round plantings. In the case of a high-rise structure, an engraved plaque that coordinates with the building can be very attractive; printing the apartment name on an awning is another way to identify the high-rise apartment complex. The majority of renters will come as a result of just driving by the development. This sign will be one of their first contacts with your property. If given $5,000 to spend on both an entry sign and a brochure, a property manager would be better off spending $4,900 on the sign and only $100 on the brochure. The sign will draw more traffic and make a greater impact than most of your other promotional activities.

Other identification signs include building address signs and those that identify recreational and supporting amenities, such as swimming pools and laundry rooms. Signs identifying the rental information center, visitor parking, and recreation center are also in this category. These signs, as well as all other forms of signage, should be used sparingly to avoid cluttering the landscape.

A telephone number is also an important element on rental signs because people frequently drive through neighborhoods when they're selecting a location. Once a prospect establishes a preferred area, he or she begins to note the best-looking rental communities. It is becoming more and more common for prospects to make rental inquiries using telephones that are installed in their cars.

Informational Signs.   These signs have the least value and generally should be avoided. The most common of these are called *command signs*. They include notices put up by property managers who like to give commands. Command signs say: "Keep off the grass," "Close the door," "Put garbage in dumpster," "Don't post messages on mailbox," or "No boots in hallway."

Usually the manager posts such a sign to deal with an immediate problem and then forgets about it. Often the signs are crudely made and sometimes they can be confusing. One manager posted a "No hot water" sign when the plumbing in the laundry room was being repaired and forgot to take the sign down later. Imagine the bewilderment of residents trying to do laundry a few days later after the plumbing was back in order! Residents quickly learn to ignore such signs if they read them in the first place.

Managers should stay away from these "don't" signs. Instead of posting a "Close the door" sign, get a door closer. Rather than using a sign telling residents not to put their boots in the hallway, state this rule in a letter sent to residents at the start of the snow season. If there are signs telling people to put their garbage in the dumpster or not to post notices

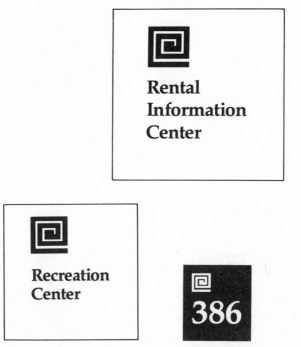

Identification Signs

These signs are used to identify important buildings and locations as well as individual apartment buildings. They can be installed either as plaques affixed to buildings or as free-standing signs on standards. The design and the use of logo, color, and type style should be consistent with the development's graphic plan.

on the mailboxes, remove them immediately. They only create a negative image for the property.

Some informational signs are necessary and required by law (e.g., swimming pool rule signs). Comply with the law, but do not add any unnecessary signs or posters.

Finally, there is another type of informational sign that finds its way into apartment complexes. Contractors, suppliers, and others like to post signs on developments to advertise themselves. Furniture rental companies and apartment locator services are other examples. Calendars, scratch pads, and ashtrays carrying other firms' advertising have no place in the office or rental areas. Don't allow them, and remove them if they appear. Establish a policy forbidding the placement of other firms' advertising on your property, and stick to it.

Rental Information Center

Some rental offices look cold, harsh, and commercial. The furnishings are severe and may include a metal desk and some uninviting side chairs. The

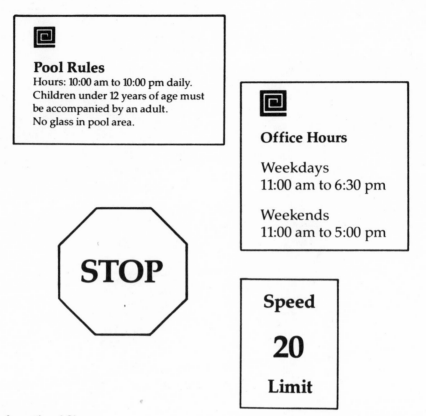

Informational Signs
Shown here are examples of informational signs. Such signs should be used sparingly; use them when they are extremely important or required by law. Too often, informational signs are command signs that are hand-lettered on-site. They frequently are graphically inconsistent, rarely obeyed, and irritating to residents.

desk is covered with calendars, appointment books, application forms, and five-day notices. Everything shouts: "This is the place where the landlord conducts business!"

Prospects do not necessarily come to rent; they come for information. The appearance of most rental offices makes many prospects feel uncomfortable. They are on guard and antagonistic in an office situation that makes them think they're applying for a loan.

Furnishings for your rental information center should be residential in scale. Choose comfortable chairs and round tables. Create a warm, inviting atmosphere that says "Welcome!" Use bright colors to liven up the surroundings. Serve coffee in the winter, iced tea or lemonade in the summer, plus cookies. This will help put prospects at ease.

Round tables are especially important. When you and the prospect sit down to discuss the apartment and lease application, having a desk between you creates a head-to-head selling situation. You want to be on the prospect's side, and a round table accomplishes this automatically.

Providing a place for children to play is a definite asset and well worth the expense. Parents can ask questions without interruption, and the manager does not have to worry about bothersome noise or possible breakage.

Exhibits in the rental information center are important. They are needed to give information about the development and provide a diversion for waiting visitors while you're involved with other prospects. No one wants to stand around gaping at plain walls; people welcome the opportunity to look at something informative. Exhibits serve another function; they give prospects a somewhat private area in which to discuss the lease terms.

For exhibits, you can use scale models of the development, a site plan, photos of the building, enlargements of floor plans, photos or sketches of amenities, lists of features, and an area facilities map. One of the best exhibits is a large aerial photograph of the development showing its relation to the rest of the community. People enjoy looking at where they are on the photo and identifying familiar sites.

Some apartment developments go so far as to have brochures of competing developments on display. This enables the rental agent to compare the development with others and to respond to prospects who say they want to see what the competition has to offer before making a decision.

If model apartments are in the same building as the rental information center, you may want to extend the graphics or exhibits into the connecting corridor so prospects continue to receive a favorable impression as they walk to the model apartments.

Model Apartments

A well-furnished model apartment is an essential part of the marketing program for developments in their initial rent-up periods, for larger complexes that must deal with a steady flow of apartment turnover, or for those suffering from an undue number of vacancies. An attractive model expresses a lifestyle that cannot be verbalized, only experienced. Observe the following points when you're setting up your models.

- *One Model or Two?* First you must decide how many models to prepare. The budget will probably dictate the answer to this question. Two models allow you to demonstrate two completely different decorating solutions. Taking prospects from one to the other, you can demonstrate the adaptability of the apartment design. Also, furnishing two models allows you to show two different lifestyles: one that appeals to the younger renter and another that caters to a more mature person. Having more than one model makes for a longer tour which in turn gives your rental staff more time with the customer.

When the models are decorated in completely different color and decorating schemes, it allows the leasing agent to ask for an opinion, which can be very helpful when it's time to help the prospect arrive at a decision.

If you have a full range of unit sizes and they all enjoy about the same market appeal, model the smaller units. Efficiency apartments, in particular, tend to look small when they're empty. Also, a creative furniture layout and decorating solution can change a one-room apartment into a cozy, functional home. If you have efficiency apartments and choose to prepare a decorated model, you must certainly do a one- or two-bedroom unit as well. A furnished and decorated efficiency apartment will help in the marketing of that type of unit but will be of little value to a prospect who is interested in something else. In fact, if you take a prospect to an efficiency unit after the desire for a one-bedroom apartment has been expressed, he or she will probably become irritated, believing that time is being wasted.

Whether you model a one- or two-bedroom unit, decorate only one bedroom as a bedroom. Bedroom decorating is usually boring (so there is little to be gained by showing more than one bedroom setting). Apartments with two bedrooms and one bath are sometimes more difficult to rent. Showing a unit with the second bedroom furnished as a den, hobby room, get-away-room, etc., will do much more to attract renters than decorating another bedroom. If people need the room for a bedroom, they can certainly visualize how it will appear. They probably already have the bedroom furnishings and most bedroom layouts allow for little variation. Because of this, there is no reason to furnish three- or four-bedroom units. Doing so simply increases the overall costs.

- *For a model apartment, select one of the least-desirable units, not one of the best.* This may sound odd, but it isn't. Prospects are quick to detect the advantages of an apartment with an exceptional layout and location. Decorated model apartments will help equalize the worst apartment layouts. The poorer layout will gain desirability when creatively decorated. The better layout can stand on its own without the help of sample furnishings. Owners and developers often model only the best layouts. This leads to an unbalanced rent-up; the better layouts rent quickly and the less-desirable units move slowly and don't realize their rent potential.
- *Stay close to the office.* Surveys have shown repeatedly that model apartments are often left out of the rental presentation, usually because the decorator model was too far away and the prospect had a tight schedule. In all likelihood, the rental agent was trying to shorten the showing time by eliminating the trip to one or more models. When the model is not shown, you negate the expense of having cre-

ated it and lose all the benefits a model offers to the marketing process.

• *Choose first floor units.* In walk-up properties, it is important to have your models on the first or ground floors because they offer easy access. Some apartment managers might be afraid that first-floor apartments present too great a risk of break-in or burglary. This is a terrible endorsement even if the prospect never learns of that fear. The fact that the manager's thinking runs in that direction is an indication of the lifestyle being offered. If the model furnishings are not safe on the first floor, how safe are the possessions of the residents?

Having the models on the lower floors is also important for customer convenience and accessibility. Some prospects have difficulty negotiating stairs and in those cases, upstairs models will not play a role in the marketing process.

• *Make the decorating and furnishings of the model truly outstanding, not mediocre, regardless of your market.* The more dramatic the approach, the better. While the model may be beyond the average prospect's means, it should not be beyond his or her dreams.

A *model apartment is intended to be looked at—it is not for living.* Common furnishings, such as a triple dresser in a bedroom or a TV set in the living room, take up space and do little to enhance the atmosphere of a model. Even a shower curtain that is fanned across the bathtub does much more damage than one might imagine. Most apartment bathrooms are tiny, maybe five by seven feet, and hanging a shower curtain visually reduces the room size. Place stacks of colorful towels in the tub instead. They aren't going to get wet because no one is going to be showering here.

In the past, property managers and developers would hire furniture stores to decorate model apartments. Managers got the job done for little or nothing in return for promoting the store name in the models and in advertising. As a result, most models looked homey and comfortable, but they made little impact on prospects. Too often, this arrangement reflected the inventory of the store rather than the goals of the rental program.

The use of rented furniture yields the same results. The style and quality are often mediocre and add absolutely nothing to the appeal of the apartment.

I recommend *hiring a competent interior designer*—give this professional free rein to decorate the apartment and make the most of its advantages. The results may be startling; no doubt they will be memorable as well. People will come to see the model apartments and talk about them—and this builds traffic. Prospects may not want to live in such a daringly decorated apartment, but people will remember it. High-income prospects will expect to see something innovative in decorating, and moderate-income prospects will be flattered by this approach. Either way, you'll impress your prospects and give them something to remember.

If you have used unusual decor, don't worry about recovering the cost of the furnishings. When the time comes to close the model, chances are that you can recover 60 percent or more of their original cost. With mediocre furnishings, you will be lucky to recover 30 percent. The difference is that people are willing to pay more for decorator merchandise, whereas they know they can get conventional furnishings anywhere.

- *Do a complete decorating job.* Decorate right down to the accessories. This includes flowers and place settings on the tables, books on the shelves, guest towels in the bathroom, and interesting utensils in the kitchen.

  Don't go too far, however. Some managers think it's a good idea to put food in the refrigerator, towels in the closet, even a half-eaten cookie on a plate to convey the sense that someone lives in the apartment. This is not wise. Prospects will think they are intruders in someone's private home. If they open a closet and find towels inside, they'll often shut the door quickly. Furnish the apartment like a model, not like a home. This means no magazines or clutter. Remember, a weekly magazine is only one week away from being out-of-date. People want new and up-to-date ideas, and they will be less inclined to garner them from models that seem to be old. Also, keep in mind that clutter is one of the reasons people move. House and garage sales are evidence of this. The opportunity to reorganize possessions and discard things that are no longer needed is one of the few advantages to moving. Keep this in mind; your models should look clean and uncluttered.

- *If someone wants it, rent it.* Imagine that you work in a clothing store and a gentlemen walks in and wants to buy the outfit on the mannequin. Would you sell it to him? Chances are excellent that you would. In fact, why not? The mannequin is a selling tool and its purpose is to show off the clothes to their best advantage. In the example it did just that. Obviously, if the same items were hanging on the rack, they would be sold before dismantling the display; but if the mannequin displayed the only such merchandise in the store, it would be sold. Mannequins have the advantage of displaying an entire ensemble (which is what a model apartment often presents).

  The same rule applies to renting a model apartment, and renting offers advantages that compensate for the extra work involved in creating a new model. First of all, you should be able to rent the model with its special decorating for a premium rental rate. Whenever you can improve an apartment so that you can charge a greater rent for it, that is known as *value added*. It's one of the most important things you can do in the operation of rental properties. Remove the furnishings and use them in your next model with some new twists or modifications—now you have the opportunity to create an even better, more-creative model. New and exciting models renew the enthusiasm of the entire staff—especially the leasing agents. After showing the same model for months (and maybe even years), agents are certainly bored and often embarrassed about its age and condition. Thus begins the tendency to skip the model tour.

- *Once a model is set up, keep it in first-class condition.* Have the maintenance crew vacuum the carpets every day and make sure that ashtrays are clean, bathroom fixtures are sparkling, and everything else is in good order. Expect to discover the loss of some accessories, and replace them quickly when that occurs. Don't let the model apartment take on a run-down appearance.

- *Use model apartments only so long as they are useful in the leasing program.* When occupancy reaches 90 to 92 percent, you will be in a good position to sell the model furnishings. The remaining apartments can be rented by showing vacant units. At that point, the models probably will show wear and tear as well as age. Despite their innovative good looks when new, styles will change and your models will begin to look dowdy. So, it's a good time to close the model.

Some model apartments are shown long past the time when they should have been put back into the income stream. Managers may insist that models are necessary when, in fact, they are maintained as a crutch because the manager is slow to put the vacant apartments in proper market-ready condition.

In some cases, models are maintained beyond their useful lives because they are used as guest apartments for the convenience of important guests or visiting owners or even supervising managers. This is not recommended. Prospects inspecting these apartments will see partially used bars of soap and rolls of toilet paper, as well as soiled glassware and utensils. It doesn't take long to deduce that someone lives in the apartment. At this point, prospects feel they are invading someone's privacy and become anxious to leave. Also, as mentioned earlier, avoid an office and model combination. Each has its own function, and the two do not mix.

In my opinion, there are two situations in which it may be necessary to maintain model apartments permanently. The first situation is occasioned by a structural feature. If the normal ceiling height in your apartments is nine feet rather than the more standard eight feet, the extra height can make empty units appear smaller than actual size. People think that higher ceilings *always* make rooms look more spacious, but I disagree with this in the case of empty rooms. Empty rooms with higher ceilings appear smaller because people have become accustomed to eight-foot ceilings. When a room is vacant, prospects will tend to refer to a room's height to gauge its length and width. A furnished model apartment demonstrates that standard furniture, and particularly queen- or king-size beds will fit nicely. When prospects see a furnished room with higher ceilings, they use the furniture as a gauge. Suddenly the ceiling height works to your advantage and the room appears larger.

The other permanent model situation is in a high-turnover project. Such a project should always have a model unit for showing to prospects. It is especially important that these models are always on the leading edge in order to achieve the maximum impact on rental prospects.

If you are managing a development in which new buildings are being opened in successive years, relocate the models to the newest building. You may reuse some of the old furniture by having it cleaned or recovered, but you'll want to emphasize the newness of the new buildings by having up-to-date models. Doing this creates one unavoidable risk: Renters living in buildings that were opened earlier will be attracted to the new models and may want to transfer to the new building. The risk is worth taking in view of the drawing power these new models will have to entice new prospects to the most recently opened buildings.

Brochures and Collateral Material

Contrary to what many people think, a brochure has little value in renting apartments. Admittedly, this is not true for condominiums or new houses. In these cases, a brochure is an important selling tool because the decision to buy is rarely made on the first visit.

In the case of renting apartments, however, about 65 percent of all rentals are made on first visits. For these people, a brochure is a post-selling tool. It helps reassure people that they've made the right decision, and it covers any questions that may not have been answered.

The remaining 35 percent of rentals are to people who require a bit of extra convincing, and the brochure is intended for these people. They visit five or six developments in a day's time, are confused by what they see, can't remember one project from the next, and use the brochures they have collected to help them sort out what they have seen.

The brochure should be *simple, direct, clear, and inexpensive.* A very slick and superlative-packed brochure can do more harm than good. Prospects don't want to be sold; they want to be informed. Give them the facts with a straightforward narrative message that is specific to your property. Don't try to win them over with gimmicky copy. For example, here's the kind of brochure copy to be <u>avoided</u>:

> Four hundred acres of natural beauty. The cool tranquility of a mile-long lake and winding streams. Oak trees, pine trees, and willows. Brooks, glens, and glades. Wildlife. Flowers. Heavenly Manor offers apartments in the midst of one of the most beautiful settings in our area.

That's a lot of descriptive copy, especially considering that it describes nothing about the complex. Such copy says little and is a turnoff to the reader. Instead, use copy like this:

> We're at Lake Drive and Lynn Lane, with easy access to shopping, business, churches, and schools. Lake Louise, just five minutes away, offers sailing, fishing, golf, a park, and picnic areas. The airport and downtown are twenty minutes away. Choose from four large floor plans—one-, two-, and three-bedroom units, each with a den. Each has lots of closet space. Washer and dryer in every unit, hi-tech kitchens, and individual climate controls.

When it comes to illustrating the brochure, use actual photographs wherever possible; stay away from renderings of buildings. People are often suspicious of artwork.

One word of caution: *Don't illustrate anything in the brochure or write about anything that won't be in your development.* The brochure will likely end up in a prospect's drawer only to be interpreted later as an implied warranty. For example, if you picture a woman with a tennis racquet and you don't actually have a tennis court, the prospect may use this to claim that you promised tennis courts. The same is true for any other feature or service that is mentioned, or implied, but not actually provided.

Finally, be sure the brochure includes *the name of your development; complete street address, city, state, and zip code; and telephone number with area code.* This is particularly important for prospects who visit a number of developments in different suburbs or cities. Without this information, prospects may not remember who or where you are.

The same identifying information should be on *floor plans* and the *site plan* if these are inserts to the brochure. Floor plans should be as large as possible; larger than six by eight inches is recommended. People have problems interpreting small floor plans, so make them big. The larger the floor plan, the larger the apartment appears in the prospect's mind. Also, remember to include dimensions on the floor plans for all major rooms.

Site plans are good for a multibuilding development. A site plan identifies all the amenities and helps orient the prospect to a particular building and its location relative to other buildings.

Besides the brochure, floor plans, and site plan, other items that come under the general heading of collateral sales material include:

- *Letters* or cards sent to prospects after they leave to thank them for their visit. These should be signed by the rental agent who helped them.
- *Postcards* with a picture of the development. These can be picked up by prospects in the rental information center, or they can be used by new residents to notify friends of their new address.
- *Hard candy* wrapped in paper imprinted with the building or project name and logo.

You'll discover other collateral promotional items, too. Just make sure they tie in with the development's theme and conform to the unified graphics system.

The Two Types of Advertising

In chapter 4, it was noted that 54 percent of the people who rent apartments do so because they liked what they saw when they drove by. This leaves 46 percent whose visits to the property were prompted by other reasons. As a matter of fact, experience shows that only 20 percent of those prospects who become residents are attracted by paid advertising, and then it's usually the classified ads in the newspaper. So, while advertising has a role to play, its value in renting apartments has been greatly overrated. Keep this point in mind when you attempt to step up a lagging rental program by increasing the advertising.

Another guideline will help direct your advertising strategies: In a stabilized program (i.e., an established development), only 0.75 percent of the gross income constitutes the size of a typical advertising budget. Such budgeting guidelines are not meant as absolutes, however. Weak or "soft" markets will always call for greater advertising expenses, while just the opposite is true in strong markets.

Many types of advertising can be used for your property: daily newspapers, radio, television, billboards, direct mail, and the telephone directory. The merits of these will be discussed one by one. But first, consider the two major types of advertising.

Institutional Advertising.   Its purpose is to establish an image, theme, status appeal, lifestyle, character, and reputation for a development. It does not focus on specific apartments for rent or call for an immediate response. Rather, it seeks to remind the public about the development.

Institutional advertising is appropriate for a large project that will take several years to complete, such as a high-rise tower, planned-unit development (PUD), or a garden complex opening in phases. This kind of advertising helps to establish the name of the project and keeps it before the public. In some cases, it may compel a person who is in the market for a new apartment to come out and see the property. The purpose of institutional advertising, however, is not to prompt an immediate response but rather to establish a long-term image.

Promotional Advertising.   The objective here is to produce immediate interest in a specific product or service. Promotional advertising focuses on one or two items, is run in media conveying a sense of immediacy (such as the newspaper), and calls for prompt action.

It is easier to understand the difference between institutional advertising and promotional advertising with examples.

Institutional advertising says: "Come live in Happy Acres, where we have one-, two-, and three-bedroom apartments renting from $500 to $850 per month."

Promotional advertising says: "For rent—two-bedroom apartment, utilities included, washer-dryer in apartment, recreational facilities, $780 per month. Happy Acres, 415 Lynn Road, Westbury, CT., (555) 555-5555."

The institutional ad covers generalities, the promotional ad addresses specifics. You'll discover that promotional advertising will usually be more effective than institutional advertising in renting apartments.

This refers strictly to the advertising of rental properties, not condominiums or other for-sale properties. These require an entirely different kind of advertising philosophy and approach.

Newspaper Advertising

Some property managers believe that a continuing program of newspaper advertising, especially on weekends, is absolutely essential in order to rent apartments. They believe that if they run an ad on Saturday or Sunday, prospects will rush in to rent apartments.

This isn't so. To find out for yourself, conduct this test. Discontinue all newspaper advertising for one or two weekends and take note of the difference in traffic count. You probably will see no change in rental traffic.

There are several reasons for this. First, most rental prospects are drive-bys; they come in whether you advertise or not. Many are drawn by the advertisements of your competitors; while they're in the neighborhood, they stop in to visit your development. This works in reverse when you advertise: Your ads will draw traffic that will visit the competition. The

Your Place

1- & 2-Bedroom Apts.

Very large and bright apartments. Natural, wooded setting. Fifteen minutes to Downtown via Expressway. Close to schools and shopping.
• Central Air Conditioning
• Self-clean Oven
• Two-door, No-frost Refrig.
• Dishwasher
• Private Patios or Balconies
• Swimming Pool
• Lighted Tennis Courts

From $500

Open daily 11 A.M. to 6 P.M.

Directions: Take I 101 to the Main Street exit and go west 1½ blocks.
200 Place Drive
555-5555

Your Place

1- and 2-bedroom apartments available for immediate occupancy. Self-cleaning oven. No-frost refrigerator. Central air conditioning. Tennis courts. Swimming pool. From $500.

Open Daily 11 A.M. to 6 P.M.

Take I 101 to the Main St. exit   go west 1½ blocks. 200 Place Drive.
555-5555.

Classified Ads

Classified ads are the most common and typically most useful form of promotional advertising for rental apartments. Every ad, regardless of size, must answer the three basic questions prospective residents ask: What do I get? How much does it cost? and, Where do I find it? A series of different ads of varying sizes is recommended to attract maximum readership.

best-looking property will come out ahead in this traffic trading. Finally, many prospects are already aware of your property and will not be influenced one way or the other by advertising or a lack of it.

This doesn't mean that you can skip advertising altogether. Before you can check the consequences of discontinuing ads, you have to start a newspaper advertising program to get your name established. Beyond a certain point, however, newspaper advertising seldom produces any additional traffic and, in fact, may be discontinued for short periods without affecting rental traffic. Some advertising must be done because of that 20 percent segment of residents who are drawn by it and have no other way of learning about you, but don't just rely on newspaper advertising to generate prospects.

Let's look at the limited impact of newspaper advertising from another angle. You don't really sell apartments; you give prospects the information they need to make their housing decisions. Actually, people make up their minds to change living quarters several months before setting out on their first trip to look at available housing. People can be expected to scan newspaper ads for a full six weeks before they leave their living rooms.

What prompts people to start looking for new apartments? The action is triggered by a series of incidents. Prospective renters may be vaguely discontented with their present apartments. The closets are small and overstuffed. Perhaps the owner or property manager is not responsive to requests. Maybe their children are having bad experiences at school, or the long drive home from work is just too much. One or more of these dissatisfactions can build up, reaching a peak in the two- to four-month period before apartment hunting actually begins.

During this time, renters have been aware of institutional ads proclaiming the wonders of this community and that one. Those ads contribute to a general feeling of dissatisfaction, but they don't spur prospects to action. As a matter of fact, they can have the opposite effect. Because of the size and image-building character of institutional ads, they may convince prospects that the development is beyond their budget. The most that institutional ads can do is plant a seed that a better lifestyle exists.

Finally, in the few weeks before the actual shopping begins, prospects start studying classified ads. Instinct says that if there are any real bargains, they will be in the smaller classified ads, and not in the larger display classified ads placed by major complexes or realty companies. Then one weekend when the weather is nice (but not too nice), or the present manager has failed again, or a particular ad promises an unusual value—the shopping begins.

The people who respond to your ads undoubtedly have followed similar patterns. Their need or desire for a different place to live began months before, followed by weeks of comparing ads, and ending now with actual physical inspections. If your ad appears on the weekend the prospects decide to shop, they might show up at your doorstep in response. This requires a bit of coincidence, the right timing, and some skill in the art of writing an effective ad. Coincidence is pure luck, timing will come with experience, and the skills of preparing an ad can be learned. Consider these points in understanding the three types of newspaper advertising.

- *Classified.* The name comes from the fact that this kind of advertising is classified by subject matter—jobs wanted, jobs available, goods for sale, homes for sale, apartments to rent, etc. The ads are grouped together in one section of the paper and generally run in one-column widths, using the uniform typeface and format of the newspaper.
- *Display.* These ads appear throughout the newspaper; they use illustrations and a variety of type styles.
- *Display Classified.* This is a hybrid type of ad that is located in the classified section of the newspaper and utilizes the artwork and type style variety that a display ad might have.

In most cases you will find that classified advertising is the most productive of the three types. It is recommended for all promotional advertising.

Regardless of what type of newspaper ad you run, the ad should answer the prospect's three primary questions:

1. *What do I get?* This means describing all the features of the property, beginning with the apartment. Start with the number of bedrooms; that's the first thing prospects want to know. Then specify such things as the number of baths, kitchen equipment, carpeting, drapes, air conditioning, method of climate control, utilities, fireplace, washer/dryer connections, and storage space. Go on to list the recreational amenities: swimming pool, sauna, tennis courts, playground, sun deck, lake, or putting green.

   These features can be set down in either a narrative or paragraph style, or in a bulletin or list style. It's a good idea to vary the form so your ad doesn't look the same each weekend.

   Don't use too many abbreviations! BR, Kit., fpl., tn.ct., and A/C may be intelligible to you, but the reader may not understand. In any event, abbreviations impede easy reading of the ad. Generally understood abbreviations are permissible (e.g., Apt., St., Ave., Blvd., Dr.).

   To attract different markets and add variety, try switching what you have to offer from week to week. For example, advertise one- and two-bedroom apartments to attract one segment of the market one week. Then you can advertise three- and four-bedroom units to appeal to the family market the next week. Don't put everything you have to offer in a single ad, or you'll confuse the prospect. Remember, each prospect is looking for only one apartment and is not really impressed by your ability to accommodate all family sizes. If you have different-sized apartments to offer, it is better to run separate ads in successive weeks than to promote all of them in one ad.

2. *What does it cost?* Some property managers are not sufficiently confident of their rental pricing to list the rent in the ad. They hope that prospects will accept the rent after seeing the apartment. However, for every prospect who is drawn by an ad without a price, the manager will lose ten to fifteen others who won't come because the rent isn't listed. This is a terrible waste. Make the ad work for you, not against you.

   If you don't want to list a specific price, it's perfectly all right to use a leader price: "From $485." Or, you can give a rent range: "Apartments from $525 to $780." In fact, promoting the top of your rental price range can add to the status of the property. Even if prospects can only afford the lower end of the range, they will en-

Your Place

A place with carefully designed apartments and custom features. A place where you can swim, play tennis, party, or quietly stroll down a wooded path. A place that is meticulously maintained and professionally managed. A special place that will enhance your lifestyle.

Your Place, with 1 and 2 bedroom apartments starting from $500 per month.

During our Grand Opening Celebration we invite you to see for yourself why Your Place is "a place to call home." Furnished models open daily from 11:00 am to 6:00 pm.

Take I-101 to Main Street exit, go west 1½ blocks to Your Place. 555-5555

Display Ad

Display ads create awareness. They are generally used for a grand opening campaign or on an ongoing basis for a large multiphase development. The sample ad shown here (obviously reduced in size) might be used as a full-page ad in a magazine or newspaper. Note that this ad answers the three basic questions prospective residents ask.

joy being associated with a complex that commands higher rents.

3. *How do I find it?* It's hard to believe, but the directions in many ads for suburban garden complexes are incorrect. Often, the person who writes the ad knows the route well and, because of this knowledge, omits a vital step in spelling out the directions. This point can be proved by going to a strange city and attempting to locate an apartment complex from the instructions in a newspaper ad.

Location instructions should be crystal clear. Start from a major expressway or major arterial street. Identify this street by its most commonly known name and route number. Sometimes a major expressway or street is known by different names as it passes through different communities within the same city, making a route number helpful. Make sure the mileage noted in the ad is correct.

Identify the exit by name and number. Be sure this name and number are visible to the person on the expressway. You may know the exit as Main Street because you travel this route every day, but all the prospect has to go by is Exit 14. Drive by the exit sign yourself to make sure the driving instructions in the ad are correct.

Also, make sure the exit is identified from all directions. A prospect driving westbound may be able to turn off at Exit 14, but an eastbound prospect may see a different number or, worse yet, there may be no exit from that direction. In that case, you'll have to include a different routing. Tell the prospect whether to turn right or left from the exit, then continue to specify all the streets leading to your property. Spell out the instructions carefully. It helps to have your directional signs along the way, too; but as noted earlier, these signs can be removed or knocked down, so don't count too heavily on them. Make sure the instructions are clear and complete so the prospect can find your property without signs.

There may be a choice of routes to get to your development. The most direct route may lead prospects past unattractive scenes or competing developments. Real estate agents who sell homes are careful to take prospects along the most scenic route, even though it may take longer. One problem with suggesting scenic routes is that the directions may run counter to directional signage.

If prospects still have difficulty finding your apartments, the answer may be a display classified ad that includes a map. The map should be to scale, not distorted, and it should indicate mileage distances so prospects have some indication of how they're proceeding and their location in relation to major landmarks.

Advertising Tips

It's crucial to keep the three basic questions in mind when developing your ads, but there is much more to learn about the inexhaustible subject of newspaper advertising. The following are recommendations regarding the appearance and placement of ads. We'll also address a few less conventional types of newspaper ads and their applications.

- *Headlines.* Catchy headlines don't catch. They may make prospects think that some clever salesperson is out to get them. Serious classified ad readers don't want to be entertained. They want to know how many rooms your apartments have, the features, amenities, price, and location. For a headline, it's better to use the number of bedrooms, the name of your property, the area of town if it is very desirable, or the street address if it is well known and follows the established numbering system.

- *The importance of a telephone number.* What about telephone numbers in ads? People have little time to waste these days, and they use the telephone to avoid unnecessary trips. The telephone number has become an important ingredient in rental advertisements, even though it would be preferable to have the prospect visit personally. I will expand on telephone techniques later in this section.

  Listing the telephone number is also helpful to prospects who start out for your complex but get lost and need additional instructions. More and more, telephone calls originate from the prospect's car telephone.

- *Ad size.* Prospects think that the true bargains are in the smaller ads. The one exception to this rule, grand-opening ads, will be discussed later. No matter how small the ad is, just make sure it answers those three important questions.

  The most successful classified ads are the smallest and advertise the fewest units. As stated earlier, try to avoid advertising more than one type of unit. Each prospect will only rent one apartment. By advertising one unit, you create a sense of urgency, which is exactly what you want to do.

  Large ads are self-defeating. The prospect who sees a large ad is apt to think that you have a correspondingly large number of apartments to rent or that the ad is expensive, so the rent must be, too. Apartments in plentiful supply or ones that appear to be moving slowly attract little response. Prospects are looking for the rare find. A small ad helps convey that impression.

  Newspapers traditionally arrange classified ads by size, with the large ads at the top of the page and the smaller ones toward the bottom. It's a good idea to vary the size of your ad from week to week so the newspaper will move it around on the page. This way there is a better chance of catching the roving eye of the prospect, and your ad won't be stuck in one position.

- *Type size.* The newspaper ad salesman will tell you that large type is easier to read. Naturally, he or she wants to sell large type in order

Your Place

1 & 2 Bedroom Apartments

Your Place offers you all you would expect in apartment living and more, "a place to call home." Each Apartment is carefully designed to offer you the most in custom features including:

- Central Air Conditioning
- Self-Cleaning Oven
- Dishwasher
- 2-Door No-Frost Refrigerator
- Garbage Disposal
- Cable Television

For your leisure time, Your Place offers a beautifully decorated club house with a large pool and lighted tennis courts.

From $500

Your Place is conveniently located only minutes from schools, shopping and expressways.

Directions: Take I-101 to Main St. exit—go west 1½ blocks to Your Place. Only minutes to schools and shopping.

Furnished models open daily 11:00 am to 6:00 pm.

Your Place
200 Place Drive
555-5555

Display Classified Ad
This type of ad is a hybrid of both classified and display ads. It appears in the classified section of the newspaper. Normally, an ad of this type and size is too expensive for weekly use and should be reserved for grand openings or other institutional advertising programs. A smaller classified ad will generally bring out more prospects than the larger, more expensive display classified ad. Use the latter sparingly.

to make the ad larger and sell more space. Don't be afraid to use standard-sized newspaper type for classified ads. When prospects read the classified pages, their eyes adjust to the small type, and they'll have little trouble reading your ad.

- *White space.* The newspaper ad salesman also may advise you to use plenty of white space in your ad. This can be overdone. Classified ads call for the judicious use of white space. A classified ad that is crowded from corner to corner can be very effective. Display ads, however, may benefit from the dramatic appeal of some extra white space.

- *Choice of newspaper.* In most metropolitan areas with more than one daily newspaper, one is usually recognized as the leader in apartment ads. That's the paper to use. You're wasting money advertising in the others.

  Community newspapers offer another opportunity. These papers are often published weekly or biweekly, and they cover a smaller geographic area than the dailies. A prospect who is looking for an apartment in a specific area may well check a local paper first.

  If you use both the leading daily and a community paper, alternate your placement so ads do not run in both papers the same week. This will stretch your advertising dollars and allow a better evaluation of the response level.

- *Frequency.* Sunday advertising is essential; that's the day most prospects look for apartments. Other than Sunday, one weekday is all that is ever recommended. Don't advertise more than twice a week in one newspaper.

  Advertising on one weekday can be effective. This weekday ad can be smaller than the Sunday ad because there generally are fewer weekday ads to compete against. Also, the person who looks for apartments during the week is a more serious shopper than a Sunday prospect. Many transferees, students, military families, and others who must locate housing quickly shop during the week.

  When scheduling ads, take holidays, season of the year, and weather into account. Don't blame the advertising if the weekend offers the first balmy days after a dreary winter—people would rather stroll in the park than visit apartments. Don't expect advertising to attract prospects in July and during the first two weeks of August when many people are on vacation. On the other hand, the last two weeks of August and the first part of September are typically good periods for attracting prospects, especially those anxious to register their children for the fall term in a nearby school.

- *Grand opening ads.* These are exceptions to my rule that the smaller the apartment ad the better. You may want to use a large display or display classified ad for a series of weekends to make your presence known. People expect a large ad in connection with a grand opening, but if the large ad continues to appear long after the grand opening is over, the ad will become stale and lose effectiveness, or the public may lose interest and avoid you.

- *Preleasing.* These ads try to attract prospects for apartments that are not yet available. You are advised against using them. When you bring in prospects, you need apartments to show; without apartments, you are wasting advertising money. Rely on drive-by traffic for any preleasing business you hope to do.

- *Shock advertising.* In difficult markets, especially those in which a large number of ads for competing developments crowd the rental section of the popular newspaper, you may be tempted to try shock advertising. This can involve humor, irreverence, a dramatic giveaway, or a next-to-nothing move-in package. The point is to capture the prospect's attention and gain a telephone call or visit. The technique often results in increased prospect traffic, and many people seem to enjoy a little humor in the usually humorless classifieds. However, on average, the prospect attracted by such an advertisement tends to be a less-desirable resident who doesn't stay for long.

- *The best ad.* An unusual but effective ad might contain the following message: "Thank you for your tremendous response. We're all filled up. If you want to get on our waiting list, stop by and leave your name." Such an ad often produces considerable traffic. People want what they can't have, and they'll come to see why your apartments are so popular.

Radio Advertising

Radio rates are low—much lower than people think. Many FM radio stations offer rates even lower than AM stations. Radio is also one of the most effective traffic builders. There have been cases in which weekend rental traffic built up tremendously minutes after a message was broadcast. Why? Because many radio listeners are in their cars when they hear something interesting, and they respond to it immediately.

While radio creates a lot of traffic, this traffic seldom rents apartments. It consists mainly of curiosity-seekers who want to know what's going on and are interested in any premium being offered. Certainly, teenagers who are drawn by radio messages aren't prime rental prospects.

In one situation I know of, mature renters were attracted by ads run on a popular radio station with a country and western format. Another winning approach is regular sponsorship of a half-hour program of music in the early evening. The program might present "beautiful" or "easy-listening" music, or you might choose a classical format. Base your choice on the musical preferences of your target market. While it is difficult to track the number of rentals from this kind of advertising, it undoubtedly improves the property image as well as its rentals—particularly in high-rent apartments.

Radio can be especially effective in connection with grand openings. The heavy traffic built up by radio can help convey a feeling of success. A profusion of activity may convince serious prospects that they should rent before all the apartments are taken.

If you decide to use radio, it's a good idea to buy broadcast time in such a way that your spot is aired with increasing frequency from Thursday to Saturday and then stops mid-afternoon on Sunday. Pay particular attention when buying radio time. Many stations have restrictions on when you can buy time. Some popular programs are filled up, with no time available. You may have to buy a package of undesirable time periods in order to get the time you want. Sometimes, the station will schedule your commercials at its convenience. Be aware of these possibilities and take them into account when planning your campaign.

Television Advertising

Television is a great selling medium—but expensive. Commercials for apartment developments are almost always institutional advertising. Only rarely are they intended to promote the leasing of individual apartments. In most metropolitan areas, the cost of television advertising is prohibitive; the only exception would be the promotion of luxury properties that have large advertising budgets. In smaller cities and towns, television advertising is somewhat more reasonable. Remember, in addition to the cost of broadcast time, there are production expenses. Making a good television commercial costs a lot of money, and it must be done with great care to show your property to its best advantage. One way to cut costs is to make commercials using videotape rather than film. In fact, most TV stations will offer to do this for you. Another way to cut costs is to advertise on UHF stations or cable stations that have lower rates and smaller audiences than VHF stations.

Be wary of certain television traps. One is the low rate for late-night shows and for Friday and Saturday nights. The reason that rates are low during these times is that the audience is small, and chances are your prospect market isn't watching.

A second trap is a series of real estate commercials run during the same program. You want to be the only real estate advertiser; you don't want to compete with two or three other developments.

A third pitfall is the tendency to purchase advertising time during your favorite shows and on your favorite stations, without regard for the target market. Don't let personal viewing or listening preferences dictate your television or radio advertising strategy.

Local public broadcasting TV stations may offer promotional opportunities that don't require cash outlays. One such opportunity is a charity benefit auction. Local merchants are asked to contribute goods and services that are then auctioned to viewers. If you participate, the station will generally prepare a commercial to promote your complex. This commercial could be run several times each day during the telecast auction in return for your donation of, say, one year of free rent on a one-bedroom apartment. This can present an opportunity for tremendous television exposure and may also include the production of a taped commercial—all achieved while benefitting a worthwhile charity.

In any case, if you do want to use television, be sure to get competent advice from an advertising agency or other communications professional before making any plans.

Magazine and Program Advertising

Included here are regional and city editions of national publications such as *Time* and *Newsweek;* magazines put out for specific cities by local publishers; and programs for concerts, operas, and plays.

In most cases, these media are restricted to major cities, and in all cases are very expensive and effective only for institutional advertising. You are borrowing the prestige of the publication and associating it with your development. The effect is one of long-term image-building, but expect little immediate response. For this kind of advertising to be productive it must be done on a sustained basis. Again, such advertising probably is most beneficial to luxury apartments.

Direct Mail

This is one of the most effective—and most expensive—forms of advertising. Many people are surprised at this, especially when they think of the amount of "junk mail" they receive. But postage is expensive, whether it's first class or third class. Add to this the cost of paper, envelopes, printing, addressing, and handling, and the cost per person reached is far higher than any other kind of advertising.

The advantage of direct mail is its extreme selectivity: It enables you to *reach only the people you want to reach*. Newspapers, magazines, radio, television, and billboards all present your message to thousands of people, many of whom have no interest whatever in your development. Direct mail advertising can target your audience.

A direct mail campaign for an apartment complex should consist of mailing between 300 and 500 letters per week. This is an adequate number on which to base an evaluation. Fewer than 300 people is too small an evaluation base and even a successful mailing may reach too few prospects. More than 500 risks wasting advertising money if the mailing is unsuccessful; and you may get too much of a response if it does the job. The 300 to 500 range is a safe middle ground.

Offering an incentive such as a house plant, T-Shirt or pair of sunglasses will increase the response to your direct mail campaign. You will need to experiment with such offers to determine whether the added cost is justified by the addition of qualified prospect traffic, and more importantly, by extra rentals. A word of caution: Avoid offers that will detract from the quality image of your development. Remember, your product is very different from many others regularly promoted with direct mail incentives. People are not going to move their families in order to qualify for free pots and pans or even a microwave oven. Today, you can purchase mailing lists from a wide variety of sources including demographic specialists. You can reach just about any audience profile. You can dictate the addressees by zip code, occupation, salary, etc. These lists are rather expensive for the first mailing, but you typically receive a considerable discount when you purchase two sets of the same mailing list.

Do your mailing on a Tuesday for arrival Thursday and definitely no later than Friday. This gives a prospect plenty of time to plan for a visit on the weekend. It's basically a waste if a letter inviting the recipient to visit an apartment complex arrives on a Monday. The invitation is usually forgotten by the weekend.

A well-planned direct mail campaign should attract a 4 percent response; that is, if you mail to 500 names, 20 prospects should visit. If you score 4 percent or better, mail the same letter to the same list the following week. Most likely, there will be the same response on the second weekend. This is because the second group originally intended to come out the first weekend but for some reason postponed it.

If the response is less than 4 percent, consider other approaches. You may want to switch to another list of names or change the approach of your letter. Remember the effect of weather on your weekend traffic, and take this into account when judging the response level.

There's no magic formula for successful direct mail. You'll have to work out your own, but by sticking to the 300 to 500 sample, keeping the letter simple, and experimenting with different approaches, you will find a workable formula.

Yellow Page (Classified Telephone Directory) Advertising

People normally don't look in the yellow pages for unfurnished apartments. The most desirable residents are the least likely to consult the yellow pages. A possible exception is if a number of your units have been prepared as corporate apartments. Housing directors, business people, and students who plan rather lengthy stays often use the yellow pages to search for furnished apartments. A small ad may attract a number of excellent short-term residents.

For most situations, the value of a yellow pages ad becomes questionable—especially in light of the high cost of a display ad. In large cities, the proliferation of different and competing yellow page publications has generally frustrated the consumer, reducing the value of this advertising medium.

A simple listing of the apartment development's name in bold-face type is adequate. It may be a good idea to include an emergency telephone number for the benefit of residents who may use the yellow pages instead of the regular telephone directory. You may also want to include your rental information center hours.

Apartment Guides

Many communities have apartment guides, often published quarterly or semiannually, that contain display ads for different apartment developments. These guides are distributed free or for a nominal charge at high-traffic points (e.g., shopping centers, airports, train stations, convenience stores, drug stores). In some communities, these guides are very effective; in others they are not. The people who read them are nearly always in the market.

Experience will have to prove whether the apartment guide in your area is a useful tool. If it is, arrange to advertise in it. The cost is usually a fraction of the cost of a newspaper ad, and the guide may be usable for a month, a quarter, and possibly as long as half a year.

Handbills and Flyers

Throwaway literature is not recommended except for grand-openings and special promotions. Handbills and flyers tend to lower the image of your property when used on a sustained basis.

Newsletters

Desktop publishing programs have made it possible to produce a professional-quality newsletter for apartment communities—even for rather small ones. The trick is to resist the temptation of letting the piece read as if it were titled "The Landlord Speaks." Don't use it as an announcement vehicle for your new rules and regulations. Activities, gatherings, civic events, menus, resident profiles, or even short stories are fine. Stay away from manager talk. If you violate this principle, you may very well prompt a resident group to use the same new software to produce a newsletter for airing their grievances.

Prospects often look at newsletters as sales literature that is more institutional and less commercial than brochures. A newsletter tends to create the impression of a viable community, which may be an important point to make. Also, a newsletter format permits periodic updating to reflect the current status of the development. If the development's rental program runs long enough, successive editions of the newsletter can report on construction progress, renters moving in, opening of amenities, the relationship of the development to the surrounding community, and so on. Additionally, a newsletter can be used for follow-up mailings to prospects who have paid you a visit.

Some important advice: If you choose to publish a newsletter, do it well and make sure it reflects your unified graphics system.

Billboards

Billboards can carry an institutional message as part of an overall campaign. More commonly they are used as directional signage near highly traveled roads as explained earlier. A billboard's primary value is to direct people who already are heading your way.

Be aware of the limitations of billboard advertising. If a salesperson claims that 10,000 people see the sign every day, it's likely the same 10,000 who are on their way to and from work. A billboard loses its impact almost as soon as it is displayed because people get used to it. Also, the sign needs lighting at night in order to get full value from it. You may have to accept a package of billboard placements on a rotating basis, which can mean poor locations as well as good ones. Finally, billboard advertising is expensive. The number of billboards is being reduced because of pressures exerted by environmental protectionists, and this has increased rates for the remaining billboards.

All of this suggests that billboards have limited value for apartment renting. What is a powerful vehicle for selling soft drinks is not necessarily right for marketing apartments.

Banners

When renting becomes difficult, apartment owners and managers always seem to come up with the idea of putting a banner on one or more buildings to attract the attention of potential renters. "Now Renting," "One Month Free," and "Win A Trip" are common messages. The community next door, not to be outdone, soon hangs their banner with an even more urgent slogan. Business rarely increases, at least in terms of the quality of the applicants; but a signal is sent to all renters announcing the fact that deal time is here. Your existing residents may begin to wonder if they can achieve a better housing deal by moving. Even if they don't move, they will demand more from you since they feel that new residents are receiving special benefits. Many of your very best residents will be embarrassed by

Promotional Billboards
Not intended to direct or to inform, promotional billboards help reinforce awareness and identity. They must be large, properly placed, and contain few enough words to be read and understood quickly. The use of "reverse" color combinations, as shown on the lower sign, will attract more attention from a greater distance. Remember to keep the message short.

these banners and their special offers. They certainly will be upset with the lower-quality neighbors who are attracted by this form of last-ditch advertising. The biggest and best "banner" should be the property itself. Put your effort into making the property look better and you'll stand out among the rest.

Human Directionals

One of the most desperate marketing strategies is to hire someone to dress up in a trendy or eye-catching costume and direct prospect traffic to your complex. People have used clowns, giant rabbits, and even an imitation Pope. Common sense should tell most apartment operators that very few prospective renters will be encouraged to visit a property and possibly lease an apartment just because a clown standing in the street suggested they do so. These attempts are usually made by operators who simply do not understand the sensitive nature of the housing business. Because property managers deal with one of the most personal of commodities, marketing techniques must be chosen carefully. Using human directionals insults virtually all housing customers.

Transit Advertising

Like billboards, transit ads are generally read by the same people all the time. Many of the people who use public transportation are not in the market for apartments in your development, especially if it is a suburban garden complex. Transit ads on the outside of buses get dirty quickly and reflect poorly on the development's image. The person stuck in a traffic jam behind a bus spewing exhaust fumes is not likely to react favorably to your ad. Also, you may not be able to get the routes you want for the best advertising exposure. For all of these reasons, transit advertising is not recommended for renting apartments.

Airport Displays

These displays reach one of the most active and affluent segments of the housing market, including executives being transferred. In large metropolitan airports, the cost of this advertising is prohibitive. In smaller cities, airport displays, including kiosks in airport lobbies, are reasonable in cost and effective as part of a major advertising program.

Benches

Advertising on benches at bus stops and elsewhere only reminds the public of your existence. An apartment ad on a bench at a key corner close to your development can help draw traffic. If you can afford to erect a bench and bus-stop shelter with architecture and landscaping that matches the character of your development, so much the better. Remember, bench advertising can be damaging when the inferior condition of the bench or its surroundings reduces the development's status.

Miscellaneous Advertising

Included here are skywriting, sponsorship of baseball and bowling teams, sponsoring a float in a parade, and similar practices. Their value is limited—it's strictly institutional. Don't expect prospects to come running out to rent an apartment just because they saw your apartment development's name on a float in a parade.

Traffic Builders

Other strategies and techniques can be used to draw traffic and prospects; these things can work well alone or as part of an advertising program.

- *Premiums.* You may consider offering a premium in newspaper advertising or direct mail to get people to visit your development. Premiums have been used successfully by savings and loan associations, banks, gasoline stations, and appliance dealers to attract customers. However, no one will move for the sake of a premium. All premiums will do is help increase traffic. If that's your goal, fine.

  Don't use premiums as an enticement for people to sign a lease application. Nothing will be an inducement if the apartment doesn't fit their needs. If they do sign, they probably would have signed without the premium incentive.

- *Giveaways.* Included here are buttons, balloons, and T-shirts. While premiums are relatively high-quality gifts, these are harmless attention-getters. People accept them as token gestures; but if done excessively, such commercialism can damage your image.

- *Celebrity appearances.* These are successful traffic builders for grand openings. They also may be good if the celebrity lives in the building and is willing to appear for the benefit of the other residents. Otherwise, a constant stream of celebrity appearances gives your building a Las Vegas atmosphere, which many prospects and residents won't like.

- *Charitable and public service activities.* If your development is conveniently located, you may be asked to make it accessible for various public service activities. The local public health service may ask if it can set up a trailer to conduct blood pressure or cholesterol tests on your premises, or the Red Cross chapter may need a room to hold a blood donor drive, either of which would draw outsiders as well. Perhaps your development might be considered a donation spot during an annual drive to collect Christmas toys for underprivileged children or the starting point for a charity run or bicycle ride.

  All of these are legitimate activities to stimulate public awareness of your property and increase the number of visitors. It may be difficult to attribute rentals to such activities, but if they don't cost anything and don't downgrade your image, go ahead and permit them.

  One thing to be very cautious of is any activity that draws large crowds of people (e.g., a rock concert). This will drive away prospects, irritate residents, and probably do physical damage to your property.

- *Trips and contests.* Here's the basic rental strategy: The greater the prospect traffic, the greater the number of renters. It would appear that in weak market situations, whatever it takes to increase traffic is acceptable. Offering a wonderful trip as a renting inducement would appear to be an effective way to attract additional renters. You will probably get a discount on these trips because of a special arrangement for volume, but, they are expensive. The money used for a trip could certainly be better spent by improving the property as a whole or the individual apartment units. Doing this will avoid the negative feelings harbored by existing residents who have seen the advertisement offering new, untried residents a vacation. I have also seen these programs backfire when the travel arrangements go sour or the trips do not include all that was implied. There have been cases in which resident organizations were formed by groups of residents who first became acquainted during a less-than-perfect trip.

Running a contest for a nice prize is a less-expensive approach, but it has little influence on rental results. The prize might be a year's free rent, a luxury trip, or a new automobile. Unfortunately, contests rarely produce any measurable increase in prospect traffic or rentals. After all, many states offer the chance to win a million or more dollars with the purchase of a one-dollar lottery ticket. These contests are public and highly regulated. Why would someone wish to participate in your contest?

Finding Prospects: Other Sources

Besides drive-by traffic and advertising, there are several other sources for prospects.

Apartment Locator Services. Firms have been established in many communities to assist prospects who are searching for apartments. These firms are usually grouped separately in the yellow pages or in the classified section of the newspaper and they are commonly called apartment locators or apartment finders. Apartment locators offer their services to the prospect by providing a central source for rental listings. The fee, however, is paid by the owner of the apartment complex that gains the prospect as a resident (and the fee is typically a percentage of the first month's rent). In a way, this is very similar to a home sale in which the real estate broker appears to be helping the buyer, but is in fact the agent of the seller. Apartment locator services are not offered in every community and the quality of these firms varies. The fact that service availability differs from one community to another is obvious to me when I teach property management courses and some of my students are unfamiliar with these services. I explain the value of apartment locator services as follows:

- *Time saving.* Blindly following apartment advertisements can waste a great deal of time. Ads typically reveal all of the benefits and none of the drawbacks of advertised apartments; advertising copy can be very deceiving. A quality locator service will take the time to learn each prospect's criteria for an apartment and will qualify the customer according to price, location, unit availability, etc. Current information about those apartment complexes that meet the prospect's requirements is shared to narrow the search and save the prospect time. Some locator services even have videos and exterior and interior color pictures on computer so that they can give the prospect a presentation of available units.

- *Identifying special needs.* A number of would-be renters have unusual requirements. Perhaps a prospect has a large dog and has been turned down again and again. Maybe the prospect has a very large family and is experiencing difficulty finding an affordable unit that has enough room. Possibly the prospect requires a short-term lease because he or she is building a house and construction has been delayed.

- *Relocation assistance.* Apartment locator services are most popular among prospects who are relocating from one place to another and have little knowledge of their new community. A locator is often in the best position to provide unbiased assistance in finding just the right accommodations. Corporations with transferees will commonly engage a locator service to help their employees find new living quarters.

When quality services are available, many managers of small apartments will depend on apartment locators to market their properties. Larger companies should use locator services only to supplement their own rental efforts. The trouble begins when the property manager becomes dependent on the locator service and exerts less effort to attract prospects.

Resident Referrals.   Probably no one is a better prospect than the person who walks into the rental information center after being referred by one of your good residents. This prospect is probably the same caliber as the present resident. Moreover, the prospect usually has seen the resident's apartment, likes the development, and is ready to rent. The resident has already done the job of informing and exciting the prospect. Such a prospect is much more desirable than one referred by a locator service or one who merely drives by.

To let residents know that you welcome and reward referrals, periodically send the residents a letter or flyer announcing this. To qualify, the resident must personally bring in and introduce the prospect, so there's no question of whether a proper referral has been made. You don't want a situation in which a prospect comes in alone and rents an apartment, and then later a resident claims to have referred that prospect. A personal introduction eliminates this possibility. When the prospect signs the lease, the resident who made the referral gets a bonus.

The bonus can take many different forms. The current trend is to make the reward a very nice improvement to the apartment—possibly a new appliance or a special decorator treatment. Townhouse developments sometimes offer to plant a fair-sized tree in the yard outside the referring person's unit or to add some special landscaping as a reward. Many complexes offer the same reward to both the referring party and the new resident. This makes it much easier for a person to refer someone, knowing that both parties benefit.

It should be noted that when rewards are offered, particularly cash rewards, the greatest proliferation of renewal prospects will come from some of your least desirable residents. Hence, you may want to examine the present caliber of your residents. Assume you have just finished upgrading your property and you want to attract a new and better grade of resident to replace some of the less-desirable current residents. You offer your existing residents a generous referral program—one month's free rent. Your offer is really directed to the new residents who have been carefully screened. Unfortunately, top-quality residents are usually very slow to recommend their friends, particularly when they are being paid to do so. The less-desirable residents do not seem to be guided by this principle, and you soon begin to receive a stream of referrals of similar caliber. Your development, hanging at a balance point, begins to shift toward the less-desirable resident, and the investment starts to slip backward. This problem only seems to occur when the referral prize is cash or a cash equivalent. The solution: Make the reward an improvement to the apartment.

Be aware that some states have regulations that may limit the use of resident referrals. The restrictions may relate directly to state licensing requirements and can prohibit the distribution of cash awards for referrals.

Housing Directors.   Included here are housing directors and personnel managers of nearby corporations, hospitals, military bases, and colleges who seek housing for people transferring into the area. Contacts with these people usually are dominated by full-service real estate firms that offer a variety of services, including home sales and mortgage financing in addition to apartments to rent.

If the location of your development is within easy driving distance of a major employer, it certainly would pay to call upon the housing or personnel director and establish a relationship. Your cause will be dramatically improved if you can point to some of their employees who are currently your residents. Don't expect instant results. You should plan to make regular calls, say every two months, to drop off literature and renew acquaintances. Be sure to inquire about affiliate companies as well as firms that supply or support them. The personnel director will often have advance word of relocations, expansions, or special assignments involving other firms that provide associated services.

You might consider establishing a "preferred employer program" in which you offer special benefits to the employees of select companies. Typically, these include: no security deposit (or a greatly reduced security deposit), discounts up to 10 percent, and the right to cancel without penalty in the event of a company transfer. If you decide to initiate such a program, seek the cooperation of the personnel department to help you promote the plan. It will be your job to prepare the printed materials and posters, but you will need the company's help in distributing these materials. If you choose to go this route, it is really important that you make a full promotional effort. If you don't, you may find that you have returned security deposits and lowered rents of existing residents who are employed by that firm, without gaining any new ones.

Waiting List.   Unless an apartment becomes available within a day or two after a prospect signs a waiting list, fewer than 1 percent of the names on such a list ever remain likely prospects. They'll look elsewhere. The primary advantage in maintaining a waiting list is to add to status appeal. People want what is in demand and hard to get. Word of this will get around, and this will increase interest and traffic.

Follow-up List.   This is a list of people who say they'll be back, but never show. The chances of converting these people to renters is very slim. Once they've left your rental information center, they lose interest. If you couldn't reach an agreement with them while they were on the premises, it will be difficult to rekindle their interest over the telephone. A good many will resent your call. Out of the one hundred prospects you call, twenty may agree to visit again, twelve may actually appear, and three or four may sign. During periods of slow traffic, however, it may be worthwhile to spend time on follow-up to gain this additional traffic and the added rental results.

Rent-up Specialists.   In many markets there are firms that will take over the leasing function for your property. Usually they arrive with a team of well-trained leasing specialists who know the techniques of renting and, in particular, the art of asking for a commitment. The fee typically covers their out-of-pocket costs plus a commission for every rental they produce. Most firms will tolerate your existing staff, but they almost never share customers or their knowledge of renting techniques. These firms and their staffs must produce or they won't be in business long. Most representatives of these firms are much more effective than the typical rental agent because they have had better training and they are closely supervised.

Employing such a firm might sound like just the ticket. You can hire one of these leasing specialists, fill your property quickly, terminate the relationship, and handle the slower-paced renewals with your own staff. There are, however, some drawbacks to be considered. The cost of this service is high. Often in very soft markets the rental progress is not much better than what you were accomplishing on your own. Also, when you utilize outsiders you are not developing an experienced staff of your own. The most damaging side effect, however, is the high turnover rate of the residents attracted in one of these rental campaigns. I've seen countless examples in which more than 80 percent of the residents who rented under these programs were no longer living in the same apartment after a period of one year. The leasing specialists counter with the argument that they were successful in attracting renters and if there is any blame for an undue rate of move-outs it should be directed at the quality of management. Whatever the cause, apartments lease faster with leasing specialists, but the turnover rate increases as well.

Public Relations

When applied to a merchandising campaign, *public relations (PR)* refers to publicity used to call attention to a development, establish its image and theme, and keep it in the news. Public relations is much more than merchandising. It includes policy-making, product design, personal relations with prospects and residents, complaint handling, and community relations. It involves finding opportunities for you and your property to make a good impression; it is positive image-building. Because our focus is on merchandising the product and attracting prospects, we'll look only at the merchandising role of public relations.

The power of public relations is in its believability. People often believe what they read in the newspaper or hear from a friend, but claims made in an ad are regarded with some skepticism. For public relations to have this believability, it must be divorced from advertising. If people know that a newspaper regularly trades off editorial space in exchange for advertising, they view the publicity as advertising and discount it accordingly.

To a great extent, the success of a PR program for an apartment development depends on the manager's ability to produce stories and photo opportunities for local newspapers, as well as radio and television stations. This is no job for an amateur. Just as property managers shouldn't design a development's symbol and graphics (unless they are professional designers), they shouldn't dabble in PR either (unless they are PR professionals). To be effective you should have the best talent available.

Public relations and publicity campaigns aren't free. True, newspapers don't charge you when they mention your development in an article, but someone must be paid to create the publicity that led to your inclusion in that article. If you try to save money in this area, you'll wind up getting few or no results.

Once the right PR talent has been hired, make it clear that you want publicity to build traffic, not to tickle someone's ego. You want publicity that focuses on the development and its features and appears in newspapers where the public can see it. Ego-building publicity focuses on the developer, manager, and owner and is restricted to real estate news corners or trade publications that the general public doesn't even read.

Beyond local publicity, a PR counselor may be able to interest a national magazine in doing a story about your development. While these magazines reach a far larger audience than the target market, the prestige will boost the image of the apartment development. In addition, reprints of national magazine stories can be distributed as information pieces in the rental information center and included in direct mail campaigns.

CONVERTING PROSPECTS TO RESIDENTS

During this discussion of marketing, I have spent considerable time dealing with areas that do not involve direct contact with the customer. The reason for this is that the final stage of marketing, actual contact with prospects, will undoubtedly be the least controllable part of the rental effort. It is to be hoped that the product and atmosphere that have been created will "carry the day." The reason for this is simple. Preparing the product is the culmination of months and often years of planning, thought, and revisions by highly trained experts. Choosing and decorating models, creating ads, outfitting rental centers, and preparing colorful collateral materials, are also the product of specialists working at a measured pace with a carefully planned goal in mind. When the customer finally appears, either by telephone or in person, the controllable portion of the marketing program decreases. The apartment manager must now have impromptu interaction with the real star, the customer.

Customers come in about every size, shape, mood, and background. They're driven by endless wants, needs, limitations, and abilities. The property's staff must match each customer's needs to the rental community using knowledge of the area, the product, alternate choices, and basic selling techniques. That's tough. An advantage does exist, however. When you hear from a potential renter, that person has indicated a possible desire for a change in his or her housing arrangements. At least there has been some "sorting" done. Imagine how much more difficult apartment marketing would be if it was necessary to start from scratch as is often the case with people who sell encyclopedias or life insurance. They must search out an audience, plant the idea of need for their product, and then proceed to fill the need with their particular product. On the other hand, we in the apartment management business deal with a product of necessity, housing—and more often than not, our customers come to us.

The apartment-hunting process is time consuming because of the distances between rental communities and the number of options that are usually available to a prospective renter. The telephone is often used to save time during the initial scouting efforts. The prospect has usually established a set of criteria that arises from his or her particular situation. This list includes requirements as well as desires and frequently reflects a "stretch" in actual needs. This is no different from the way people shop for automobiles. The car-shopping process starts with gathering information about the latest features; it includes a plan to avoid the problems inherent in inexpensive models, and extends to ultimate resale values. After a period of some investigation, a decision will be made, but the criteria and expectations will probably be compromised. The brutal reality of affordability will eventually play its role in the decision. Similarly, the point at which the rental prospect's call is fielded will determine the degree of compromise in his or her original wants and needs. For example, if this is the caller's first weekend or two in the rental market, he or she will stick pretty close to the mental or written criteria list. After all, his or her demands are justified and buoyed by all of the specials detailed in the classified ads. It will be some time before the customer actually gets a handle on the market and begins to sort out priorities.

Recognizing this, leasing agents must adjust their approach accordingly and try not to become depressed when a caller hangs up or demands apartment packages that are unrealistic. Chances are that the prospect has not left his or her living room and the realities of the market are yet to be learned. It's tempting to start selling the product during those exploratory phone calls. While that will certainly make the leasing agent feel better, it will not do very much to help the rental effort. The telephone is a valuable tool, but its primary advantage is the help it provides in securing appointments.

The Telephone Inquiry

When the telephone rings and it's a rental prospect, understand that the prospect wants to shorten the shopping time by garnering as much information as possible about the property. The prospect will want an ample apartment with a long list of amenities, all at a very special price. The staff member on the phone wants to make an appointment for the prospect to come and see the value package offered by the rental community. To do this, it is necessary to engage in a conversation that answers some, but not all, of the prospect's questions while at the same time probing for the answers to certain critical questions to help in *qualifying* the prospect. The following topics represent the information that the leasing agent should get from the prospect (though not necessarily in the order stated) as well as the appropriate follow-up activities.

- *Introduction.* When taking calls, the leasing agent should ask for the prospect's name, and he or she should be given the agent's name. The prospect might be hesitant about giving his or her name or, more importantly, telephone number or address, until he or she can determine a certain level of interest. One shouldn't dwell on the caller's identification and present whereabouts at the point that the exchange of names takes place.

- *Requirements and needs.* At this point, the question to be asked is, "How might I help you find your next home?" Remember, the response the prospect provides will rarely describe what the prospect will actually accept, so the property should not be disqualified just because there isn't an exact "fit." Rather than allowing the prospect to ask all of the questions, the leasing agent should begin an exchange that will reveal the caller's requirements and needs. If the prospect is asking all the questions, the leasing agent should first answer that inquiry and follow up with a series of his or her own questions to begin the qualifying process.

- *Timing and situation.* The rental agent can often break up a prospect's recitation of needs by asking about the prospect's intended moving date or interjecting a question about what prompted the need for a move. The answers to these questions will usually be honest and will help to "flesh out" a profile of this particular prospect. This information will become very valuable as the rental process advances.

- *Budget.* The leasing agent should ask the caller for an acceptable rental range, knowing that the estimate will probably be conservative. Prospects do not want to miss any bargains or specials, and they want to pressure the leasing person to come up with the very best deal. Actually, the prospect's strategy is reasonable, and it is probably much the same approach you would take.

- *How to contact the prospect.* If there is even a semblance of a "fit," the leasing agent should learn how to contact the caller. At first, it is important to establish a rapport and begin an exchange of information with the caller. If it appears that the leasing agent can help the caller find a new home in your property, the questions "Where can you be contacted during the day?" or, "Is it better to contact you during work hours or at home?" can be fit into the conversation. These inquiries might work better as part of the appointment process that follows. It is natural to ask for a phone number when people make appointments in case an emergency would force a postponement.

- *The appointment.* All that anyone can do on the telephone is "sell an appointment." Renting an apartment simply cannot be done by phone. In order to get almost anything today, you must ask for it. This certainly includes getting rental prospects out to visit the property. Skilled rental agents often ask for an appointment using a compound question: "Is one day of the week better than another and, is there a time of day that works better for you?" With the answer to one or both of these questions, the rental agent can *suggest a specific time and day for an appointment.* If the prospect avoids making a specific appointment, it's a good idea to ask for a general appointment. In other words, get the caller to commit to coming out on a particular weekend or one evening during a given week. An effective way to get a commitment from a prospect is to promise to set aside the necessary time to familiarize him or her with the general rental market as well as all that your rental community has to offer. A willingness to share time and knowledge often produces a corresponding commitment.

- *Directions to the property.* After making an appointment, the leasing agent should confirm that the prospect knows how to get to the complex. The agent should ask where the prospect will be coming from and summarize the appropriate directions.
- *Re-introduction.* At the end of the call, the leasing agent should state his or her name again. Many callers will have forgotten the name of the person at the other end of the line, but will not admit to this memory lapse and ask for the name. Again, a rental prospect is much more likely to keep an appointment if he or she knows the agent's name.
- *Record information.* Leasing personnel must develop the discipline to record the information gathered during a telephone inquiry. Maintain a set of cards, either blank or printed, on which to record the information derived from telephone inquiries. If the recording process begins while the prospect is on the telephone, the problems and delays associated with completing a registration card during the prospect's visit won't become an issue; the leasing agent can get right to the business of helping the prospect find a suitable home.

This brings up the issue of one of the disadvantages of paying leasing people a salary rather than a commission. Leasing people who are paid only if they play a role in producing renters will record and register everyone they meet. These people are simply not going to take the chance that a person with whom they have worked on the telephone might arrive at the office without knowing the leasing agent's name. Leasing agents paid on a salary will often do a creditable job of "talking-in" a prospect, but will not record the information that was learned about the prospect during the telephone inquiry. This omission is worse than starting over. One of the forces that motivated the prospect's arrival at the property had to do with a feeling or relationship that developed during the telephone conversation. If the leasing agent fails to record the information obtained during a telephone conversation with a prospect, the relationship is reset to zero when that customer walks through the door.

Preparing for the Visit

When the door opens and a rental prospect walks in, the "selling" job is almost half over. Why? Because his or her very presence indicates that a number of milestones have been reached. The neighborhood must be acceptable, or the prospect would not have visited. The prospect must find the property's appearance and condition to be favorable, or he or she would be saving time by going elsewhere. Obviously, the prospect hasn't heard anything negative about the reputation of the complex and its manager, or again, he or she would not have bothered to visit. What remains to be discovered by the prospect is the specific unit's appearance, availability, price, the atmosphere of the community, and the leasing agent's dedication to solving housing problems. Assuming you have done your homework in preparing the product and putting the available units into marketable condition, a great deal depends on the relationship between leasing agent and client.

Seller or Helper

After working with a great many leasing people, certain trends have become evident to me. Those agents who consistently achieve the greatest results present themselves more as helpers than as sellers. Their approach is to find out why the prospect wants a different place to live, identify any special needs and restrictions, and then make an effort to meet the established requirements.

Take a minute to think about the merchants you have dealt with who take the extra time and interest to see that you choose the right product, style, or size. In addition to assisting your initial purchase, these salespeople sometimes go one step further by helping you select coordinating items or accessories. This has become so rare an event in today's high-speed world, one is amazed and flattered by any interest or concern. Some novices may call this kind of approach high-pressure selling; but if the customer doesn't feel pressured, how can that be? A true salesperson who becomes involved in helping the customer satisfy a need or desire will always perform better than one who simply offers a product or service without putting forth any helpful sales effort.

It is not uncommon for top rental agents to suggest competing rental communities when the units in their complex do not match the prospect's requirements. These agents don't stop helping a client when the fit isn't there; they get on the telephone and make some calls. The prospect's knowledge of the neighborhood is no match for that of the professional leasing agent; the leasing person's assistance can save this prospect many hours of fruitless apartment hunting. Taking the time to help a prospect locate housing that will satisfy his or her current needs will pay dividends in the future. First of all, the prospect will probably tell others about the way he or she was treated and helped. This may not be the last time that he or she will need housing; next time one of your units may fit the bill. Also, the competitors you call will be grateful for the referrals and that may earn you referrals in return. The goodwill generated from this action is immeasurable. I have seen leasing people disciplined and even dismissed because they sent prospects to competing developments. Their superiors just didn't understand that when the apartment doesn't "fit," the agent's relationship to the prospect will be destroyed if attempts are made to force the issue.

Knowing the Product

Leasing agents can't be much help if they have limited knowledge of both the property they are renting and the neighborhood in which it is situated. It often appears that the more information that is given to the leasing agent at the time of initial employment, the less that person seems to learn about the property. When details are available in neat packages, information doesn't always register in a person's memory bank. The best results are usually obtained when rental agents are challenged to prepare their own data base about the property and neighborhood. Let that person measure and record room sizes, ceiling heights, square footage of cabinet space, and lineal footage of closets; assess the attributes and limitations of the various unit types; and judge which ones will rent most easily. Rental people must know the property from their own thorough study, not merely as a result of their many tours with rental prospects.

The same is true of knowing the neighborhood. The agent must actually ride the bus downtown and to the shopping areas. Agents should walk into the schools and inquire about the grade levels, school district boundaries, school bus routes, etc. They need to know about the businesses, churches, organizations, and local government. As we said at the beginning of this chapter, agents must also visit competitors. If they aren't allowed time for this orientation, the rental results will be limited to what can be achieved by a desk-bound clerk.

The Tour

Product and neighborhood information will be used throughout the presentation, much of which will take place during a tour of the property. The routes and the features to be included in a particular tour will vary with each customer, but the agent must plan for a number of combinations well in advance.

Ideally, the leasing agent hopes to have the opportunity to pause a moment with the prospect, become acquainted, and determine his or her needs. Unfortunately, many prospects are hurried at first because they want to assure themselves that there is a "possible fit" before taking the full tour and hearing the sales pitch. Prospects come to view apartment units, not recreational facilities and support amenities. It's sometimes difficult to slow the process sufficiently to allow prospects to feel the sense of the community. Respect the prospect's sense of urgency: The leasing agent cannot afford to waste time searching for keys or deciding what units are available. That work must take place daily, before the doors are opened for business.

There should be few surprises during the course of the prospect tours, and the surprises encountered should be truly beyond the realm of the leasing agent's control. Each agent should make a habit of walking the grounds and following the various routes available for showing the property to a prospect. This includes recreational facilities, parking areas, laundry rooms, sidewalks, steps and landings, model units and, of course, the units that are for rent. Obviously, the apartments should be in market-ready condition. This bit of advice has that textbook sound. Few people will argue with the premise that a preliminary tour should be made each day; but almost no one puts this into practice.

Sometimes the available apartment is still occupied and this requires even more advance planning. Usually, the best plan is to meet with the current resident and explain the need for his or her cooperation when the apartment is shown to potential renters. A great many renters feel that this is an imposition and some may have to be reminded that the lease clearly provides for this situation. Residents would much prefer that you wait until after they have moved to begin your re-leasing process. More time should be taken to qualify prospects when the tour involves occupied units. With luck, a match will be found after just a few showings, and residents can be spared further intrusions. The more advance notice, the better the reception will be. Choose reasonable hours to call for permission to show an apartment, and do your best *not* to schedule showings during a child's nap time or during meal times.

What happens in the case of an existing resident who is a poor housekeeper, or one who has proved to be unsatisfactory—perhaps even subject to an eviction suit? You have to forget showing that apartment. If the housekeeping is terrible, it will surely offend a quality prospect. If there is even a hint of odor, do not show the apartment to a prospective renter. Wait, clean it thoroughly, air it out, and allow time to eliminate the problem. Granted, taking an apartment out of the income stream is expensive; but it must be understood that quality residents simply will not choose an unpleasant apartment. When good prospects see a completely unacceptable unit, they are not likely to rent anything in the same development. If you are successful in leasing such an apartment before its problems are corrected, the chances are excellent that the incoming resident will present an even greater problem than the previous one.

If you have them, show model units first. This accomplishes two things. Prospects are anxious to find out what the units look like. Showing the models satisfies that need and gives the agent some time to promote the amenity package and get better acquainted with the prospect before deciding which available units should be shown. Usually, the choice should be limited to two units, so it is essential that the agent determine the prospect's needs quickly. The agent shouldn't be carrying a long list of available units or a handful of keys because this would indicate a number of vacant units. People want what is in demand; the leasing agent probably won't improve the occupancy level with the prospect who learns that there is considerable inventory. Of the two apartments to be shown, the best should be saved for last. Actually, the first apartment is often a trial. The prospect's reaction to it will signal what to show next. A third unit should be shown only when the agent learns of additional criteria during the first two showings. In most cases confusion will set in after two showings, making it difficult for the prospect to come to a decision. When prospects go away to think over different options, they rarely return. Also, revealing the availability of several units weakens your bargaining position and undermines the apartment's appeal.

Showing an apartment demands a blend of enthusiasm, feature demonstration, and the ability to allow the prospect some freedom to look around. Virtually everyone can identify the primary rooms, so statements such as "this is the kitchen" either insult the prospect or guarantee that he or she won't listen to additional comments. Prospective residents usually appreciate an agent who directs attention to energy-saving furnaces, insulated windows, frost-free refrigerators, or self-cleaning ovens. Reports about easy maintenance and creative room uses will also be appreciated. People aren't interested in knowing the total area of an apartment, but room dimensions are always of interest. If a prospect begins to point out features on his or her own, the agent should take note and slow down the presentation. Prospects can sell themselves on apartments more effectively than a leasing agent could ever hope to. This frequently occurs when one person does the scouting and returns with the other decision-maker in a semifinal round of looking. Listen carefully, and the prospects will identify their favorite features as well as their reservations.

Collateral Package

If there is printed material available to hand out, brochure sets should be prepared in advance and be ready to hand to the customer. There are mixed feelings about the timing of handing out materials. Some agents want customers to have the material in hand, so they can refer to it or make notes about features, unit numbers, rent, etc. Others believe brochures distract the prospect and eliminate the reason to return to the rental center after viewing the units.

Guest Cards

When customers walk in the door, you are going to need a method of recording their names and particulars. It's standard to use a printed guest card with spaces for information about the prospect and his or her needs. You may also want to record how the prospect learned about the development (advertising, drive-by, direct mail campaign, etc.) because this enables you to track the success of your promotional efforts. You have to determine who completes these cards and when it should be done. In some cases the card is completed by the agent shortly after the initial introductions. The true pros never go through the formality of filling out the guest card, though they may jot down information as they talk. It is not uncommon for the agent to delay completing the card until the prospect leaves. This requires much more concentration on the part of the agent, but it makes the sales presentation smoother and eliminates the interruption of completing such a form.

Walking Through a Prospect Arrival

Now that we have addressed the different aspects of dealing with a prospect, let's consider what happens when one walks through the door.

Presentation.   The entry of the rental prospect triggers an opportunity to demonstrate your rental community. The leasing agent must be quick to act and ready to learn the answers to a number of very important questions.

Introductions.   Unlike introductions over the telephone, the exchange of introductions during a visit to the rental center must be handled immediately and completely. The longer one delays getting the customer's name, the more awkward it becomes. If the prospect's name is difficult to say, or is not pronounced clearly, the leasing agent must take the time to learn the name and know its spelling. A person with a difficult name is no doubt accustomed to helping others learn his or her name and will take the necessary time to do so. While the importance of knowing and using a prospect's name may seem too rudimentary in a discussion directed toward professional leasing people, you should know that many surveys reveal that leasing agents do not learn the prospect's name until after the application is completed. It is difficult to demonstrate a sincere interest in the prospect and his or her housing situation on a nameless basis.

The Presentation

Name:		Intro: ☐
Timing:	Budget:	
Ready:	Looking:	
Situation:		
Motivating Force:		
Benefits:	Surprise:	Close:
Urgency:		Deposit: ☐
New Appointment: ☐ When:		

Ready or Looking?   A question that must be asked very early in the presentation process is, "When are you planning to move?" or "How quickly do you want to relocate from your present address?" There are prospects who need housing within a matter of weeks, and then there are those who have many months to go on a lease. Everyone who has taken the time to walk through your door deserves courteous treatment. Knowing the approximate timetable benefits you as well as your prospects.

Early in the presentation, the leasing agent should ask the prospects if they are ready to make a commitment if the right apartment comes along. If the answer is "yes," the leasing agent will know how to handle the response when he or she asks the prospects for the order—which in the rental apartment business is a deposit and a completed application. When the leasing agent asks for the order and the prospects resist, the agent already knows that the need exists; the problem is that the benefits demonstrated thus far have missed the mark in some way. On the other hand, if the answer to the question about commitment is "no" because the prospects won't need an apartment until next spring, there is little reason to even ask for the order. In this case, the leasing agent should be helpful and polite, but the fact that a decision will not be made immediately makes the approach somewhat different.

Budget.   The leasing agent should ask about the prospect's price range in the first few moments of the presentation. If the answer is $450 and your units start at $600, that issue should be dealt with immediately. The longer the matter of price is delayed, the more difficult it is for the prospect to admit that an apartment is beyond his or her means. People recognize that the leasing agent's time is valuable and that he or she is putting forth a lot of effort to help them find suitable housing. If the presentation proceeds too far, prospects who simply cannot afford the product have a difficult time admitting they are not rental candidates. When the price issue is delayed too long, the prospect often listens to the whole presentation and begs off with a statement like: "I am very interested, but I just need some time to look at what other properties have to offer." Too many of these responses, and the leasing agent's confidence level begins to erode.

If the prospect's budget falls within, say, 20 percent of your published rent, it usually pays for the leasing agent to continue with the full marketing effort. Most people are conservative when announcing their budget limitations and the leasing agent may be able to help with a little creative structuring. When prospects can't afford your apartments, the leasing agent should steer them to neighboring complexes that are within their means. As I said earlier, a leasing agent should do more than steer—he or she should ask the customers for permission to make some calls to help them find quality rental housing at a price they can afford. This will take some tact, because today *people are very sensitive about their inability to afford something other people consider basic.*

Motivating Force.   Moving is expensive, time-consuming, tiring, and unpleasant. So, when someone arrives at your door looking for an apartment, you can believe that there is an important force at work. It is critical that the leasing agent know and understand the reasons for the move and the major benefits being sought. It is not enough to know that the customer wants or needs a change in living quarters. In workshops with experienced leasing agents, I have counted more than 200 possible reasons for moving. The sales approach one takes with a prospect who is about to be married is very different from the method employed when a person is beginning divorce proceedings. A couple hoping for a home of their own some day won't have the same "hot buttons" as a retired couple who just sold their large house. The leasing agent's job is to demonstrate the benefits of an apartment. Knowing the motivating force behind a move enables the agent to emphasize those benefits that should be of interest to the customer.

Urgency.   The leasing agent's approach must have a sense of urgency. A change in housing is a big—sometimes painful—decision, one that can be easily postponed if there aren't sufficient reasons or benefits to justify the move. When there is just one available apartment, the level of urgency is obvious and can be very effective. When there is a "desperation banner" hanging on the side of the building and the newspapers are loaded with ads offering every possible incentive, it is far more difficult to convey such a sense of urgency. In fact, this is one of the primary reasons I recommend spending money to give each of your apartments its own personality. Then, even though there are other apartments available, the apartment being shown is special.

Surprise.   As the relationship between the leasing agent and the customer develops, the agent should be thinking about announcing some kind of personalized "surprise." For example, let's say that the prospect has indicated that he or she hates to waste anything, especially money. A skilled agent may respond by explaining the benefits of the energy-efficient heating plant. Later in the presentation, the agent might add the surprise of an unusually high "R" rating (a measure of heat loss) of wall and ceiling insulation. Maybe the agent surprises the customer by offering to provide some wallpaper or allow the prospect to move in a few days early. There are dozens of possible surprises. These should be planned in advance and introduced at the moment the prospect is deciding whether to sign or keep looking.

Questions and Objections.   If a prospect begins asking questions and raising objections, this is a positive sign. Questions and objections are often used as a ploy to avoid making a decision. They signal that the prospect wants to say "yes" but can't quite make a decision. Most people display hesitancy when faced with major decisions such as choosing housing, automobiles, and expensive clothing. Most rental agents misinterpret objections as negative reactions. This is not usually the case. An uninterested prospect simply listens to your presentation without comments, objections, or interruptions. When prospects take the time to spell out objections, they are interested but they need help.

Most rental agents can recite all their competitor's special features and all the negative aspects of their own property. This results from absorbing prospect objections. Rental agents must learn the most fundamental principle of marketing: *People need help in making decisions.* When objections and questions are raised, the prospect is ready. Knowledge of the prospect, the neighborhood, and the competition will all come into play. The ability to overcome objections and to answer the prospect's questions depends on product knowledge. The better prepared you are, the easier the task. Each case will be somewhat different, and experimentation is necessary. In time, experience will help point the way. Remember, all objections do not have to be overcome. Often prospects express objections to create a smoke screen that postpones decision-making.

Closing.   The two most frequent reasons for a disappointing leasing performance are: the condition of the apartment being shown and the failure on the part of the leasing agent to ask for the order. I mentioned earlier that success in getting an appointment depends on a willingness to ask for one. The same principle applies to the conclusion of the leasing agent's presentation. A customer has walked in the door, driven by a need for a change in housing accommodations; the leasing agent acts as an assistant in solving the prospect's housing problems. The leasing agent has qualified the prospect in terms of the immediacy of the prospect's needs, budget parameters, and the benefits to be gained by the move. Assuming our product is worthy of the prospect's consideration, shouldn't the leasing agent ask him or her to join the community? If the prospect is hesitant, is it because the agent has failed to answer a question or satisfy an objection? Will the prospect volunteer or identify the reason behind his or her reluctance, or must the agent initiate a probe? Unfortunately, many leasing people complete their tour of the models and an apartment or two and, if the customer doesn't say "I'll take it," the presentation is over. This stems from a lack of training and the fear of rejection.

The best way to help a novice leasing agent is to have him or her go out and visit new housing developments to witness the selling pros at work. Have the leasing agent record the "close attempts" and the words and phrases that are used. Equipped with a dozen or so of these techniques, the agent should be able to convert what he or she has learned to the business of renting apartments.

There is a period of nervousness that affects most leasing people when asking for the order, but it cannot be avoided if the person is to be successful. Sooner or later, the agent is going to strike the right relationship with the prospect and summon the courage to ask for a deposit and commitment—and the customer's answer is going to be, "yes." The best time to make a deal is immediately after completing another—thus the pattern of success begins.

The main message here is that the leasing agent *must* ask for the order. The apartment unit will not "rent itself."

Deposit.   Making a commitment to rent and placing a deposit are closely related. If the customer says yes to the "close question," but departs without leaving a deposit, little has been accomplished. The amount of the deposit is not particularly important, although a substantial figure certainly demonstrates a strong degree of commitment. A chronic deficiency revealed in the results of many shopper surveys is the fact that the customer wasn't asked for a deposit. That means that the prospect remains just that, a prospect. The prospect may come back and rent; or he or she might very well make one more stop and be "steered" to a better deal. When a person puts down a deposit, there is an element of closure or finality.

When it is difficult to get a commitment from a prospect because the rent is too high or the prospect wants a series of improvements, many experienced leasing agents will ask for a deposit and an application, making acceptance contingent upon the prospect getting his or her "deal." This accomplishes some important things. First, the prospect goes home and discontinues apartment hunting for the moment. That means he or she is not going to be lost to a competing property—at least today. Also, if the prospect will entertain the idea of putting down a deposit, it indicates serious interest. If the prospect brings up objections, yet refuses to write a deposit check that is refundable if his or her terms aren't met, the prospect may just be looking for a way to say goodbye. Finally, once a person has put down a deposit on an apartment or, for that matter, almost any other commodity, there is a sense of relief that comes with making a decision. The prospect begins to "live" the advantages and benefits of the new apartment even though it is necessary to wait for the acceptance of his or her terms. After a few days, a compromise between the offer on the table and a middle-ground counteroffer is much more likely to be achieved.

New Appointment.   When it becomes obvious to a skilled leasing agent that the customers are not going to make an immediate decision, the agent should do his or her best to make another appointment for the prospects to come out again. The prospects might say that they want time to visit some other developments for comparison purposes or that they want a friend or relative to have a chance to see the unit. The agent should then try to fix a specific time or at least a day for the return visit.

EVALUATING RESULTS

Here are some suggestions for assessing your progress.

Prospect Traffic

When times are tough and renting slows down, the standard industry cry is for more prospect traffic. If the number of people calling or walking through the door can be increased, it would appear that the odds of getting more rentals must naturally improve. Remember, when the call for more traffic goes out, the "market winds are still" and that is the very reason for concern. It's tempting to offer specials or free rent or to undertake a major promotional campaign. This approach has to produce more people on the phone and at your door or the program will be discontinued very quickly. The problem lies in the quality of the people who are attracted by such methods. These promotional efforts are acceptable in merchandising appliances, automobiles, and electronic gear, but they haven't proved successful in directing a person to where he or she is going to live. When traffic slows, take stock of each point in the marketing program. A new sign message often helps. You can almost count on the fact that your advertising has become stale. Scrap what you have and work on a new approach. Don't lose your image by adopting a shock approach or getting caught up in give-away mania. Most importantly, check the product. In the property management business, aging properties are said to "have whiskers." Remember, most people who choose not to rent in your property believe that they can get more for their rent money somewhere else. That doesn't mean that these prospects want lower rent; it says they believe that they can find a property that receives better care and maintenance for the same money. If you have money for trips, gifts, or free rent, try spending it to give the units special personalities. Finally, review the basics of renting. Did the leasing agent ask for an appointment? Did he or she know the motivating force behind the move? Can the agent list the benefits that each prospect is after? Did he or she attempt to close and ask for the order? In soft market periods, it may be very difficult to get more people through the door each week without a fire sale approach, but you can become much more effective with the traffic that you have. After all, if traffic is slow, you should have plenty of time to work on sales presentations.

Prospects Who Become Residents: Conversion Ratio

Many owners and some market analysts choose to dwell on the conversion ratio between the number of presentations that are made and the number of new residents gained. Over a long period of time such a ratio can prove beneficial in spotting a problem or sorting out ineffective leasing agents, but it should be used with caution. New properties have a much higher ratio of "lookers to renters." It's common to record as many as ten lookers for every deal made in a new, high-profile development. In a property that has stabilized, the conversion ratio will be something more like five or six prospects for each lease signed. The secret to interpreting these ratios lies in not advertising them. Some owners and supervisory managers announce their opinion of the proper conversion ratio. Then, when the leasing agents learn the magic number, they quickly adjust the weekly traffic figures to generate the desired ratio. Work with the conversion ratio, use it as a tool, but do not force it. If you are achieving a rental for every three or four people who walk through the door, study the competition and your rent levels—the chances are good that your rents are too low. If, on the other hand, you only rent a single apartment for every nine or ten showings, it is a pretty good bet that the property has some serious flaws. Either would indicate the need for some major changes.

Using Shoppers

Most rental agents dislike the use of shoppers. Let your rental agents know in advance that you plan to use shoppers to spot mistakes for the sake of correcting them, not to punish anyone.

As a matter of fact, it's a smart idea to use shoppers even if rental agents are converting prospects to residents at a ratio of five- or six-to-one. A shopper might discover that if the agents were doing everything they are supposed to do, they would be converting at an even better ratio. In that case, the rents may be too low and you can raise them safely. Have your development shopped two or three times a year, just to make sure agents are doing their best.

The shoppers might be young couples who look like prospects. If they have a baby or small child with them, so much the better. Have them dress casually and act like prospects; your shoppers should always match your resident profile. Also have two or three teams of shoppers who can visit the development on the same day but at different times. The reason for this is that it will help to substantiate the existence of selling patterns that need attention or correction. This will also help to counteract the denials that can be expected when a rental agent is confronted with a negative report. If the same report is made by more than one shopper, the agent has little argument.

The shopper should note the date and time of the visit, and the name of the rental agent. The shopper's report should be a strict narrative with no subjective comments. You will be amazed at what the shopper's report can reveal. Here are some actual examples. In one case, shoppers were denied their request for a tour of the models. In another case, a rental agent walked around without shoes; and in yet another, the rental information center was closed during the middle of the day.

Be sure to review the written report individually and privately with your rental agents so each understands what is being done—both correctly and incorrectly. Don't let the agent adopt a defensive or negative posture. Explain what was wrong and point out the correct techniques.

Setting Goals

After you are satisfied that the rental staff is doing a good job, have the staff set their own performance goals. Ask them how many apartments they would *like to rent* this month. Chances are the staff will set a high goal, much higher than you'd set for them. Then ask them to say just how many they actually *expect to rent*. The new figure will be somewhat lower than what they would like to rent, because you are asking for a specific commitment. The staff will usually meet their own commitments. If they fall below that figure, help them analyze their performance to find out why.

To improve the productivity of your rental staff, consider incentives other than money. Truly, money is one of the least powerful motivators when used as a bonus or extra inducement. Contests that involve the spirit of competition are much better to spur high achievement. By publishing results and awarding prizes, much can be done to improve performance. Remember, all people fear being last even more than they want to be first.

A Final Check

If, after doing all of the above, you're still not happy with the traffic and conversion rate, check every link in the rental chain step-by-step—

policies, rents, product preparation, merchandising, or even the product itself. If you find something that can be improved, change this item without changing anything else. Then change other elements one at a time until the desired results are achieved. Remember, the weakest link is usually the rental staff. Product preparation is next in line. Concentrate on these two aspects, and most marketing problems will be solved.

9

Rent and Investment Economics

Investment in rental housing involves a great deal of capital, either in cash or borrowed funds, and the commitment can be for many years. The day-to-day customer contact is continual and is commonly delegated to a manager who tends to the on-site affairs of the property. The development of this position marked the beginning of the property management industry. It has been the manager's constant challenge to learn more about the financial details and overall structure of the apartment business in an effort to achieve a more balanced approach to apartment management—addressing both the operational aspects of the property and the business aspects of its management (e.g., rent levels, expenses, debt service, and return on capital).

Rental properties and the problems associated with their operation are too big today to be trusted to just anyone. Professional managers are quickly replacing the people who have casually handled rental apartment properties in the past. Professionals understand the sensitive nature of a business that provides people with one of the most personal of commodities. They are schooled in policy making and implementation, and they are trained in the importance of presenting a properly prepared product. Today's manager is the premier source of rental property knowledge in terms of income potential and operating expense requirements. This chapter will review some of the numerous and often complicated aspects of the economics of apartment properties.

CASH-ON-CASH RETURN

The best way to begin is to learn where it all must end. Today's investors are making it pretty clear that they want a cash-on-cash return on their invested dollars. (Cash-on-cash return is determined by dividing cash flow by the money invested.) They will make some allowance for real estate's tradition of being one of the best hedges on inflation and the fact that real estate, unlike most other investment vehicles, allows for a considerable degree of control. Also, many investors will forego some immediate return for the promise of a higher return at the point of eventual sale. The key word here is "cash." To a great degree, the amount of money that will be available for distribution depends on the amount of rent money that is collected. Many mistakes can be offset in the process of budgeting operating expenses or handling unforeseen problems if there is some maneuvering room on the rent side of the ledger. Unfortunately, because of some managers' timidity regarding the subject of rent levels and the pressure that unforgiving market forces bring to bear, the key to achieving higher cash returns is not as straightforward as raising the rent.

INCOME GROUPS

There is no single procedure for determining the proper rent level and direction. Among residents there are at least four, and probably more, income groups that must be identified and dealt with separately because they each require a different approach. Some groups present severe restrictions when it comes to the subject of rent. The current position of each group must be examined as well as the alternatives available to them.

Low-Income Group

A house is a house—there are few differences between the costs of producing and operating one housing unit and another. Basic building components are the same regardless of where they are placed. Amenities and larger rooms probably only create a 25 percent difference between the cost of producing a rental unit that is part of a low-income development and one that is targeted to the middle- to upper-middle-income group. Even though the land may cost less in a lower-income neighborhood, land cost savings are quickly offset by higher insurance costs, vandalism losses, and labor and material charges that are often higher due to local political influences. As a result, only an amazing breakthrough in construction technology will make the development of self-supporting low-income rental housing possible. This means subsidization of one sort or another is necessary. Subsidies mean controls and controls mean rules and delays.

Many developers prefer to eliminate the problems of dealing with the government and restrict their activities to market-rate conventional housing. This in turn forces the government to "sweeten the pie" to attract investors back to the business of housing those who need varying degrees of financial assistance.

It is a given that a series of housing programs will be forthcoming to attempt to find a fair, manageable, and effective way of housing people with limited financial resources. In my experience, these people comprise about 14 percent of the rental market. Periodic adjustments in rent levels must be part of those programs to compensate for increased operating costs. Therefore, the owner must be more concerned with understanding the system's procedure than with balancing market forces. The supply and demand principles that typically drive real estate rents have little effect in low-income housing.

Limited-Income Group

Many apartment buildings have been around for a long time or were built during a time when "cheap" was the operative word. Both of these types of buildings are now struggling for survival. Without an infusion of cash to make desperately needed repairs, these properties have more difficulty attracting residents who will move in and "stick." The alternative is to take just anyone—and many new residents in this category can be counted on to cause more damage. These properties become homes to those who don't have a lot of income or, for that matter, choice. New rent levels must be closely tied to increases in the residents' effective spendable income because there is little room for adjustment in their household budgets. Residents in the limited-income group (about 53 percent of the market) are extremely price sensitive—a ten-dollar increase in the monthly rent can force them to seek housing elsewhere. This puts the manager in a very ticklish position. Say, for example, he or she knows that operating costs have risen to such a point that a $30 per unit per month increase is required to remain even. The manager also knows that $30 is more than his or her residents can afford and that such a rent increase will force a number of them to move to a development with lower rents, or at least to one that is offering a move-in discount or rent holiday (concession). When managing housing for the limited-income group, there is something to be considered in addition to the law of supply and demand—ability to pay.

After a move-out, the added costs of preparing the vacated unit usually mean a loss of revenue between residents, and the new resident is often a person of lower expectations and demands. This means a lower bottom line when there may not have been much of a bottom line in the first place. Unlike major corporations that may experience operating losses during one or more fiscal quarters, managers of rental properties usually have to stop spending when the money runs out because most rental properties do not maintain much of an operating reserve. A shortage of needed collections doesn't have much of an effect on the utility bills, recurring services, insurance, or taxes at first, but it has an immediate effect on the level of upkeep and the funds available for maintenance and repairs. This starts another cycle in a downward spiral.

Adequate-Income Group

People in this group don't have money to waste, but they have some discretionary income in their monthly budgets. Depending on individual priorities, people in the adequate-income group usually opt to spend those extra dollars on one or more indulgences. A fancier car, a nicer place to live, better home furnishings, and extended vacations are a few of those options. In terms of housing, people in the adequate-income group may opt to make an extra effort to accumulate a down payment for a home, or they may choose to rent rather than be committed to the hours of work associated with homeownership. Virtually all of the marketing efforts directed toward renters are designed to attract this income group. Many owners and managers spend large sums of money attempting to attract renters in the adequate-income group, even though the properties being promoted are in a location or display a level of maintenance that only qualifies for people in the limited-income group.

The people who make up the adequate-income group (about 25 percent of the market) can and often do pay rent amounts that will not only cover ongoing expenses and debt service, but also return a profit to the investor. These renters stay longer and cause less damage. Their incomes are such that they can keep pace with cost-of-living increases.

Almost all species on earth have predators of one kind or another; the same is true for market segments. The adequate-income group attracts more builders and marketers to satisfy its needs than any other. There are townhouses, manor and coach houses, and old and new free-standing homes to buy, plus rental accommodations that change and improve every day. These competitors are staffed with many professionals, and their livelihood depends upon presenting the best deal. This is the industry's prime market arena. If the value of the product is not in balance with the rent, the people who make up this group will quickly choose one of their many alternatives. The law of supply and demand governs this income group.

Ample-Income Group

The people in this group (approximately 8 percent of the market) don't concern themselves with questions of owning or renting—they do whatever suits their needs and desires. If they decide to rent, these people will surely make the necessary modifications to fit the apartment to their life-style and furnishings. The manager of rental housing that meets the de-mands of this income group need not spend a lot of time searching for the latest features and appointments. People with ample incomes will have their own designers and decorators help them remake a unit into their home. They are not fools when it comes to spending, but money is not their primary consideration. In this group, more prospects and residents are lost through skimping than overcharging. "Elegant," "quiet," "gra-cious," and "secure" are the buzz words here. These people do not choose housing that is trendy and they seldom move; people of ample means understand and can afford rising prices. The ample-income group repre-sents a very small segment of the rental market.

SETTING RENTS FOR THE FIRST TIME

As a manager, you may be asked to participate in the job of establishing rents for a property that is being constructed or one that has undergone a major renovation and is now targeted to a different rental audience. If the property is designed to house the low-income group, there is probably little for you to do in terms of establishing rent levels—except to develop an understanding of the rules and limitations imposed by the regulating authority controlling the funds or incentives that made the complex pos-sible. If the past is any indicator, the limited-income group will continue to occupy older housing at the going rate. The main rent-setting activity will take place in housing built for those enjoying adequate or ample incomes.

Costs will certainly be a prime ingredient in determining the ultimate rent schedule, but it is to be hoped that the market will allow the devel-oper an opportunity to recoup more than enough for expenses and mort-gage payments. In the past, rent projections—or pro formas as they are commonly called—were often made in the quiet of an office, where the addition of an extra $30 or $40 to the rent schedule involved only an era-sure. Rents are often the "plug" number to balance the owner's books. If costs exceed projections, rents may be pushed a little higher—initially as well as in subsequent years. Sometimes the manager is ostensibly "asked," but is actually told, to endorse a rent schedule that has no relationship to the actual marketplace.

When a new property comes into the market, there is a degree of the unknown regarding the amount of rent that can be achieved. The rents that the manager uses for comparison usually belong to properties that are older, even if by only a few months. The manager's product is brand-new, and it should have some features and appointments that haven't yet been seen in the marketplace. If nothing else, "brand-new" typically commands a higher price. New things generally cost more as time marches on, so the new property should qualify for higher rent on that score alone. The manager's experience as a manager of existing rental units may affect his or her judgment in establishing the rent levels of a new property that is just coming into the market. While managers tend to be conservative (low) in their estimate of rents, owners tend to err on the high side. If the problems associated with the wrong rent schedule are to be avoided, managers and owners should both work harder to acquire rent-setting skills.

The next sections will examine the most commonly used methods of establishing a schedule of rents for a property that is new to the market.

Cost versus What the Market Will Bear

The most common initial pricing method in the rental business has little scientific basis and focuses almost exclusively on what is possible in the marketplace. It combines a knowledge of what is needed to pay the bills and retire the debt with the awareness that all can be lost if vacant units linger too long in the market. This method, even with its lack of "science," occasionally produces an acceptable rent schedule. This is because a good part of achieving more rent is simply having the nerve to ask for it. If costs are high, the need for more rent exists. A little "stretch" in the asking rent usually produces more revenue. Use of this arithmetic simplicity often continues, however, and that is where problems arise.

Most developers and managers want to find a rent pattern that meets their objectives on paper and has been developed using some element of reason. This usually produces two or at most three rent levels for each apartment style. If, for example, the subject property is a two-story garden complex and the second floor units are in the greatest demand, a rent spread of, say, 2 percent may be initiated between the first and second floor units. A second layer of price differences may be adopted to adjust for the greater desirability of units facing a park rather than the parking lot. Next, another amount is chosen to separate the different-sized units. There might be a fifty-dollar difference between the efficiency and the one-bedroom units and a ninety-dollar difference between the one- and two-bedroom apartments. All the rents added together total the rent schedule that is necessary to make things balance. That's it. It's simple; it's fast, and it is to be hoped that the customer will accept the results of the formula.

Unfortunately, this system rarely works. Rental customers are keen shoppers, and they will quickly discover the flaws of such a system. The flaws come in the form of perceived bargains; prospects will quickly take advantage of the bargain units. After examining a number of units, the prospects will recognize that all of the one-bedroom apartments are not equal—some may have better views than others or there may be units with a little something extra. When there is no price differential to equalize desirability, the better units will be taken first, while the now over-priced, less-desirable units remain vacant. Unless you are marketing a development with units of identical layout, view, and access, the pricing must reflect the differences that exist among the apartments. This means a pricing system with a bit more "science."

Total Square Feet

Another common method used to set rent is to divide the total rent dollars needed by the sum of the square feet of all the units. That gives the rent pricing practitioner the necessary rent per square foot. After that, it is an easy matter to calculate the rent levels of each apartment size rounded to the nearest $5 or $10. The thought behind this is that people are really renting space, so the rents should reflect only the amount of space rented. The square foot method will get owners and managers into a good bit of trouble, however. Yes, people do rent space for money, but there are many other variables that come into play that make this system almost worthless. Apartments that are smaller in terms of number of rooms as well as square feet carry a disproportionately higher share of the rent burden. The difference in square footage between a two-bedroom split and a two-bedroom, one-bathroom apartment can be slight, but the marketplace rent levels are likely to be significantly different. This is because certain layouts are in favor and as a result command more rent, regardless of size. Also, an exclusive consideration of size does not take two important things into account: utilization of space and the fact that in every marketplace there is a maximum rent limit that tenants will pay. Computer programs do exist that can make mathematical adjustments between unit types, but the weighting process for different features depends upon empirical data that must be constantly updated to reflect current market trends.

Comparison Grid Analysis

The comparison grid analysis system is a technique to help assure that a competitive schedule of rental rates is developed. The idea is this: A manager who is responsible for establishing rent levels for a property that is either new to the market or has undergone a remodeling program should be able to put the rent on his or her property through a series of plus and minus adjustments. This idea was developed back in the 1930s and was originally applied to office buildings. Later, it became a favorite of appraisers as they searched for ways to equalize and quantify rent levels in the market in relation to those of the property being appraised.

By making adjustments to the rental rates of comparable properties, allowing for varying features, sizes, and appointments, the analyst tries to simulate a typical prospect's application of value. For example, the manager may decide that an extra 150 square feet in an apartment is worth

Comparison Grid

Unit Type: _____

Item	Subject	Comparable #1		Comparable #2		Comparable #3	
	Description	Description	+ (−) Adj.	Description	+ (−) Adj.	Description	+ (−) Adj.
Property							
Current Rent							
Location							
Age and Condition							
Appearance							
Parking							
Amenities							
Area of Unit							
Carpeting							
Appliances							
Drapes or Blinds							
Storage or Deck							
Utilities							
Net Adj. (Tot.)							
Adj. Rent	$						
Per Sq Ft							

$12.50 per month, or that a dishwasher is worth $5.50 per month. The evaluation process differs depending on the person completing the comparison(s) and, more particularly, the style preferred by the person who trained that individual. The more common approach is to *subtract allowances in categories in which the comparable units are better than the subject apartment and to add an allowance when the comparable properties are less desirable than the subject.*

There are some important drawbacks to this system that should be discussed. The most obvious is the weighting of the endless possible differences that exist among apartment properties. Furthermore, for the analysis to have any degree of accuracy, it should be performed individually for each apartment style and size. For example, the weighting for a dishwasher in a two-bedroom apartment might carry a value of $7.50, while the same appliance may only be given a value of $4 in an efficiency apartment. Setting the dollar amount of the adjustments poses an even bigger problem. Many people who use this system limit their adjustments to five-dollar or ten-dollar increments. This almost always produces an incorrect indication of the proper rent level. The schedule of charges and credits must not only be broad but also deal with some rather finite estimates of the value of different features and appointments. An extra foot or two of closet space is probably not worth $5 per month, but it is worth something to a prospect who has a lot of clothes. Added counter space, a frost-free refrigerator, gas versus electricity for cooking, a good layout versus a marginal one—all of these features are worth something. Sometimes differences are valued in pennies, sometimes in dollars. The estimates are almost always arbitrary and usually reflect only the opinion of the manager who is making the schedule—and is probably not in the market for an apartment. The system also depends on the ability of the competition to set rents properly because the rents being developed are based on those of the competition. Finally, it is important to remember that rents are being set for the future while the comparisons are based on rents that were set some time ago.

While the comparison grid analysis calls attention to the importance and value of different features and appointments, it is most difficult to implement properly. This method is widely taught but is little used in practice because it is so difficult to document and quantify the myriad differences.

Best-of-Type Pricing

As with setting any price, the most fundamental ingredient of setting rent is a thorough understanding of the marketplace and the rates being charged by competitors. Once equipped with this information, the practitioner can do a creditable job of setting rent, regardless of the exact name of the method. Best-of-type pricing involves breaking the units down into groups of like kind. In other words, all of the one-bedroom units with an alcove would make up one group and one-bedroom units with a den would constitute another. Once these groups are identified, the person responsible for setting the rents should visit each and every unit. It is necessary to identify the best individual unit in each group. Remember, the units are basically the same; that is how they came to be in the same group. The differences will exist, however, in their access, view, or some subtle feature or benefit. Perhaps only a limited number of the units in the grouping have an extra window, closet, or niche. After carefully reviewing each unit, the manager should determine which apartment is the most desirable. That knowledge, coupled with an understanding of the marketplace in general, should lead to a determination of the highest rent that can be achieved. It is important to consider the total number of units in each size category. In a development of, say, one hundred units, ten units of a certain type should produce a more aggressive rent than fifty units of a given type. Unless the unit layout is completely unacceptable, a shortage of supply usually increases a unit's desirability and thus adds to the rent. After taking the supply of a unit type into consideration, a rent amount should be set for the best apartment of that type. Then the runner-up should be revisited to determine how much it's worth relative to the absolute best. The answer might very well be that there is too little difference to quantify. If that is the case, then it should have the same rent as the very best unit in this group. Continuing to the second runner-up, deductions should be made to balance its desirability against that of the best in its grouping. Again, the deductions can and should be small if the differences are small. The system should not be compromised to gain a rhythm or to establish an easily remembered pattern. Computers are available to do the arithmetic; one should concentrate on simulating what the customer will do in terms of weighting the difference. Moving in descending order of desirability to the worst unit in the group, appropriate deductions should be made along the way. The process is repeated for each apartment type.

The major problem with best-of-type pricing is that it is slow, requires repeated trips to the apartment units, and cannot be done sitting in the office. If done correctly, it will almost always produce the largest total rent dollars and it will contribute to a more balanced rent-up of the property. This happens because an attempt has been made to do what the renting public will do: desirability has been regulated with the use of different rent levels. This should prevent renters from snapping up bargain-priced units while the less-desirable units are vacant and priced at a rent that is unacceptable to the renting public. Best-of-type pricing takes the following issues into consideration.

Status and Rent.   In setting apartment rents, there are a number of valuable lessons to be learned. First of all, housing is very much a status symbol. It is one of the principal ways to display personal achievement. Luxury high-rise buildings satisfy the desire for status identification with their impressive entryways and lobbies and with amenities such as doormen and a concierge. Garden complexes offer gatehouses, private clubs, and elaborate recreational facilities. These extras receive the most attention when residents boast about the facilities to their friends; actual use by residents is less significant than their status appeal. If there was no desire for status identification, housing requirements could be met with functional, sterile cubes. Property managers should recognize this fact before they begin setting rents for their housing units.

The American buying public believes that if something costs more, it must be better. This method of determining value is based partly on national tradition and partly on status appeal. If rents are competitive (i.e., the same as or less expensive than most other developments), the property may lose more than needed revenue—status appeal is also lost. This loss is crucial because status appeal is often factored into the decision-making process—sometimes consciously, sometimes unconsciously.

An example, something that has been used successfully for a number of years, proves the importance of these principles. The manager of a high-rise building has only to redecorate the common areas of the top floor or even the top two floors—install superior carpeting and wall covering in the public corridors; add some costly but dramatic improvements such as a marble wall or rich woodwork around the elevator doors, maybe some expensive-looking corridor lighting or decorative ashtray urns; and replace the entrance to each apartment with wood-grained doors and high-quality hardware including a distinctive door-knocker. Even though these improvements are only in the common corridor, the manager can charge 3 to 6 percent more rent per month for each of these apartments. The apartments themselves are identical to those on the lower floors. Nevertheless, the premier floors will not only command exceptional rent but also be in the greatest demand. Why? Status identification—a person's need to show superiority. Friends who visit the residents on your specially decorated floors will appreciate the extravagance and understand that there is an associated cost. This is the essence of status appeal.

Garden apartment properties often capitalize on the status principle by creating a special area of *limited-edition units*. Usually the manager will choose a secluded location or one that has a better natural setting than the rest of the development. This area may be fenced-off or in some way separated from most of the other units. Special additions might include landscaping, individualized entryways, jumbo patios, wooden decks, screened-in porches, bay windows, and private gardens. Interior upgrades can also increase the variety and value of such apartments.

The desire to impress others is demonstrated in many ways. You don't have to work in property management very long to know about the proliferation of requests for service around major holidays. During these times residents want problems corrected and improvements made to their apartments because friends and relatives will be visiting. Your residents want everything to look just right. People's homes reflect their achievements; your residents won't appear very successful if they are living in a broken-down apartment. A property manager's sensitivity to these preferences will prove effective in setting and achieving maximum rents.

Absorption Rate and Rent Level.   It is essential to have a good sense of the number of units that can be absorbed into the marketplace at your initial rent levels. In addition to introducing new units at an acceptable level, rents must be set so they represent good value and, as a result, produce a well-paced rent-up. What must be avoided is a problem known as "biting your tail." You don't want to bring too many units "on stream," nor do you want to price apartments so high that you find yourself with units that have never been rented at the same time you face the problem of dealing with lease renewals on units rented earlier in the leasing campaign.

When you are in the rent-up stage for more than one year (with a single phase), it is usually a sure sign that your development is at odds with the forces of supply and demand. The problems are considerable when you are trying to rent the last of the units and you must begin negotiating renewals with those early renters. Chances are that if the initial rent-up has taken almost a year to complete, you have offered bonuses, specials, or concessions; the existing residents will want their share as part of their renewal requirements. Ideally, you want to select a schedule of rents that represents enough of a bargain so that the units are all rented before the renewal cycle begins. This can make the difference between a successful complex and one that is constantly fighting a vacancy problem.

Views.   People place considerable value on the views from their apartments. There is more to this subject, however, than you might expect. Where they exist, lake, ocean, or mountain views are very important during the day and even more so at times of sunrise and sunset. Yet these views often have little value after dark when most people return from work. Hence, it is important to visit each of the units at night during the rent-setting process, to witness the evening view and to determine its appropriate value. In urban environments, a city view with its endless patterns of light has as much appeal as a lake or mountain view does elsewhere.

It has long been assumed that a person who rents an apartment on a higher floor gets a better view. However, as one proceeds above the mid-point in a high-rise building, the improvement in the view is negligible. You can test this theory yourself by taking someone to the fifteenth floor of a high-rise building to look out the window and note the view. The next step is to blindfold your companion and go up and down in the elevator to confuse his or her sense of location. Finally, go to the nineteenth floor and remove the blindfold so your companion can look out the window. Without the help of a relatively significant landmark, chances are it will be impossible for that individual to detect the additional four floors of height.

Fifteenth floor views and nineteenth floor views on the same side of the same building are essentially the same. The only way to discern the difference in location is by the apartment number on the door. Therefore, any rent differences between two such units should be slight. There should be little or no discount for loss of view and only a small discount to account for the loss of status appeal that results from not being higher in the building.

Floor or Pattern Pricing

Because there is a pattern of units on each floor or in each building, it's tempting to strive for a neat pattern when setting rental rates. Rents that follow a uniform pattern on paper rarely reflect the actual attributes of individual units. Pattern pricing is usually the result of an owner or manager choosing to do the pricing in the comfort of an office. Since prospective residents will make their decisions by carefully checking availabilities and weighing what they see against the rent being charged, the person setting the rent should be just as careful.

Let's look at an example, a building 25 stories tall with 24 floors of 12 apartments each—a total of 288 units. The residential floors are numbered 1 through 24, and the four corner units on each floor are two-bedroom apartments. The remainder are one-bedroom units. For convenience, I'll discuss only the two-bedroom units on the front corners of the building. The front of the building faces a row of similar buildings across a wide boulevard. Twenty-five feet away from one side of the building is an aging nine-story apartment residence. On the other side, there is a picturesque church set in a large park.

Pricing by floor results in the rent structure for these two tiers of two-bedroom units as shown in the figure on the next page; rents increase floor-by-floor in six-dollar increments moving upward from the midpoint of the building, with a ten-dollar increment for the top two floors. Descending from the midpoint, rents decrease floor-by-floor by the same six-dollar increment used in the escalation of rent, with a ten-dollar reduction in rent for the bottom floor. The midpoint or base rent is slightly higher on the side of the building facing the park and church than it is on the side facing the old building.

This rent schedule was simple to put together and it follows a pattern that's easy to remember. The benefits stop there, however. For purposes of comparison, let's use some of the principles we discussed earlier and apply the best-of-type pricing method to the same building.

Pattern Pricing

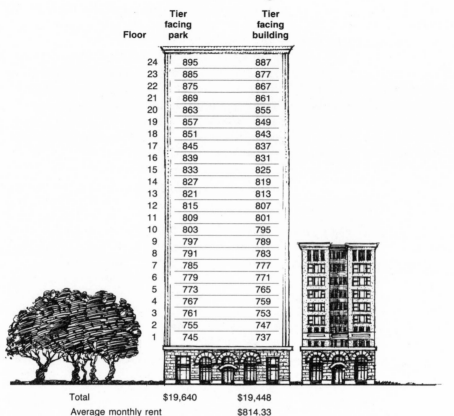

Floor	Tier facing park	Tier facing building
24	895	887
23	885	877
22	875	867
21	869	861
20	863	855
19	857	849
18	851	843
17	845	837
16	839	831
15	833	825
14	827	819
13	821	813
12	815	807
11	809	801
10	803	795
9	797	789
8	791	783
7	785	777
6	779	771
5	773	765
4	767	759
3	761	753
2	755	747
1	745	737

Total	$19,640	$19,448
Average monthly rent		$814.33

Matching Price to Value

The best-of-type pricing method achieves the closest correlation between price and value. Let's apply this to the two tiers of two-bedroom apartments in the previous example. First of all, we'll change the floor numbering system. Apartments on higher floors have greater status appeal, and that means more rent dollars. Because the lobby level is about one and a half stories in height, the numbering sequence can logically begin with the third floor; the thirteenth floor can be omitted because superstitious people avoid it. The resulting top floor number is twenty-seven rather than twenty-four, as was the case in the earlier example.

After thoroughly studying the competition, the property manager identifies the best two-bedroom apartments in the building—the top apartments overlooking the church and park. Based on complete knowledge of the market, the rent for those apartments is estimated at the highest rate the market will bear. Before setting the rent, however, improvements are made to the top two floors to create special penthouse-type units. When the improvements have been made, the manager evaluates their market value. After comparing both floors and finding virtually no difference in view, the manager establishes identical rents for all of the two-bedroom penthouse-type units. Moving downward, the corner units on the next three floors are found to share the same view as the top floors, so their rent is reduced by the market value of the penthouse upgrades only. Continuing the inspection, the manager discovers that the view suffers slightly on the next three floors and the rent is lowered appropriately. Further rent reductions are applied to blocks of units to adjust for loss of view and the reduced status appeal of lower floors as we approach the middle of the building (see figure on the following page).

So far the principal difference between this pricing technique and pattern pricing relates to diverging view and status adjustments that translate into different levels of desirability. Best-of-type pricing produced a higher average rent. I haven't mentioned any rent realignment to account for the different views from the two sides of the building. Why? Because in the inspection, it was discovered that the older building does not impede views or have a negative influence above the fifteenth floor. On the fifteenth floor and below, the presence of the older building is obvious, and the rent adjustments begin to reflect this.

Pattern pricing established a difference between the sides that was maintained throughout the building. This was unnecessary on the higher floors because the view and appeal would not be affected by a nine-story building. On the floors with a view of the adjacent building's roof, careful consideration reveals that a small rent deduction is not adequate compensation for the undesirable view. When rents for apartments above the fifteenth floor on this side of the building are not reduced, it means that apartment rents on the lower floors can be discounted substantially to compensate for the loss of view.

Once again, the manager doesn't want to make the mistake of allowing bargain-rent apartments to exist. The bargains will be snapped up, leaving behind the most difficult-to-rent apartments.

In the best-of-type pricing method, substantial adjustments were made for the less-desirable units, and at the same time the rent rates were higher overall than those determined by pattern pricing. Even more important is the fact that the building will undoubtedly rent up faster using the best-of-type rent schedule. While pattern pricing looks good on paper, the best-of-type method simulates what prospects do—namely, match price to value.

You may wonder if maintaining different rates for units of similar size will confuse prospects. The answer is yes. Most complexes have little variance in their pricing structure, so there will be some resistance to establishing a proper pricing system. Rental agents may also be confused. However, prospects are not shown every unit in the building, and discussion of rents should be in the context of a specific unit. When you prepare rent

Matching Price to Value (Best-of-Type Pricing)

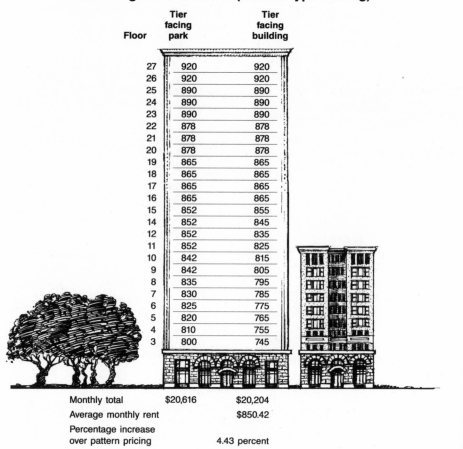

Floor	Tier facing park	Tier facing building
27	920	920
26	920	920
25	890	890
24	890	890
23	890	890
22	878	878
21	878	878
20	878	878
19	865	865
18	865	865
17	865	865
16	865	865
15	852	855
14	852	845
12	852	835
11	852	825
10	842	815
9	842	805
8	835	795
7	830	785
6	825	775
5	820	765
4	810	755
3	800	745

Monthly total	$20,616	$20,204
Average monthly rent		$850.42
Percentage increase over pattern pricing		4.43 percent

schedules detailing the rent for each unit, much of the confusion is eliminated; at the same time, prospects can be assured that your rents are firmly established and not subject to negotiation.

The same principles that are used in setting rents in large high-rise buildings will also work for smaller buildings or garden-type housing. There are differences in virtually every housing unit for the same reasons: view, layout, access, size, and floor level. The pricing procedure remains essentially the same.

MAKING ADJUSTMENTS

Mistakes will be made—no matter how careful the manager is in the initial pricing of a property. For instance, it is quite possible to misjudge the desirability of certain units. Constant review and adjustment is necessary to prevent such a mistake from becoming a costly problem. Unfortunately, the unskilled property manager does not always recognize mistakes. To illustrate this point, ask a manager which units are in the greatest demand, and often the quick response will be that one specific type of unit is always full. The manager should realize that when units rent too quickly, or if demand is extremely heavy, those apartments are underpriced.

Assuming that you have a good product and you present it well, the pace of the rent-up period will be controlled by the rent schedule. If certain unit types lease overnight, the best units have been given away at bargain prices. Prospective residents have discovered something in that particular unit type that makes it more desirable than the other apartments of the same size—the rent is too low. Maybe the renting public is willing to spend more than the manager thought for larger kitchens, extra closets, and so forth. Or maybe renters know from experience that the city view from a high-rise is worth more than a lake view—something the manager failed to take into account.

While it's important to rent as many apartments as quickly as possible, it is equally important to ensure a relatively even rent-up pace. Admittedly, the state of the economy nationally and locally will play a role in the amount of demand for different unit sizes, and this should be taken into account. Generally speaking, each unit type should rent at approximately the same rate. A rapid rent-up of a particular layout or unit type indicates a faulty rent schedule.

Upward Adjustments

The easiest way to make fast-renting units less desirable is to raise the rent. This makes the slower-renting units more desirable because of the wider gap between specific rents. Reaction time is most important. If the manager reacts slowly, the fast-moving units will be completely rented before the rents can be raised. On the other hand, there must be enough time to identify a genuine trend.

If the manager cannot determine why one type of unit is renting faster than the others, the rent for the fast-moving unit should be increased in small amounts—for example, four-dollar and eight-dollar increments—until the proper balance is reached. The reasons some units are more popular and rent up faster can often be determined by asking applicants why they made their choices. People will usually provide a ready answer. Typically, apartments with layouts similar to those in the decorated models rent faster than others. Prospects choose such layouts hoping to duplicate the decorating ideas seen in the model. Generally, the manager should anticipate this extra demand and set higher rents for the apartments similar to the models. These increases should be made after the initial rent schedule has been created. Normally, a premium of $6 or $7 per month can be safely added to the rents for these units. You may be puzzled by this idea in light of my recommendation that you use less-desirable units for your models; truly, I am not contradicting myself. All units with the same layout as the model will command higher rent because the exciting decorating possibilities of that particular layout are immediately apparent to prospects.

Rental progress and rent rates should be reviewed each week. If rent-up is progressing rapidly, a daily review would be reasonable. The property manager's job is to maximize rental income, and constant attention and review are needed in order to ensure that outcome.

To summarize:

- If certain apartments are renting much faster than others, raising the rents of the fast movers will increase the desirability of the slow movers and produce an even flow of rentals.
- If the entire property is renting much faster than the competition, consider increasing all rents until you begin to experience some resistance. The property manager's task is not only to rent all the units but also to achieve maximum rental income.

There are comparatively few problems with rent adjustments when they are increases. There are always difficulties associated with a weakening market, however, when downward adjustments would appear to be indicated. There is little complaint from existing residents when new residents rent the same unit type for more money, but residents will definitely raise objections when new renters pay less.

Downward Adjustments

Just as upward rent adjustments are made in response to market changes, certain conditions may dictate the need for downward adjustments. If the product is in top-notch shape and is being presented properly, yet some or all of the apartments are not renting, a downward rent adjustment may be in order. Rent reductions are generally only appropriate in situations of substantial vacancies when an over-ambitious rent schedule is interfering with a steady rent-up.

Assume, for example, that a manager has a total of 240 apartments, eighty of which are one-bedroom units with a den. The manager believes that this unit type is more desirable and therefore worth more rent. Initial rent-up of this unit type is slow, however; of those eighty, only ten have been rented. A check of the market reveals that the competition is experiencing pretty much the same problem. Remember, rent levels determine how quickly a residential property rents. In our example, assume that the manager had been successful in leasing the regular one-bedroom units at a lower rent. It is only in attempting to rent the one-bedroom-plus-den apartments that resistance was encountered. While the manager knows there are people who need only a single bedroom but would like the luxury of a separate den, he or she doesn't know precisely how much more these people are willing to pay for a den. Pricing the one-bedroom apartments with a den the same as the one-bedroom apartments without a den should produce a flurry of rentals, but instinct might indicate that a slightly higher rent could be achieved for the larger unit. The question becomes, how much more?

When errors are detected, the rent schedule should be adjusted accordingly. In our example of a building in which only ten of eighty apartments were rented, a rent reduction was obviously necessary. Once the nature of the problem is identified, the manager must determine the extent of the required adjustment.

Adjustments do not necessarily have to be in the form of rent reductions, however. Rent reductions have a negative effect on the value of the property and should be used *only* when other choices are not available. Before making a downward adjustment in rent, the manager should ask one question: "Is there a way that I can improve the apartment I am offering so that it is worth the rent I am asking?" If the answer to this question is "yes," the manager should make the improvement rather than reduce the rent.

Sometimes a rent reduction may prove to be the manager's only alternative. This is particularly true in new complexes where it is difficult to improve the property. In a new development, rent reductions should be extended to those people who rented earlier at the higher rents. Using the previous example, the ten people who initially rented the one-bedroom-plus-den apartments should now be charged the same rent as is set for the seventy apartments that have yet to be rented. Ideally, they should also receive a refund for the excess rent they have already paid. The manager may choose to handle the refund by issuing rent credits or rent coupons. Again, retroactive refunds are necessary if the complex has been open for only a few months; they are not recommended when rents are lowered in established developments.

Failure to pass rent reductions along to existing residents may cause many problems. In particular, it guarantees poor resident relations. Ultimately, resident dissatisfaction will cost you more than the money you forfeited by reducing all rents for a unit type. If the need for the reduction is due to an initial pricing error, early residents should not have to suffer as a result of your faulty pricing policy.

Rent Level and Property Value

Rental property is an investment, and its value as an investment is directly related to rental income. That is why any reduction in rent has such wide-reaching effects.

A common method of ascertaining the value of an apartment building is by using the *income capitalization approach*. In this method, value is estimated by dividing the net operating income by a desired *capitalization rate*. "Cap" rates are established by investors in the market, and they vary with the type, age, and location of a particular building. Assume for the moment that the desired capitalization rate is 10 percent. This means that informed investors are currently seeking a 10 percent return on their investments. Using that 10 percent "cap" rate, every dollar of rent reduction has the effect of reducing the value of the building $120 ($1.00 X 12 months = $12.00 ÷ by .10 = $120). As you can see, a hasty and unsupported reduction in rent can cause a serious decline in value. It is necessary to pursue every available opportunity to maintain the rent schedule, even if it involves costly improvements.

Concessions

When the rental market begins to soften, the banners and advertisements offering free rent appear. This is certainly the oldest and most commonly used method to attract new renters while preserving the basic rent level. Owners sitting with an unusual number of vacancies are willing to give one or more month's rent for the security of a lease and the knowledge that the rent loss will stop soon. The concession has both its good and bad points.

Concessions, or *rent holidays* as they are often called, became particularly prevalent during the Great Depression of the 1930s. Several month's free rent served as an enticement to gain extra rentals in a most competitive marketplace. Most owners were eager to sell their property and recoup what they could after the stock market crash. There was little market for half empty buildings, so owners and managers did what they could to fill their properties, including granting concessions. Many buyers were hurt during this period, having based their expectations on artificially inflated rent rolls; these buyers did their arithmetic using twelve months of the stated rent when, in fact, considering the concessions that were granted to attract new residents, the effective annual rent only included eleven or in some cases just ten months' rent. The problem became so severe, laws were commonly enacted that required owners to mark the face of the lease in large letters indicating that a concession was granted. The words "concession granted" were to alert the buyer to investigate the amount and extent of the concessions and to act as a warning to use extra care when calculating the purchase price and terms. Most of these laws are still on the books. During a downturn in the economy, it wouldn't take too long before another round of litigation would be initiated by buyers who thought that they had been duped.

The concession enjoys its day in the sun when times are tough and vacancies are many. That is the same time that a rental property owner is struggling to keep his or her development and pay the bills. It is exactly the wrong time to be giving away rent. The whole idea behind concessions is to use them as a means to attract new rent-paying residents and stop the losses. This presents a dilemma: How do you get the word out to potential new residents without rubbing it in to your existing residents that they do not qualify for the same treatment that is now being offered to perfect strangers? Some owners and managers just ignore their existing residents and hang a banner or insert an advertisement announcing the concession. Some even add words that specifically exclude present residents in case they would try to claim the same deal for themselves. It is very difficult to explain why an existing resident is not entitled to the same benefit offered to the public at large, and this can certainly result in residents deciding to move when their leases are up—to seek "revenge" and to take advantage of similar offers being made by nearby competitors. *There is no way to promote a concession to the public while keeping it a secret from your existing residents.*

The concession can, however, bridge a short-lived downturn in rental activity, thus protecting the integrity of the established rent roll. Giving a month's free rent up front is better in many ways than reducing the monthly rent by a prorated one-twelfth each month. First of all, people need "chunks" of money, not "dribbles." In other words, a single savings of $600 is much better than twelve fifty-dollar reductions. The money will come in handy to cover the costs of the move or perhaps some new furnishings. Small amounts over time have a way of getting lost with the everyday bills, so the advantage has much less impact. Meanwhile, the manager is hoping that the market will strengthen quickly so that when the lease comes up for renewal, further concessions will not be necessary. Knowing that he or she must give up a month's rent, the smart manager opts to get it over with immediately. While twelve months of a smaller prorated amount might be more helpful in the ongoing cash crunch, it is much better to miss the first month's rent and get the resident accustomed to paying the higher monthly amount. When residents ask what their new neighbors are paying, it is clearly better to quote the "retail" rent rather than the net discounted rent. If an increase is achievable at renewal time, the manager wants the increase to be added to the basic rent, not to the discounted figure.

The concession is probably the best possible closing tool. Granted, it shouldn't be used to get more people to walk in the door, but it can have quite an effect on a prospect who is debating whether to rent or keep on looking. However, it is rare indeed to find a leasing person who truly knows how and when to use the concession as a leasing tool. Given the authority to offer a prospect a month's free rent, the agent may blurt out the offer in the first few moments of the leasing interview, and this naturally has an adverse effect on the closing process. When they are shopping, people want what is in demand, not what must be given away. The offer of a free month's rent in the early part of the interview leads the prospect to the conclusion that the available apartments have not been very well accepted. It serves as a signal to the prospect that he or she should look for reasons why the apartments are not renting.

The leasing agent must continue with the basics of renting: developing a rapport, determining the prospect's motivating force and timing, demonstrating the benefits, and asking for the order. In order to be effective, the offer of free rent must be presented as a *personal accommodation* to that particular prospect; it should appear as a gesture of goodwill to help the new resident get started. The term "free rent," or the word "concession" should not be mentioned.

One form of concession is frequently granted but not thought of as such. An example of this occurs when a prospect arrives and announces that he or she doesn't need the apartment for another two months. If the manager is willing to commit a particular apartment to that individual today, for a move-in date in the future, he or she is effectively granting a concession. The manager is giving up the hope of rent during the interim months in return for the prospect's commitment to lease. This is a business decision and there is certainly nothing wrong with doing this. The problems often develop after the decision has been made.

Let's say that the prospect subsequently asks for permission to move in early or to take possession of the apartment and begin making some improvements before the actual starting date on the lease. Many managers answer with a loud "no," or they ask for a prorated rent for the extra days of occupancy. It is my opinion that the rent is lost once you have made the business decision to give it up by agreeing to a later move-in date—so why not allow the early occupancy? Doing so will cost you absolutely nothing and may very well save the property the utility charges on that unit for the time in question. It will also strengthen your hand with renewals because it precludes existing residents from bringing up the fact that units around them have been vacant for extended periods of time. This situation is much the same as going to a hotel that has your room made-up and available at nine in the morning on the day of check-in. The management can demand that you wait until the posted check-in time of 3:00 P.M., but to what advantage? They might as well extend the courtesy of early occupancy to you. Is there any reason that apartment managers shouldn't do the same?

Coupons.   These are merely concessions in a prepackaged form. They range from very primitive "rent dollars" printed at a local quick-printer to elaborately engraved certificates that are numbered and bear the name of the recipient. There are many situations in the operation of an apartment complex where dollar-value coupons can be used effectively. You might choose to offer a renewal reward to an existing resident for his or her commitment to a lease renewal. You may find yourself at a competitive disadvantage because you have electric heat, and residents serve notice that they intend to move when they receive a high bill in January or February. Coupons that can be applied toward rent would certainly help residents balance their budgets during those months and possibly prevent a number of move-outs. Residents may be rewarded with a dollar-value coupon when they pay their rent before the beginning of the month. New residents can be awarded coupons as a method of concession. This maintains the rent roll while letting the resident pick the months in which the discount will have the most favorable effect on their budgets. Referral bonuses to both the existing resident and the person being referred can be readily paid in the form of coupons. Discounts offered through an arrangement with local employers is another way coupons can be used. Some developments even allow holders of coupons to purchase improvements or upgrades for their units.

A coupon program is most effective when the production and distribution of the coupons is done with the same care that would be given to real currency, treating them like traveler's checks, for example. Spend the money necessary to produce a coupon with an engraved appearance on the best quality paper. Apply serial numbers and designate space for the signatures of both issuer and recipient. Twenty-dollar and fifty-dollar denominations are usually sufficient for most transactions. The coupons are often bound in an inexpensive wallet or binder, again just like traveler's checks. Typical limitations would be that no more than two coupons can be redeemed in any one month and that the coupons are neither assignable nor transferable.

Deficiency Discount.   A deficiency discount is a different form of concession in which the resident's rent is reduced in return for accepting an apartment with a real or imagined deficiency. The thought is that a resident willing to move into an apartment with a stain on the carpet or a burned spot on a countertop should get a break. The rationale is simple: The owner saves money on repairs.

Deficiency discounts should never be permitted. Look at it this way: By reducing the rent, the manager is not only reducing the net operating income but also lowering the value of the building. Eventually the repairs will have to be made. Repair costs will never be less than they are today; chances are they'll be greater. Also, the person who is willing to live with a deficiency may not be the most desirable resident. Repair the defect and rent the apartment at market value.

Exchange for Service.   The exchange of rent for service is *the practice of renting an apartment at a reduced rate to someone who promises to perform needed services* for the building. For example, a member of the police force might provide part-time security service to the complex in return for a rent reduction.

These practices began in developments with more vacant apartments than money, and they are unacceptable. The complex rarely gets full value on a sustaining basis. It is an unprofessional approach that detracts from the quality of the development.

Sometimes a free apartment is provided to avoid employee withholding taxes, thereby giving the recipient a form of tax-free income. As I said in chapter 3, income taxes on the value of the apartment are always required unless living in the on-site housing is a condition of employment for the benefit of and as a convenience to the owner. When housing is traded for services, the value of that housing is taxable and social security contributions are always required on the value of the apartment. Failure to pay either of these is illegal.

If the apartment complex falls under federal Wage and Hour regulations, there is also the risk of violating the Wage and Hour Act with regard to the minimum wage and premium pay after forty hours. Granted, the services being traded for are needed, but trading is the wrong approach. The manager should hire and pay for the needed services just as with other obligations and collect rent for all of the apartments. The manager who heeds this advice will bring in more money and provide better quality service overall.

RAISING RENTS IN ESTABLISHED PROPERTIES

The discussion so far has dealt with structuring rents in a new apartment complex and the up-and-down adjustments necessary to achieve proper pricing. I'll now turn my attention to the methods and timing for increasing the existing rents in established rental properties. This is an unpopular subject but probably one of the most important concerns managers have in the operation of multifamily housing. It is unpopular, of course, from a resident's standpoint because residents dislike rent increases. Apartment managers also find the idea of raising rents unpleasant and, therefore, resist rent increases as much as possible.

Raising rent is necessary to offset increases in operating expenses, to help absorb higher debt service costs, and to maintain a fair margin of profit in an inflationary economy. All of these are valid points, but they are not operative if certain market indicators say otherwise. In other words, additional rent may be warranted; but if the market signals read "stop" or "caution," the owner and manager must respect the indications or face an even greater loss through increased vacancy. I have found there to be four basic indicators that tell the manager whether or not the time is right to raise rent. They work together to tell you the time to proceed with a rent increase, when to proceed with caution and some degree of restraint, and when to forego an increase altogether. Note that this discussion of raising rents assumes there are no rent control laws governing the amount one is allowed to charge for space; rent increases for rent-controlled properties must be considered within the guidelines of the law.

Vacancies

Empirical data over a number of years indicate that the vacancy level of a property is the most important single indicator. The ratio of vacant units to the total number of units reveals the state of the market, the management and condition of the property, and acceptability of the current rent levels.

The references to vacancy here are to physical vacancy rather than economic vacancy. The difference between the two is as follows. Physical vacancy is the percentage of the total number of units that are vacant and available for rent. For example, if there are five units vacant and available for rent in a development with a total of one hundred units, it is said that the physical vacancy is 5 percent. Economic vacancy indicates the number of units that are out of the income stream. Using the same example, in addition to the five vacant units, there might be two units that have been rented for the month after next—these units are vacant, but no longer available. They are not producing any income at this point in time, so their lost revenue is part of the economic loss. Other components of economic vacancy are: units used as models, offices, or staff apartments; units that are damaged or unrentable; and units occupied by residents who are behind in their rent.

The decision whether to proceed with a rent increase should follow the guidelines below.

Less Than 5 Percent (Physical Vacancy)	Proceed With Rent Increase
Between 5 Percent and 8 Percent	Proceed With Caution
More Than 8 Percent	Wait For Improved Market (Review Again In Three Months)

Vacancies, or more specifically, excess vacancies, carry the strongest weighting of the four market signals. Generally, it is advisable to defer the implementation of a rent increase when physical vacancies exceed 8 percent. This vacancy record is signaling that something is seriously wrong in either the marketplace, the property, or both. To push for higher rents at this time will only work to exacerbate an already difficult situation. A rent increase could very well lead to an easing of resident selectivity, increased move-outs, loss of image, higher operating costs, and considerable economic recovery. When vacancies are above 8 percent, work to improve your present position before proceeding with a rent increase.

Concessions

When concessions are being granted, there is a reason—they usually signal a weak market. A specific examination of concessions provides a backstop to the possibility that vacancies are low because the manager has been granting extensive concessions. In such cases, the occupancy level does not reflect the state of the market. Earlier in this chapter, I talked about one type of concession: renting an apartment for an agreed date in the future. Anything over forty days (the typical lead time in renting an apartment) would indicate a market weakness and should be included as a concession. The guidelines in this category are these.

No Concessions	Proceed With Rent Increase
One Month Concession	Proceed, But With Caution
More Than One Month	Do Not Proceed If There Are Any Other "Stop" Indicators

Delinquencies

When times are tough, most managers ease-up their collection efforts, and that quickly increases the amount of collection losses. The delinquency indicator provides the fastest feedback of market trends and should be carefully monitored.

The percentages listed below refer to the amount of money that is outstanding at the end of a given month. For example, if the gross possible income totals $40,000 and $400 is outstanding at the end of the month, it is said that the delinquency rate is 1 percent. In the same example, $800 outstanding would indicate a delinquency rate of 2 percent. If there is an ongoing legal problem with one or two residents who owe considerable amounts, these totals can be deducted from the monthly total. The same is true if your accounting system continues to build up monthly balances of residents who have skipped out and there are only minimal chances of recovering rent payments from these former residents.

Guidelines for increasing rent when there are delinquencies are detailed below.

Less Than 1 Percent Delinquency	Proceed With Rent Increase
Between 1 Percent and 2 Percent	Proceed, But With Caution
More Than 2 Percent	Do Not Proceed If There Are Any Other "Stop" Indicators

New Construction

This guideline exists to prevent the manager from making a judgment about the current marketplace without looking at what is in the "pipeline." The absorption rate of new apartments is a painfully slow one, and just a few new developments nearby can create havoc with the occupancy level of many existing developments. If a new 100-unit complex arrives on the scene, it can reduce the occupancy level of twenty similar-sized developments from a cash-flowing 95 percent to a money-losing 90 percent almost overnight. The new property has several built-in advantages. Its interest payments during the rent-up period are probably included in the construction loan, so concessions do not present the same economic hardship they do to an existing development. The new complex is blessed with all move-ins and almost no move-outs, so its weekly rent revenue appears as net gains without any offsets. The manager of a new property can be a little more cavalier with reduced rent or specials because operating expenses—especially real estate taxes, make-ready expenses, and repairs—are only a fraction of those of an established complex.

I have termed the amounts of new construction in any community "little," "some," and "lots." Quantifying these terms depends upon the size of the rental community and the absorption rate of new rental units. In a city the size of Des Moines, Iowa, "little" might be 200 units, while in a city the size of Atlanta, Georgia, "little" might refer to 2,000 units. The "some" category might be 300 units in Des Moines and 4,000 units in Atlanta. It will take some experience in a particular rental environment to quantify these three classifications. Absorption rates for new rental properties are much lower than most people think, so if you err, make sure it is on the conservative side. The final set of market signal guidelines for rent increases are as follows.

Little (New Construction)	Proceed With Rent Increase
Some	Proceed, But With Caution
Lots	Do Not Proceed If There Are Any Other "Stop" Indicators

Guideline Evaluation

If the answer to each of these guidelines is "proceed," then a rent increase is not only possible, it should be rather aggressive. The percentage of the increase should diminish as the number of "proceed" responses is replaced by "proceed with caution" indicators. One "stop" indicator is usually the absolute maximum when deciding whether to raise rents. If that one stop indicator is for vacancies, you are usually best advised to postpone a rent increase until the overall occupancy level improves. Ignoring these market signals can cause irreparable damage to an apartment community.

Once an analysis has been made and you have established the indications for market acceptance of a rent increase, the next step is to determine the amount of the increase.

DETERMINING RENT INCREASES

As with the market indicators, experience over the years provides owners and managers with some reliable benchmarks to help set the proper amount of a rent increase. These restrictions work in concert with one another, and the new rent amount should be the lowest figure after first applying each of the following tests.

First Increase

This test is provided more for precautionary reasons than as a guide. A great many developments get off to the wrong start because they ignore this principle. When considering a rent increase on the first lease anniversary of either a new property or one that has undergone a complete renovation and is now back in service, the amount of the increase must be twice the amount of what is necessary. In other words if you determine that an increase of $30 per month is needed, you should double that figure and ask for $60. Why? Because a thirty-dollar increase will only produce the desired $30 revenue if all of the leases are renewed at the beginning of the new year. This is highly unlikely because very few residential leases expire on the first of January; expirations are typically spaced throughout the year, with the largest concentration occurring during the late spring and early fall. On average, the amount of increased revenue derived from the first round of the rent increase is only one-half of what is sought. Doubling the needed increase, however, might be too much in a competitive market.

This problem only exists when leases are renewed for the first time following the property's introduction or re-introduction into the marketplace. With subsequent increases, the added revenue of the previous year's rental increase fills in the missing gaps. For example, if the lease on unit 102 does not expire until the end of June, the amount of the last rent increase continues to add new revenue relative to the previous year. This money, plus the added revenue of the next increase, approximates the desired income in the current budget year.

Income Group Influence

Income group classification will play a critical role in determining how much rents can be increased. In the subsidized classification, your decision will typically depend upon the governing body's regulations. Normally, rent increases involve an increase in the resident subsidy, and they are most often tied to either an index or some degree of proof that the property's operating expenses have increased. Other increases are a fixed percentage figure, while some are granted to maintain a given return on investment to the owner. The manager's job is really one of understanding the amount allowable as well as the timing and implementation process.

Residents in the limited- and adequate-income groups are subject to forces of supply and demand that have different limitations, depending on the particular classification. As I have said, the people who fall into the limited-income classification are struggling and very price sensitive. The demands on their income are considerable, so there is almost no room for rent increases. An increase in rent means something else must be compromised. In past years, the limited-income group has not been able to keep pace with the Consumer Price Index (CPI). When directed to the limited-income group, rent increases that have paralleled the CPI have met with resistance and have resulted in an undue level of move-outs. The safest level of rent increase appears to be 1 to 1.5 percent *less* than the current rate of increase indicated by the CPI for that locale.

Those in the adequate-income group can better afford a rent increase, and experience shows that they can tolerate increases that equal about 1 percent *more* than the current increase in the CPI. However, there are other indicators that must also be recognized before a final determination can be made as to the exact amount of a renewal increase.

The people in the ample-income group follow much the same pattern evidenced by those in the adequate-income group, but the daily lifestyle of those of ample means is less affected by the rate of increase in the CPI; these people are not as likely to move because of a rent increase that exceeds the index. People of ample income do, however, possess the wherewithal to move at their pleasure, should they decide that their rent dollars are not being well spent.

I should offer a word of caution when discussing rent increases that are related to the CPI or some other index. Occasionally newspaper reporters write stories tracking the pattern of rent increases and comparing rent increases to other items in the CPI. Of course these stories enjoy wide readership and usually earn a prominent position in the newspaper. The problem is that the information, while statistically correct, may present a deceptive picture. To illustrate this, let's assume a small city used to have a total rental housing stock of 20,000 apartments. These units were renting at an average rate of $480 per month. Now, after a building boom that has taken place over the past three years, an additional supply of 4,000 very nice apartments has come into the market. These units are brand-new and are clearly superior to anything built in prior years. These new units, on average, rent for $850 per month. The addition of these higher priced units has the effect of increasing the overall rent average from the old $480 to $542. This raises the average rent in this sample town almost 13 percent, and yet the residents of the older rental stock haven't suffered a single dollar of rent increase. The headline, "Rents Up 13 Percent!" will certainly stir up the rental community; even worse, some apartment managers may be tempted to try for the "average increase" and suffer major move-outs in the process.

Amount of Last Increase

Regardless of the other indicators, you must establish limits on the amount of a rent increase based on your pattern of previous increases. For example, if you have set a pattern of twenty-dollar increases in the last round or two of rent increases, you will have difficulty getting more than 125 percent of the past increase, or in this case, $25. When you push for a larger amount, even though some of the other indicators appear to allow for more, you will most likely face an undue level of turnover. These steps are designed to help you strike the right balance between achieving the greatest possible increase in annual revenue and suffering the least possible loss as a result of move-outs.

Typical Rent versus Street Rent

This is one of the best all around indicators to help a manager determine the proper rent level. It works on the principle that there should always be a margin between the typical rent—the most common rent currently being collected for each unit type—and the street rent being asked of prospects walking in the door today. The range that delivers the best results for me is 106 percent. The calculation works as follows. Assume that most one-bedroom units in your development are generating $700 per month. There may be a sprinkling of units going for as little as $650 per month and some recent rentals ranging above $700, but the mode (most frequent entry) is that $700 figure. To determine the street rent, the rent that you should be asking of today's rental prospects, multiply the $700 base rent by 1.06. A rent of $742 is indicated by this calculation. If this amount strikes you as too high and you would be worried about market acceptance, that is your signal to ease-up on the amount of rent increases to your renewing residents. If, on the other hand, you have been successful in obtaining rents from incoming residents at a higher level, say $750, you should assume a more aggressive posture with your next round of renewal rent increases. The idea is to maintain a differential of about 6 percent between your typical rent and your street rent. Working within these parameters, you now have the limiting factors necessary to establish the correct amount of the next increase.

Tips for Raising Rent

There are also a number of tips that will prove helpful when preparing to raise rents.

Limit Increases to Once a Year.   Pay increases tend to happen once a year and I think rent increases should too. Housing is a long-term commodity, and residents have come to expect annual rent adjustments. Some apartment managers believe that a series of closely spaced, smaller increases will result in lower resident turnover. The suggestion of a rent increase carries with it a certain irritation factor, regardless of the amount. Presenting this news twice in a period of one year almost guarantees a negative reaction—and that means needlessly high move-outs. Studies continually show that one raise of say, $30, results in far fewer moves than two semiannual raises of, say, $12.50 each.

Allow Long Lead Time.   Sixty to seventy days is the proper notice to give when a rent increase is one of the changes in the lease renewal contract. This runs contrary to the thinking of some apartment managers who believe that the shortest possible notice results in the fewest move-outs. The thought is that if people do not have much time to react, they will sign a lease rather than scurry around to look for a new home. Too many housing alternatives exist for that tactic to work; also, some residents may not be that satisfied with their current relationship with management, and will react negatively to the "rush-act."

Most people spend what they make, and they need time to adjust their budgets to accommodate a rent increase. Many residents become irate, at least initially, when faced with a rent increase. This mood will mellow as they see their neighbors accept the same increase, and brand-new residents—who have obviously shopped around for the best value—move in at similar rent levels. A long lead time prior to the start of a rent increase will help, not hurt.

Use Odd Rent Amounts.   You might get the idea that rent increases in five-dollar and ten-dollar increments are nice because they are more easily remembered, and the bookkeeping department will have an easier time with them. Unfortunately, rent increases, and for that matter initial rent amounts, cause an adverse reaction when they are in nice bracketed amounts. People interpret a twenty-five-dollar rent increase as an example of the owner getting richer and the resident getting poorer. At the same time, an increase of $26 is often perceived as an amount to answer a specific need, probably to cover increased operating costs of the same amount. Round or bracketed amounts ($25, $30, $50) are associated with the owner wanting more money at the resident's expense. Odd numbers, both in the amount of the increase and the resulting rent, suggest a closely calculated operating budget. So use $17 instead of $15, $21 instead of $20, etc. If you use a computer, you will have little trouble handling the odd amounts.

Adjust for Desirability.   The popularity of different unit types and prime locations changes from time to time and you, as manager, should be ready to adjust the rent levels accordingly. One year the two-bedroom, one-bath apartment may be the most popular. A few years later the two-bathroom units may be the "hot" apartments, and the rent levels should be adjusted to reflect this shift in favor. Sometimes second-floor units are more popular than first-floor units. If your experience bears this out, adjust the rent at renewal time to compensate for anticipated increases and decreases in demand. If you have a lot of vacancies in one type of unit and virtually no availability in another, increase the latter's rent at a higher rate and go easy on the increase for the hard-to-rent unit. It is a rare occurrence when the market and your pricing are so in balance that you can apply a percentage increase uniformly to all unit types. If you fail to make yearly adjustments, this problem becomes exaggerated when individual unit type analysis is skipped in favor of across-the-board rent increases.

Use Graduated Rents.   If you feel that the necessary rent increase will pose a hardship for the residents and cause a high rate of move-outs, use a graduated rent increase. This will involve a letter explaining that costs have risen at such a rate that a substantial rent increase is needed. The letter should state that rent will be raised in two stages because you are mindful of residents' budget restrictions. For example, you might explain that during the first seven months an additional $13 will be due each month, and during the last five months an extra $11 will be due (in other words, for the last five months of the year the total rent increase will be $24). This does not violate the one raise per year rule because the increase is announced at one time, even though it is implemented in two stages. Note the use of an odd break in the number of months and the odd rent increase amounts. Finally, the graduated rent increase should not be used two years in a row. It should be reserved for inflationary times or just after a major renovation or upgrade program has taken place.

Test the Increases on Vacancies First.   The place to test the acceptability of a higher rent is with the vacant units. After all, the people who shape the market are those who are out shopping and looking to find a different home. The person moving is exposed to much higher costs than the residents who remain where they are. If, in spite of the extra costs of moving, prospects are choosing your development—even with the new higher rent level—it is an indication that you are offering good value. This, of course, assumes that you have not lowered your entry or selection criteria. Try several units at the new price to be sure it wasn't just an anomaly and determine whether you can sustain the new rate. People with leases coming up for renewal are actively following the classified ads and they will quickly become aware of your new "going rate." When they see new high-caliber residents moving in at regular intervals, they will be reassured that your rental community and, more specifically, their apartment size and type, represent good value for the money.

Fix Up Before the Increase.   One of the reasons for raising rents is that rising costs erode the budget and prevent you from properly operating the complex. The shortage of funds almost always appears in the general maintenance level and the "showy extras." The problem is that you need the money from the rent increase to put things right and demonstrate how nice a complex you manage. It's tempting to raise the rent first, and then, with money in hand, begin the fix-up and upgrade work. That absolutely won't work. Beg or borrow the money, but the fix-up program must take place before the increase is announced.

Charge for Apartment Improvements.   When preparing a vacant apartment for the next renter, it is both common and recommended practice to make improvements to the unit that will help it rent quicker and attract a high caliber of new resident. That's fine, but with each improvement there must be a corresponding increase in the rent. For example, if you replace the floor covering in the kitchen, you must increase the rent by say, $3.50. A new carpet might necessitate an increase of $13; a new medicine cabinet, $4; new window coverings, $2.50; etc. This is done because existing residents see virtually everything that goes on in the rental community, and they certainly will learn what you have done to improve the nearby vacant unit. Your residents may just stick their heads in and look around while the work is underway, or they may be visitors in their new neighbor's apartment. You, as manager, must be in a position to offer current residents the same improvements if they inquire why their apartments don't have the same nice appointments as the new resident's. Even with the offer of a discount, most residents will likely decline when they learn that the improvements are available at an added cost. It's important for the existing residents to know that the improvements being offered to new residents are available to everyone. Most people will make do with what they have and continue to pay less rent; an occasional few will opt for something new. The trouble begins when the rent remains the same for the new resident getting a made-over apartment.

Drafting.   There is a process called drafting that offered some help with raising rent in the past but, unfortunately, is not always effective. To describe the process, imagine that units in a certain vintage property rent for, say, $500. A newer property is constructed in the neighborhood and it has all of the latest "bells and whistles." This, plus the fact that it is new, might be enough for its units to command rents of $700. At the next round of renewals, the older property might normally be entitled to a 5 percent or $25 rent increase, but it may be able to "draft" behind the newer, more expensive property and charge an extra premium of $35 or even $50. Drafting has proved to be helpful to many properties with rents that have fallen behind the increases suffered in operating costs.

Drafting works best when there is little difference between the older product and the new property being built. For a long period of time, the typical rental property was comprised of stacks of "cookie-cutter" white cubes. The carpet changed colors and patterns, the plastic laminate on the kitchen counters differed, and so did the color of the appliances. Some developers added more common amenities, but the differences between an older property and a new one usually involved the fact that one had a fresh new appearance. As renters became more discerning and developers began to understand that they must offer features closer to those of the home builder, the differences between old and new properties became noticeably greater. Sliding doors, so typical in the older product, were replaced by fifteen-panel French doors with arched tops. Bay windows, vaulted ceilings, giant bathrooms, gourmet kitchens, and private verandas have all been introduced. These features damage the value and appeal of the older, second- or third-generation "standard."

Drafting doesn't work because the differences between yesterday's product and today's are just too striking. It is possible, if the neighborhood can support it, to totally remodel a property and give it many of the features of the newer developments, but the change in look and function must be complete and not just cosmetic. If the building still has small bathrooms or old galley kitchens with a layer of new wall covering, it simply won't work. Changes that include a redesign of the exterior facade can put a well-located property back into competition with the newer properties, and then rent levels can pick up the "push" from drafting. An easy way to illustrate this is to consider some of the very old warehouses or industrial buildings in your area that have been completely renovated into high-priced rental residences. The process is expensive. It only works in neighborhoods that are riding high or are involved in a total renewal and therefore does not offer a solution for the majority of the country's stock of aging rental housing.

Timing.   The final item in this discussion of raising rents has to do with the timing of the actual increase. The industry standard is clear: annual increases timed to take effect on the anniversary of the original move-in date. This assumes that the move-in occurs on the first day of the month. If it didn't, the date should reflect the first full month of occupancy. Some managers adjust the first lease to avoid lease expirations in winter months when it would be more difficult to find replacement residents. If the adjusted lease term is shorter than one year, you will be faced with the decision of whether to raise the rent with the lease renewal (which means that the resident will not get the advantage of a fixed rent amount for one year), or to have two rent levels in the renewal lease. Leases with two rent levels certainly open the door to some confusion. Incidentally, winter renewals are often not as bad as some believe; your current renters do not like to move out in winter any more than new ones like to move in. Many people are preoccupied with the holidays and therefore reluctant to move.

If your residents are now on a month-to-month basis, you may elect a common date each year for a general rent increase. This is not normally advisable. While it gets the extra work connected with a rent increase out of the way in one operation, the risks are considerable. The biggest risk is the chance of a rent strike if the raise is interpreted as too high. Choosing a single date for a general rent increase consolidates your yearly move-outs into one period, and you'll suffer a comparatively high vacancy rate— stripping you of the urgency of very little availability that is so critical when closing deals. It almost surely forces you to seek outside help to do the cleaning, painting, and carpet care on the vacated units.

Rent increases for housing directed toward students or seasonal occupants can be ideally timed to begin at the end of either the final quarter before the summer recess or the busy season. The idea is to have people commit to their unit before they head for home and thus be responsible for the rent during the slow period or, if nothing else, to give the owner the comfort of knowing what units are rented. This works fine when the market is tight but fails consistently in soft market situations. The inducement of a dramatic two-tier rent schedule may help implement an off-season rent increase program. In other words, rent might be $600 per month from September through June and only $200 per month during July and August. Such a rent schedule will induce people to keep the apartment for the summer rather than move-out and rerent in the fall.

Regardless of the situation, keeping pace with needed rent increases is essential. As a manager you will assume many important responsibilities—raising rents will be one of the most significant.

REAL ESTATE INVESTMENT ECONOMICS

With this better understanding of rents, we are now ready to address some of the issues that relate to the economics of real estate investment.

Real Estate Investment Terminology

Let's begin this discussion by charting the flow of income and expenditure items common in most investment real estate today:

Street Rent, Standard Rent, Optimum Rent

(These three terms are synonymous. It is helpful to compare the street rent—your target rent—with scheduled receipts when you are looking at the income and expenditures of each property you manage.)

Income and expenditure flowchart:

	Scheduled Receipts (Gross Possible Income)
Less	Vacancy and Collection Losses
Plus	Unscheduled, Sundry, or Ancillary Income
Equals	Actual Receipts, Collections, or Effective Income
Less	Operating Expenses
Equals	Net Operating Income (NOI)
Less	Debt Service or Mortgage Payments
Equals	*Cash Flow*

All of these items are interrelated and each has an effect on the final item—cash flow. To understand how each affects the cash flow and, ultimately, the return to the investor, I offer the following discussion.

Street Rent, Standard Rent, or Optimum Rent. The term "street rent" was introduced earlier in this chapter. This term plus "standard rent" and "optimum rent" are used interchangeably to describe the rent that will be quoted to new prospects and that new residents will pay. For example, consider the situation in which all of the apartments in a twenty-four-unit building are occupied and have varying lease expirations. The *street rent* is the rental rate you plan to achieve when these leases expire or a unit suddenly becomes available due to a resident move-out. Establishing today's rent—whether you call it street rent, standard rent, optimum rent, or some other name—for every unit is very important because it helps to prevent leasing personnel from rerenting vacant units today at yesterday's rate. Earlier, we discussed guidelines for estimating street rent using 106 percent of the typical rent asked for a certain type of unit.

The total street rent includes rent values for every unit in the development: even models, employee housing, office space, and any unrentable units. Though the street rent total is not a part of the income and expenditure flowchart, it is typically presented above the scheduled receipts for purposes of comparison. Street rent is the rent you would be trying to get if everyone moved out of your building today; it's always helpful to contrast the rent you're getting with your target rent.

Scheduled Receipts or Gross Possible Income.   These two terms are synonymous and identify the current total rent roll. Included in this total is the monthly rent of each unit under lease plus the current street value of each vacant and non-revenue-producing unit.

Vacancy and Collection Losses.   This item reflects the amount of money that is lost, or is expected to be lost, as a result of vacancies and collection losses. Vacancy and collection losses are a fact of life in the rental housing business. As strange as it may seem, 100 percent occupancy usually means that a property is not achieving its maximum rent potential. While full occupancy month after month may be the result of the property's exceptional location, facilities, and services, it is just as likely to be a signal that rents are too low.

Two distinct types of vacancies have been established: *physical vacancy* and *economic vacancy*. When vacancies are reported, they are usually physical vacancies. Economic vacancy indicates the percentage of units that are not producing income. Data collected by my firm indicate that in larger developments (more than eighty units) with moderate vacancies (not more than 7 to 10 percent) the following rule can be employed: The economic vacancy rate will usually amount to twice the physical vacancy rate. Therefore, a property with a 5 percent physical vacancy will usually suffer a 10 percent economic loss.

There is one notable exception to this result: An economic vacancy almost always exists, even if there is no physical vacancy. This occurs for a number of reasons. If an apartment is rented in March for occupancy in May, it is not listed as a vacant apartment available for rent, yet it generates no income for the month of April. If a resident is behind in rent payments, there is no income, but the unit must be classified as occupied. Those apartments given to employees or used as models or for office or storage space, in addition to unrentable or cannibalized apartments, are not available for rent yet produce no income. Finally, vacancy problems frequently center around the most expensive units. This creates a disproportionate dollar loss when compared to the actual number of vacant apartments.

In determining vacancy and collection losses, the property manager is less interested in the number of units that are vacant and available (physical vacancy) than in the number and value of units that reasonably can be expected to be non-revenue-producing. I have found that in larger properties, it is practically impossible to operate regularly with less than 5 percent economic vacancy. Even in a fairly tight market, an economic vacancy of 7 to 9 percent is more realistic. In privately operated student housing, an economic vacancy of 20 percent is standard, and this assumes zero physical vacancy at the start of the fall term.

There is a tendency to group vacancies and to analyze them as a total. This can result in misreading some very serious problems. Vacancies should always be detailed by unit type, indicating the total number of each type in the complex, the number of each type of unit that is vacant, and the vacancy expressed as a percentage of the total. It's even more important to do a monthly listing of vacant units and to keep a running total of rent lost from the day each unit was last rented. Some computer programs track the number of days each unit has been vacant, but that fact is not nearly as valuable as the amount of money lost. Some units will suffer enormous losses in between rentals. It is crucial to learn why.

Unscheduled, Sundry, or Ancillary Income.   Any one of these three terms may be used to identify income that is derived from a source other than rent. Ancillary income includes money or commissions received from concessions such as coin-operated laundry equipment, periodic rentals of party rooms or recreational facilities, key deposits, charges for NSF checks, forfeited security deposits, settlements, and resident damage reimbursements.

Actual Receipts, Collections, or Effective Income.   These three terms are used interchangeably to refer to the net amount of income collected after subtracting for vacancy and collection losses and adding the unscheduled or ancillary income.

Net Operating Income (NOI).   Occasionally, some real estate practitioners will attempt to coin a new phrase to replace the term net operating income (NOI), but this term has survived and is used and accepted almost universally. It represents the amount of money that remains after operating expenses are subtracted from actual receipts.

Net operating income is the primary measure of a property's performance. The property manager understands that it is his or her responsibility to produce the highest possible NOI over the economic life of the property. In other words, the manager works to maximize collections and minimize operating expenses. This, of course, must be done in such a way that it does not jeopardize the long-range economic potential of the particular property.

Real estate appraisers generally establish values on income-producing real estate *in direct proportion to the property's ability to produce NOI.* The primary method of arriving at a value for investment real estate is the income capitalization approach I discussed earlier in this chapter. Using this approach, investors, appraisers, managers, lenders, and others arrive at a property's value by selecting a desired yield or capitalization rate. This rate is divided into the property's net operating income, thereby arriving at an indication of value. The formula is:

$$\frac{\text{Net Operating Income (I)}}{\text{Capitalization Rate (R)}} = \text{Value (V)}$$

Let's take an example. Assume that the NOI (collections less operating expenses) of an apartment building is $36,000. Assume further that typical investors expect a yield on their investments or a capitalization rate of 10 percent. The property's value is determined as follows:

$$\frac{\$36,000 \text{ (I)}}{.10 \text{ (R)}} = \$360,000 \text{ (V)}$$

Let's continue by assuming that the manager is successful in combining rent increases with a series of skillful cutbacks in operating expenses. These changes increase the NOI to, say, $40,000 per year. Using the same cap rate of 10 percent, the property now becomes more valuable:

$$\frac{\$40,000 \text{ (I)}}{.10 \text{ (R)}} = \$400,000 \text{ (V)}$$

As you might imagine, investors search for skilled managers who have the ability to "create value" by instituting changes that will bring about steady and sustained increases in NOI and, hence, increase the value of their properties.

Debt Service or Mortgage Payments.   Debt service and mortgage payments are used synonymously to describe payments of principal and interest on outstanding loans. Most real estate people isolate mortgage payments because they are considered personal obligations of the owner and should not affect the real estate's ability to produce NOI.

Cash Flow.   After the mortgage principal and interest are deducted from the NOI, the amount of money remaining is termed *cash flow*. Most owners and investors are interested in this amount primarily because it represents spendable income. Once again, this annual cash return, when divided by the original cash equity invested, produces *cash-on-cash return or yield.*

The cash-on-cash return is the most commonly used method of calculating and measuring investment performance, but the reader should be aware that there are other methods. These other methods, while they recognize cash flow, also consider after-tax consequences and the property's appreciation.

The purpose of explaining the flow of income and expenditure items here is to provide an introduction to the all-important financial aspects of real estate investment. You are encouraged to continue studying the economics of real estate investment. In doing so, your value as a property manager will be enhanced, as will your ability to serve clients. Understanding the profit-and-loss aspects of multifamily housing is vital if the manager is to play a role in maximizing rental income and improving profitability.

10

Insurance

Like so many issues in the property management business, insurance coverage is constantly changing and becoming more complex. While some property managers have made insurance a secondary business and have been schooled in its intricacies, most have only a very basic knowledge of the subject. The owner's insurance coverage may seem to be a matter strictly between the owner and his or her insurance specialist, but the realities of operating investment real estate indicate something different.

You, as the manager, will almost surely be the one to maintain the actual policies for the apartment property. Even if you don't hold the policies and pay the premiums, it is imperative that you understand the property's coverage in the event of a loss, because insurance questions will surely be directed to you. For example, if an unidentified truck knocks over a light standard in the parking lot of a property you manage, you will need to know which policy covers such damages, the insurance carrier, the agent, policy number, policy expiration date, any deductibles, and the method or form for reporting the incident. Similar information will be needed in the case of injuries to people (employees, residents, or guests) or damage to the property from any one of a number of possible causes. Operating without the insurance information makes things far more difficult. Most managers readily appreciate the need for insurance knowledge and are rather quickly appointed "the keeper of the policies." It is implied that the manager will not only keep these policies in an orderly and safe manner but also assume the responsibility of monitoring expiration dates and, perhaps, coverage amounts. What starts out as someone else's concern quickly becomes a rather considerable obligation.

Learning about insurance is made even more difficult because the people in the insurance industry work every day to improve the products they offer, to ward off competition, and to maintain profit margins. Your learning process must parallel the incessant changes. In years past, insurance coverage was available for a number of basic losses or casualties that could disrupt or destroy the well-being of the property or the financial status of the owner or mortgagee. This coverage often took the form of individual policies with specifically chosen limits, and these policies were obtained from one or more carriers. Today, insurance companies are offering package policies that include most of the commonly sought forms of coverage in one comprehensive policy. One of these businessowners' or habitational policies (as residential rental property policies are sometimes called) can include almost all needed forms of coverage. As is the case with luxury automobile merchandising, these policies are offered with fewer and fewer options. Most of the different types of coverage are built into the basic policy and only special needs are accommodated through extra-cost add-ons. Very large properties must still piece together separate policies to create a customized *multiperil policy;* but even these properties may soon be able to take advantage of the convenience and lower cost of the comprehensive package policy.

Broadly interpreted, insurance coverage for an apartment property breaks down into two components—options that provide for necessary repairs when damage is done to the physical components of the property and those that protect the owner and others from liability arising out of the ownership and operation of the rental property. Of course, the mortgagee (the lender), is most interested in the insurance protection for the property or physical plant. This, in most cases, represents the limit of the lender's collateral. If a loss occurs, the lender must be assured that the money necessary to put the property back into rentable condition will be forthcoming. On the other hand, the manager, employees, residents, and the general public are more concerned about the liability aspects of the property's insurance coverage. In the discussion that follows, I'll address the different types of coverage within these two major classifications of apartment complex insurance. It is important to understand that they are frequently combined into one comprehensive insurance policy.

INSURING AGAINST PROPERTY LOSS

I will begin with the primary insurance concern of the lender—coverage for loss of the physical property. This insurance covers damage caused by those things most of us think of first when we consider the need for insurance: loss from fire, storm, or vandalism.

Fire, Extended Coverage (EC), and Vandalism or Malicious Mischief (VMM)

These types of insurance cover the basic *perils* that can damage or destroy an income-producing property. In every hour of every day more than 275 fires will occur in this country; and rental apartments are certainly involved in a good share of these losses. Common causes of fires include kitchen accidents, smoking in bed, grilling on a patio or balcony, overloaded electrical circuits, and malfunctioning heating equipment. As a property's concentration of residents increases, so do the chances of a serious fire. The added risk of loss from other causes is also very real. Sooner or later, the apartment manager will be confronted with the need for insurance and a working knowledge of how to deal with a loss.

Fire.   Coverage limits for fire are stated as the maximum amount the insurance company will be responsible to pay in the event of loss from a fire. Unfortunately, it is not quite so simple as this. There is also the question of how the property is to be restored. For years, the insurance industry used the term *actual cash value (ACV)* which means replacement costs that have been reduced by a depreciation deduction (made in accord with a depreciation schedule). Most of us know of someone who took particularly good care of his or her automobile only to be told the car was "totaled" after a relatively minor accident. This person was probably offered a settlement that wouldn't begin to repair the car. The collision portion of the automobile policy is an example of actual cash value (ACV) reimbursement. The insurance company determines the value of the automobile by consulting a guide that quantifies the automobile's depreciation based on the age and model of the car. The owner of the car receives the guidebook amount and the case is closed. Substantial arguments result from automobile claims, so you can imagine the problems with a large apartment property that has suffered a loss.

The current trend in real property insurance is toward *replacement cost coverage*. This eliminates virtually all depreciation deductions in the settlement of losses. For example, under the older style policies, the subject of the replacement cycle for carpeting would become a settlement issue. If you typically replaced the carpets in your apartments on a six-year cycle and the carpet had been down for three years when you made your insurance claim, you would only be entitled to one-half of the carpet costs because of the deduction taken for depreciation. The same is true for painting and a number of other depreciable items. Under the replacement-cost form of coverage, if you started with carpeting on the floor before the casualty, you will have carpeting after the settlement. Because you can't buy used carpeting, the replacement will be new goods similar to the previous carpeting in type and quality. You can't apply three-year old paint, so here again you would benefit from an "undepreciated" replacement.

Extended Coverage (EC).   In addition to the loss of property due to fire, buildings are susceptible to damage by other means including windstorm, hail, lightning, collapse, explosion, riot, smoke, aircraft, broken pipes, and fire hoses. Just as these risks are commonly added to your insurance under an extended coverage provision of the basic fire policy, war and nuclear disaster are usually special exclusions to the insurance carried to protect against property loss.

Vandalism or Malicious Mischief (VMM).   As the name implies, this coverage, which usually requires an endorsement to the basic policy, insures against damage caused by vandals or burglars.

Coinsurance

This is an insurance feature that, despite good intentions, has caused innumerable problems. Coinsurance had its beginnings as a vehicle to encourage property owners to carry the proper amount of insurance coverage. When this form of coverage was chosen, a special clause was added to the policy; the clause provided that the owner would pay a considerably lower rate for each one hundred dollars of coverage if he or she would agree to maintain coverage limits that at least equaled a given percentage of the actual cash value (ACV) of the property. A typical figure is 80 percent of the actual cash value. Again, ACV is the replacement cost, less a deduction for depreciation. As we discuss coverage limits, you should remember that *the value of the land is excluded,* because the land will remain even after a major loss. If the property owner maintains the agreed amount of coverage, the insurance company will pay 100 percent of the loss *up to but never exceeding the limits of the policy.* If the owner lets the coverage slip behind as construction and material costs rise, *the owner will become a coinsurer* with the insurance company in the same proportion that the property is underinsured according to the agreed-upon percentage established in the coinsurance clause. The formula, plus two examples—one showing proper coverage and one showing inadequate coverage—will help to demonstrate this calculation.

Assume you own a building that has an ACV of $800,000 (remember, this is not market value; it is replacement value less depreciation deductions) and you agree to the 80 percent coinsurance provision. Then you must maintain at least 80 percent of $800,000, or $640,000, worth of coverage. If you do, you will be covered on losses up to the limits of the policy ($640,000) by the insurance company. The formula is:

$$\frac{\text{Amount carried}}{\text{Amount to be carried}} = \begin{array}{l}\text{Percentage of loss to be paid by the} \\ \text{insurance company up to the limits} \\ \text{of the policy}\end{array}$$

Or, inserting some numbers:

$$\frac{\$640,000 \text{ (Amount carried)}}{\$640,000 \text{ (To be carried)}} = \begin{array}{l}100\% \text{ of loss to be paid by the} \\ \text{insurance company (up to the limits} \\ \text{of the policy, or, in this case,} \\ \$640,000)\end{array}$$

Let's assume that the cost of restoring buildings has increased. Your building now has an ACV of $1,100,000, but the insurance coverage has remained at $640,000. You are committed to maintain coverage of at least 80 percent of the current ACV, or $880,000. Now apply the formula again:

$$\frac{\$640,000 \text{ (Amount carried)}}{\$880,000 \text{ (To be carried)}} = \begin{array}{l}73\% \text{ of loss to be paid by the} \\ \text{insurance company (up to the limits} \\ \text{of the policy, or, in this case,} \\ \$640,000)\end{array}$$

In this case, if a loss amounted to only $20,000, the insurance company would pay 73 percent, or $14,600. You would have to make up the difference. If the loss was $200,000, the insurance would cover $146,000, and your share as coinsurer would be $54,000.

Investment property owners as well as homeowners were quick to take advantage of the lower insurance premiums created by the coinsurance provision. Unfortunately for many, either the principle was inadequately explained by insurance agents, or the policyholders did not fully appreciate the consequences of failing to meet the agreement to maintain adequate coverage as construction prices rose. Many people had a rude awakening when they submitted claims that were well below the total dollar limits of the policy and those claims were subjected to sizable coinsurance deductions. The general public's misunderstanding became a public relations nightmare for the insurance carriers, who in turn directed a good part of their advertising budgets at further explaining the principle of coinsurance and the need for constantly updating coverage limits. In an effort to avoid a dispute at the time of a loss, insurance carriers then began to seek *agreed-amount endorsements* in which the insurance company and the insured would agree, in advance, on an actual cash value. The insurance company's position was to set this amount high enough to cover inflationary restoration costs—and thus boost premium revenue. The insured party, on the other hand, was not all that eager to raise insurance expenditures and pushed to keep value estimates rather low.

The insurance industry seems to be headed toward elimination of the coinsurance provision and conversion of actual cash value with its depreciation deductions to replacement value cost coverage. The problem of increasing restoration costs is often handled with an *inflation guard* provision that increases the coverage on a periodic basis (e.g., quarterly). This assures the property owner that the coverage will be adequate to properly restore destroyed components, but it also means that, at renewal time, the premium will increase because the amount of required coverage has grown.

Inclusions and Exclusions

While on the subject of insurance coverage, we should also discuss those items that are typically included or excluded from coverage. It is very easy to misinterpret what is covered after a quick reading of either the policy itself or a single-page summary of it. The insurance industry has developed some guidelines to help in its communication. Over the years, "building," as defined by the insurance industry, has pretty well identified the additions and extensions that are to be considered part of the building for insurance purposes. These usually include overhangs and marquees, mailboxes, intercom systems, aerials, machinery, equipment, construction materials, outdoor furniture, yard fixtures (with meaningful exceptions discussed below), and personal property used in the maintenance or service of the building.

Even more important, however, is what is typically *not* covered in a basic insurance policy. Many of these exclusions fall into the category of yard fixtures and include fences, detached retaining walls, swimming pools, and paved surfaces (e.g., walks, roadways, aprons, and parking lots). Piers, wharves, docks, and beach areas or diving platforms are examples of improvements that are excluded from many policies. Similarly, foundations, underground pilings, sewers, or drainage systems are not covered. Unless specifically insured by a special policy extension, outdoor signs, lawns, trees, and plants are also commonly excluded from coverage. When these things are covered, the policy usually contains a limit to the amount that can be recovered if a loss occurs.

In addition, some coverage is lost after a building remains vacant or is unoccupied for a period of time, commonly in excess of thirty days. Vandalism or malicious mischief and plate glass coverage are two such examples. Special endorsements can be added to the policy to continue such coverage when needed.

Deductibles

Claims processing is expensive, and the number of comparatively small losses far exceeds the number of major incidents. If an insurance company can avoid losing the processing expense and the payment of the smaller claims, it is in a position to offer coverage at a lower premium. This is accomplished by setting a minimum dollar amount for claims called a deductible. Deductibles can range from $100 to more than $1,000,000. Some property owners and institutions can set aside adequate amounts and choose to self-insure against all but the most catastrophic losses. Others set up a loss pool among several properties and cover the lot using a blanket policy with a substantial deductible. This drives down their annual premiums, and losses up to the deductible amount are funded by the loss pool.

Rent Loss

This protection is almost standard for rental properties. Lenders invariably require rent loss insurance as a condition of their making a loan on the property. A great many loans on rental property are termed *non-recourse,* which means that the lender's sole recourse to satisfy the debt is the property that is pledged as collateral; the lender has no claim to the borrower's other assets. If the property has been damaged by a casualty and is left partially or totally uninhabitable, rental income will be interrupted; and the funds for making mortgage payments will be reduced or discontinued altogether. The rent loss coverage substitutes for the lost rental revenue after the damage is sustained and until the building can be readied for occupancy again. Frequently, this coverage applies for up to twelve months, although it should be stated that there are many differences among rent loss coverages.

Optional Coverage

With the seemingly endless combination of building types, locations, climates, inclusions, and values, there is a corresponding number of insurance option combinations. The insurance industry has measured the risks of many of these exposures, and underwriters have calculated extra premiums and customized special coverage for almost any situation—most, of course, at an additional cost. In addition to the special forms of coverage already mentioned, here are some other examples of the more commonly requested options.

Improvements and Betterment. This coverage is carried by occupants to insure any special improvements they have made to their apartments. These treatments can include anything that becomes a part of the real estate such as floor covering, paneling, built-ins, climate control devices, upgraded bathrooms or kitchens, and more. This is seen more in condominium properties than in rental apartments.

Boiler and Machinery.   This can usually be selected as optional coverage for losses sustained in connection with damage to a building's boiler, pressure vessels, and air-conditioning systems. The added cost is established by the insurance carrier's underwriting department and is related to the cost of such apparatus and the exposure to damage.

Plate Glass.   Exterior plate glass insurance is commonly *added to a package policy*. Coverage is usually limited to a fixed dollar amount per lite of glass or to a total loss amount per occurrence or during the term of the policy.

Contents.   This coverage might be needed to insure lobby furniture, recreation building furnishings, exercise equipment, office or model furnishings, apartment furnishings (should you have any furnished units), and the like. A value is usually established, and coverage frequently involves a deductible amount to eliminate small claims. The policy may also be endorsed to include *fine arts coverage* for paintings or sculptures that are used to decorate the lobby or common areas.

Mini-Computers or Personal Computers.   Computers are the focus of many apartment office break-ins because they are light, highly portable, and can produce instant dollars for thieves. This kind of equipment is usually named in a schedule provided by the insured; each piece of equipment is identified by a description, serial number, and model number. Coverage can be added to include software programs and the time required to restore lost data.

Volume Purchases.   As with most commodities, greater volume results in lower prices. Insurance companies are no different; they prefer volume and will discount premiums to attract bulk business. Many owners of multiple properties have elected to group their properties together under one *blanket policy* to gain the lowest annual premium. Such an owner might also be able to include one or two higher risk properties in the package at a much lower rate than what should be expected.

Natural Disasters.   Floods, earthquakes, volcanic eruptions, mud slides, etc. were once referred to as "acts of God." Now they are referred to as "causes of loss" and individually identified in the policy. Losses involving these types of hazards may be included under a "difference in condition" (DIC) endorsement. Insurance covering natural disasters often involves very high deductibles.

Flood insurance is unique because qualifying for coverage means that the insured property must be in an area that is prone to flooding and in compliance with government guidelines for flood prevention. Insurance can be provided by the National Flood Insurance Program or by private companies.

INSURING AGAINST OTHER CLAIMS

Everything we have discussed thus far has involved possible loss or damage to the property itself, but there are many more risks. Rental property is a business, and in the course of operating that business we are exposed to a myriad of potential financial losses—often very serious ones.

Liability Coverage

Liability insurance protects the property owner and those involved with the property's operation, (e.g., the managing agent), from claims arising from injuries or even death. Other people, such as tenants, tenant guests, visitors, some vendors, and the general public are covered by this form of insurance. If a person were to slip and fall on a walk or stairway in the complex, it is this liability insurance that would absorb the medical bills. It would also defend the owner as well as any other *named insured* in the event of a lawsuit arising from such an accident. The managing agent will surely be included in any such litigation, because it can be argued that the manager had day-to-day responsibility for the upkeep of the property and thus played a role in the injury. Also, it is not uncommon for the managing agent's employer, as a company, to possess a greater net worth than the owner of the property being managed. Lawsuits tend to include everyone, even those with the most remote connection, and especially those individuals and entities with some degree of wealth. For that reason, the manager as well as his or her employer must insist upon being *named as additional insured* on the property's general liability policy. The lender, on the other hand, is not in a position of daily control; generally, liability coverage is not extended to financial institutions.

We face an increasingly litigious society. The total claims and awards for commonly sustained injuries range into the millions of dollars; this exceeds the limits of most basic liability coverage.

Umbrella Protection

There is always the possibility of a major liability claim exceeding the basic liability coverage. To protect against this, the property should have additional umbrella coverage which is available from either the basic policy carrier or a second one. This coverage, which is its own separate policy, would undertake the payment of claims that exceed the basic liability coverage. The limits of umbrella protection can be as high as, if not higher than, 20 million dollars; the premium is usually quoted as a specific dollar amount per million dollars of added liability coverage. Because these personal injury losses can reach such enormous amounts, even the insurance companies will reinsure themselves against a major claim.

Errors and Omissions

Managing real estate is a complicated business with myriad responsibilities. As agent, you are very definitely exposed to financial risks if you should make an error or fail to perform a crucial function within your scope of authority. As is the case with most risks, there are insurance carriers willing to protect you against such losses—for a price. This coverage is called errors and omissions insurance and it is typically purchased and paid for by the managing agent. Because of the substantial awards made by juries in liability cases—especially those awarded in decisions against the medical profession—errors and omissions coverage is expensive and offered by only a handful of insurance companies. This coverage usually involves a large deductible to eliminate small nuisance claims. The policy carefully delineates what constitutes an error or an omission; gross negligence on the part of the agent is often excluded—as, of course, is fraud.

Non-Owned or Hired Auto

This is a rather special form of third party liability and property damage insurance that allows an employer to buy insurance coverage as protection from claims arising out of accidents involving vehicles that are *not* owned by the property (e.g., an employees's automobile). It is commonplace in the operation of an apartment property to send one of the maintenance people to the hardware store or to the gas station. The manager might ask the bookkeeper to make a bank deposit at lunch time. Examples of "hired auto" also include asking a person to borrow or rent a vehicle to perform a particular task. If any of these people are involved in an accident while performing a work-related duty, the liability can quickly shift to the employer.

Coverage for these risks is comparatively inexpensive, but the loss potential is substantial. This is particularly true when the employee has inadequate coverage or none at all. You should also know that if your firm, the managing agent, is involved in sending your people on such errands, you will also need protection either as a named insured on the complex's non-owned auto policy or through separate coverage.

Insurance to protect vehicles owned by an apartment property as well as those who drive these vehicles is a separate policy and not often part of the non-owned auto coverage.

Host and Liquor Liability Insurance

Another common occurrence, and hence a liability exposure, is the accident that results from the consumption of alcoholic beverages. Perhaps alcohol is served in your complex's clubhouse or during the social activities offered by the development. If an accident causing injury or death occurs—and it can be proved that the responsible party was consuming alcohol in your development prior to the accident—you can be sure that those involved, including the managing agent, will be included in any resulting lawsuits. Host and liquor liability insurance protects those involved only when the beverages are given away, not sold. To sell liquor, you need not only a license but a completely different kind of insurance—*dram shop insurance.* Let's assume that you do not have a recreational facility and you don't plan to include parties in your regular resident activities. If you do not have a recreational facility, and you don't plan to host parties as part of your resident activities but you choose to host a single party, you are advised to contact your insurance agent to purchase host and liquor liability insurance for that single event rather than run the risk of catastrophic loss.

Fire Legal Liability

What if your property suffers a major fire and the dense, black soot discolors the white building next door? The fire damage to your building would be covered by the property's fire insurance, but what about the building next door? Your insurance carrier did not agree to repair all of the buildings in the neighborhood. Fire legal liability, which is optional coverage, can be obtained to handle such situations.

Crime Coverage

Depending upon the types of coverage included in your policy, this insurance protects the apartment owner from some twelve to fourteen different risks, the most common of which are employee dishonesty and burglary, and destruction, theft, and disappearance of currency.

WORKERS' COMPENSATION

This coverage is last in our list of the basic insurance forms because it is unique in so many ways. First of all, workers' compensation is always a separate policy and is not included in either a businessowners' policy or a special multiperil policy. It is also one of the only types of insurance that is not assignable to a new owner. This insurance is required by state law; in some states, however, an employer may be allowed to carry the risk independently if sufficient financial ability is demonstrated. The insurance protects employees who are injured during the course of their work-related activities by paying the medical costs and providing salary benefits while the employee is recovering (or continuing benefits if the employee is partially or permanently disabled). The premium is determined by the job hazards inherent in the work being performed and the amount of money paid in wages. For example, the rate per $100 of salary for a building engineer is much greater than the rate applied to the earnings of a leasing agent. The engineer's job involves whirling machines and pumps and a host of potential injuries while the leasing agent's greatest risk might be the possibility of falling down a few steps. The initial or deposit premium is determined by listing the different classes of worker exposure and estimating your workers' annual wages during the upcoming year. At the end of each year, the insurance company audits the payroll records to arrive at an adjusted premium. Either this is invoiced to make up any difference owed, or a credit memo is issued for an overpayment. It is not uncommon for properties with no employees to maintain workers' compensation insurance. The possibility of hiring a student or some other casual laborer to help out with a particular project might result in an injury and a workers' compensation claim.

It is absolutely essential that you *secure current certificates of insurance from all of the contractors and subcontractors who perform work* on the properties you manage. There are several situations in which the liability of an independent contractor can be transferred to the owner and operator of the property. Some states have laws stating that a contractor without a license and insurance is deemed to be an employee of the property. During the workers' compensation audit, some insurance carriers include the value of work performed by individuals and contractors as if they were direct employees when these people show no evidence of insurance. If you do not constantly verify the existence of current policies and sufficient coverage for each tradesperson who works at your properties, you may well find yourself providing that insurance or, at least, undertaking the associated risks.

HANDLING INSURED LOSSES

Knowing what to expect and how to proceed in the event of a loss is one of the most important aspects of property management. Managers have some very definite responsibilities in this area, and the failure to handle them correctly can shift much of the liability to the management firm. In most cases, a period of learning and an allowance for mistakes are part of the process of becoming a property manager. However, mistakes in handling an insurance claim can result in huge economic losses to both the property owner and the management company.

Report All Losses

The advice to report all losses may sound too simple, but this first procedure following a loss is omitted regularly in the operation of rental property. Let's say one of your groundskeepers sustains a cut on the hand while using a weed trimmer. A common response might be to administer a little first aid and hope that the healing process is quick and pain-free. Perhaps you hear about a person who fell on a slippery spot in the parking lot. You don't know the time the accident occurred, the exact location, or even the identity of the individual involved. What can you report? The simple answer is, report everything you know and everything you heard. When insurance is purchased, the burden of responsibility shifts to the insurance carrier with a few, very important exceptions. Obviously, the premium must be paid and all incidents must be reported promptly. The final burden that remains with the owner or manager is the follow-up activity to lessen any damages should a loss occur.

The reluctance to report claims may stem from a general optimism that everything will work out, the fear that insurance rates will rise, or the unwillingness to assume the burden of additional paperwork and investigation. Wishing it so won't help. Insurance has been purchased, and a manager's job requires that potential claims be handled in a responsible manner. The failure to report a claim results when incidents are communicated vaguely or appear to be minor, not when major incidents occur. The law gives injured parties considerable time to register any claims for damages. If it is revealed that you had knowledge of an incident involving an injury and failed to report it to the insurance company, it may be determined that you breached an important condition of your insurance agreement. You can avoid such problems by reporting all incidents to the insurance carrier. It's all right if you lack much of the background data, such as the person's name, time of occurrence, extent of injuries, etc. The insurance company has people capable of securing the missing information. Your job is to report all incidents.

Don't Volunteer

When a catastrophe such as fire, windstorm, or tornado results in a casualty loss (i.e., loss of property) there is usually a great deal of commotion. The scene is anything but pretty. The weather may be inclement and such incidents frequently occur at night. As you would expect, emotions run high in a situation involving the loss of furnishings and other personal possessions. Some people may have been injured trying to escape from the peril. People may be homeless and without proper clothes to wear.

There are plenty of opportunities to volunteer, but in my opinion you should not do so. You may have vacant apartments that could be used to house those of your residents who have lost their homes, but that is not one of the provisions in your lease document. There are legal implications and ongoing consequences when you begin to go beyond the bounds of a normal landlord-tenant relationship. As a manager, you do not have the authority to commit and obligate your owner to these added burdens.

Another word of caution: Television crews may want pictures and answers to questions ranging from "What happened and why did it happen?" to "Who is responsible?" Reporters sometimes try to address all the issues in one telecast. As for the "media," it is best to let someone else do the talking. In the minutes immediately following a disaster, chances are good that your grasp of the situation will be incomplete. When the statement is aired publicly, you may regret your attempt to make a coherent statement from limited knowledge. Chances are, you will know much more in the morning, so hold your comments until then.

Beware of Public Adjusters

When you are called to the scene of an apartment complex that has been damaged by fire or some other force, you will often be approached by an individual who hands you an impressive-looking business card with a generic name involving insurance or insurance adjustments. This person will typically act calmly and be very knowledgeable about what steps should be taken next. This can be very comforting to a manager who has not experienced the emotions associated with a property loss. Unfortunately, many managers might begin to work with this stranger under the assumption that he or she is an agent of the insurance carrier. You should be aware that the adjusters who arrive at the scene are most likely public adjusters and do not represent your insurance company. Once they have secured an obligation from you, they gain a foothold in the loss settlement and restoration work—and their fee is commonly a percentage of the monetary loss. These public adjusters have numerous contacts. With just a few phone calls, workers will begin to arrive to take care of necessary chores: a tarpaulin is placed over a hole in the roof, doors and windows are boarded up to secure the building, and emergency electrical lines and portable boilers are installed to furnish heat to the damaged structure. Seeing a public adjuster seize the authority and order this repair work, the manager may be convinced that things could not be better—when in reality he or she may be obligating the management company or the property ownership to substantial fees. I strongly advise you not to become involved with these people in the first place. Your insurance carrier will let you know when their adjuster is coming to your property—do not accept the services of anyone else.

Protect the Property

The work that the public adjuster would authorize comes under the heading of protecting the property from further damage. That is the remaining obligation of the insured. There will be time between the occurrence of the crisis and the moment the insurance company's representative arrives on the scene. Until then, you are not only authorized to act but also responsible for the mitigation of any further damages to the property. You should always have the home telephone numbers of various tradespeople or contractors whom you can call during emergencies. That list should surely include a board-up service, electrician, plumber, carpenter, furnace or boiler company, and a locksmith. Talk with them in advance so that you know they will respond, have alternate firms or individuals available, and keep a copy of that list with you or in your car. There are no advance warnings for emergencies. Your job requires that you act quickly and decisively; so you must always be prepared. The cost of this work will be part of the insurance claim on a dollar-for-dollar basis.

Learn About Insurance Adjustment

Adjusting an insurance loss is a very detailed and complicated process. It is absolutely no place for a beginner. Even for experienced managers who have been through many fire or casualty losses, the adjustment procedure can be troublesome. Remember, the authorized insurance adjuster who is assigned to the loss is the employee or agent of the insurance company, not the property. The insurance company is anxious to settle the matter and to see that the restoration process is begun, but it is not going to throw money at the building. The adjuster appointed by your insurance carrier will methodically go through each and every component and decide whether it needs to be cleaned, repaired, or replaced. Insurance companies have a schedule of allowances that may or may not be sufficient to complete the work. The adjuster's estimation of what is acceptable may not be what you know to be necessary in the marketplace. Under certain policies, some items are subject to depreciation deductions which can present a rude surprise when the final settlement amount is announced. The adjuster does this every working day; you don't. So get help. Most cities have a "fire-builder" or restoration contractor who is very experienced in both the adjustment of insurance casualty claims and the actual restoration work. A few calls to the more experienced managers in town will give you the names of these people and some background information. The good ones are expensive, but they know this very specialized business. They know the rules that the insurance company will follow, and they know what you are entitled to. Their chances of achieving a proper settlement are far superior to yours unless you have considerable experience in insurance settlements. They are also very efficient in the dirty and dangerous business of fire restoration. There is a big difference between building a new building and restoring one that has been damaged in a major fire or natural disaster. The method of compensation is often a percentage of the money needed to restore the property. Some managers choose to pay a fee only for the help in adjusting the loss, and then they do the actual restoration with their own cadre of contractors or personnel.

With luck, the properties that you manage will suffer very few losses requiring the services of an adjuster. When the occasion does arise, take the time to learn more about this very important subject.

chapter 11

Budgets

I have several acquaintances who operate many millions of dollars worth of rental property without using any budgets. When challenged about this practice, they respond, "What if the boiler rusts out and needs to be replaced, but isn't budgeted?" or, "What if we get twice the normal amount of snowfall—what would you do, consult a budget?" These same people insist that they do not waste money, but rather they spend what is necessary to properly operate their properties.

Many managers who are called upon during the busy last months of the year and asked to prepare a budget for the coming year would champion a "no budget" approach. These managers wish to be left alone to operate their properties—increasing revenues and curtailing expenses—while owners trust them to produce the best possible results.

Developing and using a budget is time-consuming and potentially restraining, but a budget is a valuable tool that demands forethought, goal-planning, and control. Budgets also provide a means to monitor progress. Unfortunately, too many budgets are prepared in haste, and their relationship to reality is weak from the very beginning. Other budgets are developed only to be pared by an overly optimistic owner or superior in an effort to force unrealistic results. Such a budget will lose its value as a working tool shortly after the new budget year begins. Some budgets are created at a "higher level," while the person who is responsible for increasing rent levels or holding back on expenses makes no contribution to the budget's development. This practice leads to frustration because neither party has a realistic impression of where the other is headed. An-

other example of budgets causing problems is the result of the short tenure of some managers; it is not unusual to find a manager trying to live
within the bounds of a poorly prepared budget made by his or her prede-
cessor. Any combination of these difficulties can contribute to the appeal
of operating without the burden and restraint of a budget. Actually a budget is like a road map—it helps you get where you want to go efficiently
and within your means.

TYPES OF BUDGETS

October and November are typically referred to as budget time in the
apartment management business. In areas of the country with four distinct
seasons, the high point of rental occupancy usually occurs in mid-October.
At this time, rent increases have been put to the test and most discretionary expenditures have been made for the year. Utility, seasonal, and make-
ready costs are at their lowest. Armed with year-to-date operating data, a
manager may use every spare moment in the months of October and November to prepare a budget for the upcoming year. A variety of budget
types are commonly used in the management of rental apartments. These
include: net operating income (NOI), cash flow, annual, quarterly, rent-
up, major expenditure, and replacement reserve budgets. More than one
type of budget may be needed to effectively plan for your specific property.

Net Operating Income (NOI) Budget

This type of budget reflects the gross possible income, vacancy and collection losses, sundry income projections, resulting collection expectations,
and a listing of proposed operating expenses. The final budget line, the
NOI, is broken out by month and totaled for the year. In a budget of this
type, the monthly debt service is omitted or dealt with in a separate accounting. All inclusions up to and including the calculation of the NOI are
matters of concern to the manager, a potential buyer, an appraiser, or
others interested in the earning capability of the investment. *Including
the mortgage with its associated debt-service payments adds a personal
variable to the budget* and does not, or at least should not, affect the
proper operation of the property.

Cash Flow Budget

Most budgets for rental properties fall into this category. They follow the
same pattern as the NOI budget except the cash flow budget does track the
payment of principal and interest each month. The final budget line is referred to as *cash flow.* This is the spendable cash that constitutes the re-

Basic Budget Format

	Stable	Upgrade
Gross Possible Income		
Laundry Receipts		
Other Income		
Vacancy Loss		
Effective Income		
Total Payroll		
Staff Apartments		
Painting and Decorating		
Maintenance and Repairs		
Supplies		
Trash Removal		
Exterminating		
Grounds and Pool Maintenance		
Cleaning and Janitorial		
Utilities		
Management fee _____ %		
Miscellaneous		
Legal and Accounting		
Telephone and Office Supplies		
Advertising and Promotion		
Taxes and Insurance		
Total Expenses		
Net Operating Income		

turn on investment or the periodic income that is so critical in attracting investors. It is important that managers see this monthly expenditure requirement, but adding the debt-service payments to a basic operating budget presents some problems.

An owner who has been aggressive, or even unrealistic, in acquiring one or more levels of debt can effectively destroy the proper operation of the investment. The ability of an owner to acquire debt is not an automatic indicator that a property's income can support the accompanying payments. This problem may eventually influence the budget because most managers adhere to an unwritten rule of payment priority that goes something like this: Pay the mortgage first, or there won't be any property to manage; pay the employees next, or they won't return to work; then pay the utilities—so it won't be dark and cold; and finally, pay the insurance and real estate taxes so the lender won't make a move to change the property's ownership status. Most of these expenditures or "outflows" are very predictable in addition to representing a substantial percentage of the whole budget. Income remains a variable as well as maintenance, upkeep, and repair—which are more difficult to predict.

Having a budget with a negative cash flow is unsatisfactory to the owner, who will in turn pressure the manager to increase the income and cut back on upkeep expenses in order to balance accounts. This sometimes results in less care being taken in checking prospects' references and eliminating many needed and scheduled repairs. Properties suffer when burdened with an unreasonable debt service. In my opinion, the reason most budgets do not work well is the influence of an unrealistic debt-service load.

Annual Budget

Most budgets detail income and expense projections for each of the months in the upcoming year. Nevertheless, there are situations when a total of annual income and expense items is sufficient. Usually an annual budget is prepared for submission to lenders, appraisers, investment partners, tax assessors, or others who do not need or should not be concerned with the monthly details of income or expenses. An annual budget is far less revealing and more difficult to track than a monthly budget schedule. For that same reason, an annual budget is not very valuable to either the manager or someone closely monitoring ongoing property performance.

Quarterly Budget

This budget, prepared in advance for each of the four business quarters, has become quite popular. There are several reasons for this: (1) budget numbers correlate to both the weather cycles and the changing rental activity during each of the four quarters; (2) managers can forecast income and expenses much more accurately using the smaller blocks of time; and (3) the owner's optimism is more likely to be kept in check.

People who develop a quarterly budget are often more accountable for their predictions than are those whose budgets culminate a year from now. Shorter budget periods are also more effective in stimulating achievement. When quarterly budgets are used, there is usually an annual companion budget that includes far less detail. The conservative annual budget is used for long-range planning while the shorter, quarterly budgets function more as goal-setting targets and learning tools. Utilizing this combination is the budgeting method I favor.

Rent-Up Budget

Some situations call for "special purpose" budgets. During a rent-up campaign, even a month is too long an interval between budget reports. Most rent-up budgets are prepared on a weekly schedule for periods of thirteen weeks. These budgets typically break out all of the various unit types and track week-to-week rental progress. Tracking begins the month that each unit becomes a revenue producer, not when the lease is signed or residents begin occupancy on a concession or rent holiday.

The expenses during a rent-up campaign are entirely different from those after the property has stabilized. Major costs will be advertising, public relations, collateral materials, rental personnel, incentives, and promotions. Real estate taxes, repairs, make-ready costs, and even mortgage payments will not become an issue for some months. The primary purpose of the rent-up budget is to monitor rental progress with the season and to regulate the use of advertising and promotional funds.

Major Expenditure Budget

This is a budget that is used to consolidate the major expenditures planned in a given period. For example, major expenditures might include new siding, a complete exterior paint job, redesigned courtyard landscaping, or the replacement of ten sets of appliances. By maintaining a separate budget for these items, they can be separated from the budget items that recur every year, making budget planning and analysis easier. This budget is frequently made before the actual operating budget is prepared because the decision to do certain work should be influenced by the need for the work rather than the availability of funds. The major expenditure projects can be assigned priorities and later re-evaluated after the operating budget is prepared to determine which items can be accommodated with the projected availability of cash.

Major expenditures are often kept in a separate expense category to make year-to-year budget comparisons easier. Consider the repainting of all exterior wood surfaces, expected to cost $25,000. This expenditure should not be combined with the ongoing painting and decorating that must be done each year. In this way, the manager can follow the spending pattern for each category and recognize the difference between recurring annual maintenance items and special projects.

I prefer to draw a distinction between major and *capital expenditures* and treat them separately during the budgeting process. Because the two are often confused, it is important to distinguish between them: A capital expenditure represents a true improvement to the property; major expenditures are replacements and repairs. Hence, the $15,000 bill you incur by repainting the complex constitutes a major expenditure; the $75,000 you spend installing a new swimming pool is a capital expenditure.

Replacement Reserves

This is different from the major expenditure budget. Think of replacement reserves as something like a lay-away plan. Major expense items such as the roof, boiler, appliances, and carpeting are assigned a life expectancy. Money is set aside and it often earns interest, delivering the funds to pay for replacements when necessary. The money put away each month or year for this purpose is called a *sinking fund*. Many developments, insured under either federal or state programs, require periodic deposits into a sinking fund or, as it is more commonly called, a replacement reserve. The payments are allocated to different component categories and tracked on a reserve schedule. When a replacement becomes necessary, funds are deducted from that category and used to pay for the required item. Occasionally, permission is granted to shift money between categories to cover an unexpected replacement expense. While replacement reserves are carefully structured and regulated in government-insured housing, they are far less formal in the case of conventional rental properties. Owners frequently set aside funds over a period of time to meet a planned major expenditure. The owner may choose to set aside $1,000 per month for a year and one-half to pay for a new roof or to replace leaky hot water lines. The money is budgeted on its own reserve schedule and is not included with the listing of other operating expenses. This takes place after the NOI line, but before the line detailing cash flow. Unless the owner has a change of heart, this money will not be available as spendable cash because it is being held for the upcoming replacement. The money paid into this fund by the owner must be treated as part of the property's earned income and as such is subject to income taxes. In the year that the major expenditure occurs, a transfer entry is shown on the income side of the budget inserting the replacement funds into the operating income and a line item is added in the operating budget for the cost of that improvement. At that point, the money spent is recognized and may be treated either as an expense or a depreciable asset depending on the accounting method chosen.

Contingency

In any upgrading or remodeling budget, the final expense line item to discuss is called contingency. All budgets—most particularly budgets such as rent-up or major improvement budgets—should provide an allowance for unknown items. This figure is often a percentage of the total budget and may range from as little as 2 percent to as much as 8 percent. The answer to the question, "What is it for?" is simply, "I don't know." That is why a contingency allowance exists in an estimation of upgrading expenses—to cover the unknown. If a manager can specify one or more possible expenditures such as higher labor costs, additional drywall patching, or the like, he or she would be better advised to increase the amount budgeted for those particular expense categories or add more line items to include these specific anticipated expenses. The contingency category is for items that cannot be foreseen; these things have a way of popping up as the year gets under way.

PREPARING A BUDGET

There are a series of important considerations in the process of preparing an operating budget for a rental apartment property. Obviously, the more experience a manager has operating a particular property or type of property, the more accurate and useful the budget will be. Without the benefit of past records, the budget preparation process will require much more time and reveal greater variances and outright distortions. Some useful guidelines follow.

Use Realistic Figures

Starting with income, there is a tendency to make calculations using current rent levels and to ignore the *aging of the leases*. It is also very easy to project rentals and fail to account for free rent allowances. Experienced managers have learned to be conservative with their income projections. Owners are never upset when their managers report more income than was anticipated in the budget; the problems arise when the situation is reversed. Being conservative is even more important regarding projections of unscheduled income.

When budgeting expenses, don't skimp or ignore the price increases that will surely occur. This doesn't mean that you cannot find ways to operate a property more efficiently or investigate trends to learn about departures from "the norm." Utilities, services, insurance, and real estate taxes follow a pattern and can be tracked fairly easily, but make some telephone calls and do some investigation to avoid surprises. Payroll and related expenses often create a major problem. It is easy to account for existing salaries, but there is a tendency to forget to allow for overtime, salary increases, seasonal workers, vacation replacements, incentives, and benefits. My experience indicates that this category is typically the most underbudgeted and overspent. Supplies, repairs, and maintenance are the other expense categories that are most frequently misjudged during budget preparation. They do not always show up as budgeting errors because as the manager sees a budget problem developing, expenditures are sometimes reclassified to other categories or eliminated entirely—thus depriving the property of repairs or improvements. This can harm the property in many other ways.

Again, the best advice is to develop a workable budget with realistic projections. Don't be pressured into committing to an unrealistic budget in November, only to be forced to apologize each month in the following year.

Acceptable Variances

Just how far off can you be and still be within an acceptable variance? There are some established industry rules to help answer that question. Normally, a sense of limited variance acceptability is created by the use of *specific, rather than rounded figures.* In other words, by estimating the water bill to be $3,434, one is effectively expressing a high degree of confidence in the projection. Anyone reading the budget might assume that the water bill will reflect that figure, plus or minus a few dollars. Had the projection been $3,400, that same person might assume an acceptable variance range from $3,300 to $3,500.

Remember, budgets are estimates and a lot can happen in one year; leave a little room for the unknown. A pro's budget is filled with lots of triple zeros and double zeros. Don't try to predict income or expenses to the exact dollar.

Budget Categories

There isn't much to be gained by establishing a great number of income or expense categories. The more categories you have, the more likely things are to be misclassified; analysis is also made more difficult. This problem is exacerbated when overspending occurs in certain budget categories, and the manager begins changing expense classifications to minimize budget forecast miscalculations. Let's take a look at the basic income categories:

- Apartment income
- Other scheduled income (parking, commercial, etc.)
- Concession income (laundry, vending, etc.)
- Non-scheduled income (clubroom rentals, late charges, NSF charges, forfeited security deposits, etc.)

The list of operating expenses can be considerably longer, but many major investors choose to limit the display of expenses to five major categories:

- Utilities and services
- Payroll and related expenses
- Management, administrative and promotion
- Real estate taxes and insurance
- Repairs and maintenance

Grouping expenses in these broad categories eliminates most of the confusion concerning category identification and provides the budget reader with a quick method of monitoring expense performance. Unfortunately, when too few categories are listed, the budget isn't as great a help to a property manager. The typical breakdown for tracking and comparison are contained in these categories:

- Utilities
- Services
- Supplies
- Payroll and related expenses
- Advertising and promotion
- Management and administrative
- Legal and audit
- Insurance
- Real estate taxes
- Repairs and maintenance
- Miscellaneous

Seasonality

For each category of expense, it must be decided whether projections should reflect the trends exhibited in the previous months or in the same period during the preceding year. The latter focus is called seasonality. For example, when preparing a budget for heating expense, one should be more interested in what happened a year ago January than in the "lead-up" months of November and December (months that are typically warmer than January). Lease-up expenditures, yard maintenance, exterior repairs, and utilities are a few examples of expenses that correlate more to a season than to the previous month's pattern. Even expenses such as insurance and real estate taxes have seasonality because these charges do not accrue monthly. Laundry income is something else that follows a definite seasonal pattern. In locations with weather patterns that change with the seasons, January usually shows the smallest laundry collections because heavier winter clothing tends to be less washable, and many people receive new clothing over the holidays. July is one of the most lucrative laundry months because people change their washable summer clothing much more frequently. These patterns are well established and can and should be accounted for in monthly budget projections.

On the other hand, services, supplies, and many maintenance expenditures follow a monthly pattern. Income items follow their own patterns as well. Renewals and inflation often have a way of increasing rent each month; this makes month-to-month progression much more indicative of current trends than the amount collected at this time last year.

In most areas of the United States, the fuel consumed to heat a property during the first ninety days of the year is about one-half of the annual total, with January's fuel expense being the highest. In order to be a useful planning and tracking tool, the budget must reflect consumption expectations rather than the annual heating costs divided by six to reflect the heating season, or even worse, by twelve for the entire year. The same is true of air-conditioning expenses during the warm months. Generally, property managers estimate monthly heating expenses with the help of "heating degree day" statistics that are recorded by several government agencies, most notably the United States Weather Bureau and the National Oceanic and Atmospheric Administration (NOAA). These records have been collected for over 100 years for most communities.

Heating degree days are calculated for the heating season in this way: Starting with the *base temperature of 65 degrees Fahrenheit,* subtract the average temperature for a given day to produce that particular day's heating degree days. For example, assume the average temperature in your city on February 28 is 45 degrees Fahrenheit. Subtracting 45 from 65, there are twenty heating degree days for your city on February 28th.

Daily temperatures and heating degree days are recorded and reported at airports and many other locations. Many major newspapers report degree days every day and often print temperature variances from a normal or average year. Subscription services are also available to provide wind and moisture information as well as very specific degree day data for each hour of the day. While this is interesting, it is much more than anyone needs for budgeting purposes. Knowing the average heating degree days for each month makes it easier to estimate heating costs. We can also determine how much fuel will cost or how many Btu's (British thermal units) it takes to satisfy one heating degree day. For example, if you know that the total gas heating cost is $22,000 (i.e., the total bill, exclusive of the gas consumed for cooking, heating water, and drying clothes) and the average number of heating degree days in your location is 4,900, you can ascertain that about $4.50 is required to satisfy a single degree day. Knowing this, one is in a much better position to estimate the variable expense of heat and to enter an accurate budget forecast in each month's column. You can do a similar analysis by carefully examining the monthly fuel bills for one or more years. It is important that you use the total fuel bill, including any charges, fuel adjustments, taxes, meter charges, etc. These extras often add up considerably; omitting them would significantly distort your projections.

Cooling degree days are calculated in much the same way, except that the base temperature of 65 degrees is subtracted from the average daily summer temperature to calculate that day's number of degree day units (e.g., a day with an average temperature of 85 degrees would have twenty cooling degree days).

Development Size

You might expect this section to address the issue of economy of size, and to some extent it does. Nevertheless, there are limits to the advantage of

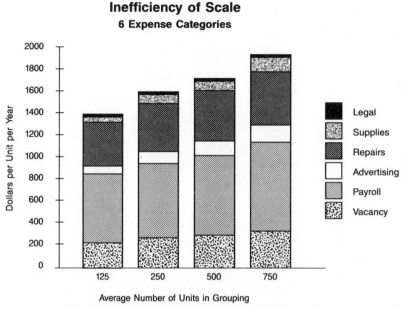

Inefficiency of Scale
6 Expense Categories

Legend:
- Legal
- Supplies
- Repairs
- Advertising
- Payroll
- Vacancy

Average Number of Units in Grouping
1989 Operating Expenses 36,000 Unit Study

size; the per-apartment costs of operating a large development tend to be higher than those of a smaller development. A very definite pattern emerged when I studied and monitored the expense ledgers for 36,000 units in several hundred apartment properties ranging in size from six apartments to as many as one thousand. Small properties, those under fifty units, enjoyed very little savings due to size. Those developments with more than fifty units showed an increasing efficiency of operation up through approximately the 110-unit point. After that high point, the operating efficiency—in per-unit operational costs—began a slow but consistent downturn that accelerated after passing the 130-unit point. This pattern, or at least the high point on the chart, showed some movement during the years 1983 to 1988. The high point moved from 88 units to 110.

The very large developments, those with 300 units and more, spent many hundreds of dollars more per unit per year than did their smaller, correlative apartment communities. The differences in spending occurred in six distinct areas: vacancies, payroll, repairs, supplies, advertising, and legal expenses. There was also a disparity between the rent amounts collected for similar unit types. Differences became very pronounced as the size of the properties being compared increased.

Let's take a closer look at my study. Starting with base figures from the communities with about 125 units, the cost increases experienced by properties larger than that were examined. The results strongly indicate that the apartment management industry has not increased management skills as fast as the building industry has increased its ability to build bigger developments. I will clarify this by providing some data from the study and pointing out the ways these figures relate to the expense categories affected most by the size of the development.

Vacancies. The average number of rent loss days between the departure of an old resident and arrival of a new one ranged from twenty-two days in the 125-unit properties to fifty-one days in the 750-unit group. The time required to get a vacant unit into market-ready condition was twelve days for the smaller properties and thirty-five days for the larger ones.

Managers of the smaller apartment communities reported impending move-outs considerably sooner than their counterparts managing larger properties. After interviewing managers, it was concluded that the manager of a smaller rental community was likely to have a more personal relationship with his or her residents than was the manager of a large community. Consequently, the manager of the smaller property is alerted to potential move-outs sooner, giving that manager a head start in a situation that is already favorable because he or she has fewer units to prepare each month. This difference in preparation time means money lost for the larger property.

Payroll.   You might expect the number of apartments per staff member to increase in the case of larger properties, but in fact the opposite trend was observed. Staff members with highly specialized responsibilities were basically nonexistent in the smaller properties but became increasingly more commonplace as the size of the community increased. In the large properties there were staff members who handled only a single task. There is often little job flexibility within these developments, even when certain jobs such as bookkeeping or leasing demonstrated clear patterns of slow and busy times.

Repairs.   It was concluded that smaller properties tend to repair things while larger properties are more likely to replace components. Perhaps the maintenance staff of smaller properties learn to fix things in place because they have little or no room to store replacements. Also, larger properties spend considerably more in hiring outside mechanics and tradespeople than do the smaller 125-unit properties.

Supplies.   You might expect the manager of a large apartment complex to attract the attention of a wholesale supplier offering considerable discounts from the prices charged at the local hardware store. Though savings may exist in terms of price per item purchased, the study found that larger properties purchased larger quantities on an apartment per year basis. Waste, over-ordering, and subsequent pilferage were far more prevalent in the large developments.

Advertising.   During the comparative examination of advertising, it was discovered that the larger 750-unit developments purchased more than three times the number of lines of print space per vacant apartment than the smaller 125-unit complexes. Ads for the smaller properties typically highlighted a particular unit and usually ran in weekend newspaper editions only. These ads were small—rarely over ten lines in length. It would seem that the size of the community dictated the size of the advertisement. Ad size did appear to have a relationship to the number of prospects who responded—more prospects responded to the larger ads—but the prospect-to-resident conversion ratio was clearly better in the smaller properties.

Legal Expense.   Although legal fees make up a very small percentage of an apartment community's overall expenditures, the pattern of higher legal costs followed the increase in the size of the developments being studied. It is interesting to note that in the five years of the study there were very few evictions in the smaller apartment communities. During the same five years, there was an almost monthly procession of court cases and evictions in the larger properties. This is attributable to the more personal relationship that exists between residents and managers in the smaller properties.

Rent Revenue.   An additional observation from this study is worth sharing. The smaller apartment communities were consistently successful in achieving greater amounts of rent per apartment, probably because smaller developments offer more identity than do large ones.

Time and training will diminish the expense imbalance between smaller and larger properties, but the person putting together an operating budget must take size-related patterns into account. The budgeting method cannot be as simple as developing a set of per-unit expense figures for each category and multiplying them by the number of units in the development. I believe more owners and managers should begin to divide their larger properties into smaller, more economical sections. This can be done most easily when there is some geographical boundary such as a corner lot with entrances on two major streets, or if architecture varies from one section of the development to another.

Building Age and the Budget

There is a tendency to budget for all apartment communities basically the same way once buildings are built and completed. Nevertheless, when it comes to repairs and maintenance, there are significant differences among apartment properties that are the result of differences in their ages. Budgeting for repairs and maintenance for years two through four is fairly simple. Most equipment and components still function almost like new, and those items that do malfunction are often under warranty. Parts are readily available and repairs usually involve only a part or two rather than complete systems. Ceiling and closet painting can often be skipped; carpets need shampooing rather than replacement. After the first four years, however, the repair and maintenance pace picks up considerably in continuing four-year cycles. Assuming constant dollars (in other words, ignoring any inflationary effect), these two expense categories, considered together, increase about 7 percent per year. That means in five years, repairs and maintenance costs will have risen 35 percent—before any cost of living increases are taken into account. Over ten years, plan on a 70 percent increase in the costs of repair and general maintenance. Older buildings simply cost more to maintain, and an accurate budget will reflect that fact. Unfortunately, just about the time this becomes obvious, another trend becomes clear: Achieving rent increases also becomes correspondingly more difficult as a building ages.

BUDGET ANALYSIS

Once a budget is prepared, there is still the job of comparing it to actual results and learning ways to analyze budget variances. Some variances occur because the budget does not account for the natural lag between the month in which an expense is expected and the month when the bill for that expense is actually received and paid. The utility bill paid this month usually covers the preceding month's charges. This is true of many bills—with the exception of payroll, management fees, real estate taxes, and debt-service payments. This effect levels out when analyzing an entire year because one has accounted for all twelve months. Variances arise when the budget is examined a month at a time. It is usually better to adjust the budget to reflect the month when a charge or invoice will be received or paid rather than the time the commodity or service is delivered or performed. If the estimate of income and expenses does not reflect reality, the budget loses much of its month-to-month usefulness as a tracking tool.

Same Period Last Year

In addition to the item-by-item tracking of budget to actual, the most widely watched variable is a comparison of this year's figures to the figures in a corresponding category the previous year. This practice reveals the beginnings of patterns that can lead to potential problems. If certain categories start to "slip" as the actual expenses begin to accumulate each month, it may be necessary to revise the budget. The budget is not etched in stone and should not be used to demonstrate just how far actual figures can vary from budget estimates. A budget is a tool that isn't worth much when it fails to project what is actually occurring. Sticking to a budget that isn't working is a waste of time.

Percentage of Income

The percentage of gross possible income is useful because it indicates trends in the larger and more important categories (e.g., real estate taxes equal 15 percent of gross possible income). This method is best used when comparing the year-to-year changes that occur for a single property or for properties with very similar rental ranges. However, such an analysis will cause problems when applied to properties that have a wide disparity in their rent levels. Most computer programs for financial analysis provide a column to express both income and expense as a percentage of the gross possible income. Some software, however, indicates the percentage of collections; this can be very misleading and may cause considerable confusion.

My studies of garden apartment complexes indicate that the total operating expenses expressed as a percentage of the gross possible income can vary by as much as 18 percent, depending on the average rent level. Properties for the limited-income group tend to be older, need more repair and, more importantly, have a lower rent schedule than do some of the newer, more up-to-date complexes. While the rent in a limited-income complex may be half that of the more-expensive and more-luxurious developments, certain expenses remain virtually the same. The charges for services such as rubbish removal or pest control are probably the same throughout a municipality, and the utility companies charge standard rates for heat, light, and water. The difference lies in expressing the expenses as a percentage of each property's gross income. Owners who have several properties with a wide range of rent levels often have trouble understanding why one property requires 42 percent of its income for operating expenses while another property in the same town requires 56 percent. The truth of the matter is, the percentage of gross possible income that is required to cover expenses goes down only as the average rent level goes up.

This changes when analyzing urban properties with major rent differentials, however. High-rise buildings are not only much more expensive to build, they also frequently add expensive amenities such as door attendants, parking garages, and a host of specialized services. These added expenses neutralize some of the variance I just described.

Dollars per Room

One of the standby indicators for comparing the operating results of one property to those of another is dollars per room per year. This is not nearly as popular a method as percentage of gross possible income. Though less affected by differences in rent levels, this method does not take size of rooms into consideration, nor does it consider bathrooms (a meaningful source of problems and expense). It requires uniformity in preparing the count of rooms, or much of its analytical value is lost. (The reader is reminded of the discussion in chapter 1 recommending a room-counting method.)

Cents (or Dollars) per Square Foot

Appraisers commonly use cents—or dollars—per square foot as another method of comparing operating expenses. It should be emphasized that square foot references in real estate are made on a yearly basis with one major exception, apartment rents, which are expressed monthly. Apartment rents, when displayed in a square foot format, are detailed in *cents (or dollars) per rentable square foot.* In other words, the rent is calculated using only the space that is contained in the occupied unit, and no allowance is made for the areas that feed and support the living space—often referred to as *common area or nonyield space.*

While the residential manager receives rent for only the rentable square feet, he or she must operate and maintain the entire complex. Hence, operating expenses are expressed on a gross square foot basis—it is probably one of the most popular methods of examining operating expenses and is especially useful when comparing properties. Breaking expenses down to rentable square feet will lead to problems because of the constant adjustments necessary to compensate for differences in architectural styles and varying proportions of nonyield space. I am not aware of any data base collecting apartment expense information on a rentable square foot basis.

Cost per Apartment

Analyzing an apartment's operating expenses based on the cost per apartment per year might appear simplistic, but it does produce surprisingly accurate results. The key to this method is expressing all of the property's expenses as one total. Within a single apartment community, the cost to operate a smaller apartment is about the same as the cost to operate a larger one. Because turnover rates are higher in smaller units, make-ready expenses are incurred more frequently. This offsets the higher per-unit preparation cost for a larger unit. Repairs to mechanical systems and appliances do not vary much between apartments of different size—making these costs fairly similar. Significant differences in operating expenses will be revealed if comparisons are made by line item, but these expenses have a tendency to equalize when treated as a total.

Cost per Plumbing Fixture

In my opinion, analyzing operating expenses on a cost-per-plumbing-fixture basis produces some very reliable results for a number of reasons. This method involves looking at the number of plumbing fixtures per unit, a figure that will be closely related to both the size of an apartment and the rent level. In addition to adjusting for the extra damage and breakdown exposure of added plumbing connections, the relationship of plumbing fixtures to costs is a real one.

A count of plumbing connections would include the obvious, such as the kitchen sink, bathroom vanity, tub, and water closet as well as those connections necessary for disposals, dishwashers, hot water dispensers, ice makers, washers, bar sink, bidet, hot tub, fountains, etc. Larger bathrooms often have multiple sinks or bathing facilities, and each one should be counted as a plumbing connection. Most of these items require additional apartment area and this signals increased operating costs. As the number of these devices increases, your residents are likely to be more affluent, and your rent level—the prime indicator of a property's quality of operation—is apt to be higher. I believe that this method of budget analysis will become more and more popular.

As you can see from this example, budgets and budget analysis can take many forms. The point to be made is that budgets are necessary to plan the financial operation of any complex. Learning to use them as management tools is a necessary lesson for every property manager.

Computer

CHAPTER

12

Computers, Accounting, and Records

COMPUTERS

On the way home from the closing, the new owner of an apartment property would be well advised to make one more purchase that day—a personal computer. The job of administering the paperwork and accounting tasks of a large apartment building is formidable, and a computer can greatly simplify these tasks. Now, with the computer as a mainstay of most management operations, those who continue to resist this technology find themselves on the outside looking in.

What makes the computer so important is its ability to handle repetitive tasks using only a fraction of the time the same job would take manually. As one might gather through reading this book, there is a lot to the apartment management business, and most managers need more time on the property to see that everything is being done correctly. That's difficult when you are saddled with paperwork, schedules, lists, letters, and basic record keeping.

Equipment

Every day, the technology and variety of computers and printers advances to yet another level. The day you purchase a computer, the product is usually on its way to becoming obsolete—the manufacturer has already directed its staff to find ways to improve or replace the machine you just purchased. Nevertheless, don't fall into the trap of waiting for the "next generation" of technology. The longer you wait, the more difficult it will be to catch up with everyone else in the property management business.

The computer equipment used to handle the chores of the property management business should have considerable speed and substantial memory capacity. A good part of the work you will want the computer to perform will involve a data base system of one design or another to maintain resident and accounting records. This processing can be slow with the old-style microchips, and property management files can use up a great deal of memory in a very short time. You surely want to maximize productivity during the time you utilize the computer; you are best advised to purchase equipment at the leading edge of technology in terms of speed and memory capacity.

The manufacturer of the equipment is not quite as important as the *operating system* that is employed by that firm's machines. Stay in the mainstream. Talk with a number of your associates in the property management business before making a decision. Find out what kind of equipment they use and ask the names of compatible software. There is a great deal of sharing of customized spreadsheets, privately written programs, and advice among professionals in the property management business; but if you are to participate in that sharing, you will need compatible computer operating systems and equipment. (Note: Do be mindful of the way copyright laws govern the exchange of programs.) If your equipment is made by a major manufacturer, it will probably be easier to obtain advice on how to install and operate it. You do not want to be the proud owner of equipment that worked fine during the "canned" showroom presentation but won't print your rent roll when you're back at the office.

Your hardware requirements will include a printer. This equipment is clearly moving toward continued advancement of laser technology. The printing process is quick and quiet, and the printed page appears as if it has been typeset. Because so much of a management firm's work ends up in printed form, it would be foolish to damage your image with the output of a bottom-of-the-line printer. Compatibility is less of a problem with printers because most software developers have made the effort to ensure that their product will work with the widest assortment of printers and configurations.

Software

One of the most difficult aspects of converting accounting chores to a computer is selecting software. With the dozens and dozens of programs on the market, you shouldn't choose to develop your own custom program. I know of firms that have been "developing" a workable accounting program for years. Meanwhile, they must struggle along with a manual or quasi-automatic system while they are waiting. There are many programs available today that will handle all but the most specialized tasks, and you can be "up and running" in several weeks. The wheel has been invented; save yourself the time and trouble of reinvention.

Choosing the right software for your operation remains a very difficult task, however. Suppliers carefully package software to show off the strong and unique attributes of their products; the limitations are not publicized. These limitations are for you to discover when you get the new program back to the office. This is why it is so important to speak with fellow property managers. If they have had a system for some time, they will quickly recite its deficiencies and at the same time explain what it really can do. You should also ask the software dealer for a complete collection of print-outs that can be generated by their program. Study and compare a number of these to determine if they will deliver what you need or expect. Your study will also prompt a number of questions that you should be asking dealers. It is the salesperson's job to sell; it is your job to sift through the many different functions of these programs to be sure they will perform the work the way you want it done. Choosing the wrong software program can have serious consequences—if you find another program next year that suits you better, it is very complicated to switch. Take a little more time with your initial decision.

Spreadsheet.   In addition to your accounting software, you will need what is referred to as an electronic spreadsheet. Basically, the electronic spreadsheet is set up along the lines of a columnar pad with rows and columns. This is the program that you will spend most of your time using. Monday morning reports, budgets, listings of availabilities, time records, analyses, evaluations, financial reports, and presentations are just a few examples of the daily tasks that can be accomplished very quickly using spreadsheets. Many managers have gone a step further and have automated data entry or calculations by writing program macros, a set of commands making up a kind of mini-program to instruct the computer to perform a series of tasks. The commands might be in the form of user prompts requesting the input of different information. After all of the information has been gathered, the computer usually follows additional instructions to sort the data, perform the calculations, and print a schedule of processed information. These programs can be written in a few hours and customized to perform some very specialized and time-consuming tasks. Personnel with very little computer training can quickly learn to handle the input. Property managers develop many of these specialized programs over the course of a year or two and they commonly trade these privately written and macro-driven programs with other managers. This is another reason why it is so important to select initial equipment and basic software that is compatible with the mainstays of the real estate industry.

Ideally, you will want an accounting package that is compatible with your electronic spreadsheet program. You should insist upon the capability of *importing and exporting data* to and from your spreadsheets. For example, you may develop a customized budget that lists all of your budget categories and has room for insertions in separate monthly columns plus the yearly totals. After filling in the spreadsheet, you may want to export these numbers to the accounting program. Without the ability to export this information directly to the accounting program, you must re-enter all of your data—and avoiding this was one of your reasons for choosing automation. The same thing is true in reverse. Computer accounting systems contain a host of data, including all of your information regarding residents, collections, expenses, etc. You may need a listing that specifies where each resident works, or an itemization of expenses on a per-square-foot, room, or plumbing-fixture basis. Your program should be capable of extracting data from the records that exist in the accounting program in a manner that can be used by the spreadsheet program.

There is a major risk inherent in spreadsheets: Their looks can be deceiving. Spreadsheets often present columns of figures that line up nicely, but may not be correct. Because they look good and are the product of a computer calculation, people tend to accept figures displayed on a spreadsheet without checking them. Unfortunately, the formula in the cell calling for the total of a column may not extend to all of the rows of figures—or the formula may be wrong. Another difficulty exists with macros that are prepared to handle a specific job, perhaps in connection with a particular property. You might decide that with a few changes you can use such a macro for other jobs or properties. If this is not done carefully, a variable associated with the original may be forgotten—making the modifications incorrect. Computers are wonderful tools, but they can't protect you against yourself.

Word Processing.   Next on the list of required software is a program that will perform your word processing. Like other types of software, there is a constant procession of new programs and new generations of old programs. Every person who has taken the time to become proficient with a particular program believes it to be the best. It will take some investigation to determine what is best for you. The standard advice applies here as well: *Stick with the programs that have proven themselves.* There are books, newsletters, and user groups to help you with the best-known programs—so why waste your time being a pioneer?

There are programs that will do just about anything you want to accomplish with words or numbers. You can write single letters, form letters, or newsletters. You can produce labels, invoices, forms, or even letterheads. Some will allow you to print not only the standard input concerning the parties to the agreement and the terms of the lease, but also the entire lease form in a single printing. So much of our work is repetitive; the word processor can handle most writing tasks with just a few commands. You will be able to personalize letters that were once handled as general form letters. You can ask the machine to insert custom salutations and to use the resident's or client's name in the body of the letter and the letter's spacing will adjust automatically. Management offices now collect certain letters dealing with common situations and catalog them for future use.

Most management offices keep their records in unit number order because the unit is permanent and the resident isn't. That's fine when the resident is standing in front of you or he or she is on the telephone and you can request the unit number, but what about inquiries from a parcel delivery service driver? Word processing programs can usually produce an alphabetized listing of your residents or your vendors in a matter of minutes. Such programs will also help you with your spelling, word selection, and even grammar. Word processors have become so popular in property management offices that often the biggest problem is producing a single, typed envelope.

Graphics.   Property managers spend a considerable part of the workweek preparing presentations to explain or promote ideas, plans, and results. Boring rows and columns of numbers can come alive with the use of computer graphics. Beautiful color visuals can be customized and produced in minutes using basic hardware, a plotter or a color printer, and one of the many graphics programs available. Signs, charts, title pages, and even floor plans are easily generated. In fact, some managers have their floor plans on file in the computer so that they can work with prospective renters and plan positioning of the prospects' furniture in various unit layouts. This same capability is often used to redesign troublesome units.

Computer Skills Tell a Story

A property manager with little or no computer skill has severely impaired his or her career potential. There is no doubt that the computer will play an increasingly important role in property management. Those waiting for their employer to provide the equipment and training could be left far behind. When interviewing for new staff members, progressive executive managers will surely inquire about computer familiarity. A lack of meaningful computer skills will hurt your chances in the selection process.

On the other hand, we have all seen the manager who goes overboard learning about the machine and all of its intricacies. Hiding behind a computer while producing reams of reports cannot replace on-the-job common sense. After all, apartment management is a business of people contact. Property managers should use computers to provide more time to spend with customers, not machines.

ACCOUNTING

Personal computers make your work easier, but they can't think for you. To begin to put your machine(s) to work, you must consider all the aspects of accounting for the income and expenses of your property.

Types of Income

In the process of managing rental apartments, you will collect and spend a great deal of other people's money. The collections fall into two basic categories: scheduled income (the rent roll) and unscheduled income (any income received other than rent). The design of any accounting system should be based on tracking the *fixed factor* (which is, in this case, the apartment units), and not the *variable factor* (in this case, the residents). If there are 120 units, we must account for 120 unit months (43,800 days) of potential income. It is to be hoped that most units will be occupied by rent-paying residents, but all units—vacant, office, model, unrentable, storage, etc.—must be accounted for each month. A system that does not maintain a running financial history of each and every rental unit can be easily compromised.

The second form of income, unscheduled receipts, presents more problems and accounting risks. More money is misappropriated, "lost," or stolen from this area than any other.

Unscheduled revenues come from several sources: resident payments to cover damages, fees from concessionaires, charges for use of a hospitality or recreation room, lease settlements or cancellation fees, back-rent payments on accounts that have been written off, and income from building-owned laundry equipment, among others. Much of this money comes in the form of cash. It can amount to many thousands of dollars over a one-year period. Because of this and the fact that collection cannot always be anticipated, the opportunity for loss through theft or misuse is great. Be aware that the situation exists and that the risk is also there. No system is foolproof, but you should take the time to develop a system that will at least minimize the risk.

Handling Security Deposit Funds

Security deposit funds are a daily part of a manager's work. The manager starts by issuing a receipt for this money to the individual resident. The money is then typically deposited into the property's operating account or, in some jurisdictions, it must be maintained in a separate escrow account. Some laws now require that the entity collecting the security deposit (e.g., the management firm) remain responsible for the reimbursement at the time of move-out. Such laws are a response to complaints by renters who have lost their security deposit money because the property was sold or the owner became insolvent. Traditionally, new security deposit funds were deposited to the operating account as income, and refund checks were cut from the operating revenues of the move-out month. If all went well, a new resident was in position to move in, and effectively that person's security deposit money was used to repay the vacating resident. During periods of rising vacancies, however, the collection of new security deposit funds does not equal the money being refunded. That means operating expense money must be diverted at a time when it is most needed. When refunds are not made promptly, word spreads quickly and this affects both new rentals and renewals. It has been common practice for legislatures to enact stricter regulations governing the return of security deposits. Many of these involve rather severe penalties if prompt refunds are not made.

Virtually all real estate accounting systems prepare a monthly schedule itemizing each resident's security deposit account and listing a total of the security deposit liability. This money belongs to others, so a fiduciary responsibility is involved. As manager, you may be held responsible if this money is not available at the time the resident completes his or her occupancy requirement.

More and more communities have passed laws requiring the owner to pay interest on security deposit funds. Usually, this means actually preparing a check each year, not just crediting the security deposit account with the earned interest. Either way, if the interest exceeds $10, the owner—or more commonly the agent—must promptly issue a Form 1099 signaling to the Internal Revenue Service that interest has been paid.

Owner's Custodial Account

All monies collected on behalf of the owner should be placed in a custodial or trust account separate from the funds of the managing agent. There should be no commingling of the owner's and management company's funds. Separate custodial accounts for a property owner's funds are required by most state laws and ethics codes and by the United States Department of Housing and Urban Development for all federally insured or assisted apartment properties.

It's not necessary for every building to have its own bank account, although this is sometimes done and may be required in some areas or by some management agreements. It is more desirable to deposit all funds from properties under your management in a single bank account. This practice greatly simplifies check-writing and record-keeping procedures. Each owner then receives a statement showing his or her cash position. The single bank account for all owners' funds is a matter of convenience for the managing agent.

One word of caution: With several different owners' funds in a single custodial account, it is possible to inadvertently overdraw one owner's funds using the surplus funds of another. Unless you have approval for this, you are making an unauthorized loan of an owner's money. As an alternative, some management firms have invested in equipment that is capable of imprinting the magnetic bank account code number on blank, continuous form checks. This provides the convenience of writing checks on individual bank accounts for each property without the problem of constantly loading the printer with different checks.

Accrual versus Cash Accounting

For the most part, accrual accounting has replaced cash-basis accounting, because the Internal Revenue Service requires it in most cases and it is the preferred general accounting practice. It certainly provides a truer financial picture than cash-basis accounting. Accrual accounting is also essential if the accounting records are to be audited. Many computerized management programs are a mixture of the two forms of accounting. These systems track rents on an accrual basis but account for many expenses on a cash basis or when paid. It is then the job of the owner's accountant to sort out the differences at income tax time.

Purchase Orders

In order to provide true accrual accounting, the accounting of expenditures should begin at the time a product or service is ordered or a commitment is made. Without such information, the owner or his or her accounting consultant does not have a realistic picture of the property's financial position at any given point in time. Many computer programs require that purchases be made with a purchase order system that begins tracking a potential obligation from the time it is issued—not when the invoice is received or the bill is actually paid.

It is important to make all purchases with a *written and numbered purchase order.* This is essential if you are to keep track of what is ordered, what orders are outstanding, and whether the invoices agree with the quoted price. If you have a file of such orders and a building is sold, you can easily contact vendors whose shipments have not been delivered and cancel the orders. Otherwise, vendors may fill the orders and then bill you or the former owner, a situation that could lead to disputes. The new owner may refuse to pay the bill, claiming not to have authorized the order; the vendor might then put a lien on the building, further complicating matters. This unpleasantness can be avoided if you cancel unfilled orders. Without a purchase order file, you'll have trouble remembering what orders are open. The remedy is to put everything in writing.

Every purchase order placed by a managing agent should contain a notice to the effect that *the management company is acting as an agent, not as the principal, and that it will disclose the identity of the principal if requested.* This signals to the supplier that your company is an agent and that the principal, not the managing agent, is responsible for payment of the invoice. (Obviously, the notice is not necessary if the manager is a direct employee of the owner.) Without this notice, the supplier can assume that the managing agent is acting on his or her own behalf and will look to the agent for collection if the invoice isn't paid. It's very rare that a supplier will ask the identity of the principal but, if you are asked, you should be allowed to disclose this information.

Bill Payments

As managing agent, you need policies and procedures for paying bills. The major points to be considered follow.

- *Choose a period to pay bills when money is available and when you have the time to do the paperwork.* Do not have suppliers submit bills by the tenth of the month for payment on the first of the following month. While it's true that bank balances are highest in the beginning days of the month, this is also the busiest time because the manager is handling move-outs and move-ins, collecting rents, taking complaints, and doing extra paperwork. It would be better to select a time that's less hectic—perhaps the middle of the month—for bill payments.

  In the same regard, it's unfortunate that most mortgage payments are due on the first of each month. Invariably, there isn't enough money collected and in the bank to meet the first-of-the-month payment date. At the time the mortgage was originally made, it would have been an easy matter to arrange for payments to be due later in the month. Even if the mortgage is established, it's worth a try to have the payment date set forward. By setting the date at the fifteenth, there will be more money on hand, and the payment can be handled more comfortably.

- *Inform all vendors of your bill-paying procedures.* This will discourage calls from vendors who want to know when they will be paid.

- *Be aware of discounts and gross and net billings.* The manager should take advantage of these discounts merely as good business. If you can't take discounts because of a short turnaround period or because of a lack of funds, notify owners of this right away. Otherwise, if they find out that you're not taking advantage of discounts, they may put in a claim for the money because you were negligent. Negotiating discounts and payment terms is frequently part of the property manager's responsibility.

To take advantage of discounts, you may have to deviate from your established bill-paying schedule. For example, many discounts are only available if payment is made within ten days of the invoice date; if you pay in fifteen days, the discount won't be granted. Some vendors, however, will honor a discount even if payment is made thirty days later, feeling that money is money. Others will strictly observe the discount period.

Utility companies may bill on a gross and net basis. The lower net amount must be paid by the stated due date; the higher gross amount is due some days later. If your operation is large enough, the utility company may extend the net period.

Another point about utility bills: You may be billed for a vacant apartment even though it is leased to a new resident. The same thing may happen if a resident moves in early. To avoid this, have the resident sign the utility application and turn-on card when the lease is signed, so his or her utility service and charges will begin with the date the lease is in effect or the move-in date, whichever is earlier. It is to your advantage to have utility company forms in your office and mail the signed forms to the utility company yourself. Residents will appreciate the fact that you've saved them some time, while you ensure that the chore will be addressed immediately.

- *Avoid paying bills that are cash on delivery (COD).* Some vendors insist on COD payment, especially if they've had bad experiences with apartment owners and managers. Once you are in the habit of paying COD, vendors will insist on it because it's the quickest way to get cash; there's no incentive for them to change. Paying COD will complicate your record-keeping and bill-paying procedures.

  If necessary, change vendors in order to avoid COD billings. With a new vendor, allow time for the vendor to run a credit check and approve the account. This is recommended for purchases of all supplies, materials, and services. The only exceptions would be payments for one-time items, such as emergency, noncontract snowplowing for which the driver demands cash.

- *Don't use petty cash funds to pay vendors.* If you do, you will need a large cash fund on hand to pay all the vendors who will soon demand cash. These funds are subject to theft and misuse. It also leads to poor record keeping. Petty cash is for incidental purchases such as postage stamps and postage due, small shipping charges, gas for lawn mowers, and minor office expenses. A revolving fund of $200 should be adequate for most properties.

- *Have bills approved by the site manager who ordered the work before they are processed for payment.* If checks are prepared centrally, don't send the checks back to the site manager for review prior to forwarding to the vendor. Some firms do this, claiming that it enables the site manager to know who is being paid and to hold back a check if there is a last-minute question about performance. This should have been determined before the bill was approved for payment.

The danger of letting the site manager approve the check or forward it to the vendor is that it provides the chance to extract a kickback from the vendor, even if it's nothing more than a free lunch. By simply calling the vendor and saying, "I've got your check," the site manager exerts some pressure on the vendor. This leads to a poor business relationship, which in turn will cost the owner money.

Form 1099

Vendors who are not corporations must be issued a Form 1099, Miscellaneous Income, detailing the amount of money that was paid to them in the year. This form must be in their hands shortly after the end of the calendar year. Many computer programs can prepare these forms to be sent to vendors, the IRS, and state authorities (where applicable). The Internal Revenue Service does exempt minor amounts from this accounting of miscellaneous income; always be aware of the current IRS definition of a "minor amount." The IRS rigidly enforces its regulations and there are penalties for noncompliance.

Taxes and Reporting Forms

As managing agent, you will most likely prepare payroll checks and this will involve making regular deposits of monies withheld for federal and state income taxes as well as accounting for both employer and employee social security contributions (FICA), employer contributions to Federal Unemployment Insurance Tax (FUTA), and other payroll taxes. Most management firms are also responsible for filing Form 941, Employer's Quarterly Payroll Tax Return, which reconciles tax liability. Shortly after the end of each calendar year, every employee is entitled to receive a Form W-2, Wage and Tax Statement, detailing gross wages earned as well as the total amount of taxes withheld and contributions made into his or her social security account. In municipalities that have instituted a form of taxation on employers and employees, that money must be accounted for and reported. State and local sales tax on rents has been a subject of much discussion and, if enacted, will involve filing even more reports.

Management Statement

Basically, managing agents produce a *statement of receipts and disbursements* for the owner; it is not intended to replace all other accounting documents or procedures. The problem is settling upon an accounting format that will provide the necessary information and satisfy most clients. A large percentage of management business is centered around major institutional owners who have hundreds of properties in cities and towns across the country. The asset managers for such owners prefer that you conform to their company's style and format of accounting so that the preparation of their own consolidated management reports is made easier. They must detail total figures for all the properties in their portfolio. Computerized accounting systems are simply not capable of major modification. Therefore, managers often must deviate from their standard system and manually produce a special report in order to secure institutional management business.

Some systems can extract data and rearrange display output to meet specific requirements. Now, with advancements in technology, some managers are in a race to see how many different reports and report variations can be conceived to dazzle owners. It is not uncommon to find monthly management reports for a 150-unit apartment property that are one-inch thick. Many owners are not impressed; they are overwhelmed.

The management statement is actually a collection of reports, usually starting with a narrative summary to explain the month's activities to the owner and including separate reports detailing such items as rent roll, disbursements and miscellaneous receipts, reserve account transactions, etc. Management statements are typically prepared and sent to the owner shortly after the end of each monthly reporting period. Many firms end their accounting month before the last calendar day so that the management report can be prepared during the slow business days rather than the busy first few days of the month. Once the pattern is established, however, it is critical that it be maintained because owners will become accustomed to that schedule. This monthly package typically includes the original copies of the paid invoices and a check for any payment due to the owner.

The basic components of the monthly management statement (excluding the introductory narrative) are explained below.

- *Rent roll.* Each apartment and all other rental spaces should be listed in numerical sequence, regardless of whether the unit is leased.

Once this order has been adopted, it should not vary much from month to month. Listed with each apartment or entry should be all other fixed information, such as unit size, floor number, and address.

Following on the same line is the variable information—including the resident's name, amount of security deposit, term of lease, rent, and rent status. If a particular unit is vacant, this portion would be blank. The more sophisticated programs often detail the amount of rent lost since the unit was last occupied. Possibly, under a single apartment unit, information would be given for more than one resident in the same month (e.g., residents moving during the month, collection from a delinquent previous resident).

The information concerning the resident is a running history. It should show the status listed at the end of the previous month, all transactions during the current month, and the ending status. Without such a detailed description, an owner cannot properly monitor the activities of the property, nor can he or she evaluate the managing agent's performance.

Some agents do not list the entire rent roll but instead *report by exception*. This type of report is easier for an agent to prepare and easier for an owner to read, but it lacks the unit-by-unit detail necessary to really explain what is going on.

- *Disbursements and miscellaneous receipts.* This is a chronological listing of all checks written and all monies received from sources other than rental units (e.g., collections from laundry equipment, vending machines, recreation room fees). This list details the name of the vendor, the amount paid, and often the check number. It also specifies the source and amount of each miscellaneous receipt.

  This statement will include items other than routine building operating expenses. Common examples are debt-service payments, payments for capital expenditures, and distributions to owners. (Most managing agents establish a *chart of accounts* to classify items of expense. By so doing, purchases can be categorized for budgetary and accounting purposes by using the assigned account numbers for each category.)

  Many disbursement listings are on a cash basis and do not reflect unpaid bills. This omission can give an owner the impression that there are no outstanding debts. One way to avoid this is to include a total of unpaid bills at the end of the statement so the owner becomes aware of them.

- *Reserve account transactions.* Items on this list might include the monthly deposit into the owner's real estate tax fund, with an indication of the current balance; deposits for future capital expenditures; or a regular monthly accounting of an established reserve-for-replacement account. These items show the owner how much money is being accumulated for major expenditures. Generally, when these major expenditures are made, a portion of the reserve fund is transferred into the operating account where it will be used to pay a particular bill.

• *Running summary of all financial transactions.* This summary usually contains a beginning balance for the month, total of collections, total of disbursements, an update of the escrow or reserve account, remittances to owners, and the ending balance.

In addition to this essential information, many managers add the following extra reports and schedules to provide a more complete picture of the property's fiscal and market position.

• Complete general ledger
• Security deposit liability report
• Separate delinquency report with monthly aging
• Listing of accounts payable
• Square foot income-expense analysis
• Vacancy analysis
• Comparability analysis
• Prospect traffic and conversion report

RECORDS

As a property manager, you become the "keeper of the records" and there is no shortage of items that need to be maintained, filed, stored, protected, and rotated. When you first become manager, the owner usually entrusts you with many of the records that he or she has accumulated as part of the ownership and operation of the particular property. These files might include leases, contracts, insurance policies, warranties, payment books, real estate tax information, correspondence, etc. As time goes on, many of these files and documents will move to storage boxes after being replaced by more current paperwork. All of these materials must be maintained in a manner that ensures their safekeeping and ease of retrieval. In the following paragraphs, I will discuss the more important records and offer some thoughts about the maintenance of such files.

Leases

Documents dealing with the occupancy of the apartments (and perhaps parking or commercial enterprises such as laundry facilities) are important legal papers. Basically, they represent the income potential of the property. As such, they are valuable and should be carefully protected. If the leases were to be lost, stolen, or destroyed, you would have difficulty duplicating these records, and the job of enforcement and tracking would become much more onerous. Many managers maintain the lease files in locked, fire-resistant cabinets. The permanent, active-lease file is usually set up by building, and then by unit number within that building, not by an alphabetized resident list. Files are organized in this fashion to provide a complete and permanent record for each unit. This method often requires a cross-index to facilitate locating a particular person's lease. As leases expire and are replaced by new ones, the outdated leases are typically maintained in a less secure fashion in alphabetical order by resident. Inquiries involving expired leases are almost always initiated with the name of the resident rather than the unit identification. The lease documents are the property of the building and they must be turned over to the owner when they are requested. Laws vary regarding the length of time one must hold leases; some people choose to hold them indefinitely (this is the practice I advocate).

Warranties and Owner's Manuals

Managers who oversee the structures that constitute most investment real estate tend to accumulate a substantial number of warranties and owner's manuals. These documents may not be needed for many years but they are valuable and must be protected. For example, a new roof may carry a ten- or even twenty-year warranty; many air-conditioning compressors or refrigeration units come with a five-year or longer warranty; and sealed window units frequently carry long warranty periods. Virtually every pump, motor, and appliance comes with some sort of factory warranty. Sometimes, the manufacturer can determine age by the model or serial number, but that doesn't always work. Frequently, the warranty period is extended when delays are incurred in the finishing and occupancy of the building; you will need the paperwork to help enforce a claim.

When you buy a new device, you expect it to work or you will quickly demand repair or replacement. At that point, you know who the product contact is, and this representative arranges to get things going again. A few years later, the arrangements will almost assuredly be more complicated. When a breakdown occurs and you have the owner's manual filed in a safe place, you will be several steps ahead of the game. Top managers guard these reference materials carefully and make sure that they are transferred with the property if there is a sale or management transition.

Plans or Occupancy Certificates

When a building is under construction, almost everyone seems to have a set of plans and specifications. As the years slip by, the sets of plans become more and more tattered as they are moved to different locations. A complete set of plans is often heavy, certainly bulky, and rarely fits in a standard file cabinet. It is, however, very valuable and it should be protected and not stored behind a door or sent to the maintenance area. The need for plans will become apparent later in the building's life when renovation, retrofitting, or replacement of some hidden, but major, mechanical item must be undertaken. As the manager, do your part to protect the original drawings.

Occupancy certificates or zoning documents are other examples of papers that have a way of getting lost. Holding these papers can save countless hours in later years; they should be preserved in a permanent file.

Contracts

Operating an apartment building means removing trash, exterminating bugs, cleaning windows, keeping the grounds, and maintaining complicated machinery. These activities usually involve outside vendors—and that means contracts and letters of agreement. Having access to these documents can avoid misunderstandings; they have legal significance, and they bind the owner of the property. Contracts need to be filed for safekeeping—even after the contract period has passed. They belong to the owner and should be turned over to the owner should there be a transition in the property's management.

Correspondence and Memos to the File

Property management involves a great deal of letter writing to a wide audience: owners, residents (future, present, and past), neighbors, bankers, insurance carriers, governmental agencies, vendors, etc. Many agents choose to file correspondence by year; others do their filing by property. Either is fine so long as the pattern is consistent and retrieval is fairly easy and gets predictable results.

Memos to the file are an important part of record keeping. Today's society is becoming increasingly litigious, and our minds are simply not capable of recalling exactly what was said or agreed upon during a discussion. Whenever a situation shows any potential for developing a misunderstanding in the future, write or dictate a memo that records your understanding of the circumstances; then file the memo away for future reference. You will never have a clearer understanding of a conversation or negotiation than you do in the moments immediately following it. Memos to the file require an additional time commitment—a burden considering the number of activities that you must pack into each day—but memos are essential if you are to be in a position to defend yourself if a problem should occur. In fact, many top professionals make a regular habit of recording the highlights of virtually every discussion they have in a chronological diary maintained in a binder or steno pad. These diaries are then labeled with the starting and ending dates and filed for future reference. Without such a record, you may find yourself defenseless in a situation that develops years after the fact. Take the time—make yourself a record.

Insurance Policies

As I said in chapter 10, the managing agent will probably inherit the job of maintaining the property's insurance policies. Most managers keep insurance documents under lock and key and in fire-resistant cabinets. This includes the policies that are in effect as well as those that have recently expired. The responsibility that goes with keeping the policies includes tracking policy expirations and alerting the owner to upcoming renewals. The manager who maintains the insurance records will have a difficult time dodging some level of liability in the event that a loss occurs and the applicable policy has been allowed to go unrenewed. *Tickler files* used to remind you of crucial dates must be unfailing when it comes to insurance policy expirations.

Property Taxes

Real estate and personal property taxes are commonly called *ad valorem taxes*. An ad valorem tax means "according to value" or "according to worth" (of the property), as opposed to an income tax, which is "according to income."

In some cases, real estate taxes are the largest single item of expense for the buildings you manage. Proper record keeping requires the maintenance of a separate tax file for each property. This file should contain the following information:

1. A legal description of the property.
2. The permanent tax identification number.
3. Information concerning the valuation of the land and the building.
4. Timetables and procedures for handling assessments.
5. History of the tax rate to the present day.
6. Name, address, and telephone number of the tax attorney assigned to the property.
7. Copies of paid tax bills.
8. Special assessments and other taxes.
9. Correspondence regarding protests, appeals, and complaints.

In addition to the permanent tax file, a "tickler file" is also needed here as a reminder of approaching payments and protest dates. As managing agent, you are obligated to make sure that real estate taxes are paid whether or not you receive a bill. If you don't get a bill, it's your obligation to find out what's wrong. When you do receive the tax bill, check carefully to see that it applies to your property.

Some localities also collect *personal property tax* and *sales tax* on rents. If this is true in your area, you must set up and maintain a record of payments made and returns filed.

Employee Time Records

As explained in chapter 3, building employees (including most managerial help) are entitled to at least the minimum hourly wage for the first forty hours of the workweek and time-and-a-half for overtime. In effect, this makes all building personnel hourly employees, whether they are paid a salary or an hourly wage. Therefore, it's important to keep records of all time worked and to pay overtime when necessary.

A record system is initiated by giving each person a timecard each week. Have your employees fill in the hours worked each day, and then collect the cards at the end of the workweek. Be sure to keep these cards on file and inspect the times before issuing payroll checks. If an employee works more than forty hours in one workweek, overtime must be paid.

Actual time records are essential in any investigative hearings. The vast majority of Wage and Hour Law settlements are made on "proof of the record"—that is, what the timecards show. Without a card, it's your word against an employee's.

Canceled Checks, Deposit Receipts, Copies of Paid Invoices

Provide space and a system to preserve and retrieve records of rent payments, bank deposits, and invoices that you have paid on your clients behalf. Five years is the minimum holding period. In a well-run management operation, there is little need to fall back on these records, but there will be situations when the recovery of these documents is crucial to solving a dispute or claim.

Computer Records

Almost all management records are generated and saved though the use of computers because computers are so reliable that little thought is given to protecting data stored in them. Every manual written about the business applications of computers stresses the importance of making backup diskette copies of all data stored on floppy diskettes in addition to the data on internal hard disks. Some people make backups and then store them right next to the originals. Others invest in expensive tape backup devices and then fail to make regularly scheduled backups. It is simply a matter of time until one of your disks becomes damaged or destroyed or your system "crashes," leaving you with the difficult and often impossible job of recreating your records. *Backup should be a daily requirement,* and the backup disks should be taken to an off-site location in the event that your offices are physically damaged. Arrangements should also be made to run your programs on standby equipment should your machines or your facilities become nonfunctional. Owners, employees, residents, and vendors will usually have some patience with you after learning about a major breakdown, but that grace period rarely exceeds one week.

In addressing a subject like data backup, I am reminded that the subjects of computers, accounting, and record keeping are very closely related in our business. Accounting and record keeping are more difficult and tedious tasks without computers, while record-keeping activities have a significant impact on the accuracy of one's accounting. This seems to be a fitting conclusion to *Practical Apartment Management*, because there is so much interrelatedness among the skills and responsibilities of a property manager. The discerning property manager learns how to integrate duties and employ a variety of talents to manage his or her properties successfully.

Glossary

Abandonment A relinquishment or surrender of property or rights. Abandonment of leased premises refers to the relinquishing of the premises by the tenant before the lease expires, without consent of the owner.

Abatement In real estate, a reduction of rent, interest, or an amount due; also, any reduction of amount or intensity.

Abstract of title A summary of all the deeds, wills, and legal proceedings that show the nature of a person's right to a given estate, together with the mortgages, judgments, etc., that constitute liens or encumbrances on it.

Accounts payable Monies due others for services rendered or for goods ordered and received.

Accounts receivable Monies due for services rendered or goods ordered and delivered.

ACCREDITED MANAGEMENT ORGANIZATION® (AMO®) An accreditation conferred by the Institute of Real Estate Management of the NATIONAL ASSOCIATION OF REALTORS® to real estate management firms that are under the direction of a CERTIFIED PROPERTY MANAGER® and comply with stipulated requirements as to accounting procedures, performance, and protection of funds entrusted to them.

ACCREDITED RESIDENTIAL MANAGER (ARM®) A professional service award conferred upon individuals by the Institute of Real Estate Management of the NATIONAL ASSOCIATION OF REALTORS®. Individuals who achieve the ARM® recognition meet IREM's standards of experience, ethics, and education. (See also *CERTIFIED PROPERTY MANAGER®*.)

Accrual accounting   The method of accounting that involves entering amounts of income when money is earned and amounts of expense when bills are incurred (even though the cash may not be received or paid). (See also *cash accounting*.)

Actual authority   The authority expressly or implicitly conferred by a principal on an agent to act on his or her behalf.

Ad valorem tax   A tax levied according to the value of the object taxed: a tax in proportion to the value. Most often refers to tax levied by municipalities and counties against real property and personal property.

Adjustment   In insurance, the settlement of the amount to be received by the insured.

Agency management   Management of property owned by another by an agency authorized to do so.

Agent   A person authorized to transact some business or perform some act for another (the principal) within the limits of the authority bestowed by the latter.

Aggregate rent   The total or gross rent amount for the lease term.

Amortized mortgage   A mortgage loan in which the principal as well as the interest is payable in monthly or periodic installments during the term of the loan.

Ancillary income   A common term used to describe additional, unscheduled income such as laundry room receipts and commissions; also called sundry income.

Annual mortgage constant rate   A rate equal to the percentage derived by dividing the annual payment of principal and interest on a loan by the amount of the loan; used with level payment loans.

Annual statement   In real estate, a fully detailed and annotated statement of all income and expense items involving cash and covering a twelve-consecutive-month period of operation of an individual property (including the disposition and application of net funds for the period concerned and accumulated funds from prior periods). Variations in form and content are effected to conform with owner directives.

Arbitration   The submitting of a matter in dispute to the judgment of one, two, or more disinterested persons called arbitrators, whose decision, called an award, is binding on the parties.

Assessed value   The value placed on land and buildings by a government unit (assessor) for use in levying annual real estate taxes.

Assessment   The imposition of a tax, charge, or levy, usually according to established rates. (See also *special assessment*.)

Assignee   One to whom some right or interest is given, either for the individual's own enjoyment, or in trust; the person receiving an assignment.

Assignment   The transfer in writing of an interest in a bond, mortgage, lease, or other instrument.

Assignor   One giving some right of interest; the person making the assignment.

Authority   Power or right conferred on a person, usually by another to act on his or her behalf, so that the person authorized may perform the authorized activity without incurring liability. (See also *agent.*)

Balloon payment   The final payment of a mortgage loan that is considerably larger than the required periodic payments; this results from the fact that the loan was not fully amortized.

Beneficiary   A person designated to receive funds or other property under a trust, insurance policy, mortgage loan, etc.

Best use   In real estate, economically the most productive use in terms of net income or net return over a foreseeable period of time without prejudice to the total capital investment or fair market value of a property; also called highest and best use.

Betterment   Improvements upon real property other than mere repairs.

Blanket mortgage   A mortgage covering several pieces of property.

Blanket policy   An insurance policy covering all of a specified quantity or class of property, or a variety of risks, or both.

British thermal unit (Btu)   The energy needed to raise the temperature of one pound of water by one degree Fahrenheit.

Cannibalization   To strip equipment or housing units of parts for use in other equipment or units to help keep the latter in service.

Capital improvement   A structural addition or betterment to real property other than a repair or replacement; also, the use of capital for a betterment that did not exist before.

Capitalization   The process employed in estimating the value of a property by the use of a proper investment rate of return and the annual net operating income expected to be produced by the property, the formula being expressed:

$$\frac{\text{Net Operating Income}}{\text{Rate}} = \text{Value}$$

Cash accounting   The method of accounting that recognizes income and expenses when money is received or paid. (See also *accrual accounting.*)

Cash flow   The amount of cash available after all payments have been made for operating expenses and mortgage principal and interest.

Cash-on-cash return   The annual cash flow divided by the original cash equity investment.

Certified copy   A document signed and certified as true by the official in whose custody the original is held.

CERTIFIED PROPERTY MANAGER® (CPM®)   A professional designation conferred upon individuals by the Institute of Real Estate Management of the NATIONAL ASSOCIATION OF REALTORS®. For over fifty years IREM has awarded the CPM® designation to those property managers who meet high standards of experience, ethics, and education. (See also *ACCREDITED RESIDENTIAL MANAGER®*.)

Chart of accounts   An arbitrary classification or arrangement of account items according to grade or class.

Collateral   Security given as a pledge for the fulfillment of an obligation.

Collateral materials   As applied to advertising and promotion, includes printing and devices such as brochures, leaflets, floor plans, posters, photographs, lapel pins, book matches, etc.

Commingle   To mix or combine; combining the money of more than one person or entity into a common fund.

Comparison grid   A method of price analysis in which the features of a subject property are compared to similar features in three or more comparable properties in the same market. The price (or rent) for each comparable property helps to determine an appropriate price (or rent) for the subject. This method involves assigning values for different attributes such as square footage, amenities, patios, parking, floor and window treatments, appliances, location, and view; the process should take market trends into consideration and is obviously subjective. Each comparable property is compared to the subject, feature by feature. When the feature being examined is superior in the comparable property, the comparable price should be reduced by the amount that particular feature is worth in the marketplace. When the feature being examined is superior in the subject property, the comparable price should be appropriately increased. Pricing of the subject property is determined by tallying the adjustments to the price of each comparable and then either averaging the adjusted prices or using the final price of the comparable that has had the fewest adjustments—because this comparable is most like the subject property.

Compound interest   Interest upon interest; when the simple interest on a sum of money is added to the principal as it becomes due, then bears interest itself, becoming sort of a secondary principal. Simple interest is paid on the principal only.

Condemnation   The taking of private property for public use; also the official act to terminate the use of real property for nonconformance with governmental regulations or because of hazards to public health and safety.

Condemnation clause   A provision in a lease stating the agreed rights, privileges, and limitations of the owner and tenant, respectively, in the event of the taking of the subject property for public use.

Condominium   Outright ownership of an individual unit within a multiple-unit structure along with prorated shared ownership of the common areas of the structure.

Consideration   Something that suffices to make an agreement legally binding; something given in exchange for a promise.

Constant   See *annual mortgage constant rate.*

Constructive eviction   Inability of a tenant to obtain or maintain possession by reason of a condition of the property making occupancy hazardous or unfit for its intended use.

Construction loan   A short-term loan made to finance the cost of new construction or rehabilitation, as distinguished from permanent financing on a completed building. Money is normally sent to the builder as costs are incurred during construction.

Constructive notice   Notice given to the world by recorded documents. All persons are charged with knowledge of such documents and their contents whether or not they have actually examined them. Possession of property is also considered notice that the person in possession has an interest in the property.

Consumer Price Index (CPI)   A ratio of the cost of consumer goods at the present time in relation to a base period, said to be 100. This index is published monthly by the United States Department of Labor, Bureau of Labor Statistics.

Contingent liability   A liability that can fall to one as an implied participant or contributor; conditional liability.

Conventional mortgage   A mortgage loan not insured or guaranteed by governmental agencies (FHA or VA).

Conveyance   The instrument or document by which a transfer is made or title passed from one person to another.

Cooperative   Ownership of a share or shares of stock in a corporation that holds the title to a multiple-unit residential structure; shareholders do not own their units outright but have the right to occupy them.

Corporation   A legal entity that is chartered by a state and treated by courts as an artificial person or body of persons separate and distinct from the persons who own it.

Cost approach   The process of estimating the value of a property by adding to the estimated land value the appraiser's estimate of the replacement cost of the building less depreciation.

Covenant   An agreement written into deeds and other instruments promising performance or nonperformance of certain acts, or stipulating certain uses or non-uses of the property.

Death clause   A special clause in a lease that provides for termination of the lease before its expiration date in the event of the tenant's death.

Deed of trust   A written document by which title to land is conveyed as security for the repayment of a loan.

Deed restrictions   Clauses in a deed limiting the future uses of the property. Deed restrictions may limit the density of buildings, dictate the types of structures that can be erected, or prevent buildings from being used for specific purposes (or at all). Deed restrictions may impose numerous limitations and conditions.

Default   The nonperformance of a duty, whether arising under a contract, or otherwise; failure to meet an obligation when due.

Defect of title   A claim, restricted use provision, or other imperfection that adversely affects the customary use and marketability of a property.

Deferred maintenance   Ordinary maintenance of a building that, because it has not been effected, noticeably affects the use, occupancy, welfare, and value of the property.

Deficiency judgment   A personal judgment levied against the mortgagor when the foreclosure sale does not produce sufficient funds to pay the mortgage debt in full.

Delinquency   An overdue debt, as rent not paid on the due date.

Demised premises   Property conveyed by a lease.

Density   The number of dwelling units constructed per acre.

Department of Housing and Urban Development (HUD)   A federal department created in 1968 to supervise the Federal Housing Authority (FHA) and a number of other agencies that administer various housing programs.

Depreciation   Loss of value due to all causes, usually considered to include: (1) physical deterioration (ordinary wear and tear), (2) functional depreciation (see *obsolescence*), and (3) economic obsolescence; also, the tax deduction that allows for exhaustion of property.

Direct-reduction loan   Loan in which payments are equal in amounts, with a portion applied first to the current interest, and the remainder to the reduction of the principal; also called level-payment or self-amortizing loan.

Disability clause   A special lease covenant that provides for the alteration of the lease terms or the termination of the lease before expiration, in the event that the tenant is physically disabled and unable to continue his or her use of the leased premises; most often included in leases of residential property.

Discount rate   Any rate used to translate a future dollar amount into an equivalent present value. Also, the interest rate the Federal Reserve Bank charges banks.

Down payment   An agreed initial increment payment to secure the delivery of property or goods upon payment of the total agreed price in accordance with a specific agreement.

Duly authorized   Properly authorized to act for another in accordance with legal requirements and in conformance with a written series of conditions and covenants (e.g., power of attorney).

Easement   A right or interest in land owned by another that entitles the holder (or occupant) of that land to some use, privilege, or benefit out of or over it.

Economic life   The number of years during which a building will continue to produce an acceptable yield.

Economic obsolescence   Impairment of desirability or useful life, or loss in the use and value, of property arising from economic forces outside of the building or property, such as changes in optimum land use, legislative enactments that restrict or impair property rights, and changes in supply-demand relationships. (See also *obsolescence.*)

Economic turnover   A type of turnover that involves either tenants moving from a rented apartment to a purchased single-family home, townhouse, or condominium; or tenants moving to another part of the country. (See also *lateral turnover* and *turnover.*)

Economic vacancy   The number of units in a building or a development that are not producing income. This includes vacancies, models, offices, delinquencies, staff apartments, cannibalized units, and units being used for storage; usually expressed as a percentage of the total number of units. (See also *physical vacancy.*)

Efficiency apartment   A small, bedroomless apartment usually with less than a standard-size kitchen. (See also *studio apartment.*)

Efficiency factor   The percentage of gross building area that is actually rentable.

$$\frac{\text{Rentable Area}}{\text{Gross Building Area}} = \text{Efficiency Factor}$$

Elevation   A drawing or design representing a vertical side or portion of a building; a place above the level of the surrounding ground.

Eminent domain   The right of a government or municipal quasi-public body to acquire private property for public use through a court action called condemnation in which the court determines that the use is a public use and determines the price or compensation to be paid to the owner.

Empty-nesters   Persons whose children have left home permanently.

Encroachment   A building or some portion of it, or a wall or fence that illegally extends beyond the owner's land onto another's land or a street or alley.

Encumbrance   Any lien, such as a mortgage, tax lien, or judgment lien; also, an easement, a restriction on the use of a land, or an outstanding dower right which may diminish the value of the property.

Endorse   To approve or guarantee payment; to alter a document by adding a covenant.

Environmental Protection Agency (EPA)   The agency of the United States government established in 1970 to enforce laws that preserve and protect the environment.

Equalization   The raising or lowering of assessed values for tax purposes in a particular county or taxing district to make them equal to assessments in other counties or districts.

Equity   The interest or value that an owner has in real estate over and above the mortgage against it.

Errors and omissions insurance   A form of liability insurance. In the case of the property manager, errors and omissions insurance protects against liabilities resulting from honest mistakes and oversights (but provides no protection in cases of gross negligence).

Escalator clause   A clause in a contract, lease, or mortgage providing for increases in wages, rent, or interest based on fluctuations in certain economic indexes, costs, or taxes.

Eviction   A legal process to reclaim real estate from a tenant or person holding a mortgage who has not performed under the agreed-upon terms.

Exclusive agent   An agent with exclusive rights for a fixed period of time to sell or lease property owned by another.

Exculpate   To free from blame. Hold harmless clauses are exculpatory.

Execution   The signing and delivery of an instrument; also, a legal order directing an official to enforce a judgment against the property of a debtor.

Experience exchange   A compilation of operating data on comparable properties generated through annual surveys of property managers. An example is *Income/Expense Analysis: Conventional Apartments* published every year by IREM.

Extended coverage (EC)   An endorsement to a standard form of fire insurance policy adding to the insurance coverage against financial loss from certain other specified hazards.

Fair Credit Reporting Act   Enacted in 1971, this federal law gives people the right to see and correct their credit records at credit reporting bureaus.

Fair Debt Collection Practices Act   As originally passed in 1978, this federal law created a series of guidelines for debt collectors to follow and was designed to prevent collection agencies from harassing debtors. In 1986, the law was expanded to include any organization that collects consumer debt (including property managers). The law is governed and regulated by the Federal Trade Commission (FTC).

Fair housing laws   Any law that prohibits discrimination grounded on race, religion, national origin, family status, etc. against people seeking housing. There are federal, state, and local fair housing laws, all of which must be adhered to.

Fair Labor Standards Act   Enacted in 1938, this federal law establishes minimum wages per hour and maximum hours of work. It also provides that employees who work in excess of forty hours per week are to be paid one and one-half times their regular hourly wage. This is frequently referred to as *Wage and Hour Law*.

Fair market value   The price paid, or one that might be anticipated as necessarily payable, by a willing and informed buyer to a willing and informed seller, neither of whom is under any compulsion to act, and if the object sold has been reasonably exposed to the market.

Feasibility study A study to discover the practicality, possibility, and reasonableness of a proposed undertaking.

Fee simple The largest possible estate or rights of ownership of real property continuing without time limitation. Sometimes called fee or fee simple absolute.

Federal Housing Administration (FHA) An agency—part of the United States Department of Housing and Urban Development—that administers a variety of housing loan programs.

Fidelity bond A casualty insurance guaranteeing one individual against financial loss that might result from dishonest acts of another specific individual.

Fiduciary One charged with a relationship of trust and confidence, as between a principal and agent, trustee and beneficiary, or attorney and client.

Financial analysis Projection of income and expense, financing considerations, tax implementations, and value charged; used in a management survey.

Financing The availability, amount, and terms under which money may be borrowed to assist in the purchase of real property and using the property itself as the security for such borrowing.

Fire and extended coverage insurance (Fire and EC) Insurance for property that covers not only loss by fire but also windstorm, hail, explosion, riot, civil commotion, aircraft, vehicles, and smoke.

Fire insurance Insurance on property against all direct loss or damage by fire.

First mortgage A mortgage that has priority as a lien over all other mortgages.

Fixed assets Properties, goods, or other things of value that cannot be readily sold or otherwise converted on short notice at their true and fair value. Things possessed mainly of value in their use as is, and of little value if removed, such as trade fixtures and machinery.

Fixture An article of personal property attached permanently to a building or to land so that it becomes part of the real estate.

Float In banking, the time that lapses after a deposit or withdrawal is made and before the transaction is credited or deducted.

Foreclosure A court action initiated by the mortgagee, or a lienor, for the purpose of having the court order the debtor's real estate sold to pay the mortgage or other lien (e.g., mechanic's lien or judgment).

Fraud Intentional deception to cause a person to give up property or a lawful right.

Functional obsolescence Defects in a building or structure that detract from its value or marketability.

General partnership The business activity of two or more persons who agree to pool capital, talents, and other assets according to some agreed-to formula, and similarly to divide profits and losses, and to commit the partnership to certain obligations. General partners assume unlimited liability.

Graduated rent   Rent that has two or more levels in the same lease term.

Gross building area   Area equal to length times width of the building(s) times the number of living floors, expressed in square feet.

Gross income   The total monthly or annual revenue from all sources, such as rents and other receipts, before any deductions, allowances, or charges.

Gross National Product (GNP)   The total value of a nation's annual output of goods and services.

Gross possible income   The total monthly or annual possible income before uncollected income is deducted.

Gross receipts   The total cash income from all sources during a specific period of time such as monthly or annually.

Gross rent multiplier   A figure that, when used as a multiplier of the gross income of a property, produces an estimated value of that property.

Half-bath   A term used in real estate to describe a bathroom with a basin and water closet but no bathing facilities such as a tub or shower.

Head rent   Rent charged to a person or persons occupying the same premises independently of each other.

Hold harmless   A declaration that one is not liable for things beyond his or her control.

Holdover tenancy   A tenancy whereby the tenant retains possession of leased premises after his or her lease has expired, and the landlord, by continuing to accept rent from the tenant, thereby agrees to the tenant's continued occupancy as defined by state law.

Income approach   The process of estimating the value of an income-producing property by capitalization of the annual net income expected to be produced by the property during its remaining useful life.

Independent contractor   A person who contracts to do a piece of work for another by using his or her own methods and without being under the control of the other person regarding how the work should be done. Unlike an employee, an independent contractor pays for all expenses, income and social security taxes, and receives no employee benefits.

In-house management   Management originating from within an organization or company (i.e., by the staff or the corporation owning the property rather than by someone brought in from outside).

Institute of Real Estate Management (IREM)   A professional association of men and women, affiliated with the NATIONAL ASSOCIATION OF REALTORS®, who meet established standards of experience, education, and ethics with the objective of continually improving their respective managerial skills by mutual education and exchange of ideas and experiences.

Insurable value   A term commonly used to describe the actual cash value (ACV) of a property; the cost to replace the building or structure, less certain depreciation factors.

Insurance   An agreement to assume a foreseeable financial loss in the event of fire, casualty, liability, or property damage in consideration of a premium payment by the one insured (the insured) to the one insuring (the insurer, carrier, insurance company, etc.).

Interest   A share in the ownership of property; a payment for the use of money borrowed.

Joint tenants   Two or more owners of a parcel of land who have been specifically named in one conveyance as joint tenants. Upon the death of a joint tenant, his or her interest passes to the surviving joint tenant or tenants by the right of survivorship, which is the important element of joint tenancy.

Joint venture   An association of persons or other entities to carry out a single business enterprise for profit, for which purpose they combine their property, money, and skills.

Judgment clause   A provision in notes, leases, and contracts by which the debtor, tenant, and others authorize any attorney to go into court and confess a judgment against them for a default in payment; sometimes called a *cognovit*. The use of this clause is prohibited in many jurisdictions.

Jurisdiction   The district over which the power of the court extends.

Landlord-tenant law   Laws enacted by various jurisdictions that regulate the relationship between landlord and tenant.

Latent defects   Physical deficiencies or construction defects not readily detected from a reasonable inspection of the property, such as a defective septic tank, underground sewage system, improper plumbing, or electrical wiring; also called hidden defects.

Lateral turnover   A type of turnover that occurs when tenants move from one rented apartment to a similar rented apartment in the same general market. (See also *economic turnover* and *turnover*.)

Lease   A contract, written or oral, for the possession of a landowner's land or property for a stipulated period of time in consideration of the payment of rent or other income by the tenant. Leases for more than one year generally must be in writing to be enforceable; may be called an occupancy agreement.

Lease conditions   The provisions or covenants setting forth the agreed privileges, obligations, and restrictions under which a lease is made; also called lease terms.

Lease extension agreement   A covenant or other written and executed instrument extending or agreeing to extend the lease term beyond the expiration date as provided in the body of the original lease.

Legal description   The description used to identify the property in such legal instruments as deeds or mortgages.

Lender's loss payable   An endorsement to a policy of hazard insurance providing that any compensation for losses sustained shall be made to the order of a lender to whom the property has been pledged as security for a loan.

Lessee   The tenant in a lease.

Lessor   The landlord in a lease.

Let   To lease; to grant the use of a thing for compensation.

Level-payment loan   See *direct-reduction loan.*

License   Official authorization to engage in a business, profession, or other activity with or for the public or affecting the public interest; freedom to act or express oneself; also, the revocable permission for a temporary use—a personal right that cannot be sold.

Lien   The legal right of a creditor to have his or her debt paid out of the property of the debtor.

Limited partnership   A partnership arrangement that limits certain of the partners' liability to the amount they have invested and limits the profit they can make. Limited partnerships are managed and operated by one or more general partners whose liability is not limited. The limited partners are not permitted to have a voice in the management.

Limited power of attorney   A legal authorization to act on behalf of another for a specified purpose.

Loan commitment   An agreement to lend an amount of money, usually under stated terms and conditions.

Loan cost   The cost in money for securing a loan, as in loan fees, legal charges, title or abstract costs, recording charges or notary fees; the total charges for effecting a loan, customarily paid by the borrower.

Loan payment   The payment of an installment on the principal balance plus accrued interest on the entire unpaid balance that accrued since the immediately preceding interest payment.

Majority   The age set by state law at which individuals have the legal right to manage their own affairs and are responsible for their own actions. The age of majority varies from state to state. (See also *minor.*)

Management agreement   A contract or letter of understanding between the owner(s) of a property and the designated managing agent, describing the duties and establishing powers, responsibilities, rights, and obligations of the parties thereto.

Management company A real estate organization that specializes in the professional management of real properties for others.

Management fee The monetary consideration paid monthly or otherwise for the performance of management duties.

Managing agent An agent duly appointed to direct and control all matters pertaining to a property that is owned or controlled by another.

Market analysis A determination of the characteristics, purchasing power, and habits of the population segment expected to be tenants of a property, used in a management survey.

Market value The highest price that a buyer—ready, willing, and able, but not compelled to buy—would pay, and the lowest a seller—ready, willing, and able, but not compelled to sell—would accept.

Mechanic's lien A lien created by statute that exists in favor of contractors, laborers, or material suppliers who have performed work or furnished materials in the erection or repair of a building.

Minor One who has not reached the age set by state law to be legally recognized as an adult; therefore, one not legally responsible for contracting debts or signing contracts. (See also *majority*.)

Month-to-month tenancy An agreement to rent or lease for consecutive and continuing monthly periods until terminated by proper prior notice by either the landlord or the tenant. Notice of termination must precede the commencement date of the final month of occupancy. The time period of prior notice is usually established by state law.

Mortgage A conditional transfer or pledge of real property as security for the payment of a debt; also, the document used to create a mortgage loan.

Mortgagee The lender in a mortgage loan transaction.

Mortgagor The borrower, the owner of the real estate who conveys his or her property as security for the loan.

NATIONAL ASSOCIATION OF REALTORS® The national nonprofit corporation whose membership is principally composed of individual real estate agents who are members in subscribing local real estate boards throughout the United States and its possessions and dedicated to the highest principles and performance by real estate licensee members.

Net cost Cost after all incidental charges are added and all allowable credits are deducted.

Net operating income (NOI) Total collections less operating expenses.

Net prior to debt service (NPDS) The cash available from collected rental income after all operating expenses have been deducted and before capital expenses and debt service have been deducted; the net operating income.

Notary public   An officer licensed by the state to certify documents to make them authentic and to take affidavits.

Notice to vacate   A legal notice requiring a tenant to remove himself or herself and all removable possessions from the premises within a stated period of time or upon a specified day and date, and to deliver the premises to the owner or agent or to a designated successor.

Obsolescence   Lessening of value due to being out-of-date (obsolete) as a result of changes in design and use; also, an element of depreciation. (See also *economic obsolescence* and *functional obsolescence.*)

Occupancy agreement   A lease agreement that spells out the conditions of occupancy of a property for a specified length of time for a specified amount of rent.

Occupational Safety and Health Act of 1970 (OSHA)   A law requiring employers to comply with job safety and health standards issued by the U.S. Department of Labor.

Off-site management   Management of a property by persons not residing or keeping office hours at the subject property.

Option   The right to purchase or lease something at a future date for a specified price and terms; the right may or may not be exercised at the option holder's (optionee's) discretion. Options may be received or purchased.

Owner, landlord, and tenant liability (OLT)   Insurance protecting claims against a property owner, a landlord, or a tenant arising from personal injury to a person or persons in or about a subject property and including the improvements on the land and any other contiguous areas for which the insured is legally responsible, such as sidewalks.

Parking ratio   The number of parking spaces provided for each dwelling unit constructed.

Peaceful enjoyment   The use of real property without illegal or unreasonable interference or annoyance within the control of the party granting the use.

Personal property   Movable property belonging to an individual, family, etc., that is not permanently affixed to real property, such as clothing, furniture, furnishings, and appliances.

Physical vacancy   The number of vacant units in a building or development that are available for rent, usually expressed as a percentage of the total number of units. (See also *economic vacancy.*)

Planned unit development (PUD)   A group of buildings, sometimes with varying uses (e.g. apartment, offices, shops, schools), that are completely planned before groundbreaking. Generally, they are large in scale and built in several phases over a number of years.

Plumbing chase   A duct space or enclosure inside partition walls to house plumbing lines and vent stacks.

Points In real estate lending, fees charged by the lender to increase the overall yield to that lender: A point is 1 percent of the loan principal; also called discount points.

Power of attorney A written instrument authorizing another to act in one's behalf as his or her agent or attorney.

Prepayment penalty An extra stipulated charge for paying off all or part of a loan on real property in advance; a cash penalty for paying off a mortgage loan before its date of maturity.

Present value The worth of money to be received in the future discounted by a given discount rate—the value determined is the value of the money today.

Prime rate The lowest interest rate currently being charged to the most financially responsible persons or with the security of highly rated and easily converted securities on loans repayable on demand by the lender.

Principal (1) A sum of money lent or employed as a fund or investment—as distinguished from its income or profits; (2) the original amount, or remaining balance of a loan; or (3) a party to a transaction—as distinguished from an agent.

Property analysis A study conducted by a property manager referring to items such as deferred maintenance, functional and economic obsolescence, land location and zoning, exterior construction and condition, plant and equipment, unit mix, facilities, and expected income and expenses.

Property damage insurance Insurance against liability for damage to property of others that may result from occurrences in or about a specified property and for which the insured is legally liable.

Property manager The chief operating officer or administrator of a particular property or group of properties.

Public area A space in a property for general public use and not restricted for use by any lease or other agreements, as a lobby, corridor, or court.

Pullman kitchen A small non-walk-in kitchen, often in a closet-sized space, with appliances and equipment that are smaller than standard.

Real estate Land; a portion of the earth's surface extending downward to the center of the earth and upward into space including all things permanently attached to the land by nature or by mankind; also, freehold estates in land.

Real estate broker Any person, partnership, association, or corporation who for a compensation or valuable consideration sells or offers for sale, buys or offers to buy, or negotiates the purchase, sale, or exchange of real estate, or who leases or offers to rent any real estate or the improvements on it for others. Such a broker may have to have a state license.

Real estate investment trust (REIT) An entity that sells shares to investors and uses the funds to invest in real estate. Real estate investment trusts must meet certain requirements such as a minimum number of investors and widely dispersed ownership. No corporate taxes need to be paid as long as a series of complex Internal Revenue Service qualifications are met.

REALTOR®   A registered trademark reserved for the sole use of active members of local boards of REALTORS® affiliated with the NATIONAL ASSOCIATION OF REALTORS®.

Recapitulation statement   An annual balanced cash statement customarily prepared by real estate managers showing all receipts, disbursements, and reserves accumulated for an established twelve-month period; also called "recap" statement.

Recurring expenses   Operating expenses that recur monthly or periodically, such as those for utilities, supplies, salaries, scavenger services, insurance, and taxes.

Redemption period   A period established by state laws during which the property owner has the right to redeem his or her real estate from a foreclosure or a tax sale by paying the sale price, interest, and costs. (Many states do not have mortgage redemption laws.)

Regional analysis   A detailed study of a region, usually surrounding and including one or more neighboring cities, to determine the force of various factors affecting the economic welfare of a section of the region, such as population growth and movement, employment, industrial and business activity, transportation facilities, tax structures, topography, improvements, and trends.

Re-lease or re-let   To rent again. Usually involving a cancellation of the previous lease.

Rent ledger   Record of rent received, date, period covered, and other related information.

Rent loss   The deficiency increment resulting from vacancies, bad debts, etc., between total projected rental income (for a given period) and the actual rents collected or collectible.

Rent roll   A list of each rental unit described by size and type. This also includes the following information if the unit is being rented: amount of monthly rent, tenant name, and lease expiration date; also called rent schedule. The rent roll—unlike the rent ledger—does not include the status of rent payment.

Rentable area   The combined rentable area of all dwelling units in a project. The rentable area of a unit is calculated by multiplying length times width of the apartment, with no discounts for interior partitions, plumbing chases, and other small niches. Balconies, patios, and unheated porches are not included in these measurements. Sometimes called net rentable area.

Replacement cost   The estimated cost to replace or restore a building to its exact pre-existing condition and appearance.

Rescind   Invalidate, annul, cancel, repeal, etc.

Resident manager   An employee residing in a building for the purpose of overseeing and administering the day-to-day building affairs in accordance with directions from the manager or owner; also called on-site manager, site manager, and residential manager.

Right of re-entry   The act of resuming possession of lands, or tenements, in pursuance of a right reserved by the owner on parting with the possession. Leases usually contain a clause providing that the owner may terminate the lease and re-enter for nonpayment of rent or breach of any of the covenants by the tenant.

Second mortgage   A mortgage loan secured by real estate that has previously been made security for a prior mortgage loan; also called a junior mortgage or junior lien.

Security deposit   A preset amount of money advanced by the tenant and held by an owner or manager for a specified period to cover damages and to ensure the faithful performance of the lease terms by the tenant.

Site plan   A plan, prepared to scale, showing locations of buildings, roadways, parking areas, and other improvements.

Special assessment   A charge against real estate made by a unit of government to cover the proportionate cost of an improvement such as a street or sewer.

Square-foot cost   The cost per square foot of area to build, buy, rent, etc.

Studio apartment   Commonly used term to describe an efficiency or bedroomless apartment. In certain areas, the term refers to a small apartment with two levels.

Subdivision   A tract of land divided by the owner into blocks, building lots, and streets by a recorded subdivision plat; compliance with local regulations is required.

Subletting   The leasing of premises by a tenant to a third party for part of the tenant's remaining term.

Subordination clause   A lease covenant in which the tenant agrees to take any action required to subordinate his or her claims against the property to the rights of the lender under a first mortgage or deed of trust, so long as it does not affect his or her right to possession.

Subrogation   The substitution of one creditor for another. The substituted person succeeds to the legal rights and claims of the original claimant. Subrogation is used by insurers to acquire from the insured party rights to sue to recover any claims they have paid.

Tenant   One who pays rent to occupy or gain possession of real estate. The estate or interest held is called a tenancy.

Tenant improvements   Additions or alterations to a leased premises for the use of the tenant, at the cost and expense of the tenant and becoming a part of the realty unless otherwise agreed to in writing.

Tenant organization   A group of tenants formed to use their collective powers against an owner to achieve certain goals such as improved conditions, expanded facilities, and lower rent.

Tenant profile   A study and listing of the similar and dissimilar characteristics of the present tenants in a property.

Tenant selectivity   An established set of standards used in the selection of tenants for a particular property.

Title   The evidence of right that a person has to the ownership and possession of land.

Title insurance   A policy insuring an owner or mortgagee against the loss by reason of defects in the title to a parcel of real estate, other than encumbrances, defects, and matters that are specifically excluded by the policy.

Townhouse   A one-, two-, or three-story dwelling with a separate outside entryway sharing common or partitioning walls with other similar dwellings.

Turnover   The number of units vacated during a specific period of time, usually one year. Most turnover rates are expressed as the ratio between the number of new tenants and the total number of units in a property. (See also *economic turnover* and *lateral turnover.*)

Umbrella liability insurance   Extra liability coverage that exceeds the limits of one's basic liability policy.

Unit mix   A number or percentage total of each unit size or type contained in a particular property.

Unit size   A listing of the number of bedrooms and baths an apartment contains.

Vacancy   An area in a building that is unoccupied and available for rent.

Wage and Hour Law   See *Fair Labor Standards Act.*

Walk-up   An apartment building of two or more floors in which the only access to the upper floors is by means of stairways.

Work order   A written form, letter, or other instrument for authorizing work to be performed. A means for controlling and recording work ordered.

Workers' compensation   Liability insurance obtained by an employer that will cover compensation and benefits awarded to an employee for a sickness or injury that occurred as a result of or in the course of employment.

Yield   The total economic return to an investor.

Zoning ordinance   Exercise of power by a municipality in regulating and controlling the character and use of property.

Index